Pokémon™

SUPER DELUXE ESSENTIAL HANDBOOK

The need-to-know stats and facts on over 800 characters!

SCHOLASTIC INC.

W9-BES-863

© 1997 Nintendo, Creatures, GAME FREAK, TV Tokyo, ShoPro, JR Kikaku. © Pokémon. TM and ® are trademarks of Nintendo.

For sale in India only.

All rights reserved.

Published by Scholastic India Pvt. Ltd. under licence from Dream Theatre Private Limited Scholastic India Pvt. Ltd. is a subsidiary of Scholastic Inc., New York, 10012 (USA).

No part of this publication may be reproduced in whole or in part, or stored in a retrieval system, or transmitted in any form or by any means, electronic, mechanical, photocopying, recording, or otherwise without the written permission of the publisher.

For information regarding permission, write to:
Scholastic India Pvt. Ltd.
A-27, Ground Floor, Bharti Sigma Centre
Infocity-1, Sector 34, Gurgaon-122001 (India)

First edition: September 2019
This edition July 2022
ISBN-13: 978-93-8929-733-1

Designed by Carolyn Bull and DeMonico Design, Co.

Printed at Sanat Printers, Kundli, Haryana

WELCOME TO THE WORLD OF POKÉMON!

Kanto ... Johto ... Hoenn ... Sinnoh ... Unova ... Kalos ... and now, Alola!

There are seven known Pokémon regions bursting with fascinating Pokémon— creatures that come in all shapes, sizes, and personalities. Some live in oceans; others in caves, old towers, rivers, or tall grass.

Trainers can find, capture, train, trade, collect, and use Pokémon in battle against their rivals in the quest to become the best.

The key to success with Pokémon is staying informed. Information about each Pokémon's type, category, height, and weight can make all the difference in catching, raising, battling, and evolving your Pokémon.

In this book, you'll get all the stats and facts you need about over 800 Pokémon. You'll discover how each Pokémon evolves and which moves it uses.

So get ready, Trainers: With this *Super Deluxe Essential Handbook*, you'll be ready to master almost any Pokémon challenge!

HOW TO USE THIS BOOK

This book provides the basic stats and facts you need to know to start your Pokémon journey. Here's what you'll discover about each Pokémon:

NAME

CATEGORY

All Pokémon belong to a certain category.

TYPE

Each Pokémon has a type, and some even have two. (Pokémon with two types are called dual-type Pokémon.) Every Pokémon type comes with advantages and disadvantages. We'll break them all down for you here.

DESCRIPTION

Knowledge is power. Pokémon Trainers have to know their stuff. Find out everything you need to know about your Pokémon here.

HOW TO SAY IT

When it comes to Pokémon pronunciation, it's easy to get tongue-tied! There are many Pokémon with unusual names, so we'll help you sound them out. Soon you'll be saying Pokémon names so perfectly, you'll sound like a professor.

HEIGHT AND WEIGHT

How does each Pokémon measure up? Find out by checking its height and weight stats. And remember, good things come in all shapes and sizes. It's up to every Trainer to work with his or her Pokémon and play up its strengths.

POSSIBLE MOVES

Every Pokémon has its own unique combination of moves. Before you hit the battlefield, we'll tell you all about each Pokémon's awesome attacks. And don't forget—with a good Trainer, they can always learn more!

EVOLUTION

If your Pokémon has an evolved form or pre-evolved form, we'll show you its place in the chain and how it evolves.

PIKACHU
Mouse Pokémon

REGIONS:
Alola
Kalos
(Central)
Kanto

TYPE: ELECTRIC

Pikachu naturally stores up electricity in its body, and it needs to discharge that energy on a regular basis to maintain good health. To take advantage of this, some have suggested creating a Pikachu-fueled power plant.

How to Say It: PEE-ka-choo
Imperial Height: 1'04''
Imperial Weight: 13.2 lbs.
Metric Height: 0.4 m
Metric Weight: 6.0 kg

Possible Moves: Tail Whip, Thunder Shock, Growl, Play Nice, Quick Attack, Electro Ball, Thunder Wave, Feint, Double Team, Spark, Nuzzle, Discharge, Slam, Thunderbolt, Agility, Wild Charge, Light Screen, Thunder

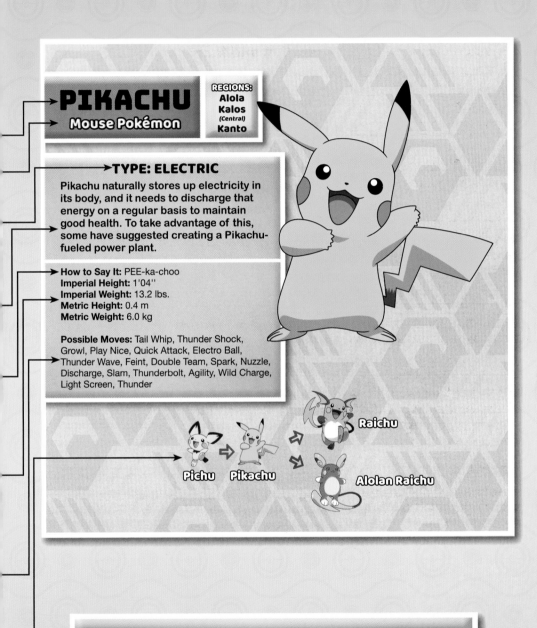

Pichu   Pikachu   Raichu

Alolan Raichu

Curious about what Pokémon types you'll spot on your journey? Find out more about all eighteen types on the next page...

GUIDE TO POKÉMON TYPES

A Pokémon's type can tell you a lot about it—from where to find it in the wild to the moves it'll be able to use on the battlefield. Type is the key to unlocking a Pokémon's power.

A clever Trainer should always consider type when picking a Pokémon for a match, because type is one way to determine Pokémon's strengths and weaknesses. For example, a Fire-type may melt an Ice-type, but against a Water-type, it might find it's the one in hot water. And while a Water-type usually has the upper hand in battle with a Fire-type, a Water-type move would act like a sprinkler on a Grass-type Pokémon. But when that same Grass-type is battling a Fire-type, it just might get scorched.

FIRE

GRASS

WATER

NORMAL

ELECTRIC

BUG

GHOST

FLYING

FIGHTING

PSYCHIC

STEEL

ROCK

GROUND

ICE

POISON

DARK

DRAGON

FAIRY

BATTLE BASICS

WHY BATTLE?

There are two basic reasons for a Pokémon to battle. One is for sport. You can battle another Trainer in a friendly competition. Your Pokémon do the fighting, but you decide which Pokémon and which moves to use.

The second reason is to catch wild Pokémon. Wild Pokémon have no training and no owners. They can be found pretty much anywhere. Battle is one of the main ways to catch a Pokémon. But other Trainers' Pokémon are off-limits. You can't capture their Pokémon, even if you win a competition.

CHOOSING THE BEST POKÉMON FOR THE JOB

As you prepare for your first battle, you may have several Pokémon to choose from. Use the resources in this book to help you decide which Pokémon would be best. If you're facing a Fire-type Pokémon, like Litten, you can put out its sparks with a Water-type Pokémon, like Popplio.

THE FACE-OFF

You and your Pokémon will have to face, and hopefully defeat, each and every Pokémon on the other Trainer's team. You win when your Pokémon have defeated all the other Trainer's Pokémon. But Pokémon do not get seriously hurt in battle. If they are defeated, they faint and then return to their Poké Balls to rest and be healed. An important part of a Trainer's job is to take good care of his or her Pokémon.

MEGA EVOLUTION

A select group of Pokémon possesses the ability to Mega Evolve. A Pokémon can only Mega Evolve during battle, and Mega Evolution increases its strength in ways no Trainer could imagine.

Lucario   Lucarionite   Mega Lucario

But Mega Evolution requires more than just capturing a Pokémon of a specific species. First, there must be an incredibly strong bond of trust and friendship between the Trainer and Pokémon. They must be unified on and off the battlefield.

Second, the Trainer must possess both a Key Stone and the right Mega Stone. Each Pokémon species capable of Mega Evolving has a specific Mega Stone. A Trainer must quest for the perfect one and prove him or herself worthy of its power.

ALOLAN FORMS

Alolan Pokémon can look very different and be of a different type. When Pokémon develop a distinct appearance based on the region in which they live, it's called a regional variant. For example, the reason Alolan Exeggutor have grown taller is Alola's warm and sunny climate. It's perfect for Exeggcute and Exeggutor to thrive. Some believe that Alolan Exeggutor looks exactly the way it's supposed to because of Alola's environment.

ULTRA BEASTS

Ultra Beasts possess mighty powers. These mysterious creatures come from Ultra Wormholes.

LEGENDARY AND MYTHICAL POKÉMON

These extremely rare and powerful Pokémon are a bit of a mystery. They are unusually strong, and many have had incredible influence. Some have used their power to shape history and the world. And they are so rare that few people ever glimpse them. Trainers who have spotted a Legendary or Mythical Pokémon count themselves among the lucky.

Ready to discover more about each Pokémon? Then let's begin!

11

ABOMASNOW
Frost Tree Pokémon

TYPE: GRASS-ICE

Snow-covered mountains are Abomasnow's preferred habitat. It creates blizzards to hide itself and keep others away.

How to Say It: ah-BOM-ah-snow
Imperial Height: 7'03''
Imperial Weight: 298.7 lbs.
Metric Height: 2.2 m
Metric Weight: 135.5 kg

Possible Moves: Ice Punch, Powder Snow, Leer, Razor Leaf, Icy Wind, Grass Whistle, Swagger, Mist, Ice Shard, Ingrain, Wood Hammer, Blizzard, Sheer Cold

MEGA ABOMASNOW
Frost Tree Pokémon

TYPE: GRASS-ICE

Imperial Height: 8'10''
Imperial Weight: 407.9 lbs.
Metric Height: 2.7 m
Metric Weight: 185.0 kg

Snover ⇒ **Abomasnow** ⇒ **Mega Abomasnow**

12

TYPE: PSYCHIC

Even while Abra is sleeping, which is most of the time, it can escape a foe by teleporting away. Sometimes it wakes to find itself in an unfamiliar location and gets scared.

How to Say It: AB-ra
Imperial Height: 2'11''
Imperial Weight: 43.0 lbs.

Metric Height: 0.9 m
Metric Weight: 19.5 kg

Possible Move: Teleport

ABRA
Psi Pokémon

Abra → Kadabra → Alakazam → Mega Alakazam

ABSOL
Disaster Pokémon

TYPE: DARK

Where Absol appears, disaster often follows. People blamed it for causing these disasters, so they drove it away, into the mountains—but in truth, it was only trying to warn everyone.

How to Say It: AB-sahl
Imperial Height: 3'11''
Imperial Weight: 103.6 lbs.
Metric Height: 1.2 m
Metric Weight: 47.0 kg

Possible Moves: Perish Song, Future Sight, Scratch, Feint, Leer, Quick Attack, Pursuit, Taunt, Bite, Double Team, Slash, Swords Dance, Night Slash, Detect, Psycho Cut, Me First, Sucker Punch, Razor Wind

MEGA ABSOL
Disaster Pokémon

TYPE: DARK

Imperial Height: 3'11''
Imperial Weight: 108.0 lbs.
Metric Height: 1.2 m
Metric Weight: 49.0 kg

Absol ⇨ Mega Absol

14

ACCELGOR
Shell Out Pokémon

TYPE: BUG

After coming out of its shell, Accelgor is light and quick, moving with the speed of a ninja. It wraps its body up to keep from drying out.

How to Say It: ak-SELL-gohr
Imperial Height: 2'07''
Imperial Weight: 55.8 lbs.
Metric Height: 0.8 m
Metric Weight: 25.3 kg

Possible Moves: Water Shuriken, Final Gambit, Power Swap, Absorb, Acid Spray, Double Team, Quick Attack, Struggle Bug, Mega Drain, Swift, Me First, Agility, Giga Drain, U-turn, Bug Buzz, Recover

Shelmet   Accelgor

Shield Forme

AEGISLASH
Royal Sword Pokémon

TYPE: STEEL-GHOST

Aegislash has long been seen as a symbol of royalty. In olden days, these Pokémon often accompanied the king.

How to Say It: EE-jih-SLASH
Imperial Height: 5'07''
Imperial Weight: 116.8 lbs.
Metric Height: 1.7 m
Metric Weight: 53.0 kg

Possible Moves: Fury Cutter, Pursuit, Autotomize, Shadow Sneak, Slash, Iron Defense, Night Slash, Power Trick, Iron Head

Blade Forme

Honedge   Doublade   Aegislash

15

AERODACTYL

Fossil Pokémon

TYPE: ROCK-FLYING

In its own time, this ancient Pokémon was master of the skies. The fangs that line its jaws are like the teeth of a saw, and it uses them to grip and tear at opponents.

How to Say It: AIR-row-DACK-tull
Imperial Height: 5'11''
Imperial Weight: 130.1 lbs.
Metric Height: 1.8 m
Metric Weight: 59.0 kg

Possible Moves: Iron Head, Ice Fang, Fire Fang, Thunder Fang, Wing Attack, Supersonic, Bite, Scary Face, Roar, Agility, Ancient Power, Crunch, Take Down, Sky Drop, Hyper Beam, Rock Slide, Giga Impact

MEGA AERODACTYL

Fossil Pokémon

TYPE: ROCK-FLYING

Imperial Height: 6'11''
Imperial Weight: 174.2 lbs.
Metric Height: 2.1 m
Metric Weight: 79.0 kg

Aerodactyl   Mega Aerodactyl

AGGRON
Iron Armor Pokémon

TYPE: STEEL-ROCK

Aggron is extremely protective of the mountain it claims as its territory. After a natural disaster, it will work tirelessly to restore its mountain, rebuilding the topsoil and planting trees.

How to Say It: AGG-ron
Imperial Height: 6'11''
Imperial Weight: 793.7 lbs.
Metric Height: 2.1 m
Metric Weight: 360.0 kg

Possible Moves: Tackle, Harden, Mud-Slap, Headbutt, Metal Claw, Rock Tomb, Protect, Roar, Iron Head, Rock Slide, Take Down, Metal Sound, Iron Tail, Iron Defense, Double-Edge, Autotomize, Heavy Slam, Metal Burst

MEGA AGGRON
Iron Armor Pokémon

TYPE: STEEL

Imperial Height: 7'03''
Imperial Weight: 870.8 lbs.
Metric Height: 2.2 m
Metric Weight: 395.0 kg

 Aron ⇨ **Lairon** ⇨ **Aggron** ⇨  **Mega Aggron**

AIPOM
Long Tail Pokémon

REGIONS:
Alola
Johto

TYPE: NORMAL

Aipom's tail is much handier than its actual hands, which have become clumsy from lack of use. It can use the tail to climb high up into trees and scout for food.

How to Say It: AY-pom
Imperial Height: 2'07''
Imperial Weight: 25.4 lbs.
Metric Height: 0.8 m
Metric Weight: 11.5 kg

Possible Moves: Scratch, Tail Whip, Sand Attack, Astonish, Baton Pass, Tickle, Fury Swipes, Swift, Screech, Agility, Double Hit, Fling, Nasty Plot, Last Resort

Aipom ⇨ Ambipom

ALAKAZAM
Psi Pokémon

TYPE: PSYCHIC

Alakazam's brain never stops growing, and its head has to keep expanding to contain its enormous intellect. If its psychic powers overflow, everyone nearby will get a splitting headache.

How to Say It: AL-a-kuh-ZAM
Imperial Height: 4'11''
Imperial Weight: 105.8 lbs.
Metric Height: 1.5 m
Metric Weight: 48.0 kg

Possible Moves: Kinesis, Teleport, Confusion, Disable, Psybeam, Miracle Eye, Reflect, Psycho Cut, Recover, Telekinesis, Ally Switch, Psychic, Calm Mind, Future Sight, Trick

MEGA ALAKAZAM
Psi Pokémon

TYPE: PSYCHIC
Imperial Height: 3'11''
Imperial Weight: 105.8 lbs.
Metric Height: 1.2 m
Metric Weight: 48.0 kg

Abra   ➡   Kadabra   ➡   Alakazam   ➡   Mega Alakazam

19

ALOMOMOLA

Caring Pokémon

TYPE: WATER

Alomomola has a reputation as a healer in the open sea where it lives. Pokémon that have been hurt gather around it so it can fix them up with the curative slime that covers its body.

How to Say It: uh-LOH-muh-MOH-luh
Imperial Height: 3'11''
Imperial Weight: 69.7 lbs.

Metric Height: 1.2 m
Metric Weight: 31.6 kg

Possible Moves: Play Nice, Hydro Pump, Wide Guard, Healing Wish, Helping Hand, Pound, Water Sport, Aqua Ring, Aqua Jet, Double Slap, Heal Pulse, Protect, Water Pulse, Wake-Up Slap, Soak, Wish, Brine, Safeguard, Whirlpool

Does not evolve

ALTARIA
Humming Pokémon

TYPE: DRAGON-FLYING

When Altaria sings through the sky in its beautiful soprano voice, anyone listening falls into a happy daydream. Its soft, cottony wings are perfect for catching updrafts.

How to Say It: ahl-TAR-ee-uh
Imperial Height: 3'07''
Imperial Weight: 45.4 lbs.
Metric Height: 1.1 m
Metric Weight: 20.6 kg

Possible Moves: Sky Attack, Pluck, Peck, Growl, Astonish, Sing, Fury Attack, Safeguard, Disarming Voice, Mist, Round, Natural Gift, Take Down, Refresh, Dragon Dance, Dragon Breath, Cotton Guard, Dragon Pulse, Perish Song, Moonblast

MEGA ALTARIA
Humming Pokémon

TYPE: DRAGON-FAIRY

Imperial Height: 4'11''
Imperial Weight: 45.4 lbs.
Metric Height: 1.5 m
Metric Weight: 20.6 kg

Swablu ⇨ Altaria ⇨ Mega Altaria

AMAURA
Tundra Pokémon

TYPE: ROCK-ICE

Amaura's call is said to summon the glowing colors of the aurora. These ancient Pokémon do best in cold climates that are hard to find in today's world.

How to Say It: ah-MORE-uh
Imperial Height: 4'03"
Imperial Weight: 55.6 lbs.
Metric Height: 1.3 m
Metric Weight: 25.2 kg

Possible Moves: Growl, Powder Snow, Thunder Wave, Rock Throw, Icy Wind, Take Down, Mist, Aurora Beam, Ancient Power, Round, Avalanche, Hail, Nature Power, Encore, Light Screen, Ice Beam, Hyper Beam, Blizzard

Amaura ⇨ Aurorus

AMBIPOM
Long Tail Pokémon

REGIONS:
Alola
Sinnoh

TYPE: NORMAL

Ambipom can be territorial when it's defending its favorite trees from rival Passimian, but it also has a soft side. It shows affection by hugging its Trainer tightly with both of its long tails.

How to Say It: AM-bee-pom
Imperial Height: 3'11"
Imperial Weight: 44.8 lbs.
Metric Height: 1.2 m
Metric Weight: 20.3 kg

Possible Moves: Dual Chop, Scratch, Tail Whip, Sand Attack, Astonish, Baton Pass, Tickle, Fury Swipes, Swift, Screech, Agility, Double Hit, Fling, Nasty Plot, Last Resort

Aipom ⇨ Ambipom

AMOONGUSS
Mushroom Pokémon

TYPE:
GRASS-POISON

In a swaying dance, Amoonguss waves its arm caps, which look like Poké Balls, in an attempt to lure the unwary. It doesn't often work.

How to Say It: uh-MOON-gus
Imperial Height: 2'00''
Imperial Weight: 23.1 lbs.
Metric Height: 0.6 m
Metric Weight: 10.5 kg

Possible Moves: Absorb, Growth, Astonish, Bide, Mega Drain, Ingrain, Feint Attack, Sweet Scent, Giga Drain, Toxic, Synthesis, Clear Smog, Solar Beam, Rage Powder, Spore

Foongus ⇨ Amoonguss

AMPHAROS
Light Pokémon

TYPE: ELECTRIC

Sailors have a tradition of using Ampharos as a beacon to guide them home. The light on its tail is so bright that it can be seen from a great distance.

How to Say It: AMF-fah-rahs
Imperial Height: 4'07''
Imperial Weight: 135.6 lbs.
Metric Height: 1.4 m
Metric Weight: 61.5 kg

Possible Moves: Zap Cannon, Magnetic Flux, Ion Deluge, Dragon Pulse, Fire Punch, Tackle, Growl, Thunder Wave, Thunder Shock, Cotton Spore, Charge, Take Down, Electro Ball, Confuse Ray, Thunder Punch, Power Gem, Discharge, Cotton Guard, Signal Beam, Light Screen, Thunder

MEGA AMPHAROS
Light Pokémon

TYPE: ELECTRIC-DRAGON

Imperial Height: 4'07''
Imperial Weight: 135.6 lbs.
Metric Height: 1.4 m
Metric Weight: 61.5 kg

Mareep　**Flaaffy**　**Ampharos**

Mega Ampharos

ANORITH
Old Shrimp Pokémon

TYPE: ROCK-BUG

It's possible to restore Anorith from a fossil, but this Pokémon doesn't do well in modern oceans because the environment is so different from its original home. It can swim quickly with its eight wings.

How to Say It: AN-no-rith
Imperial Height: 2'04''
Imperial Weight: 27.6 lbs.
Metric Height: 0.7 m
Metric Weight: 12.5 kg

Possible Moves: Scratch, Harden, Mud Sport, Water Gun, Fury Cutter, Smack Down, Metal Claw, Ancient Power, Bug Bite, Brine, Slash, Crush Claw, X-Scissor, Protect, Rock Blast

Anorith ⇨ Armaldo

TYPE: WATER-BUG

In battle, Araquanid uses the water bubble that surrounds its head as a weapon, headbutting its opponents or cutting off their air. When it's not battling, it uses the bubble as a shield to protect its weaker companions.

How to Say It: uh-RACK-wuh-nid
Imperial Height: 5'11''
Imperial Weight: 180.8 lbs.
Metric Height: 1.8 m
Metric Weight: 82.0 kg

Possible Moves: Wide Guard, Soak, Bubble, Infestation, Spider Web, Bug Bite, Bubble Beam, Bite, Aqua Ring, Leech Life, Crunch, Lunge, Mirror Coat, Liquidation, Entrainment

REGION:
Alola

ARAQUANID
Water Bubble Pokémon

Dewpider ⇨ Araquanid

ARBOK

Cobra Pokémon

TYPE: POISON

The patterns on Arbok's stomach can confuse and befuddle its opponents long enough for it to trap them in its coils. Nearly two dozen variations of these patterns have been observed.

How to Say It: ARE-bock
Imperial Height: 11'06''
Imperial Weight: 143.3 lbs.
Metric Height: 3.5 m
Metric Weight: 65.0 kg

Possible Moves: Ice Fang, Thunder Fang, Fire Fang, Wrap, Leer, Poison Sting, Bite, Glare, Screech, Acid, Crunch, Stockpile, Swallow, Spit Up, Acid Spray, Mud Bomb, Gastro Acid, Belch, Haze, Coil, Gunk Shot

Ekans ⇒ Arbok

ARCANINE

Legendary Pokémon

REGIONS:
Alola
Kanto

TYPE: FIRE

Beautiful and majestic, Arcanine uses the flame that burns within it as fuel to run amazing distances. Ancient Eastern folklore speaks of this powerful Pokémon.

How to Say It: ARE-ka-nine
Imperial Height: 6'03''
Imperial Weight: 341.7 lbs.
Metric Height: 1.9 m
Metric Weight: 155.0 kg

Possible Moves: Thunder Fang, Bite, Roar, Odor Sleuth, Fire Fang, Extreme Speed

Growlithe ⇒ Arcanine

TYPE: NORMAL

In the mythology of the Sinnoh region, Arceus emerged from its Egg into complete nothingness, and then shaped the world and everything in it.

How to Say It: ARK-ee-us
Imperial Height: 10'06''
Imperial Weight: 705.5 lbs.
Metric Height: 3.2 m
Metric Weight: 320.0 kg

Possible Moves: Seismic Toss, Cosmic Power, Natural Gift, Punishment, Gravity, Earth Power, Hyper Voice, Extreme Speed, Refresh, Future Sight, Recover, Hyper Beam, Perish Song, Judgment

REGION: Sinnoh

ARCEUS
Alpha Pokémon

MYTHICAL POKÉMON

Does not evolve

ARCHEN

First Bird Pokémon

REGIONS: Alola Unova

TYPE: ROCK-FLYING

Although modern-day flying Pokémon are descended from Archen, this ancient Pokémon could not truly fly. It used its wings to glide between trees or swoop onto opponents from above.

How to Say It: AR-ken
Imperial Height: 1'08''
Imperial Weight: 20.9 lbs.
Metric Height: 0.5 m
Metric Weight: 9.5 kg

Possible Moves: Quick Attack, Leer, Wing Attack, Rock Throw, Double Team, Scary Face, Pluck, Ancient Power, Agility, Quick Guard, Acrobatics, Dragon Breath, Crunch, Endeavor, U-turn, Rock Slide, Dragon Claw, Thrash

Archen   Archeops

ARCHEOPS

First Bird Pokémon

REGIONS: Alola Unova

TYPE: ROCK-FLYING

In the ancient world, Archeops could apparently fly but preferred to run, covering the ground at speeds of around twenty-five mph. They often teamed up against opponents—one would corner and distract the foe while another swooped in from above.

How to Say It: AR-kee-ops   **Metric Height:** 1.4 m
Imperial Height: 4'07''   **Metric Weight:** 32.0 kg
Imperial Weight: 70.5 lbs.

Possible Moves: Quick Attack, Leer, Wing Attack, Rock Throw, Double Team, Scary Face, Pluck, Ancient Power, Agility, Quick Guard, Acrobatics, Dragon Breath, Crunch, Endeavor, U-turn, Rock Slide, Dragon Claw, Thrash

Archen   Archeops

ARIADOS
Long Leg Pokémon

TYPE: BUG-POISON

Ariados thread is sometimes used in weaving to produce a particularly strong piece of cloth. When making its web, Ariados spins this thread from both ends of its body.

How to Say It: AIR-ree-uh-dose
Imperial Height: 3'07''
Imperial Weight: 73.9 lbs.
Metric Height: 1.1 m
Metric Weight: 33.5 kg

Possible Moves: Swords Dance, Focus Energy, Venom Drench, Fell Stinger, Bug Bite, Poison Sting, String Shot, Constrict, Absorb, Infestation, Scary Face, Night Shade, Shadow Sneak, Fury Swipes, Sucker Punch, Spider Web, Agility, Pin Missile, Psychic, Poison Jab, Cross Poison, Sticky Web, Toxic Thread

Spinarak ➡ Ariados

ARMALDO
Plate Pokémon

TYPE: ROCK-BUG

After evolving, Armaldo lives primarily on the land, though it still hunts for food in the sea. This ancient Pokémon has been revealed as the ancestor of some modern Bug types.

How to Say It: ar-MAL-do
Imperial Height: 4'11''
Imperial Weight: 150.4 lbs.
Metric Height: 1.5 m
Metric Weight: 68.2 kg

Possible Moves: Scratch, Harden, Mud Sport, Water Gun, Fury Cutter, Smack Down, Metal Claw, Protect, Ancient Power, Bug Bite, Brine, Slash, Rock Blast, Crush Claw, X-Scissor

Anorith ➡ Armaldo

29

AROMATISSE
Fragrance Pokémon

TYPE: FAIRY

Aromatisse uses its powerful scent as a weapon in battle. It can overpower an opponent with a strategic stench.

How to Say It: uh-ROME-uh-teece
Imperial Height: 2'07''
Imperial Weight: 34.2 lbs.
Metric Height: 0.8 m
Metric Weight: 15.5 kg

Possible Moves: Aromatic Mist, Heal Pulse, Sweet Scent, Fairy Wind, Sweet Kiss, Odor Sleuth, Echoed Voice, Calm Mind, Draining Kiss, Aromatherapy, Attract, Moonblast, Charm, Flail, Misty Terrain, Skill Swap, Psychic, Disarming Voice, Reflect, Psych Up

Spritzee ⇨ Aromatisse

ARON
Iron Armor Pokémon

TYPE: STEEL-ROCK

Aron chews up metal objects, from iron ore to steel bridges, and uses the metal to build up its body. It can destroy a heavy truck with a full-speed charge.

How to Say It: AIR-ron
Imperial Height: 1'04''
Imperial Weight: 132.3 lbs.
Metric Height: 0.4 m
Metric Weight: 60.0 kg

Possible Moves: Tackle, Harden, Mud-Slap, Headbutt, Metal Claw, Rock Tomb, Protect, Roar, Iron Head, Rock Slide, Take Down, Metal Sound, Iron Tail, Iron Defense, Double-Edge, Autotomize, Heavy Slam, Metal Burst

Aron ⇨ Lairon ⇨ Aggron ⇨ Mega Aggron

TYPE: ICE-FLYING

When Articuno flaps its wings, the air turns chilly. This Legendary Pokémon often brings snowfall in its wake.

How to Say It: ART-tick-COO-no
Imperial Height: 5'07''
Imperial Weight: 122.1 lbs.
Metric Height: 1.7 m
Metric Weight: 55.4 kg

Possible Moves: Roost, Hurricane, Freeze-Dry, Tailwind, Sheer Cold, Gust, Powder Snow, Mist, Ice Shard, Mind Reader, Ancient Power, Agility, Ice Beam, Reflect, Hail, Blizzard

REGIONS:
Kalos
(Coastal)
Kanto

ARTICUNO
Freeze Pokémon

LEGENDARY POKÉMON

Does not evolve

AUDINO
Hearing Pokémon

REGIONS:
Kalos
(Central)
Unova

TYPE: NORMAL

With the sensitive feelers on their ears, Audino can listen to people's heartbeats to pick up on their current state. Egg-hatching can be predicted as well.

How to Say It: AW-dih-noh
Imperial Height: 3'07''
Imperial Weight: 68.3 lbs.
Metric Height: 1.1 m
Metric Weight: 31.0 kg

Possible Moves: Last Resort, Play Nice, Pound, Growl, Helping Hand, Refresh, Double Slap, Attract, Secret Power, Entrainment, Take Down, Heal Pulse, After You, Simple Beam, Double-Edge

MEGA AUDINO
Hearing Pokémon

TYPE: NORMAL-FAIRY

Imperial Height: 4'11''
Imperial Weight: 70.5 lbs.
Metric Height: 1.5 m
Metric Weight: 32.0 kg

Audino   **Mega Audino**

TYPE: ROCK-ICE

With its calm and gentle demeanor and beautifully colored sails, Aurorus seems like a wonderful companion for petting and snuggling. Unfortunately, its skin is hundreds of degrees below freezing.

How to Say It: ah-ROAR-us
Imperial Height: 8'10''
Imperial Weight: 496.0 lbs.
Metric Height: 2.7 m
Metric Weight: 225.0 kg

Possible Moves: Freeze-Dry, Growl, Powder Snow, Thunder Wave, Rock Throw, Icy Wind, Take Down, Mist, Aurora Beam, Ancient Power, Round, Avalanche, Hail, Nature Power, Encore, Light Screen, Ice Beam, Hyper Beam, Blizzard

REGIONS:
Alola
Kalos
(Coastal)

AURORUS
Tundra Pokémon

Amaura ⇨ Aurorus

REGION:
Kalos
(Mountain)

AVALUGG
Iceberg Pokémon

TYPE: ICE

Avalugg's broad, flat back is a common resting place for groups of Bergmite. Its big, bulky body can crush obstacles in its path.

How to Say It: AV-uh-lug
Imperial Height: 6'07''
Imperial Weight: 1,113.3 lbs.
Metric Height: 2.0 m
Metric Weight: 505.0 kg

Possible Moves: Body Slam, Wide Guard, Iron Defense, Crunch, Skull Bash, Tackle, Bite, Harden, Powder Snow, Icy Wind, Take Down, Sharpen, Curse, Ice Fang, Ice Ball, Rapid Spin, Avalanche, Blizzard, Recover, Double-Edge

Bergmite ⇨ Avalugg

AXEW

Tusk Pokémon

REGIONS:
Kalos
(Central)
Unova

TYPE: DRAGON

If one of Axew's tusks breaks off, it quickly regrows, even stronger and sharper than before. Axew uses its tusks to crush berries and mark territory.

How to Say It: AKS-yoo
Imperial Height: 2'00''
Imperial Weight: 39.7 lbs.
Metric Height: 0.6 m
Metric Weight: 18.0 kg

Possible Moves: Scratch, Leer, Assurance, Dragon Rage, Dual Chop, Scary Face, Slash, False Swipe, Dragon Claw, Dragon Dance, Taunt, Dragon Pulse, Swords Dance, Guillotine, Outrage, Giga Impact

Axew ⇨ Fraxure ⇨ Haxorus

AZELF

Willpower Pokémon

REGION:
Sinnoh

LEGENDARY POKÉMON

TYPE: PSYCHIC

According to legend, Azelf brought a lasting balance to the world. It is known as "The Being of Willpower."

How to Say It: AZ-elf
Imperial Height: 1'00''
Imperial Weight: 0.7 lbs.
Metric Height: 0.3 m
Metric Weight: 0.3 kg

Possible Moves: Rest, Confusion, Imprison, Detect, Swift, Uproar, Future Sight, Nasty Plot, Extrasensory, Last Resort, Natural Gift, Explosion

Does not evolve

AZUMARILL
Aqua Rabbit Pokémon

TYPE: WATER-FAIRY

When Azumarill spots a Pokémon struggling in the water, it creates a balloon of air so the other Pokémon can breathe. It has excellent hearing.

How to Say It: ah-ZU-mare-rill
Imperial Height: 2'07''
Imperial Weight: 62.8 lbs.
Metric Height: 0.8 m
Metric Weight: 28.5 kg

Possible Moves: Tackle, Water Gun, Tail Whip, Water Sport, Bubble, Defense Curl, Rollout, Bubble Beam, Helping Hand, Aqua Tail, Double-Edge, Aqua Ring, Rain Dance, Superpower, Hydro Pump, Play Rough

Azurill   Marill   Azumarill

TYPE: NORMAL-FAIRY

Azurill can fling itself more than ten yards by spinning the large ball at the end of its tail and then throwing it. It can also use the tail to bounce around.

How to Say It: uh-ZOO-rill
Imperial Height: 0'08''
Imperial Weight: 4.4 lbs.
Metric Height: 0.2 m
Metric Weight: 2.0 kg

Possible Moves: Splash, Water Gun, Tail Whip, Water Sport, Bubble, Charm, Bubble Beam, Helping Hand, Slam, Bounce

AZURILL
Polka Dot Pokémon

Azurill   Marill   Azumarill

35

BAGON

Rock Head Pokémon

REGIONS:
Alola
Hoenn
Kalos
(Coastal)

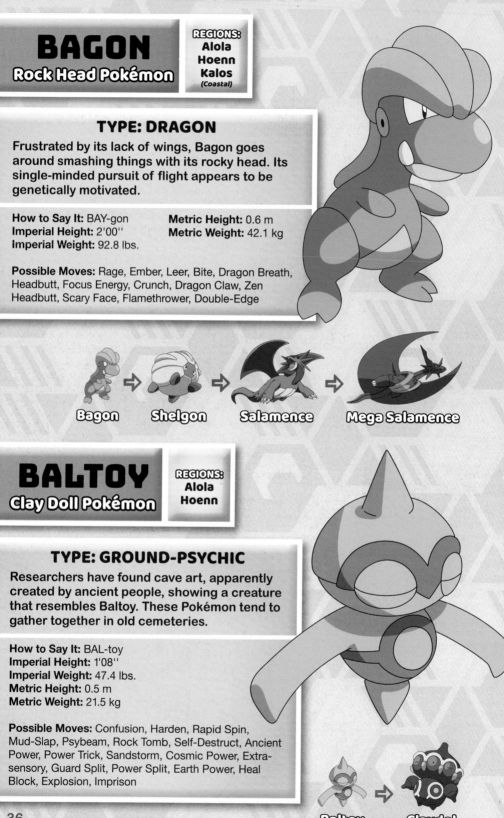

TYPE: DRAGON

Frustrated by its lack of wings, Bagon goes around smashing things with its rocky head. Its single-minded pursuit of flight appears to be genetically motivated.

How to Say It: BAY-gon
Imperial Height: 2'00''
Imperial Weight: 92.8 lbs.
Metric Height: 0.6 m
Metric Weight: 42.1 kg

Possible Moves: Rage, Ember, Leer, Bite, Dragon Breath, Headbutt, Focus Energy, Crunch, Dragon Claw, Zen Headbutt, Scary Face, Flamethrower, Double-Edge

Bagon ⇨ **Shelgon** ⇨ **Salamence** ⇨ **Mega Salamence**

BALTOY

Clay Doll Pokémon

REGIONS:
Alola
Hoenn

TYPE: GROUND-PSYCHIC

Researchers have found cave art, apparently created by ancient people, showing a creature that resembles Baltoy. These Pokémon tend to gather together in old cemeteries.

How to Say It: BAL-toy
Imperial Height: 1'08''
Imperial Weight: 47.4 lbs.
Metric Height: 0.5 m
Metric Weight: 21.5 kg

Possible Moves: Confusion, Harden, Rapid Spin, Mud-Slap, Psybeam, Rock Tomb, Self-Destruct, Ancient Power, Power Trick, Sandstorm, Cosmic Power, Extrasensory, Guard Split, Power Split, Earth Power, Heal Block, Explosion, Imprison

Baltoy ⇨ **Claydol**

BANETTE
Marionette Pokémon

TYPE: GHOST

Banette came into being from an abandoned child's toy, fueled by resentment and vengeance. Some people speculate that if Banette's Trainer takes good care of it, its spirit will be able to rest.

How to Say It: bane-NETT
Imperial Height: 3'07''
Imperial Weight: 27.6 lbs.
Metric Height: 1.1 m
Metric Weight: 12.5 kg

Possible Moves: Phantom Force, Knock Off, Screech, Night Shade, Curse, Spite, Will-O-Wisp, Shadow Sneak, Feint Attack, Hex, Shadow Ball, Sucker Punch, Embargo, Snatch, Grudge, Trick

MEGA BANETTE
Marionette Pokémon

TYPE: GHOST

Imperial Height: 3'11''
Imperial Weight: 28.7 lbs.
Metric Height: 1.2 m
Metric Weight: 13.0 kg

Shuppet ⇨ **Banette** ⇨ **Mega Banette**

BARBARACLE
Collective Pokémon

TYPE: ROCK-WATER

When seven Binacle come together to fight as one, a Barbaracle is formed. The head gives the orders, but the limbs don't always listen.

How to Say It: bar-BARE-uh-kull
Imperial Height: 4'03''
Imperial Weight: 211.6 lbs.
Metric Height: 1.3 m
Metric Weight: 96.0 kg

Possible Moves: Stone Edge, Skull Bash, Shell Smash, Scratch, Sand Attack, Water Gun, Withdraw, Fury Swipes, Slash, Mud-Slap, Clamp, Rock Polish, Ancient Power, Hone Claws, Fury Cutter, Night Slash, Razor Shell, Cross Chop

Binacle ⇨ **Barbaracle**

BARBOACH
Whiskers Pokémon

REGIONS:
**Alola
Hoenn
Kalos**
(Mountain)

TYPE: WATER-GROUND

It's so hard to hold on to a slippery Barboach that doing so has become a competition in some places! This Pokémon prefers to live in muddy water, where it uses its whiskers to sense its surroundings.

How to Say It: bar-BOACH
Imperial Height: 1'04''
Imperial Weight: 4.2 lbs.
Metric Height: 0.4 m
Metric Weight: 1.9 kg

Possible Moves: Mud-Slap, Mud Sport, Water Sport, Water Gun, Mud Bomb, Amnesia, Water Pulse, Magnitude, Rest, Snore, Aqua Tail, Earthquake, Muddy Water, Future Sight, Fissure

Barboach ⇨ **Whiscash**

Red Stripe

BASCULIN
Hostile Pokémon

TYPE: WATER

Basculin is notoriously aggressive, and schools of this Pokémon dominate any lake they come to inhabit. The Red- and Blue-Stripe forms constantly clash over territory.

How to Say It: BASS-kyoo-lin
Imperial Height: 3'03"
Imperial Weight: 39.7 lbs.
Metric Height: 1.0 m
Metric Weight: 18.0 kg

Possible Moves: Thrash, Flail, Tail Whip, Tackle, Water Gun, Uproar, Headbutt, Bite, Aqua Jet, Chip Away, Take Down, Crunch, Aqua Tail, Soak, Double-Edge, Scary Face, Final Gambit, Head Smash

Blue Stripe

Does not evolve

BASTIODON
Shield Pokémon

TYPE: ROCK-STEEL

Bastiodon is well guarded against a frontal assault, but it's vulnerable from the rear. Fossils of Bastiodon and Rampardos have been discovered in the same places, often locked together in eternal combat.

How to Say It: BAS-tee-oh-DON
Imperial Height: 4'03"
Imperial Weight: 329.6 lbs.
Metric Height: 1.3 m
Metric Weight: 149.5 kg

Possible Moves: Block, Tackle, Protect, Taunt, Metal Sound, Take Down, Iron Defense, Swagger, Ancient Power, Endure, Metal Burst, Iron Head, Heavy Slam

Shieldon ⇨ **Bastiodon**

BAYLEEF
Leaf Pokémon

REGION: Johto

TYPE: GRASS

The tree shoots that form a wreath around Bayleef's neck give off an invigorating fragrance. A tube-shaped leaf protects each shoot.

How to Say It: BAY-leaf
Imperial Height: 3'11''
Imperial Weight: 34.8 lbs.
Metric Height: 1.2 m
Metric Weight: 15.8 kg

Possible Moves: Tackle, Growl, Razor Leaf, Poison Powder, Synthesis, Reflect, Magical Leaf, Natural Gift, Sweet Scent, Light Screen, Body Slam, Safeguard, Aromatherapy, Solar Beam

Chikorita ⇨ Bayleef ⇨ Meganium

BEARTIC
Freezing Pokémon

REGIONS: Kalos (Mountain) Unova

TYPE: ICE

Beartic live in the far north, where the seas are very cold. Their fangs and claws are made of ice formed by their own freezing breath.

How to Say It: BAIR-tick
Imperial Height: 8'06''
Imperial Weight: 573.2 lbs.
Metric Height: 2.6 m
Metric Weight: 260.0 kg

Possible Moves: Sheer Cold, Thrash, Superpower, Aqua Jet, Growl, Powder Snow, Bide, Icy Wind, Play Nice, Fury Swipes, Brine, Endure, Swagger, Slash, Flail, Icicle Crash, Rest, Blizzard, Hail

Cubchoo ⇨ Beartic

BEAUTIFLY
Butterfly Pokémon

TYPE: BUG-FLYING

To attract a Beautifly, plant flowers near your windows. This Pokémon uncoils its long mouth to gather pollen from flowers.

How to Say It: BUE-tee-fly
Imperial Height: 3'03''
Imperial Weight: 62.6 lbs.

Metric Height: 1.0 m
Metric Weight: 28.4 kg

Possible Moves: Absorb, Gust, Stun Spore, Morning Sun, Air Cutter, Mega Drain, Whirlwind, Attract, Silver Wind, Giga Drain, Bug Buzz, Rage, Quiver Dance

Wurmple ⇨ Silcoon ⇨ Beautifly

BEEDRILL
Poison Bee Pokémon

TYPE: BUG-POISON

Stay far away from a Beedrill nest. These territorial Pokémon will swarm any intruder in a furious attack.

How to Say It: BEE-dril
Imperial Height: 3'03"
Imperial Weight: 65.0 lbs.
Metric Height: 1.0 m
Metric Weight: 29.5 kg

Possible Moves: Fury Attack, Focus Energy, Twineedle, Rage, Pursuit, Toxic Spikes, Pin Missile, Agility, Assurance, Poison Jab, Endeavor, Fell Stinger, Venoshock

MEGA BEEDRILL
Poison Bee Pokémon

TYPE: BUG-POISON
Imperial Height: 4'07"
Imperial Weight: 89.4 lbs.
Metric Height: 1.4 m
Metric Weight: 40.5 kg

Weedle Kakuna Beedrill

Mega Beedrill

BEHEEYEM
Cerebral Pokémon

TYPE: PSYCHIC

By flashing its fingers in multiple colors, Beheeyem has the power to control its opponents' minds and overwrite their memories. You don't remember meeting this Pokémon? How interesting . . .

How to Say It: BEE-hee-ehm
Imperial Height: 3'03''
Imperial Weight: 76.1 lbs.

Metric Height: 1.0 m
Metric Weight: 34.5 kg

Possible Moves: Psychic Terrain, Confusion, Growl, Heal Block, Miracle Eye, Psybeam, Headbutt, Hidden Power, Imprison, Simple Beam, Zen Headbutt, Psych Up, Psychic, Calm Mind, Recover, Guard Split, Power Split, Synchronoise, Wonder Room

Elgyem ➡ **Beheeyem**

TYPE: STEEL-PSYCHIC

Groups of Beldum communicate using the power of magnetism. It uses the magnetic force generated inside its cells to pull its opponent within range of its claws.

How to Say It: BELL-dum
Imperial Height: 2'00''
Imperial Weight: 209.9 lbs.
Metric Height: 0.6 m
Metric Weight: 95.2 kg

Possible Move: Take Down

BELDUM
Iron Ball Pokémon

Beldum ➡ **Metang** ➡ **Metagross** ➡ **Mega Metagross**

BELLOSSOM

Flower Pokémon

TYPE: GRASS

In strong sunlight, this Pokémon's leaves spin in a joyful dance. Bellossom that evolve from a particularly stinky Gloom will grow the most beautiful flowers.

How to Say It: bell-LAHS-um
Imperial Height: 1'04''
Imperial Weight: 12.8 lbs.
Metric Height: 0.4 m
Metric Weight: 5.8 kg

Possible Moves: Leaf Storm, Leaf Blade, Mega Drain, Sweet Scent, Stun Spore, Sunny Day, Magical Leaf, Petal Blizzard, Quiver Dance

Oddish ⇨ Gloom ⇨ Bellossom

BELLSPROUT

Flower Pokémon

TYPE: GRASS-POISON

Bellsprout's long, thin body can bend in any direction, so it's good at dodging attacks. The liquid it spits is highly corrosive.

How to Say It: BELL-sprout
Imperial Height: 2'04''
Imperial Weight: 8.8 lbs.
Metric Height: 0.7 m
Metric Weight: 4.0 kg

Possible Moves: Vine Whip, Growth, Wrap, Sleep Powder, Poison Powder, Stun Spore, Acid, Knock Off, Sweet Scent, Gastro Acid, Razor Leaf, Poison Jab, Slam, Wring Out

Bellsprout ⇨ Weepinbell ⇨ Victreebel

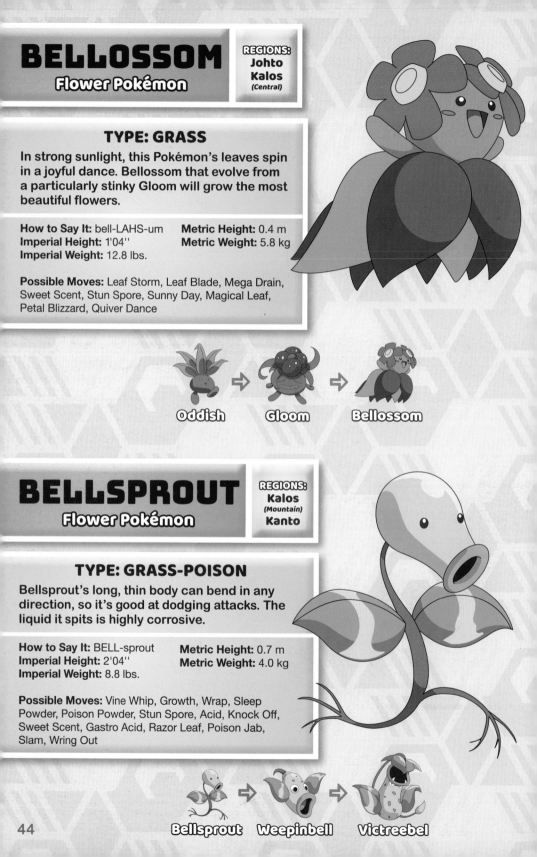

TYPE: ICE

When cracks form in Bergmite's icy body, it uses freezing air to patch itself up with new ice. It lives high in the mountains.

How to Say It: BERG-mite
Imperial Height: 3'03''
Imperial Weight: 219.4 lbs.
Metric Height: 1.0 m
Metric Weight: 99.5 kg

Possible Moves: Tackle, Bite, Harden, Powder Snow, Icy Wind, Take Down, Sharpen, Curse, Ice Fang, Ice Ball, Rapid Spin, Avalanche, Blizzard, Recover, Double-Edge

REGION: Kalos (Mountain)

BERGMITE
Ice Chunk Pokémon

Bergmite ➡ **Avalugg**

REGION: Alola

BEWEAR
Strong Arm Pokémon

TYPE: NORMAL-FIGHTING

Think twice before making friends with a Bewear. This superstrong Pokémon might be even more dangerous to those it likes, because it tends to deliver bone-crushing hugs as a sign of affection. Beware!

How to Say It: beh-WARE
Imperial Height: 6'11''
Imperial Weight: 297.6 lbs.
Metric Height: 2.1 m
Metric Weight: 135.0 kg

Possible Moves: Bind, Tackle, Leer, Bide, Baby-Doll Eyes, Brutal Swing, Flail, Payback, Take Down, Hammer Arm, Thrash, Pain Split, Double-Edge, Superpower

Stufful ➡ **Bewear**

BIBAREL
Beaver Pokémon

REGIONS:
Kalos
(Central)
Sinnoh

TYPE: NORMAL-WATER

With their large, sharp teeth, Bibarel busily cut up trees to build nests. Sometimes these nests block small streams and divert the flow of the water.

How to Say It: bee-BER-rel
Imperial Height: 3'03"
Imperial Weight: 69.4 lbs.
Metric Height: 1.0 m
Metric Weight: 31.5 kg

Possible Moves: Aqua Jet, Rototiller, Tackle, Growl, Defense Curl, Rollout, Water Gun, Headbutt, Hyper Fang, Yawn, Crunch, Take Down, Super Fang, Swords Dance, Amnesia, Superpower, Curse

Bidoof ⇨ Bibarel

BIDOOF
Plump Mouse Pokémon

REGIONS:
Kalos
(Central)
Sinnoh

TYPE: NORMAL

Bidoof live beside the water, where they gnaw on rock or wood to keep their front teeth worn down. They have a steady nature and are not easily upset.

How to Say It: BEE-doof
Imperial Height: 1'08"
Imperial Weight: 44.1 lbs.
Metric Height: 0.5 m
Metric Weight: 20.0 kg

Possible Moves: Tackle, Growl, Defense Curl, Rollout, Headbutt, Hyper Fang, Yawn, Crunch, Take Down, Super Fang, Swords Dance, Amnesia, Superpower, Curse

Bidoof ⇨ Bibarel

TYPE: ROCK-WATER

Binacle live in pairs, two on the same rock. They comb the beach for seaweed to eat.

How to Say It: BY-nuh-kull
Imperial Height: 1'08''
Imperial Weight: 68.3 lbs.
Metric Height: 0.5 m
Metric Weight: 31.0 kg

Possible Moves: Shell Smash, Scratch, Sand Attack, Water Gun, Withdraw, Fury Swipes, Slash, Mud-Slap, Clamp, Rock Polish, Ancient Power, Hone Claws, Fury Cutter, Night Slash, Razor Shell, Cross Chop

REGION:
Kalos
(Coastal)

BINACLE
Two-Handed Pokémon

Binacle **Barbaracle**

REGIONS:
Alola
Kalos
(Mountain)
Unova

BISHARP
Sword Blade Pokémon

TYPE: DARK-STEEL

Backed up by a posse of Pawniard, Bisharp remains calm and collected in battle. Despite its strength, if the blade on its head is ever chipped, it forfeits its position as the group's leader.

How to Say It: BIH-sharp
Imperial Height: 5'03''
Imperial Weight: 154.3 lbs.
Metric Height: 1.6 m
Metric Weight: 70.0 kg

Possible Moves: Guillotine, Iron Head, Metal Burst, Scratch, Leer, Fury Cutter, Torment, Feint Attack, Scary Face, Metal Claw, Slash, Assurance, Metal Sound, Embargo, Iron Defense, Night Slash, Swords Dance

Pawniard **Bisharp**

BLACEPHALON
Fireworks Pokémon

ULTRA BEAST

TYPE: FIRE-GHOST

Blacephalon, one of the mysterious Ultra Beasts, has an unexpected method of attack: It makes its own head blow up! Its opponents are so surprised by this that it can take advantage and steal their energy.

How to Say It: blass-SEF-uh-lawn
Imperial Height: 5'11''
Imperial Weight: 28.7 lbs.

Metric Height: 1.8 m
Metric Weight: 13.0 kg

Possible Moves: Ember, Astonish, Magic Coat, Stored Power, Flame Burst, Night Shade, Light Screen, Calm Mind, Fire Blast, Shadow Ball, Trick, Mind Blown

Does not evolve

BLASTOISE
Shellfish Pokémon

TYPE: WATER

From the spouts on its shell, Blastoise can fire water bullets with amazing accuracy. It can hit a target more than 160 feet away!

How to Say It: BLAS-toyce
Imperial Height: 5'03"
Imperial Weight: 188.5 lbs.
Metric Height: 1.6 m
Metric Weight: 85.5 kg

Possible Moves: Flash Cannon, Tackle, Tail Whip, Water Gun, Withdraw, Bubble, Bite, Rapid Spin, Protect, Water Pulse, Aqua Tail, Skull Bash, Iron Defense, Rain Dance, Hydro Pump

MEGA BLASTOISE
Shellfish Pokémon

TYPE: WATER
Imperial Height: 5'03"
Imperial Weight: 222.9 lbs.
Metric Height: 1.6 m
Metric Weight: 101.1 kg

Squirtle ⇨ **Wartortle** ⇨ **Blastoise** ⇨ **Mega Blastoise**

49

BLAZIKEN
Blaze Pokémon

REGION: Hoenn

TYPE: FIRE-FIGHTING

With continued strengthening of its legs, Blaziken can leap over a thirty-story building. The flames that flare from its wrists burn hotter against a worthy foe.

How to Say It: BLAZE-uh-ken
Imperial Height: 6'03''
Imperial Weight: 114.6 lbs.
Metric Height: 1.9 m
Metric Weight: 52.0 kg

Possible Moves: Blaze Kick, Double Kick, Flare Blitz, Fire Punch, High Jump Kick, Scratch, Growl, Ember, Sand Attack, Peck, Flame Charge, Quick Attack, Bulk Up, Focus Energy, Slash, Brave Bird, Sky Uppercut

MEGA BLAZIKEN
Blaze Pokémon

TYPE: FIRE-FIGHTING
Imperial Height: 6'03''
Imperial Weight: 114.6 lbs.
Metric Height: 1.9 m
Metric Weight: 52.0 kg

Torchic ➡ Combusken ➡ Blaziken ➡ Mega Blaziken

TYPE: NORMAL

Eating the egg of a Blissey has a calming effect on even the wildest of tempers. The soft, fluffy fur that covers its body is extremely sensitive to its surroundings, and it can even sense emotions this way.

How to Say It: BLISS-sey
Imperial Height: 4'11''
Imperial Weight: 103.2 lbs.
Metric Height: 1.5 m
Metric Weight: 46.8 kg

Possible Moves: Defense Curl, Pound, Growl, Tail Whip, Refresh, Double Slap, Soft-Boiled, Bestow, Minimize, Take Down, Sing, Fling, Heal Pulse, Egg Bomb, Light Screen, Healing Wish, Double-Edge

REGIONS:
Alola
Johto

BLISSEY
Happiness Pokémon

Happiny ⇨ **Chansey** ⇨ **Blissey**

TYPE: ELECTRIC

Blitzle's mane attracts lightning and stores the electricity. It can discharge this electricity in controlled flashes to communicate with others.

How to Say It: BLIT-zul
Imperial Height: 2'07''
Imperial Weight: 65.7 lbs.
Metric Height: 0.8 m
Metric Weight: 29.8 kg

Possible Moves: Quick Attack, Tail Whip, Charge, Shock Wave, Thunder Wave, Flame Charge, Pursuit, Spark, Stomp, Discharge, Agility, Wild Charge, Thrash

REGION:
Unova

BLITZLE
Electrified Pokémon

Blitzle ⇨ **Zebstrika**

BOLDORE

Ore Pokémon

TYPE: ROCK

The crystals that dot Boldore's body are masses of pure energy and could be used as an impressive fuel source if they were to come off. It's good at finding underground water, but being near water makes it uneasy.

How to Say It: BOHL-dohr
Imperial Height: 2'11''
Imperial Weight: 224.9 lbs.
Metric Height: 0.9 m
Metric Weight: 102.0 kg

Possible Moves: Power Gem, Tackle, Harden, Sand Attack, Headbutt, Rock Blast, Mud-Slap, Iron Defense, Smack Down, Rock Slide, Stealth Rock, Sandstorm, Stone Edge, Explosion

Roggenrola   Boldore   Gigalith

BONSLY

Bonsai Pokémon

TYPE: ROCK

Bonsly "sweats" by releasing moisture from its eyes, which makes it look like it's crying. It prefers a dry environment where few plants grow, but that often leaves it without camouflage.

How to Say It: BON-slye
Imperial Height: 1'08''
Imperial Weight: 33.1 lbs.
Metric Height: 0.5 m
Metric Weight: 15.0 kg

Possible Moves: Fake Tears, Copycat, Flail, Low Kick, Rock Throw, Mimic, Feint Attack, Tearful Look, Rock Tomb, Block, Rock Slide, Counter, Sucker Punch, Double-Edge

Bonsly   Sudowoodo

TYPE: NORMAL

Though Bouffalant can knock a train off the rails with the force of its headbutt, it doesn't worry about hurting itself, because its fluffy fur absorbs the impact.

How to Say It: BOO-fuh-lahnt
Imperial Height: 5'03''
Imperial Weight: 208.6 lbs.
Metric Height: 1.6 m
Metric Weight: 94.6 kg

Possible Moves: Pursuit, Leer, Rage, Fury Attack, Horn Attack, Scary Face, Revenge, Head Charge, Focus Energy, Megahorn, Reversal, Thrash, Swords Dance, Giga Impact

REGION: Unova

BOUFFALANT
Bash Buffalo Pokémon

Does not evolve

REGION: Alola

BOUNSWEET
Fruit Pokémon

TYPE: GRASS

Bounsweet smells good enough to eat—which sometimes gets it into trouble! The intensely sugary liquid it gives off can be diluted to bring the sweetness level down so people can drink it.

How to Say It: BOWN-sweet
Imperial Height: 1'00''
Imperial Weight: 7.1 lbs.
Metric Height: 0.3 m
Metric Weight: 3.2 kg

Possible Moves: Splash, Play Nice, Rapid Spin, Razor Leaf, Sweet Scent, Magical Leaf, Teeter Dance, Flail, Aromatic Mist

Bounsweet   Steenee   Tsareena

BRAIXEN
Fox Pokémon

REGION:
Kalos
(Central)

TYPE: FIRE

When Braixen pulls the twig out of its tail, the friction from its fur sets the wood on fire. It can use this flaming twig as a tool or a weapon.

How to Say It: BRAKE-sen
Imperial Height: 3'03''
Imperial Weight: 32.0 lbs.
Metric Height: 1.0 m
Metric Weight: 14.5 kg

Possible Moves: Scratch, Tail Whip, Ember, Howl, Flame Charge, Psybeam, Fire Spin, Lucky Chant, Light Screen, Psyshock, Flamethrower, Will-O-Wisp, Psychic, Sunny Day, Magic Room, Fire Blast

Fennekin ⇨ Braixen ⇨ Delphox

BRAVIARY
Valiant Pokémon

REGIONS:
Alola
Unova

TYPE: NORMAL-FLYING

In ancient Alola, Braviary was respected as "the hero of the sky." Several of these Pokémon teamed up to fight back against people who threatened their territory, or so the story goes.

How to Say It: BRAY-vee-air-ee
Imperial Height: 4'11''
Imperial Weight: 90.4 lbs.
Metric Height: 1.5 m
Metric Weight: 41.0 kg

Possible Moves: Thrash, Brave Bird, Whirlwind, Superpower, Peck, Leer, Fury Attack, Wing Attack, Hone Claws, Scary Face, Aerial Ace, Slash, Defog, Tailwind, Air Slash, Crush Claw, Sky Drop

Rufflet ⇨ Braviary

BRELOOM
Mushroom Pokémon

TYPE: GRASS-FIGHTING

If a seed falls from Breloom's tail, you really shouldn't eat it. The seeds are toxic and taste terrible. Its arms stretch to throw impressive punches.

How to Say It: brell-LOOM
Imperial Height: 3'11''
Imperial Weight: 86.4 lbs.
Metric Height: 1.2 m
Metric Weight: 39.2 kg

Possible Moves: Absorb, Tackle, Stun Spore, Leech Seed, Mega Drain, Headbutt, Mach Punch, Feint, Counter, Force Palm, Sky Uppercut, Mind Reader, Seed Bomb, Dynamic Punch

Shroomish ⇨ **Breloom**

BRIONNE
Pop Star Pokémon

TYPE: WATER

Brionne pelts its opponents with water balloons in a swift and skillful battle dance. It also shows off its dancing abilities when trying to cheer up its Trainer.

How to Say It: bree-AHN
Imperial Height: 2'00''
Imperial Weight: 38.6 lbs.
Metric Height: 0.6 m
Metric Weight: 17.5 kg

Possible Moves: Pound, Water Gun, Growl, Disarming Voice, Baby-Doll Eyes, Aqua Jet, Icy Wind, Encore, Bubble Beam, Sing, Double Slap, Hyper Voice, Moonblast, Captivate, Hydro Pump, Misty Terrain

Popplio ⇨ **Brionne** ⇨ **Primarina**

BRONZONG
Bronze Bell Pokémon

REGION: Sinnoh

TYPE: STEEL-PSYCHIC

In ancient times, people thought Bronzong was responsible for making the rain fall, so they often asked it for help to make their crops flourish.

How to Say It: brawn-ZONG
Imperial Height: 4'03''
Imperial Weight: 412.3 lbs.
Metric Height: 1.3 m
Metric Weight: 187.0 kg

Possible Moves: Block, Sunny Day, Rain Dance, Tackle, Confusion, Hypnosis, Imprison, Confuse Ray, Psywave, Iron Defense, Feint Attack, Safeguard, Future Sight, Metal Sound, Gyro Ball, Extrasensory, Payback, Heal Block, Heavy Slam

Bronzor ⇨ Bronzong

BRONZOR
Bronze Pokémon

REGION: Sinnoh

TYPE: STEEL-PSYCHIC

In ancient times, people thought a mystical power was contained within Bronzor's back pattern. Artifacts matching its shape have been discovered in tombs from that era.

How to Say It: BRAWN-zor
Imperial Height: 1'08''
Imperial Weight: 133.4 lbs.
Metric Height: 0.5 m
Metric Weight: 60.5 kg

Possible Moves: Tackle, Confusion, Hypnosis, Imprison, Confuse Ray, Psywave, Iron Defense, Feint Attack, Safeguard, Future Sight, Metal Sound, Gyro Ball, Extrasensory, Payback, Heal Block, Heavy Slam

Bronzor ⇨ Bronzong

TYPE: WATER-PSYCHIC

Don't let the beguiling grin of the brightly colored Bruxish fool you—those teeth are strong and sharp, and it can wield psychic powers mighty enough to stun an opponent in battle.

How to Say It: BRUCK-sish
Imperial Height: 2'11''
Imperial Weight: 41.9 lbs.
Metric Height: 0.9 m
Metric Weight: 19.0 kg

Possible Moves: Water Gun, Astonish, Confusion, Bite, Aqua Jet, Disable, Psywave, Crunch, Aqua Tail, Screech, Psychic Fangs, Synchronoise

REGION:
Alola

BRUXISH
Gnash Teeth Pokémon

Does not evolve

REGIONS:
Kalos
(Central)
Sinnoh

BUDEW
Bud Pokémon

TYPE: GRASS-POISON

When the weather turns cold, Budew's bud is tightly closed. In the springtime, it opens up again and gives off its pollen.

How to Say It: buh-DOO
Imperial Height: 0'08''
Imperial Weight: 2.6 lbs.
Metric Height: 0.2 m
Metric Weight: 1.2 kg

Possible Moves: Absorb, Growth, Water Sport, Stun Spore, Mega Drain, Worry Seed

Budew ➡ Roselia ➡ Roserade

57

BUIZEL

Sea Weasel Pokémon

TYPE: WATER

Buizel rapidly spins its two tails to propel itself through the water. The flotation sac around its neck keeps its head up without effort, and it can deflate the sac to dive.

How to Say It: BWEE-zul
Imperial Height: 2'04"
Imperial Weight: 65.0 lbs.
Metric Height: 0.7 m
Metric Weight: 29.5 kg

Possible Moves: Sonic Boom, Growl, Water Sport, Quick Attack, Water Gun, Pursuit, Swift, Aqua Jet, Double Hit, Whirlpool, Razor Wind, Aqua Tail, Agility, Hydro Pump

Buizel ➡ **Floatzel**

BULBASAUR

Seed Pokémon

REGIONS:
Kalos
(Central)
Kanto

TYPE: GRASS-POISON

Bulbasaur likes to take a nap in the sunshine. While it sleeps, the seed on its back catches the rays and uses the energy to grow.

How to Say It: BUL-ba-sore
Imperial Height: 2'04"
Imperial Weight: 15.2 lbs.
Metric Height: 0.7 m
Metric Weight: 6.9 kg

Possible Moves: Tackle, Growl, Leech Seed, Vine Whip, Poison Powder, Sleep Powder, Take Down, Razor Leaf, Sweet Scent, Growth, Double-Edge, Worry Seed, Synthesis, Seed Bomb

Bulbasaur ➡ **Ivysaur** ➡ **Venusaur** ➡ **Mega Venusaur**

BUNEARY
Rabbit Pokémon

TYPE: NORMAL

Buneary is cute and cuddly, but its ears pack enough punching power to pulverize a boulder. It always keeps one ear rolled up, ready to unleash a punch in response to a surprise attack.

How to Say It: buh-NEAR-ee
Imperial Height: 1'04''
Imperial Weight: 12.1 lbs.
Metric Height: 0.4 m
Metric Weight: 5.5 kg

Possible Moves: Splash, Pound, Defense Curl, Foresight, Endure, Frustration, Quick Attack, Jump Kick, Baton Pass, Agility, Dizzy Punch, After You, Charm, Entrainment, Bounce, Healing Wish, Baby-Doll Eyes

Buneary   **Lopunny**   **Mega Lopunny**

BUNNELBY
Digging Pokémon

TYPE: NORMAL

Bunnelby can use its ears like shovels to dig holes in the ground. Eventually, its ears become strong enough to cut through thick tree roots while it digs.

How to Say It: BUN-ell-bee
Imperial Height: 1'04''
Imperial Weight: 11.0 lbs.
Metric Height: 0.4 m
Metric Weight: 5.0 kg

Possible Moves: Tackle, Agility, Leer, Quick Attack, Double Slap, Mud-Slap, Take Down, Mud Shot, Double Kick, Odor Sleuth, Flail, Dig, Bounce, Super Fang, Facade, Earthquake

Bunnelby   **Diggersby**

59

BURMY (PLANT CLOAK)
Bagworm Pokémon

TYPE: BUG

Burmy creates a cloak for itself out of whatever materials it can find. The cloak protects it from chilly temperatures and shields it in battle.

How to Say It: BURR-mee
Imperial Height: 0'08''
Imperial Weight: 7.5 lbs.

Metric Height: 0.2 m
Metric Weight: 3.4 kg

Possible Moves: Protect, Tackle, Bug Bite, Hidden Power

Wormadam
Female Form

Mothim
Male Form

Burmy

BURMY (SANDY CLOAK)
Bagworm Pokémon

REGIONS:
Kalos
(Central)
Sinnoh

TYPE: BUG

Did you know that each Burmy covers up with the objects around it? This Burmy uses rocks and sand for protection.

How to Say It: BURR-mee
Imperial Height: 0'08''
Imperial Weight: 7.5 lbs.

Metric Height: 0.2 m
Metric Weight: 3.4 kg

Possible Moves: Protect, Tackle, Bug Bite, Hidden Power

Wormadam
Female Form

Mothim
Male Form

Burmy

BURMY (TRASH CLOAK)
Bagworm Pokémon

TYPE: BUG

If you're looking for Burmy with a Trash Cloak, try poking around inside a few buildings. You might get lucky!

How to Say It: BURR-mee
Imperial Height: 0'08''
Imperial Weight: 7.5 lbs.

Metric Height: 0.2 m
Metric Weight: 3.4 kg

Possible Moves: Protect, Tackle, Bug Bite, Hidden Power

Burmy

Wormadam
Female Form

Mothim
Male Form

BUTTERFREE
Butterfly Pokémon

TYPE: BUG-FLYING

Butterfree's wings are covered in scales that carry poison. When attacked, it flutters its wings madly to scatter these scales. Its large, compound eyes are formed of many tiny eyes.

How to Say It: BUT-er-free
Imperial Height: 3'07''
Imperial Weight: 70.5 lbs.

Metric Height: 1.1 m
Metric Weight: 32.0 kg

Possible Moves: Gust, Confusion, Poison Powder, Stun Spore, Sleep Powder, Psybeam, Silver Wind, Supersonic, Safeguard, Whirlwind, Bug Buzz, Rage Powder, Captivate, Tailwind, Air Slash, Quiver Dance

Caterpie   Metapod   Butterfree   61

BUZZWOLE

Swollen Pokémon

REGION: Alola

ULTRA BEAST

TYPE: BUG-FIGHTING

Buzzwole, one of the mysterious Ultra Beasts, is enormously strong, capable of demolishing heavy machinery with a punch. When it displays its impressive muscles, no one is sure whether it's just showing off—or issuing a threat.

How to Say It: BUZZ-wole
Imperial Height: 7'10''
Imperial Weight: 735.5 lbs.
Metric Height: 2.4 m
Metric Weight: 333.6 kg

Possible Moves: Fell Stinger, Thunder Punch, Ice Punch, Reversal, Harden, Power-Up Punch, Focus Energy, Comet Punch, Bulk Up, Vital Throw, Endure, Leech Life, Taunt, Mega Punch, Counter, Hammer Arm, Lunge, Dynamic Punch, Superpower, Focus Punch

Does not evolve

TYPE: GRASS

Cacnea produce the most beautiful and fragrant flowers when they live in particularly harsh and dry environments. They can shoot their thorns to attack.

How to Say It: CACK-nee-uh
Imperial Height: 1'04''
Imperial Weight: 113.1 lbs.
Metric Height: 0.4 m
Metric Weight: 51.3 kg

Possible Moves: Poison Sting, Leer, Absorb, Growth, Leech Seed, Sand Attack, Pin Missile, Ingrain, Feint Attack, Spikes, Sucker Punch, Payback, Needle Arm, Cotton Spore, Sandstorm, Destiny Bond, Energy Ball

REGION: Hoenn

CACNEA
Cactus Pokémon

Cacnea ⇨ Cacturne

REGION: Hoenn

CACTURNE
Scarecrow Pokémon

TYPE: GRASS-DARK

Cacturne stand very still during the day so as not to waste energy or moisture in the heat of the desert sun. After dark, they hunt in packs, often attacking travelers who weren't prepared for the environment.

How to Say It: CACK-turn
Imperial Height: 4'03''
Imperial Weight: 170.6 lbs.
Metric Height: 1.3 m
Metric Weight: 77.4 kg

Possible Moves: Spiky Shield, Destiny Bond, Revenge, Poison Sting, Leer, Absorb, Growth, Leech Seed, Sand Attack, Needle Arm, Feint Attack, Ingrain, Payback, Spikes, Sucker Punch, Pin Missile, Energy Ball, Cotton Spore, Sandstorm

Cacnea ⇨ Cacturne

CAMERUPT

Eruption Pokémon

REGION: Hoenn

TYPE: FIRE-GROUND

When Camerupt gets angry, the volcanic humps on its back tend to erupt. The magma that sprays out is superheated and very dangerous.

How to Say It: CAM-err-rupt
Imperial Height: 6'03''
Imperial Weight: 485.0 lbs.
Metric Height: 1.9 m
Metric Weight: 220.0 kg

Possible Moves: Rock Slide, Fissure, Eruption, Growl, Tackle, Ember, Focus Energy, Magnitude, Flame Burst, Amnesia, Lava Plume, Earth Power, Curse, Take Down, Yawn, Earthquake

MEGA CAMERUPT

Eruption Pokémon

TYPE: FIRE-GROUND

Imperial Height: 8'02''
Imperial Weight: 706.6 lbs.
Metric Height: 2.5 m
Metric Weight: 320.5 kg

Numel → Camerupt → Mega Camerupt

CARBINK
Jewel Pokémon

TYPE: ROCK-FAIRY

The extreme pressure and temperature of its underground home caused Carbink's body to compact and crystallize. Though it's not a rare Pokémon, the sparkle of its jewel-like body catches the eye.

How to Say It: CAR-bink
Imperial Height: 1'00''
Imperial Weight: 12.6 lbs.
Metric Height: 0.3 m
Metric Weight: 5.7 kg

Possible Moves: Tackle, Harden, Rock Throw, Sharpen, Smack Down, Reflect, Stealth Rock, Guard Split, Ancient Power, Flail, Skill Swap, Power Gem, Stone Edge, Moonblast, Light Screen, Safeguard

Does not evolve

REGIONS:
Kalos
(Mountain)
Sinnoh

CARNIVINE
Bug Catcher Pokémon

TYPE: GRASS

Carnivine wraps itself around trees in swampy areas. It gives off a sweet aroma that lures others close, then attacks.

How to Say It: CAR-neh-vine
Imperial Height: 4'07''
Imperial Weight: 59.5 lbs.
Metric Height: 1.4 m
Metric Weight: 27.0 kg

Possible Moves: Bind, Growth, Bite, Vine Whip, Sweet Scent, Ingrain, Feint Attack, Leaf Tornado, Stockpile, Spit Up, Swallow, Crunch, Wring Out, Power Whip

Does not evolve

CARRACOSTA
Prototurtle Pokémon

TYPE: WATER-ROCK

Carracosta can get around pretty well on land and is a strong swimmer, which gives it an advantage in battles near water. Its heavy shell is made up of the same sturdy material as its bones.

How to Say It: care-a-KOSS-tah
Imperial Height: 3'11''
Imperial Weight: 178.6 lbs.
Metric Height: 1.2 m
Metric Weight: 81.0 kg

Possible Moves: Bide, Withdraw, Water Gun, Rollout, Bite, Protect, Aqua Jet, Ancient Power, Crunch, Wide Guard, Brine, Smack Down, Curse, Shell Smash, Aqua Tail, Rock Slide, Rain Dance, Hydro Pump

Tirtouga → Carracosta

CARVANHA
Savage Pokémon

TYPE: WATER-DARK

A lone Carvanha is a bit of a wimp, but in numbers, they're terrifying. Any hint of blood in the water draws them swarming to attack. Each school defends its territory viciously.

How to Say It: car-VAH-na
Imperial Height: 2'07''
Imperial Weight: 45.9 lbs.
Metric Height: 0.8 m
Metric Weight: 20.8 kg

Possible Moves: Leer, Bite, Rage, Focus Energy, Aqua Jet, Assurance, Screech, Swagger, Ice Fang, Scary Face, Poison Fang, Crunch, Agility, Take Down

Carvanha → Sharpedo →

Mega Sharpedo

CASCOON
Cocoon Pokémon

TYPE: BUG

When Cascoon is ready to evolve, it wraps itself up in silk, which hardens around its body. If something attacks its cocoon, it takes the hit without moving so as not to use up energy . . . but it also remembers the attacker.

How to Say It: CAS-koon
Imperial Height: 2'04''
Imperial Weight: 25.4 lbs.
Metric Height: 0.7 m
Metric Weight: 11.5 kg

Possible Move: Harden

Wurmple ⇨ Cascoon ⇨ Dustox

CASTFORM
Weather Pokémon

Regular Form

TYPE: NORMAL

When the weather changes, Castform's appearance changes with it. It's so sensitive to shifts in humidity and temperature that these changes alter the structure of its cells.

How to Say It: CAST-form
Imperial Height: 1'00''
Imperial Weight: 1.8 lbs.
Metric Height: 0.3 m
Metric Weight: 0.8 kg

Possible Moves: Tackle, Water Gun, Ember, Powder Snow, Headbutt, Rain Dance, Sunny Day, Hail, Weather Ball, Hydro Pump, Fire Blast, Blizzard, Hurricane

Snowy Form

Sunny Form

Rainy Form

Does not evolve

CATERPIE
Worm Pokémon

REGIONS:
Alola
Kalos
(Central)
Kanto

TYPE: BUG

Caterpie is recommended for Trainers just starting their journey—it doesn't require much effort to catch and raise this Pokémon. To repel the Flying types that like to attack it, Caterpie produces a terrible smell from its antennae.

How to Say It: CAT-ur-pee
Imperial Height: 1'00''
Imperial Weight: 6.4 lbs.
Metric Height: 0.3 m
Metric Weight: 2.9 kg

Possible Moves: Tackle, String Shot, Bug Bite

Caterpie ⇒ Metapod ⇒ Butterfree

CELEBI
Time Travel Pokémon

MYTHICAL POKÉMON

TYPE: PSYCHIC-GRASS

Celebi traveled back in time to come to this world. According to myth, its presence is a sign of a bright future.

How to Say It: SEL-ih-bee
Imperial Height: 2'00''
Imperial Weight: 11.0 lbs.

Metric Height: 0.6 m
Metric Weight: 5.0 kg

Possible Moves: Leech Seed, Confusion, Recover, Heal Bell, Safeguard, Magical Leaf, Ancient Power, Baton Pass, Natural Gift, Heal Block, Future Sight, Healing Wish, Leaf Storm, Perish Song

Does not evolve

CELESTEELA

Launch Pokémon

REGION: Alola

ULTRA BEAST

TYPE: STEEL-FLYING

Celesteela, one of the mysterious Ultra Beasts, can shoot incendiary gases from its arms and has been known to burn down wide swaths of trees. In flight, it can reach impressive speeds.

How to Say It: sell-uh-STEEL-uh
Imperial Height: 30'02''
Imperial Weight: 2,204.4 lbs.
Metric Height: 9.2 m
Metric Weight: 999.9 kg

Possible Moves: Wide Guard, Air Slash, Ingrain, Absorb, Harden, Tackle, Smack Down, Mega Drain, Leech Seed, Metal Sound, Iron Head, Giga Drain, Flash Cannon, Autotomize, Seed Bomb, Skull Bash, Iron Defense, Heavy Slam, Double-Edge

Does not evolve

CHANDELURE
Luring Pokémon

TYPE: GHOST-FIRE

Chandelure's spooky flames can burn the spirit right out of someone. If that happens, the spirit becomes trapped in this world, endlessly wandering.

How to Say It: shan-duh-LOOR
Imperial Height: 3'03''
Imperial Weight: 75.6 lbs.
Metric Height: 1.0 m
Metric Weight: 34.3 kg

Possible Moves: Pain Split, Smog, Confuse Ray, Flame Burst, Hex

Litwick ⇨ Lampent ⇨ Chandelure

CHANSEY
Egg Pokémon

TYPE: NORMAL

Many other Pokémon just love Chansey eggs—they're full of nutrients and very tasty. Chansey move fast and can be hard to find, so catching one is a rare treat.

How to Say It: CHAN-see
Imperial Height: 3'07''
Imperial Weight: 76.3 lbs.
Metric Height: 1.1 m
Metric Weight: 34.6 kg

Possible Moves: Double-Edge, Defense Curl, Pound, Growl, Tail Whip, Refresh, Double Slap, Soft-Boiled, Bestow, Minimize, Take Down, Sing, Fling, Heal Pulse, Egg Bomb, Light Screen, Healing Wish

Happiny ⇨ Chansey ⇨ Blissey

CHARIZARD
Flame Pokémon

REGIONS:
Kalos
(Central)
Kanto

TYPE: FIRE-FLYING

Charizard seeks out stronger foes and only breathes fire during battles with worthy opponents. The fiery breath is so hot that it can turn any material to slag.

How to Say It: CHAR-iz-ard
Imperial Height: 5'07''
Imperial Weight: 199.5 lbs.
Metric Height: 1.7 m
Metric Weight: 90.5 kg

Possible Moves: Flare Blitz, Heat Wave, Dragon Claw, Shadow Claw, Air Slash, Scratch, Growl, Ember, Smokescreen, Dragon Rage, Scary Face, Fire Fang, Flame Burst, Wing Attack, Slash, Flamethrower, Fire Spin, Inferno

MEGA CHARIZARD X
Flame Pokémon

TYPE: FIRE-DRAGON

Imperial Height: 5'07''
Imperial Weight: 243.6 lbs.
Metric Height: 1.7 m
Metric Weight: 110.5 kg

MEGA CHARIZARD Y
Flame Pokémon

TYPE: FIRE-FLYING

Imperial Height: 5'07''
Imperial Weight: 221.6 lbs.
Metric Height: 1.7 m
Metric Weight: 100.5 kg

Mega Charizard X

Charmander ⇨ **Charmeleon** ⇨ **Charizard**

Mega Charizard Y

CHARJABUG
Battery Pokémon

TYPE: BUG-ELECTRIC

When Charjabug breaks down food for energy, some of that energy is stored as electricity inside its body. A Trainer who likes to go camping would appreciate having this Pokémon as a partner!

How to Say It: CHAR-juh-bug
Imperial Height: 1'08''
Imperial Weight: 23.1 lbs.
Metric Height: 0.5 m
Metric Weight: 10.5 kg

Possible Moves: Charge, Vice Grip, String Shot, Mud-Slap, Bite, Bug Bite, Spark, Acrobatics, Crunch, X-Scissor, Dig, Discharge, Iron Defense

Grubbin ⇒ **Charjabug** ⇒ **Vikavolt**

REGIONS:
Kalos
(Central)
Kanto

CHARMANDER
Lizard Pokémon

TYPE: FIRE

The flame on Charmander's tail tip indicates how the Pokémon is feeling. It flares up in a fury when Charmander is angry!

How to Say It: CHAR-man-der
Imperial Height: 2'00''
Imperial Weight: 18.7 lbs.
Metric Height: 0.6 m
Metric Weight: 8.5 kg

Possible Moves: Scratch, Growl, Ember, Smokescreen, Dragon Rage, Scary Face, Fire Fang, Flame Burst, Slash, Flamethrower, Fire Spin, Inferno

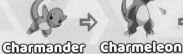

Charmander ⇒ **Charmeleon** ⇒ **Charizard** ⇒ **Mega Charizard X** / **Mega Charizard Y**

CHARMELEON

Flame Pokémon

TYPE: FIRE

When Charmeleon takes on a powerful opponent in battle, its tail flame glows white-hot. Its claws are very sharp.

How to Say It: char-MEE-lee-un
Imperial Height: 3'07''
Imperial Weight: 41.9 lbs.
Metric Height: 1.1 m
Metric Weight: 19.0 kg

Possible Moves: Scratch, Growl, Ember, Smokescreen, Dragon Rage, Scary Face, Fire Fang, Flame Burst, Slash, Flamethrower, Fire Spin, Inferno

Charmander ⇨ Charmeleon ⇨ Charizard ⇨ **Mega Charizard X**

⇨ **Mega Charizard Y**

CHATOT

Music Note Pokémon

REGIONS:
Kalos
(Coastal)
Sinnoh

TYPE: NORMAL-FLYING

Chatot can mimic other Pokémon's cries and even human speech. A group of them will often pick up the same phrase and keep repeating it among themselves.

How to Say It: CHAT-tot
Imperial Height: 1'08''
Imperial Weight: 4.2 lbs.
Metric Height: 0.5 m
Metric Weight: 1.9 kg

Possible Moves: Hyper Voice, Chatter, Confide, Taunt, Peck, Growl, Mirror Move, Sing, Fury Attack, Round, Mimic, Echoed Voice, Roost, Uproar, Synchronoise, Feather Dance

Does not evolve

CHERRIM
Blossom Pokémon

TYPE: GRASS

Cherrim keeps its petals folded around itself except in bright sunshine. When the weather is nice, its bloom opens wide to absorb as much sunlight as it can.

How to Say It: chuh-RIM
Imperial Height: 1'08''
Imperial Weight: 20.5 lbs.
Metric Height: 0.5 m
Metric Weight: 9.3 kg

Possible Moves: Morning Sun, Tackle, Growth, Leech Seed, Helping Hand, Magical Leaf, Sunny Day, Petal Dance, Worry Seed, Take Down, Solar Beam, Lucky Chant

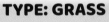

Cherubi   Cherrim

TYPE: GRASS

Cherubi stores nutrients in the small red ball attached to its head. When it's ready to evolve, it uses up all the nutrients at once, making the small ball wither.

How to Say It: chuh-ROO-bee
Imperial Height: 1'04''
Imperial Weight: 7.3 lbs.
Metric Height: 0.4 m
Metric Weight: 3.3 kg

Possible Moves: Morning Sun, Tackle, Growth, Leech Seed, Helping Hand, Magical Leaf, Sunny Day, Worry Seed, Take Down, Solar Beam, Lucky Chant, Petal Blizzard

CHERUBI
Cherry Pokémon

Cherubi   Cherrim

CHESNAUGHT
Spiny Armor Pokémon

TYPE: GRASS-FIGHTING

When its friends are in trouble, Chesnaught uses its own body as a shield. Its shell is tough enough to protect it from a powerful explosion.

How to Say It: CHESS-nawt
Imperial Height: 5'03''
Imperial Weight: 198.4 lbs.
Metric Height: 1.6 m
Metric Weight: 90.0 kg

Possible Moves: Feint, Hammer Arm, Belly Drum, Tackle, Growl, Vine Whip, Rollout, Bite, Leech Seed, Pin Missile, Needle Arm, Take Down, Seed Bomb, Spiky Shield, Mud Shot, Bulk Up, Body Slam, Pain Split, Wood Hammer, Giga Impact

Chespin ⇨ **Quilladin** ⇨ **Chesnaught**

CHESPIN
Spiny Nut Pokémon

REGION: Kalos (Central)

TYPE: GRASS

When Chespin flexes its soft quills, they become tough spikes with sharp, piercing points. It relies on its nutlike shell for protection in battle.

How to Say It: CHESS-pin
Imperial Height: 1'04''
Imperial Weight: 19.8 lbs.
Metric Height: 0.4 m
Metric Weight: 9.0 kg

Possible Moves: Growl, Vine Whip, Rollout, Bite, Leech Seed, Pin Missile, Take Down, Seed Bomb, Mud Shot, Bulk Up, Body Slam, Pain Split, Wood Hammer

  **Chespin** ⇨ **Quilladin** **Chesnaught**

TYPE: GRASS

Chikorita brandishes its leaf in battle to fend off a foe. When it does this, the leaf gives off a lovely aroma that calms everyone down.

How to Say It: CHICK-oh-REE-ta
Imperial Height: 2'11''
Imperial Weight: 14.1 lbs.
Metric Height: 0.9 m
Metric Weight: 6.4 kg

Possible Moves: Tackle, Growl, Razor Leaf, Poison Powder, Synthesis, Reflect, Magical Leaf, Natural Gift, Sweet Scent, Light Screen, Body Slam, Safeguard, Aromatherapy, Solar Beam

REGION: Johto

CHIKORITA
Leaf Pokémon

Chikorita ⇨ **Bayleef** ⇨ **Meganium**

REGION: Sinnoh

CHIMCHAR
Chimp Pokémon

TYPE: FIRE

Chimchar's rear is always on fire, even when it stands in the rain. If it's not feeling well, the flame flickers weakly.

How to Say It: CHIM-char
Imperial Height: 1'08''
Imperial Weight: 13.7 lbs.
Metric Height: 0.5 m
Metric Weight: 6.2 kg

Possible Moves: Scratch, Leer, Ember, Taunt, Fury Swipes, Flame Wheel, Nasty Plot, Torment, Facade, Fire Spin, Acrobatics, Slack Off, Flamethrower

Chimchar ⇨ **Monferno** ⇨ **Infernape**

77

CHIMECHO

Wind Chime Pokémon

REGIONS:
Hoenn
Kalos
(Coastal)

TYPE: PSYCHIC

The sucker on the top of Chimecho's head can attach to a tree branch or building. Its hollow body amplifies its chiming cries.

How to Say It: chime-ECK-ko
Imperial Height: 2'00''
Imperial Weight: 2.2 lbs.
Metric Height: 0.6 m
Metric Weight: 1.0 kg

Possible Moves: Healing Wish, Synchronoise, Wrap, Growl, Astonish, Confusion, Uproar, Take Down, Yawn, Psywave, Double-Edge, Heal Bell, Safeguard, Extrasensory, Heal Pulse

Chingling ⇨ Chimecho

CHINCHOU

Angler Pokémon

REGIONS:
Alola
Johto
Kalos
(Coastal)

TYPE: WATER-ELECTRIC

Long ago, two of Chinchou's fins developed into antennae, which flash brightly to communicate with others, or to light its way in the depths of the ocean where it lives. They can also discharge an electric shock.

How to Say It: CHIN-chow
Imperial Height: 1'08''
Imperial Weight: 26.5 lbs.
Metric Height: 0.5 m
Metric Weight: 12.0 kg

Possible Moves: Bubble, Supersonic, Thunder Wave, Electro Ball, Water Gun, Confuse Ray, Bubble Beam, Spark, Signal Beam, Flail, Discharge, Take Down, Aqua Ring, Hydro Pump, Ion Deluge, Charge

Chinchou ⇨ Lanturn

CHINGLING
Bell Pokémon

TYPE: PSYCHIC

When Chingling hops about, a small orb bounces around inside its mouth, producing a noise like the sound of bells. It uses high-pitched sounds to attack its opponents' hearing.

How to Say It: CHING-ling
Imperial Height: 0'08''
Imperial Weight: 1.3 lbs.
Metric Height: 0.2 m
Metric Weight: 0.6 kg

Possible Moves: Wrap, Growl, Astonish, Confusion, Yawn, Last Resort, Entrainment, Uproar

Chingling ➡ Chimecho

CINCCINO
Scarf Pokémon

TYPE: NORMAL

A special oil coats Cinccino's soft white fur. This oil repels dust and dirt, deflects enemy attacks, and keeps static electricity at bay.

How to Say It: chin-CHEE-noh
Imperial Height: 1'08''
Imperial Weight: 16.5 lbs.
Metric Height: 0.5 m
Metric Weight: 7.5 kg

Possible Moves: Bullet Seed, Rock Blast, Helping Hand, Tickle, Sing, Tail Slap

Minccino ➡ Cinccino

CLAMPERL
Bivalve Pokémon

REGIONS:
Alola
Hoenn
Kalos
(Coastal)

TYPE: WATER

Clamperl attacks by clamping its opponent tightly between the two sides of its shell. It can hold on like this until the opponent grows tired and gives up. The pearl inside is extremely valuable.

How to Say It: CLAM-perl
Imperial Height: 1'04''
Imperial Weight: 115.7 lbs.
Metric Height: 0.4 m
Metric Weight: 52.5 kg

Possible Moves: Clamp, Water Gun, Whirlpool, Iron Defense, Shell Smash

Clamperl   Huntail

Gorebyss

CLAUNCHER
Water Gun Pokémon

REGIONS:
Alola
Kalos
(Coastal)

TYPE: WATER

Clauncher propels itself by shooting a jet of water from just one of its claws, which gives it an unbalanced, zigzagging swimming path. If a claw becomes injured, it tries to avoid drawing attention to itself.

How to Say It: CLAWN-chur
Imperial Height: 1'08''
Imperial Weight: 18.3 lbs.
Metric Height: 0.5 m
Metric Weight: 8.3 kg

Possible Moves: Splash, Water Gun, Water Sport, Vice Grip, Bubble, Flail, Bubble Beam, Swords Dance, Crabhammer, Water Pulse, Smack Down, Aqua Jet, Muddy Water

Clauncher   Clawitzer

CLAWITZER
Howitzer Pokémon

TYPE: WATER

Clawitzer collects water in its huge right claw, then compresses it at high pressure. As a result, the water jet it shoots is strong enough to slice through solid metal.

How to Say It: CLOW-wit-zur
Imperial Height: 4'03''
Imperial Weight: 77.8 lbs.
Metric Height: 1.3 m
Metric Weight: 35.3 kg

Possible Moves: Heal Pulse, Dark Pulse, Dragon Pulse, Aura Sphere, Splash, Water Gun, Water Sport, Vice Grip, Bubble, Flail, Bubble Beam, Swords Dance, Crabhammer, Water Pulse, Smack Down, Aqua Jet, Muddy Water

Clauncher ➡ Clawitzer

REGIONS:
**Alola
Hoenn**

CLAYDOL
Clay Doll Pokémon

TYPE: GROUND-PSYCHIC

Claydol has to stay out of the rain to keep itself from melting. It creates a shield of psychic energy to keep water away. Its ancient creators were apparently inspired by an object from the sky.

How to Say It: CLAY-doll
Imperial Height: 4'11''
Imperial Weight: 238.1 lbs.
Metric Height: 1.5 m
Metric Weight: 108.0 kg

Possible Moves: Hyper Beam, Teleport, Harden, Confusion, Rapid Spin, Mud-Slap, Heal Block, Rock Tomb, Psybeam, Ancient Power, Cosmic Power, Power Trick, Self-Destruct, Extrasensory, Guard Split, Power Split, Earth Power, Sandstorm, Imprison, Explosion

Baltoy ➡ Claydol

81

CLEFABLE

Fairy Pokémon

TYPE: FAIRY

Clefable usually stay hidden, living in the mountains far from people. Tradition holds that anyone who sees two Clefable skipping along together will have a happy marriage.

How to Say It: kleh-FAY-bull
Imperial Height: 4'03"
Imperial Weight: 88.2 lbs.
Metric Height: 1.3 m
Metric Weight: 40.0 kg

Possible Moves: Spotlight, Disarming Voice, Sing, Double Slap, Minimize, Metronome

Cleffa ➡ Clefairy ➡ Clefable

CLEFAIRY

Fairy Pokémon

REGIONS:
**Alola
Kanto**

TYPE: FAIRY

Who doesn't love Clefairy? People of all ages think they're really adorable, but they can be hard to find. When they dance under the full moon, a strange magnetic force surrounds the area.

How to Say It: kleh-FAIR-ee
Imperial Height: 2'00"
Imperial Weight: 16.5 lbs.
Metric Height: 0.6 m
Metric Weight: 7.5 kg

Possible Moves: Spotlight, Disarming Voice, Pound, Growl, Encore, Sing, Double Slap, Defense Curl, Follow Me, Bestow, Wake-Up Slap, Minimize, Stored Power, Metronome, Cosmic Power, Lucky Chant, Body Slam, Moonlight, Moonblast, Gravity, Meteor Mash, Healing Wish, After You

Cleffa ➡ Clefairy ➡ Clefable

TYPE: FAIRY

REGIONS:
Alola
Johto

CLEFFA
Star Shape Pokémon

Cleffa who live in the Alola region are very fond of Minior. When shooting stars streak through the night sky, Cleffa can be found watching intently. With its five-pointed silhouette, it's said to be the rebirth of a star.

How to Say It: CLEFF-uh
Imperial Height: 1'00''
Imperial Weight: 6.6 lbs.
Metric Height: 0.3 m
Metric Weight: 3.0 kg

Possible Moves: Pound, Charm, Encore, Sing, Sweet Kiss, Copycat, Magical Leaf

Cleffa ⇨ Clefairy ⇨ Clefable

TYPE: WATER-ICE

REGIONS:
Alola
Kalos
(Coastal)
Kanto

CLOYSTER
Bivalve Pokémon

Ancient people used the spikes from Cloyster shells to make spears. The shell is strong enough to withstand a bomb blast, so what lurks within remains a mystery.

How to Say It: CLOY-stur
Imperial Height: 4'11''
Imperial Weight: 292.1 lbs.
Metric Height: 1.5 m
Metric Weight: 132.5 kg

Possible Moves: Hydro Pump, Shell Smash, Toxic Spikes, Withdraw, Supersonic, Protect, Aurora Beam, Spike Cannon, Spikes, Icicle Crash

Shellder ⇨ Cloyster

83

COBALION
Iron Will Pokémon

REGION: Unova

LEGENDARY POKÉMON

TYPE: STEEL-FIGHTING

Like its body, Cobalion's heart is tough as steel. Legends say that in the past, it protected Pokémon from harmful people.

How to Say It: koh-BAY-lee-un
Imperial Height: 6'11''
Imperial Weight: 551.2 lbs.
Metric Height: 2.1 m
Metric Weight: 250.0 kg

Possible Moves: Quick Attack, Leer, Double Kick, Metal Claw, Take Down, Helping Hand, Retaliate, Iron Head, Sacred Sword, Swords Dance, Quick Guard, Work Up, Metal Burst, Close Combat

84

Does not evolve

REGION: Unova

COFAGRIGUS
Coffin Pokémon

TYPE: GHOST

Cofagrigus resembles a coffin covered in solid gold. Stories say that when would-be thieves approach, it opens its lid and traps them inside.

How to Say It: kof-uh-GREE-guss
Imperial Height: 5'07''
Imperial Weight: 168.7 lbs.
Metric Height: 1.7 m
Metric Weight: 76.5 kg

Possible Moves: Astonish, Protect, Disable, Haze, Night Shade, Hex, Will-O-Wisp, Ominous Wind, Curse, Power Split, Guard Split, Scary Face, Shadow Ball, Grudge, Mean Look, Destiny Bond

Yamask ➡ **Cofagrigus**

TYPE: BUG-FLYING

Combee are always in search of honey, which they bring to their Vespiquen leader. They cluster together to sleep in a formation that resembles a hive.

How to Say It: COMB-bee
Imperial Height: 1'00''
Imperial Weight: 12.1 lbs.
Metric Height: 0.3 m
Metric Weight: 5.5 kg

Possible Moves:
Sweet Scent, Gust, Bug Bite, Bug Buzz

REGIONS: Kalos (Central) Sinnoh

COMBEE
Tiny Bee Pokémon

Combee ➡ **Vespiquen**

COMBUSKEN
Young Fowl Pokémon

REGION: Hoenn

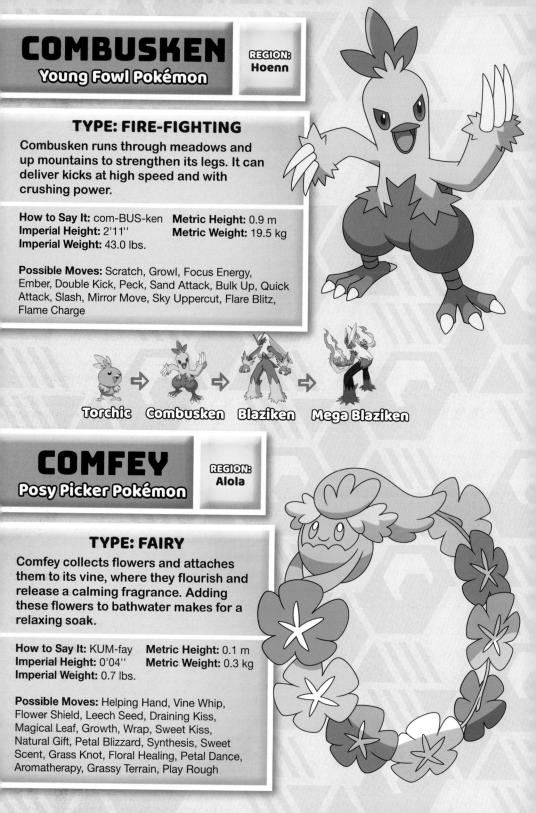

TYPE: FIRE-FIGHTING

Combusken runs through meadows and up mountains to strengthen its legs. It can deliver kicks at high speed and with crushing power.

How to Say It: com-BUS-ken
Imperial Height: 2'11''
Imperial Weight: 43.0 lbs.
Metric Height: 0.9 m
Metric Weight: 19.5 kg

Possible Moves: Scratch, Growl, Focus Energy, Ember, Double Kick, Peck, Sand Attack, Bulk Up, Quick Attack, Slash, Mirror Move, Sky Uppercut, Flare Blitz, Flame Charge

Torchic ⇒ Combusken ⇒ Blaziken ⇒ Mega Blaziken

COMFEY
Posy Picker Pokémon

REGION: Alola

TYPE: FAIRY

Comfey collects flowers and attaches them to its vine, where they flourish and release a calming fragrance. Adding these flowers to bathwater makes for a relaxing soak.

How to Say It: KUM-fay
Imperial Height: 0'04''
Imperial Weight: 0.7 lbs.
Metric Height: 0.1 m
Metric Weight: 0.3 kg

Possible Moves: Helping Hand, Vine Whip, Flower Shield, Leech Seed, Draining Kiss, Magical Leaf, Growth, Wrap, Sweet Kiss, Natural Gift, Petal Blizzard, Synthesis, Sweet Scent, Grass Knot, Floral Healing, Petal Dance, Aromatherapy, Grassy Terrain, Play Rough

Does not evolve

CONKELDURR
Muscular Pokémon

REGIONS:
Kalos
(Mountain)
Unova

TYPE: FIGHTING

Conkeldurr spin their concrete pillars to attack. It's said that long ago, people first learned about concrete from these Pokémon.

How to Say It: kon-KELL-dur
Imperial Height: 4'07''
Imperial Weight: 191.8 lbs.
Metric Height: 1.4 m
Metric Weight: 87.0 kg

Possible Moves: Pound, Leer, Focus Energy, Bide, Low Kick, Rock Throw, Wake-Up Slap, Chip Away, Bulk Up, Rock Slide, Dynamic Punch, Scary Face, Hammer Arm, Stone Edge, Focus Punch, Superpower

Timburr ⇨ Gurdurr ⇨ Conkeldurr

CORPHISH
Ruffian Pokémon

REGIONS:
Alola
Hoenn
Kalos
(Coastal)

TYPE: WATER

Corphish possesses the fortitude to survive in almost any environment, including Alola. It's likely to thrive even if released by its Trainer.

How to Say It: COR-fish
Imperial Height: 2'00''
Imperial Weight: 25.4 lbs.
Metric Height: 0.6 m
Metric Weight: 11.5 kg

Possible Moves: Bubble, Harden, Vice Grip, Leer, Bubble Beam, Protect, Double Hit, Knock Off, Night Slash, Razor Shell, Taunt, Swords Dance, Crunch, Crabhammer, Guillotine

Corphish ⇨ Crawdaunt

CORSOLA

Coral Pokémon

REGIONS:
Alola
Johto
Kalos
(Coastal)

TYPE: WATER-ROCK

The coral branches on Corsola's head are fairly fragile and often snap off, but they're good as new after a few days of regrowth. Corsola sometimes breaks off its own branches to use as a decoy when it's being chased.

How to Say It: COR-soh-la
Imperial Height: 2'00''
Imperial Weight: 11.0 lbs.
Metric Height: 0.6 m
Metric Weight: 5.0 kg

Possible Moves: Tackle, Harden, Bubble, Recover, Bubble Beam, Refresh, Ancient Power, Spike Cannon, Lucky Chant, Brine, Iron Defense, Rock Blast, Endure, Aqua Ring, Power Gem, Mirror Coat, Earth Power, Flail

Does not evolve

COSMOEM

Protostar Pokémon

REGION:
Alola

LEGENDARY POKÉMON

TYPE: PSYCHIC

Cosmoem never moves, radiating a gentle warmth as it develops inside the hard shell that surrounds it. Long ago, people referred to it as the cocoon of the stars, and some still think its origins lie in another world.

How to Say It: KOZ-mo-em
Imperial Height: 0'04''
Imperial Weight: 2,204.4 lbs.
Metric Height: 0.1 m
Metric Weight: 999.9 kg

Possible Moves: Cosmic Power, Teleport

Cosmog   Cosmoem   Solgaleo   Lunala

TYPE: PSYCHIC

Cosmog reportedly came to the Alola region from another world, but its origins are shrouded in mystery. Known as the child of the stars, it grows by gathering dust from the atmosphere.

How to Say It: KOZ-mog
Imperial Height: 0'08''
Imperial Weight: 0.2 lbs.
Metric Height: 0.2 m
Metric Weight: 0.1 kg

Possible Moves: Splash, Teleport

REGION: Alola

COSMOG
Nebula Pokémon

LEGENDARY POKÉMON

Cosmog → Cosmoem → Solgaleo

Lunala

COTTONEE
Cotton Puff Pokémon

TYPE: GRASS-FAIRY

When several Cottonee gather, they tend to huddle up and cling together in a big puffy cloud of soft, fluffy Pokémon. Such gatherings often leave behind drifts of cottony material that makes excellent stuffing for pillows and mattresses.

How to Say It: KAHT-ton-ee
Imperial Height: 1'00"
Imperial Weight: 1.3 lbs.
Metric Height: 0.3 m
Metric Weight: 0.6 kg

Possible Moves: Absorb, Fairy Wind, Growth, Leech Seed, Stun Spore, Mega Drain, Cotton Spore, Razor Leaf, Poison Powder, Giga Drain, Charm, Helping Hand, Energy Ball, Cotton Guard, Sunny Day, Endeavor, Solar Beam

Cottonee ⇨ Whimsicott

CRABOMINABLE
Woolly Crab Pokémon

REGION:
Alola

TYPE: FIGHTING-ICE

Covered in warm fur, Crabominable evolved from Crabrawler that took their goal of aiming for the top a bit too literally and found themselves at the summit of icy mountains. They can detach their pincers and shoot them at foes.

How to Say It: crab-BAH-min-uh-bull
Imperial Height: 5'07"
Imperial Weight: 396.8 lbs.
Metric Height: 1.7 m
Metric Weight: 180.0 kg

Possible Moves: Ice Punch, Bubble, Rock Smash, Leer, Pursuit, Bubble Beam, Power-Up Punch, Dizzy Punch, Avalanche, Reversal, Ice Hammer, Iron Defense, Dynamic Punch, Close Combat

Crabrawler ⇨ Crabominable

CRABRAWLER
Boxing Pokémon

TYPE: FIGHTING

Crabrawler is always looking for a fight, and it really hates to lose. Sometimes its pincers come right off because it uses them for punching so much! Fortunately, it can regrow them quickly.

How to Say It: crab-BRAW-ler
Imperial Height: 2'00''
Imperial Weight: 15.4 lbs.
Metric Height: 0.6 m
Metric Weight: 7.0 kg

Possible Moves: Bubble, Rock Smash, Leer, Pursuit, Bubble Beam, Power-Up Punch, Dizzy Punch, Payback, Reversal, Crabhammer, Iron Defense, Dynamic Punch, Close Combat

Crabrawler ⇨ Crabominable

REGIONS:
Alola
Hoenn

CRADILY
Barnacle Pokémon

TYPE: ROCK-GRASS

Cradily comes and goes with the waves. It spends most of its life in shallow seas but emerges onto land when the tide is low enough for it to find food.

How to Say It: cray-DILLY
Imperial Height: 4'11''
Imperial Weight: 133.2 lbs.
Metric Height: 1.5 m
Metric Weight: 60.4 kg

Possible Moves: Wring Out, Astonish, Constrict, Acid, Ingrain, Confuse Ray, Ancient Power, Brine, Giga Drain, Gastro Acid, Amnesia, Energy Ball, Stockpile, Spit Up, Swallow

Lileep ⇨ Cradily

91

CRANIDOS
Head Butt Pokémon

REGIONS:
Alola
Sinnoh

TYPE: ROCK

Fossilized trees, broken in half, are often found in the same area as Cranidos fossils. This Pokémon lived in the ancient jungle and also used its powerful headbutt to battle its rival, Aerodactyl.

How to Say It: CRANE-ee-dose
Imperial Height: 2'11''
Imperial Weight: 69.4 lbs.
Metric Height: 0.9 m
Metric Weight: 31.5 kg

Possible Moves: Headbutt, Leer, Focus Energy, Pursuit, Take Down, Scary Face, Assurance, Chip Away, Ancient Power, Zen Headbutt, Screech, Head Smash

Cranidos   Rampardos

CRAWDAUNT
Rogue Pokémon

REGIONS:
Alola
Hoenn
Kalos
(Central)

TYPE: WATER-DARK

Crawdaunt puts up a tough front, but if it happens to injure one of its pincers in battle, it hastily retreats in fear. It won't show its face again until the pincer is completely healed.

How to Say It: CRAW-daunt
Imperial Height: 3'07''
Imperial Weight: 72.3 lbs.
Metric Height: 1.1 m
Metric Weight: 32.8 kg

Possible Moves: Swift, Bubble, Harden, Vice Grip, Leer, Bubble Beam, Protect, Double Hit, Knock Off, Night Slash, Razor Shell, Taunt, Swords Dance, Crunch, Crabhammer, Guillotine

Corphish   Crawdaunt

CRESSELIA
Lunar Pokémon

LEGENDARY POKÉMON

TYPE: PSYCHIC

The glimmering particles that trail from Cresselia's wings resemble a veil. This Legendary Pokémon, which brings happy dreams, is said to be a symbol of the crescent moon.

How to Say It: creh-SELL-ee-ah
Imperial Height: 4'11''   **Metric Height:** 1.5 m
Imperial Weight: 188.7 lbs.   **Metric Weight:** 85.6 kg

Possible Moves: Lunar Dance, Psycho Shift, Psycho Cut, Moonlight, Confusion, Double Team, Safeguard, Mist, Aurora Beam, Future Sight, Slash, Psychic, Moonblast

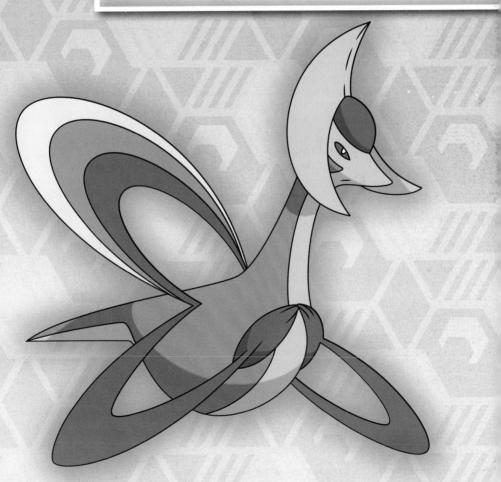

Does not evolve

CROAGUNK
Toxic Mouth Pokémon

REGIONS:
Kalos
(Central)
Sinnoh

TYPE: POISON-FIGHTING

Croagunk produces its distinctive croaking sound by inflating the poison sacs in its cheeks. The sound often startles an opponent so it can get in a poisonous jab.

How to Say It: CROW-gunk
Imperial Height: 2'04''
Imperial Weight: 50.7 lbs.
Metric Height: 0.7 m
Metric Weight: 23.0 kg

Possible Moves: Astonish, Mud-Slap, Poison Sting, Taunt, Pursuit, Feint Attack, Revenge, Swagger, Mud Bomb, Sucker Punch, Venoshock, Nasty Plot, Poison Jab, Sludge Bomb, Belch, Flatter

Croagunk ⇨ Toxicroak

CROBAT
Bat Pokémon

REGIONS:
Alola
Johto
Kalos
(Central)

TYPE: POISON-FLYING

Crobat's hind legs evolved into an extra pair of wings, so this Pokémon has a hard time getting around on the ground. In the air, though, it's a master of speed and stealth.

How to Say It: CROW-bat
Imperial Height: 5'11''
Imperial Weight: 165.3 lbs.
Metric Height: 1.8 m
Metric Weight: 75.0 kg

Possible Moves: Cross Poison, Screech, Absorb, Supersonic, Astonish, Bite, Wing Attack, Confuse Ray, Air Cutter, Swift, Poison Fang, Mean Look, Leech Life, Haze, Venoshock, Air Slash, Quick Guard

Zubat ⇨ Golbat ⇨ Crobat

CROCONAW
Big Jaw Pokémon

TYPE: WATER

Each of Croconaw's fangs ends in a barb that resembles a fishhook. When it grips a foe in its fearsome jaws, escape is nearly impossible.

How to Say It: CROCK-oh-naw
Imperial Height: 3'07''
Imperial Weight: 55.1 lbs.
Metric Height: 1.1 m
Metric Weight: 25.0 kg

Possible Moves: Scratch, Leer, Water Gun, Rage, Bite, Scary Face, Ice Fang, Flail, Crunch, Chip Away, Slash, Screech, Thrash, Aqua Tail, Superpower, Hydro Pump

Totodile ⇨ Croconaw ⇨ Feraligatr

TYPE: BUG-ROCK

Because Crustle carries a heavy slab of rock everywhere it goes, its legs are extremely strong. Battles between them are determined by whose rock breaks first.

How to Say It: KRUS-tul
Imperial Height: 4'07''
Imperial Weight: 440.9 lbs.
Metric Height: 1.4 m
Metric Weight: 200.0 kg

Possible Moves: Shell Smash, Rock Blast, Withdraw, Sand Attack, Feint Attack, Smack Down, Rock Polish, Bug Bite, Stealth Rock, Rock Slide, Slash, X-Scissor, Flail, Rock Wrecker

CRUSTLE
Stone Home Pokémon

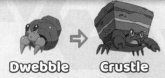

Dwebble ⇨ Crustle

CRYOGONAL

Crystallizing Pokémon

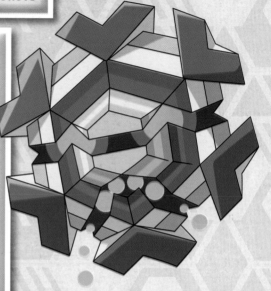

TYPE: ICE

Cryogonal's crystalline structure is made of ice formed in snow clouds. With its long chains of ice crystals, it unleashes a freezing attack.

How to Say It: kry-AH-guh-nul
Imperial Height: 3'07''
Imperial Weight: 326.3 lbs.
Metric Height: 1.1 m
Metric Weight: 148.0 kg

Possible Moves: Bind, Ice Shard, Sharpen, Rapid Spin, Icy Wind, Mist, Haze, Aurora Beam, Acid Armor, Ancient Power, Ice Beam, Light Screen, Reflect, Slash, Confuse Ray, Recover, Freeze-Dry, Solar Beam, Night Slash, Sheer Cold

Does not evolve

CUBCHOO

Chill Pokémon

REGIONS:
Kalos
(Mountain)
Unova

TYPE: ICE

Even a healthy Cubchoo always has a runny nose. Its sniffles power its freezing attacks.

How to Say It: cub-CHOO
Imperial Height: 1'08''
Imperial Weight: 18.7 lbs.
Metric Height: 0.5 m
Metric Weight: 8.5 kg

Possible Moves: Growl, Powder Snow, Bide, Icy Wind, Play Nice, Fury Swipes, Brine, Endure, Charm, Slash, Flail, Rest, Blizzard, Hail, Thrash, Sheer Cold

Cubchoo ⇨ Beartic

CUBONE
Lonely Pokémon

TYPE: GROUND

When Cubone mourns for its lost mother, its loud cries sometimes attract the attention of Mandibuzz, who swoop down to attack. Some think that learning to cope with its grief is the only way Cubone can evolve.

How to Say It: CUE-bone
Imperial Height: 1'04''
Imperial Weight: 14.3 lbs.
Metric Height: 0.4 m
Metric Weight: 6.5 kg

Possible Moves: Growl, Tail Whip, Bone Club, Headbutt, Leer, Focus Energy, Bonemerang, Rage, False Swipe, Thrash, Fling, Stomping Tantrum, Endeavor, Double-Edge, Retaliate, Bone Rush

Marowak

Cubone

Alolan Marowak

CUTIEFLY
Bee Fly Pokémon

TYPE: BUG-FAIRY

Cutiefly can sense the aura of flowers and gauge when they're ready to bloom, so it always knows where to find fresh nectar. If you notice a swarm of these Pokémon following you around, you might have a floral aura!

How to Say It: KYOO-tee-fly
Imperial Height: 0'04''
Imperial Weight: 0.4 lbs.
Metric Height: 0.1 m
Metric Weight: 0.2 kg

Possible Moves: Absorb, Fairy Wind, Stun Spore, Struggle Bug, Silver Wind, Draining Kiss, Sweet Scent, Bug Buzz, Dazzling Gleam, Aromatherapy, Quiver Dance

Cutiefly   **Ribombee**

CYNDAQUIL
Fire Mouse Pokémon

REGION: Johto

TYPE: FIRE

The protective flames on Cyndaquil's back are an indicator of its mood. A sputtering fire means it's tired, while anger makes the flames burn high and hot.

How to Say It: SIN-da-kwill
Imperial Height: 1'08''
Imperial Weight: 17.4 lbs.

Metric Height: 0.5 m
Metric Weight: 7.9 kg

Possible Moves: Tackle, Leer, Smokescreen, Ember, Quick Attack, Flame Wheel, Defense Curl, Flame Charge, Swift, Lava Plume, Flamethrower, Inferno, Rollout, Double-Edge, Burn Up, Eruption

Cyndaquil ⇨ Quilava ⇨ Typhlosion

TYPE: DARK

Darkrai defends its territory by sending intruders into a deep sleep, where they are tormented by terrible nightmares.

How to Say It: DARK-rye
Imperial Height: 4'11''
Imperial Weight: 111.3 lbs.
Metric Height: 1.5 m
Metric Weight: 50.5 kg

Possible Moves: Ominous Wind, Disable, Quick Attack, Hypnosis, Feint Attack, Nightmare, Double Team, Haze, Dark Void, Nasty Plot, Dream Eater, Dark Pulse

REGION: Sinnoh

DARKRAI
Pitch-Black Pokémon

MYTHICAL POKÉMON

Does not evolve

DARMANITAN
Blazing Pokémon

TYPE: FIRE

Fueled by its internal fire, Darmanitan can throw a punch hard enough to destroy a dump truck. To recover from a serious battle, it turns to stone so it can meditate undisturbed.

How to Say It: dar-MAN-ih-tan
Imperial Height: 4'03''
Imperial Weight: 204.8 lbs.
Metric Height: 1.3 m
Metric Weight: 92.9 kg

Possible Moves: Tackle, Rollout, Incinerate, Rage, Fire Fang, Headbutt, Swagger, Facade, Fire Punch, Work Up, Thrash, Belly Drum, Flare Blitz, Hammer Arm, Taunt, Superpower, Overheat

Darumaka ➡ Darmanitan

DARTRIX
Blade Quill Pokémon

REGION: Alola

TYPE: GRASS-FLYING

Dartrix is very conscious of its appearance and spends a lot of time keeping its wings clean. It can throw sharp-edged feathers, known as blade quills, with great accuracy.

How to Say It: DAR-trix
Imperial Height: 2'04''
Imperial Weight: 35.3 lbs.
Metric Height: 0.7 m
Metric Weight: 16.0 kg

Possible Moves: Tackle, Leafage, Growl, Peck, Astonish, Razor Leaf, Ominous Wind, Foresight, Pluck, Synthesis, Fury Attack, Sucker Punch, Leaf Blade, Feather Dance, Brave Bird, Nasty Plot

Rowlet ➡ Dartrix ➡ Decidueye

REGION:
Unova

DARUMAKA
Zen Charm Pokémon

TYPE: FIRE

Darumaka tucks its hands and feet into its body to sleep, but its internal fire still burns at searing temperatures. Long ago, people used its intense body heat to warm themselves.

How to Say It: dah-roo-MAH-kuh
Imperial Height: 2'00"
Imperial Weight: 82.7 lbs.
Metric Height: 0.6 m
Metric Weight: 37.5 kg

Possible Moves: Tackle, Rollout, Incinerate, Rage, Fire Fang, Headbutt, Uproar, Facade, Fire Punch, Work Up, Thrash, Belly Drum, Flare Blitz, Taunt, Superpower, Overheat

Darumaka ➡ **Darmanitan**

REGION:
Alola

DECIDUEYE
Arrow Quill Pokémon

TYPE: GRASS-GHOST

A natural marksman, Decidueye can shoot its arrow quills with astonishing precision, hitting a tiny target a hundred yards away. It tends to be calm and collected, but sometimes panics if it's caught off guard.

How to Say It: deh-SIH-joo-eye
Imperial Height: 5'03"
Imperial Weight: 80.7 lbs.
Metric Height: 1.6 m
Metric Weight: 36.6 kg

Possible Moves: Spirit Shackle, Phantom Force, Leaf Storm, U-turn, Shadow Sneak, Tackle, Leafage, Growl, Peck, Astonish, Razor Leaf, Ominous Wind, Foresight, Pluck, Synthesis, Fury Attack, Sucker Punch, Leaf Blade, Feather Dance, Brave Bird, Nasty Plot

Rowlet ➡ **Dartrix** ➡ **Decidueye**

DEDENNE

Antenna Pokémon

REGIONS:
Alola
Kalos
(Coastal)

TYPE: ELECTRIC-FAIRY

Dedenne uses its whiskers to sense its environment and to deliver electric shocks. This Pokémon can recharge itself with electricity from a household outlet—which can make for an unpleasant surprise when the power bill comes in!

How to Say It: deh-DEN-nay
Imperial Height: 0'08''
Imperial Weight: 4.9 lbs.
Metric Height: 0.2 m
Metric Weight: 2.2 kg

Possible Moves: Tackle, Tail Whip, Thunder Shock, Charge, Charm, Parabolic Charge, Nuzzle, Thunder Wave, Volt Switch, Rest, Snore, Charge Beam, Entrainment, Play Rough, Thunder, Discharge

Does not evolve

DEERLING

Season Pokémon

REGION:
Unova

TYPE: NORMAL-GRASS

Deerling's fur changes with the seasons. Shifts in temperature and humidity affect the color and even the scent of its fur.

How to Say It: DEER-ling
Imperial Height: 2'00''
Imperial Weight: 43.0 lbs.
Metric Height: 0.6 m
Metric Weight: 19.5 kg

Possible Moves: Tackle, Camouflage, Growl, Sand Attack, Double Kick, Leech Seed, Feint Attack, Take Down, Jump Kick, Aromatherapy, Energy Ball, Charm, Nature Power, Double-Edge, Solar Beam

Autumn Form

Summer Form

Winter Form

Spring Form

Deerling ⇨ Sawsbuck

TYPE: DARK-DRAGON

Deino can't see, so they explore their surroundings by biting and crashing into things. Because of this, they are often covered in cuts and scratches.

How to Say It: DY-noh
Imperial Height: 2'07''
Imperial Weight: 38.1 lbs.
Metric Height: 0.8 m
Metric Weight: 17.3 kg

Possible Moves: Tackle, Dragon Rage, Focus Energy, Bite, Headbutt, Dragon Breath, Roar, Crunch, Slam, Dragon Pulse, Work Up, Dragon Rush, Body Slam, Scary Face, Hyper Voice, Outrage

DEINO
Irate Pokémon

Deino ➡ Zweilous ➡ Hydreigon

DELCATTY
Prim Pokémon

TYPE: NORMAL

Delcatty lives according to its own whims, eating and sleeping as the mood strikes it. If awakened by another Pokémon, it moves elsewhere to continue its nap.

How to Say It: dell-CAT-tee
Imperial Height: 3'07''
Imperial Weight: 71.9 lbs.
Metric Height: 1.1 m
Metric Weight: 32.6 kg

Possible Moves: Fake Out, Attract, Sing, Double Slap

Skitty ➡ Delcatty

103

DELIBIRD

Delivery Pokémon

REGIONS:
Alola
Johto
Kalos
(Mountain)

TYPE: ICE-FLYING

Delibird usually live in very cold climates, but they seem to be fairly tolerant of the tropical heat of Alola. Most of their time is spent trying to build up food supplies that they then share with others.

How to Say It: DELL-ee-bird
Imperial Height: 2'11''
Imperial Weight: 35.3 lbs.
Metric Height: 0.9 m
Metric Weight: 16.0 kg

Possible Moves: Present, Drill Peck

Does not evolve

DELPHOX

Fox Pokémon

REGION:
Kalos
(Central)

TYPE: FIRE-PSYCHIC

The mystical Delphox uses a flaming branch as a focus for its psychic visions. When it gazes into the fire, it can see the future.

How to Say It: DELL-fox
Imperial Height: 4'11''
Imperial Weight: 86.0 lbs.
Metric Height: 1.5 m
Metric Weight: 39.0 kg

Possible Moves: Future Sight, Role Play, Switcheroo, Shadow Ball, Scratch, Tail Whip, Ember, Howl, Flame Charge, Psybeam, Fire Spin, Lucky Chant, Light Screen, Psyshock, Mystical Fire, Flamethrower, Will-O-Wisp, Psychic, Sunny Day, Magic Room, Fire Blast

Fennekin ➡ **Braixen** ➡ **Delphox**

TYPE: PSYCHIC

From the crystal on its chest, Deoxys can shoot out laser beams. This highly intelligent Pokémon came into being when a virus mutated during a fall from space.

How to Say It: dee-OCKS-iss
Imperial Height: 5'07''
Imperial Weight: 134.0 lbs.
Metric Height: 1.7 m
Metric Weight: 60.8 kg

Possible Moves: Leer, Wrap, Night Shade, Teleport, Knock Off, Pursuit, Psychic, Snatch, Psycho Shift, Zen Headbutt, Cosmic Power, Recover, Psycho Boost Hyper Beam

REGION: Hoenn

DEOXYS
DNA Pokémon

MYTHICAL POKÉMON

Does not evolve

DEWGONG
Sea Lion Pokémon

REGIONS:
Alola
Kanto

TYPE: WATER-ICE

When it's looking for food, Dewgong can cut through the water at a steady pace. After a meal, it pulls itself up onto the beach to rest in the sun. Warming up helps it process food.

How to Say It: DOO-gong
Imperial Height: 5'07''
Imperial Weight: 264.6 lbs.
Metric Height: 1.7 m
Metric Weight: 120.0 kg

Possible Moves: Headbutt, Growl, Signal Beam, Icy Wind, Encore, Ice Shard, Rest, Aqua Ring, Aurora Beam, Aqua Jet, Brine, Sheer Cold, Take Down, Dive, Aqua Tail, Ice Beam, Safeguard, Hail

Seel ➡ Dewgong

DEWOTT
Discipline Pokémon

REGION:
Unova

TYPE: WATER

Dewott must undergo disciplined training to master the flowing techniques it uses when wielding its two scalchops in battle.

How to Say It: DOO-wot
Imperial Height: 2'07''
Imperial Weight: 54.0 lbs.

Metric Height: 0.8 m
Metric Weight: 24.5 kg

Possible Moves: Tackle, Tail Whip, Water Gun, Water Sport, Focus Energy, Razor Shell, Fury Cutter, Water Pulse, Revenge, Aqua Jet, Encore, Aqua Tail, Retaliate, Swords Dance, Hydro Pump

Oshawott ➡ Dewott ➡ Samurott

DEWPIDER
Water Bubble Pokémon

TYPE: WATER-BUG

Mostly aquatic, Dewpider brings a water-bubble "helmet" along when it ventures onto the land to look for food. The bubble also lends extra power when Dewpider headbutts an opponent.

How to Say It: DOO-pih-der
Imperial Height: 1'00''
Imperial Weight: 8.8 lbs.
Metric Height: 0.3 m
Metric Weight: 4.0 kg

Possible Moves: Water Sport, Bubble, Infestation, Spider Web, Bug Bite, Bubble Beam, Bite, Aqua Ring, Leech Life, Crunch, Lunge, Mirror Coat, Liquidation, Entrainment

Dewpider   Araquanid

DHELMISE
Sea Creeper Pokémon

TYPE: GHOST-GRASS

When Dhelmise swings its mighty anchor, even the biggest Pokémon have to watch out! It snags seaweed floating past on the waves and scavenges detritus from the seafloor to add to its body.

How to Say It: dell-MIZE
Imperial Height: 12'10''
Imperial Weight: 463.0 lbs.
Metric Height: 3.9 m
Metric Weight: 210.0 kg

Possible Moves: Switcheroo, Absorb, Growth, Rapid Spin, Astonish, Mega Drain, Wrap, Gyro Ball, Metal Sound, Giga Drain, Whirlpool, Anchor Shot, Shadow Ball, Energy Ball, Slam, Heavy Slam, Phantom Force, Power Whip

Does not evolve

DIALGA
Temporal Pokémon

REGION: Sinnoh

LEGENDARY POKÉMON

TYPE: STEEL-DRAGON

It is said Dialga can control time with its mighty roar. In ancient times, it was revered as a legend.

How to Say It: dee-AWL-gah
Imperial Height: 17'09''
Imperial Weight: 1,505.8 lbs.
Metric Height: 5.4 m
Metric Weight: 683.0 kg

Possible Moves: Dragon Breath, Scary Face, Metal Claw, Ancient Power, Slash, Power Gem, Metal Burst, Dragon Claw, Earth Power, Aura Sphere, Iron Tail, Roar of Time, Flash Cannon

Does not evolve

DIANCIE
Jewel Pokémon

MYTHICAL POKÉMON

TYPE: ROCK-FAIRY

According to myth, when Carbink suddenly transforms into Diancie, its dazzling appearance is the most beautiful sight in existence. It has the power to compress carbon from the atmosphere, forming diamonds between its hands.

How to Say It: die-AHN-see
Imperial Height: 2'04''
Imperial Weight: 19.4 lbs.
Metric Height: 0.7 m
Metric Weight: 8.8 kg

Possible Moves: Tackle, Harden, Rock Throw, Sharpen, Smack Down, Reflect, Stealth Rock, Guard Split, Ancient Power, Flail, Skill Swap, Power Gem, Trick Room, Stone Edge, Moonblast, Diamond Storm, Light Screen, Safeguard

MEGA DIANCIE
Jewel Pokémon

TYPE: ROCK-FAIRY

Imperial Height: 3'07''
Imperial Weight: 61.3 lbs.
Metric Height: 1.1 m
Metric Weight: 27.8 kg

Diancie **Mega Diancie**

DIGGERSBY
Digging Pokémon

REGION:
Kalos
(Central)

TYPE: NORMAL-GROUND

Diggersby can use their ears like excavators to move heavy boulders. Construction workers like having them around.

How to Say It: DIH-gurz-bee
Imperial Height: 3'03''
Imperial Weight: 93.5 lbs.

Metric Height: 1.0 m
Metric Weight: 42.4 kg

Possible Moves: Hammer Arm, Rototiller, Bulldoze, Swords Dance, Tackle, Agility, Leer, Quick Attack, Double Slap, Mud-Slap, Take Down, Mud Shot, Double Kick, Odor Sleuth, Flail, Dig, Bounce, Super Fang, Facade, Earthquake

Bunnelby ⇨ Diggersby

DIGLETT
Mole Pokémon

TYPE: GROUND

To farmers, Diglett can be a blessing or a curse! The soil it lives in becomes rich and fertile, great for growing crops—but this Pokémon can also be destructive, chewing on the roots of those crops.

How to Say It: DIG-let
Imperial Height: 0'08''
Imperial Weight: 1.8 lbs.
Metric Height: 0.2 m
Metric Weight: 0.8 kg

Possible Moves: Scratch, Sand Attack, Growl, Astonish, Mud-Slap, Magnitude, Bulldoze, Sucker Punch, Mud Bomb, Earth Power, Dig, Slash, Earthquake, Fissure

Diglett ⇨ **Dugtrio**

ALOLAN DIGLETT
Mole Pokémon

TYPE: GROUND-STEEL

The metal hairs that sprout from the top of Diglett's head can be used to communicate or to sense its surroundings. It can extend just those hairs above ground to make sure everything is safe before emerging.

How to Say It: uh-LO-luhn DIG-let
Imperial Height: 0'08''
Imperial Weight: 2.2 lbs.
Metric Height: 0.2 m
Metric Weight: 1.0 kg

Possible Moves: Sand Attack, Metal Claw, Growl, Astonish, Mud-Slap, Magnitude, Bulldoze, Sucker Punch, Mud Bomb, Earth Power, Dig, Iron Head, Earthquake, Fissure

Alolan Diglett ⇨ **Alolan Dugtrio**

111

DITTO
Transform Pokémon

TYPE: NORMAL

Ditto can change its shape to resemble just about anything, and it sometimes uses this talent to befriend other Pokémon. Some are more skilled at duplication than others.

How to Say It: DIT-toe
Imperial Height: 1'00''
Imperial Weight: 8.8 lbs.
Metric Height: 0.3 m
Metric Weight: 4.0 kg

Possible Move: Transform

Does not evolve

DODRIO
Triple Bird Pokémon

TYPE: NORMAL-FLYING

Dodrio has three heads, three hearts, and three sets of lungs. It can keep watch in all directions and run a long way without getting tired.

How to Say It: doe-DREE-oh
Imperial Height: 5'11''
Imperial Weight: 187.8 lbs.
Metric Height: 1.8 m
Metric Weight: 85.2 kg

Possible Moves: Tri Attack, Peck, Growl, Quick Attack, Rage, Fury Attack, Pursuit, Pluck, Double Hit, Agility, Uproar, Acupressure, Swords Dance, Jump Kick, Drill Peck, Endeavor, Thrash

Doduo ⇨ Dodrio

DODUO
Twin Bird Pokémon

TYPE: NORMAL-FLYING

While one of Doduo's heads sleeps, the other stays alert to watch for danger. Its brains are identical.

How to Say It: doe-DOO-oh
Imperial Height: 4'07''
Imperial Weight: 86.4 lbs.

Metric Height: 1.4 m
Metric Weight: 39.2 kg

Possible Moves: Peck, Growl, Quick Attack, Rage, Fury Attack, Pursuit, Pluck, Double Hit, Agility, Uproar, Acupressure, Swords Dance, Jump Kick, Drill Peck, Endeavor, Thrash

Doduo ⇨ Dodrio

TYPE: GROUND

Donphan curls up in a ball to attack with a high-speed rolling tackle. Such an attack can knock down a house!

How to Say It: DON-fan
Imperial Height: 3'07''
Imperial Weight: 264.6 lbs.
Metric Height: 1.1 m
Metric Weight: 120.0 kg

Possible Moves: Fury Attack, Fire Fang, Thunder Fang, Horn Attack, Growl, Defense Curl, Bulldoze, Rapid Spin, Rollout, Assurance, Knock Off, Slam, Magnitude, Scary Face, Earthquake, Giga Impact

REGION:
Johto

DONPHAN
Armor Pokémon

Phanpy ⇨ Donphan

113

DOUBLADE
Sword Pokémon

REGION: **Kalos** (Central)

TYPE: STEEL-GHOST

The two swords that make up Doublade's body fight together in intricate slashing patterns that bewilder even accomplished swordsmen.

How to Say It: DUH-blade
Imperial Height: 2'07"
Imperial Weight: 9.9 lbs.
Metric Height: 0.8 m
Metric Weight: 4.5 kg

Possible Moves: Tackle, Swords Dance, Fury Cutter, Metal Sound, Pursuit, Autotomize, Shadow Sneak, Aerial Ace, Retaliate, Slash, Iron Defense, Night Slash, Power Trick, Iron Head, Sacred Sword

Honedge **Doublade** **Aegislash**

DRAGALGE
Mock Kelp Pokémon

REGIONS: **Alola** **Kalos** (Coastal)

TYPE: POISON-DRAGON

Dragalge spews a noxious poison that's corrosive enough to melt solid metal. Despite its intimidating nature, it's a favorite companion of Dhelmise.

How to Say It: druh-GAL-jee
Imperial Height: 5'11"
Imperial Weight: 179.7 lbs.
Metric Height: 1.8 m
Metric Weight: 81.5 kg

Possible Moves: Dragon Tail, Twister, Tackle, Smokescreen, Water Gun, Feint Attack, Tail Whip, Bubble, Acid, Camouflage, Poison Tail, Water Pulse, Double Team, Toxic, Aqua Tail, Sludge Bomb, Hydro Pump, Dragon Pulse

Skrelp **Dragalge**

REGIONS:
Alola
Kalos
(Mountain)
Kanto

DRAGONAIR
Dragon Pokémon

TYPE: DRAGON

With the crystalline orbs on its body, Dragonair is rumored to be able to change the weather. Because of this, farmers have long regarded this Pokémon with respect.

How to Say It: DRAG-gon-AIR
Imperial Height: 13'01''
Imperial Weight: 36.4 lbs.
Metric Height: 4.0 m
Metric Weight: 16.5 kg

Possible Moves: Wrap, Leer, Thunder Wave, Twister, Dragon Rage, Slam, Agility, Dragon Tail, Aqua Tail, Dragon Rush, Safeguard, Dragon Dance, Outrage, Hyper Beam

Dratini → Dragonair → Dragonite

REGIONS:
Alola
Kalos
(Mountain)
Kanto

DRAGONITE
Dragon Pokémon

TYPE: DRAGON-FLYING

A Dragonite once rescued a man from a shipwreck and flew him off to a Dragonite paradise on a faraway island. This calm and kindly Pokémon is slow to anger, but once roused, its wrath can be incredibly destructive.

How to Say It: DRAG-gon-ite
Imperial Height: 7'03''
Imperial Weight: 463.0 lbs.
Metric Height: 2.2 m
Metric Weight: 210.0 kg

Possible Moves: Wing Attack, Hurricane, Fire Punch, Thunder Punch, Roost, Wrap, Leer, Thunder Wave, Twister, Dragon Rage, Slam, Agility, Dragon Tail, Aqua Tail, Dragon Rush, Safeguard, Dragon Dance, Outrage, Hyper Beam, Hurricane

Dratini → Dragonair → Dragonite

115

DRAMPA
Placid Pokémon

REGION: Alola

TYPE: NORMAL-DRAGON

Even wild Drampa have a real soft spot for kids. Though they make their home far away in the mountains, they often come into town to visit and play with the local children.

How to Say It: DRAM-puh
Imperial Height: 9'10''
Imperial Weight: 407.9 lbs.
Metric Height: 3.0 m
Metric Weight: 185.0 kg

Possible Moves: Play Nice, Echoed Voice, Twister, Protect, Glare, Light Screen, Dragon Rage, Natural Gift, Dragon Breath, Safeguard, Extrasensory, Dragon Pulse, Fly, Hyper Voice, Outrage

Does not evolve

DRAPION
Ogre Scorpion Pokémon

REGIONS: Kalos (Mountain) Sinnoh

TYPE: POISON-DARK

Drapion's strong arms could tear a car into scrap metal. The claws on its arms and tail are extremely toxic.

How to Say It: DRAP-ee-on
Imperial Height: 4'03''
Imperial Weight: 135.6 lbs.
Metric Height: 1.3 m
Metric Weight: 61.5 kg

Possible Moves: Thunder Fang, Ice Fang, Fire Fang, Bite, Poison Sting, Leer, Knock Off, Pin Missile, Acupressure, Pursuit, Bug Bite, Poison Fang, Venoshock, Hone Claws, Toxic Spikes, Night Slash, Scary Face, Crunch, Fell Stinger, Cross Poison

Skorupi

Drapion

REGIONS:
Alola
Kalos
(Mountain)
Kanto

DRATINI
Dragon Pokémon

TYPE: DRAGON

Dratini's existence was mere rumor until a fisherman finally managed to catch one after fighting it for many long hours. It sheds its skin several times as it grows, and the skin is sometimes used in clothing.

How to Say It: dra-TEE-nee
Imperial Height: 5'11''
Imperial Weight: 7.3 lbs.
Metric Height: 1.8 m
Metric Weight: 3.3 kg

Possible Moves: Wrap, Leer, Thunder Wave, Twister, Dragon Rage, Slam, Agility, Dragon Tail, Aqua Tail, Dragon Rush, Safeguard, Dragon Dance, Outrage, Hyper Beam

 ➡ ➡

Dratini　　**Dragonair**　　**Dragonite**

REGIONS:
Alola
Kalos
(Coastal)
Sinnoh

DRIFBLIM
Blimp Pokémon

TYPE: GHOST-FLYING

Drifblim take to the sky at dusk, flying in large groups. They can be hard to track even for a dedicated observer, because they sometimes disappear right in front of people's eyes.

How to Say It: DRIFF-blim
Imperial Height: 3'11''
Imperial Weight: 33.1 lbs.
Metric Height: 1.2 m
Metric Weight: 15.0 kg

Possible Moves: Phantom Force, Constrict, Minimize, Astonish, Gust, Focus Energy, Payback, Ominous Wind, Stockpile, Hex, Swallow, Spit Up, Shadow Ball, Amnesia, Baton Pass, Explosion

Drifloon ➡ **Drifblim**

117

DRIFLOON

Balloon Pokémon

TYPE: GHOST-FLYING

Scary stories are told of children who took hold of Drifloon's dangling strings and were never seen again. The spirit within its floating body is only barely contained—any puncture could send it spilling out with a ghostly shriek.

How to Say It: DRIFF-loon
Imperial Height: 1'04''
Imperial Weight: 2.6 lbs.
Metric Height: 0.4 m
Metric Weight: 1.2 kg

Possible Moves: Constrict, Minimize, Astonish, Gust, Focus Energy, Payback, Ominous Wind, Stockpile, Hex, Swallow, Spit Up, Shadow Ball, Amnesia, Baton Pass, Explosion

Drifloon   Drifblim

DRILBUR

Mole Pokémon

REGION:
Unova

TYPE: GROUND

Drilbur bores through the ground by bringing its claws together to form a sharp point and rotating its entire body. In this way, it can travel underground as fast as thirty mph.

How to Say It: DRIL-bur
Imperial Height: 1'00''
Imperial Weight: 18.7 lbs.
Metric Height: 0.3 m
Metric Weight: 8.5 kg

Possible Moves: Scratch, Mud Sport, Rapid Spin, Mud-Slap, Fury Swipes, Metal Claw, Dig, Hone Claws, Slash, Rock Slide, Earthquake, Swords Dance, Sandstorm, Drill Run, Fissure

Drilbur   Excadrill

DROWZEE
Hypnosis Pokémon

TYPE: PSYCHIC

Drowzee feeds on dreams and has a particular taste for the ones that show the dreamer having a lot of fun. It sometimes shows off its favorite dreams to friends.

How to Say It: DROW-zee
Imperial Height: 3'03''
Imperial Weight: 71.4 lbs.
Metric Height: 1.0 m
Metric Weight: 32.4 kg

Possible Moves: Pound, Hypnosis, Disable, Confusion, Headbutt, Poison Gas, Meditate, Psybeam, Wake-Up Slap, Psych Up, Synchronoise, Zen Headbutt, Swagger, Psychic, Nasty Plot, Psyshock, Future Sight

Drowzee → Hypno

DRUDDIGON
Cave Pokémon

TYPE: DRAGON

Druddigon searches for food in underground tunnels created by Diglett and Dugtrio. The skin on its face is harder than rock, so it doesn't hesitate to charge foes who appear before it in the narrow caves.

How to Say It: DRUD-dih-guhn
Imperial Height: 5'03''
Imperial Weight: 306.4 lbs.
Metric Height: 1.6 m
Metric Weight: 139.0 kg

Possible Moves: Leer, Scratch, Hone Claws, Bite, Scary Face, Dragon Rage, Slash, Crunch, Dragon Claw, Chip Away, Revenge, Night Slash, Dragon Tail, Rock Climb, Superpower, Outrage

Does not evolve

DUCKLETT
Water Bird Pokémon

REGIONS:
Kalos
(Central)
Unova

TYPE: WATER-FLYING

Skilled swimmers, Ducklett dive underwater in search of delicious peat moss. When enemies approach, they kick up water with their wings to cover their retreat.

How to Say It: DUK-lit
Imperial Height: 1'08''
Imperial Weight: 12.1 lbs.
Metric Height: 0.5 m
Metric Weight: 5.5 kg

Possible Moves: Water Gun, Water Sport, Defog, Wing Attack, Water Pulse, Aerial Ace, Bubble Beam, Feather Dance, Aqua Ring, Air Slash, Roost, Rain Dance, Tailwind, Brave Bird, Hurricane

Ducklett ⇒ **Swanna**

TYPE: GROUND

By working together, the triplets that make up a Dugtrio can dig sixty miles into the ground. No one knows what this Pokémon's body looks like, because only its heads show above the dirt.

How to Say It: DUG-TREE-oh
Imperial Height: 2'04''
Imperial Weight: 73.4 lbs.
Metric Height: 0.7 m
Metric Weight: 33.3 kg

Possible Moves: Rototiller, Night Slash, Tri Attack, Scratch, Sand Attack, Growl, Astonish, Mud-Slap, Magnitude, Bulldoze, Sucker Punch, Sand Tomb, Mud Bomb, Earth Power, Dig, Slash, Earthquake, Fissure

REGIONS:
Kalos
(Mountain)
Kanto

DUGTRIO
Mole Pokémon

Diglett → **Dugtrio**

REGION:
Alola

ALOLAN DUGTRIO
Mole Pokémon

TYPE: GROUND-STEEL

Although Dugtrio's golden hair is shiny and beautiful, people aren't inclined to collect it when it falls—there are stories that doing so will bring bad luck. In Alola, this Pokémon is thought to represent the spirit of the land.

How to Say It: uh-LO-luhn DUG-TREE-oh
Imperial Height: 2'04''
Imperial Weight: 146.8 lbs.
Metric Height: 0.7 m
Metric Weight: 66.6 kg

Possible Moves: Sand Tomb, Rototiller, Night Slash, Tri Attack, Sand Attack, Metal Claw, Growl, Astonish, Mud-Slap, Magnitude, Bulldoze, Sucker Punch, Mud Bomb, Earth Power, Dig, Iron Head, Earthquake, Fissure

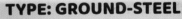

Alolan Diglett → **Alolan Dugtrio**

DUNSPARCE

Land Snake Pokémon

REGIONS:
Alola
Johto
Kalos
(Central)

Does not evolve

TYPE: NORMAL

Dunsparce burrows backward into the ground using its tail when threatened, so it's hard to catch—particularly since it views every person who approaches as a threat. Diglett sometimes share Dunsparce's tunnels.

How to Say It: DUN-sparce
Imperial Height: 4'11''
Imperial Weight: 30.9 lbs.
Metric Height: 1.5 m
Metric Weight: 14.0 kg

Possible Moves: Rage, Defense Curl, Rollout, Spite, Pursuit, Screech, Mud-Slap, Yawn, Ancient Power, Body Slam, Drill Run, Roost, Take Down, Coil, Dig, Glare, Double-Edge, Endeavor, Air Slash, Dragon Rush, Endure

DUOSION

Mitosis Pokémon

REGIONS:
Kalos
(Coastal)
Unova

TYPE: PSYCHIC

Duosion's brain is divided into two, so sometimes it tries to do two different things at the same time. When the brains are thinking together, Duosion's psychic power is at its strongest.

How to Say It: doo-OH-zhun
Imperial Height: 2'00''
Imperial Weight: 17.6 lbs.
Metric Height: 0.6 m
Metric Weight: 8.0 kg

Possible Moves: Psywave, Reflect, Rollout, Snatch, Hidden Power, Light Screen, Charm, Recover, Psyshock, Endeavor, Future Sight, Pain Split, Psychic, Skill Swap, Heal Block, Wonder Room

Solosis ➡ **Duosion** ➡ **Reuniclus**

TYPE: BUG-STEEL

The heavily armored Durant work together to keep attackers away from their colony. Durant and Heatmor are natural enemies.

How to Say It: dur-ANT
Imperial Height: 1'00''
Imperial Weight: 72.8 lbs.
Metric Height: 0.3 m
Metric Weight: 33.0 kg

Possible Moves: Guillotine, Iron Defense, Metal Sound, Vice Grip, Sand Attack, Fury Cutter, Bite, Agility, Metal Claw, Bug Bite, Crunch, Iron Head, Dig, Entrainment, X-Scissor

REGIONS:
Kalos
(Mountain)
Unova

DURANT
Iron Ant Pokémon

Does not evolve

TYPE: GHOST

There is no escape for anything absorbed into the hollow body of Dusclops. When it waves its hands and focuses its single eye, it can entrance a foe to do its will.

How to Say It: DUS-klops
Imperial Height: 5'03''
Imperial Weight: 67.5 lbs.
Metric Height: 1.6 m
Metric Weight: 30.6 kg

Possible Moves: Shadow Punch, Future Sight, Fire Punch, Ice Punch, Thunder Punch, Gravity, Bind, Leer, Night Shade, Disable, Foresight, Astonish, Foresight, Shadow Sneak, Pursuit, Will-O-Wisp, Confuse Ray, Curse, Hex, Shadow Ball, Mean Look, Payback

REGION:
Hoenn

DUSCLOPS
Beckon Pokémon

Duskull ⇨ **Dusclops** ⇨ **Dusknoir**

DUSKNOIR

Gripper Pokémon

REGION: Hoenn

TYPE: GHOST

Dusknoir senses signals from the spirit world with the antenna on its head. The signals tell it to guide lost spirits . . . and sometimes people.

How to Say It: DUSK-nwar
Imperial Height: 7'03"
Imperial Weight: 235.0 lbs.
Metric Height: 2.2 m
Metric Weight: 106.6 kg

Possible Moves: Fire Punch, Ice Punch, Thunder Punch, Gravity, Bind, Leer, Night Shade, Disable, Foresight, Astonish, Confuse Ray, Shadow Sneak, Pursuit, Curse, Will-O-Wisp, Shadow Punch, Hex, Mean Look, Payback, Future Sight, Shadow Ball

Duskull ⇨ **Dusclops** ⇨ **Dusknoir**

DUSKULL

Requiem Pokémon

REGION: Hoenn

TYPE: GHOST

Parents sometimes threaten misbehaving children with a visit from Duskull. It can pass through walls in pursuit of its target, but gives up the chase at sunrise.

How to Say It: DUS-kull
Imperial Height: 2'07"
Imperial Weight: 33.1 lbs.
Metric Height: 0.8 m
Metric Weight: 15.0 kg

Possible Moves: Leer, Night Shade, Disable, Foresight, Astonish, Confuse Ray, Shadow Sneak, Pursuit, Curse, Will-O-Wisp, Hex, Mean Look, Payback, Future Sight, Shadow Ball

Duskull ⇨ **Dusclops** ⇨ **Dusknoir**

TYPE: BUG-POISON

City lights attract Dustox in swarms. This is unfortunate, because their wings scatter poisonous dust and their feeding habits quickly strip trees bare.

How to Say It: DUS-tocks
Imperial Height: 3'11''
Imperial Weight: 69.7 lbs.
Metric Height: 1.2 m
Metric Weight: 31.6 kg

Possible Moves: Gust, Confusion, Poison Power, Moonlight, Venoshock, Psybeam, Silver Wind, Light Screen, Whirlwind, Toxic, Bug Buzz, Protect, Quiver Dance

REGION: Hoenn

DUSTOX
Poison Moth Pokémon

Wurmple **Cascoon** **Dustox**

REGIONS: Kalos *(Coastal)* Unova

DWEBBLE
Rock Inn Pokémon

TYPE: BUG-ROCK

Using a special liquid from its mouth, Dwebble hollows out a rock to use as its shell. It becomes very anxious without a proper rock.

How to Say It: DWEHB-bul
Imperial Height: 1'00''
Imperial Weight: 32.0 lbs.
Metric Height: 0.3 m
Metric Weight: 14.5 kg

Possible Moves: Fury Cutter, Rock Blast, Withdraw, Sand Attack, Feint Attack, Smack Down, Rock Polish, Bug Bite, Stealth Rock, Rock Slide, Slash, X-Scissor, Shell Smash, Flail, Rock Wrecker

Dwebble **Crustle**

125

EELEKTRIK

EleFish Pokémon

TYPE: ELECTRIC

Eelektrik wraps its long body around its opponent and gives off a paralyzing electric shock from the round markings on its sides. Its appetite is quite large.

How to Say It: ee-LEK-trik
Imperial Height: 3'11''
Imperial Weight: 48.5 lbs.
Metric Height: 1.2 m
Metric Weight: 22.0 kg

Possible Moves: Headbutt, Thunder Wave, Spark, Charge Beam, Bind, Acid, Discharge, Crunch, Thunderbolt, Acid Spray, Coil, Wild Charge, Gastro Acid, Zap Cannon, Thrash

Tynamo   Eelektrik   Eelektross

EELEKTROSS

EleFish Pokémon

TYPE: ELECTRIC

With their gaping sucker mouths, electrically charged fangs, and long arms that allow them to crawl up on land, Eelektross are dangerous opponents.

How to Say It: ee-LEK-trahs   **Metric Height:** 2.1 m
Imperial Height: 6'11''   **Metric Weight:** 80.5 kg
Imperial Weight: 177.5 lbs.

Possible Moves: Crunch, Thrash, Zap Cannon, Gastro Acid, Coil, Ion Deluge, Crush Claw, Headbutt, Acid

Tynamo   Eelektrik   Eelektross

EEVEE
Evolution Pokémon

Jolteon
Flareon
Glaceon
Vaporeon
Eevee
Espeon
Umbreon
Sylveon
Leafeon

TYPE: NORMAL

Eight different Pokémon evolve from the amazingly adaptive Eevee, according to current studies. Its unstable genetic structure allows for this incredible diversity in Evolution.

How to Say It: EE-vee
Imperial Height: 1'00''
Imperial Weight: 14.3 lbs.
Metric Height: 0.3 m
Metric Weight: 6.5 kg

Possible Moves: Covet, Helping Hand, Growl, Tackle, Tail Whip, Sand Attack, Baby-Doll Eyes, Quick Attack, Bite, Swift, Refresh, Take Down, Charm, Baton Pass, Double-Edge, Last Resort, Trump Card

EKANS
Snake Pokémon

TYPE: POISON

When it's ready for a meal, Ekans can open its mouth extra wide to swallow things that are bigger than itself. Sometimes that trick isn't enough—if a particularly big bite gets stuck, it can cause Ekans to faint.

How to Say It: ECK-kins
Imperial Height: 6'07''
Imperial Weight: 15.2 lbs.
Metric Height: 2.0 m
Metric Weight: 6.9 kg

Possible Moves: Wrap, Leer, Poison Sting, Bite, Glare, Screech, Acid, Stockpile, Swallow, Spit Up, Acid Spray, Mud Bomb, Gastro Acid, Belch, Haze, Coil, Gunk Shot

Ekans → Arbok

ELECTABUZZ
Electric Pokémon

REGIONS:
Alola
Kanto

TYPE: ELECTRIC

Electabuzz consumes electricity, but isn't very good at retaining the power within its body—it's constantly leaking electric current. If the power goes out on a calm, sunny day, it's probably the fault of Electabuzz.

How to Say It: eh-LECK-ta-buzz
Imperial Height: 3'07''
Imperial Weight: 66.1 lbs.
Metric Height: 1.1 m
Metric Weight: 30.0 kg

Possible Moves: Quick Attack, Leer, Thunder Shock, Low Kick, Swift, Shock Wave, Thunder Wave, Electro Ball, Light Screen, Thunder Punch, Discharge, Screech, Thunderbolt, Thunder

Elekid → Electabuzz → Electivire

ELECTIVIRE
Thunderbolt Pokémon

TYPE: ELECTRIC

When Electivire beats its chest in excitement, it produces a sound like thunder and showers of electric sparks. It can unleash an intense shock by pressing the tips of its two tails into its foe.

How to Say It: el-LECT-uh-vire
Imperial Height: 5'11''
Imperial Weight: 305.6 lbs.
Metric Height: 1.8 m
Metric Weight: 138.6 kg

Possible Moves: Electric Terrain, Ion Deluge, Fire Punch, Quick Attack, Leer, Thunder Shock, Low Kick, Swift, Shock Wave, Thunder Wave, Electro Ball, Light Screen, Thunder Punch, Discharge, Screech, Thunderbolt, Thunder, Giga Impact

Elekid ⇨ **Electabuzz** ⇨ **Electivire**

TYPE: ELECTRIC

With every step Electrike takes, friction causes static electricity to build up in its long fur. It runs with impressive speed, emitting a peculiar crackling sound as the static in its coat discharges.

ELECTRIKE
Lightning Pokémon

How to Say It: eh-LEK-trike
Imperial Height: 2'00''
Imperial Weight: 33.5 lbs.
Metric Height: 0.6 m
Metric Weight: 15.2 kg

Possible Moves: Tackle, Thunder Wave, Leer, Howl, Quick Attack, Spark, Odor Sleuth, Bite, Thunder Fang, Roar, Discharge, Charge, Wild Charge, Thunder

Electrike ⇨ **Manectric** ⇨ **Mega Manectric**

129

ELECTRODE
Ball Pokémon

TYPE: ELECTRIC

Electrode feeds by absorbing electricity, often from power plants or lightning storms. If it eats too much at once, it explodes.

How to Say It: ee-LECK-trode
Imperial Height: 3'11''
Imperial Weight: 146.8 lbs.
Metric Height: 1.2 m
Metric Weight: 66.6 kg

Possible Moves: Magnetic Flux, Charge, Tackle, Sonic Boom, Spark, Eerie Impulse, Rollout, Screech, Charge Beam, Light Screen, Electro Ball, Self-Destruct, Swift, Magnet Rise, Gyro Ball, Explosion, Mirror Coat, Discharge

Voltorb ⇒ Electrode

ELEKID
Electric Pokémon

REGIONS:
Alola
Johto

TYPE: ELECTRIC

An Elekid that lives with its Trainer can feed on electricity straight from the outlets in the house. These Pokémon have developed a rivalry with Togedemaru, who try to siphon off their electricity.

How to Say It: EL-eh-kid
Imperial Height: 2'00''
Imperial Weight: 51.8 lbs.
Metric Height: 0.6 m
Metric Weight: 23.5 kg

Possible Moves: Quick Attack, Leer, Thunder Shock, Low Kick, Swift, Shock Wave, Thunder Wave, Electro Ball, Light Screen, Thunder Punch, Discharge, Screech, Thunderbolt, Thunder

Elekid ⇒ Electabuzz ⇒ Electivire

ELGYEM
Cerebral Pokémon

TYPE: PSYCHIC

Elgyem, which possesses immense psychic power, is apparently responsible for many stories of alien encounters. Reports of its origins in a UFO crash a few decades ago do nothing to dispel this confusion.

How to Say It: ELL-jee-ehm
Imperial Height: 1'08''
Imperial Weight: 19.8 lbs.
Metric Height: 0.5 m
Metric Weight: 9.0 kg

Possible Moves: Confusion, Growl, Heal Block, Miracle Eye, Psybeam, Headbutt, Hidden Power, Imprison, Simple Beam, Zen Headbutt, Psych Up, Psychic, Calm Mind, Recover, Guard Split, Power Split, Synchronoise, Wonder Room

Elgyem ⇨ **Beheeyem**

REGION:
Unova

EMBOAR
Mega Fire Pig Pokémon

TYPE: FIRE-FIGHTING

With the fiery beard that covers its chin, Emboar can set its fists ablaze and throw flaming punches. Its battle moves are speedy and powerful.

How to Say It: EHM-bohr
Imperial Height: 5'03''
Imperial Weight: 330.7 lbs.
Metric Height: 1.6 m
Metric Weight: 150.0 kg

Possible Moves: Hammer Arm, Tackle, Tail Whip, Ember, Odor Sleuth, Defense Curl, Flame Charge, Arm Thrust, Smog, Rollout, Take Down, Heat Crash, Assurance, Flamethrower, Head Smash, Roar, Flare Blitz

Tepig ⇨ **Pignite** ⇨ **Emboar**

131

EMOLGA

Sky Squirrel Pokémon

REGIONS:
Alola
Kalos
(Coastal)
Unova

TYPE: ELECTRIC-FLYING

When Emolga stretches out its limbs, the membrane connecting them spreads like a cape and allows it to glide through the air. The holes that Pikipek drill in trees make handy nests for wild Emolga.

How to Say It: ee-MAHL-guh
Imperial Height: 1'04''
Imperial Weight: 11.0 lbs.
Metric Height: 0.4 m
Metric Weight: 5.0 kg

Possible Moves: Thunder Shock, Quick Attack, Tail Whip, Charge, Spark, Nuzzle, Pursuit, Double Team, Shock Wave, Electro Ball, Acrobatics, Light Screen, Encore, Volt Switch, Agility, Discharge

Does not evolve

EMPOLEON

Emperor Pokémon

REGION:
Sinnoh

TYPE: WATER-STEEL

With the sharp edges of its wings, Empoleon can slash through drifting ice as it swims faster than a speedboat. The length of its tridentlike horns indicates its power.

How to Say It: em-POH-lee-on
Imperial Height: 5'07''
Imperial Weight: 186.3 lbs.
Metric Height: 1.7 m
Metric Weight: 84.5 kg

Possible Moves: Tackle, Growl, Bubble, Swords Dance, Peck, Metal Claw, Bubble Beam, Swagger, Fury Attack, Brine, Aqua Jet, Whirlpool, Mist, Drill Peck, Hydro Pump

Piplup ⇨ Prinplup ⇨ Empoleon

TYPE: FIRE

People say that Entei came into being when a volcano erupted. This Legendary Pokémon carries the heat of magma in its fiery heart.

How to Say It: EN-tay
Imperial Height: 6'11''
Imperial Weight: 436.5 lbs.
Metric Height: 2.1 m
Metric Weight: 198.0 kg

Possible Moves: Sacred Fire, Eruption, Extrasensory, Lava Plume, Bite, Leer, Ember, Roar, Fire Spin, Stomp, Flamethrower, Swagger, Fire Fang, Fire Blast, Calm Mind

Does not evolve

ENTEI
Volcano Pokémon

LEGENDARY POKÉMON

ESCAVALIER
Cavalry Pokémon

TYPE: BUG-STEEL

The stolen Shelmet shell protects Escavalier's bodylike armor. It uses its double lances to attack.

How to Say It: ess-KAV-a-LEER
Imperial Height: 3'03''
Imperial Weight: 72.8 lbs.
Metric Height: 1.0 m
Metric Weight: 33.0 kg

Possible Moves: Double-Edge, Fell Stinger, Peck, Leer, Quick Guard, Twineedle, Fury Attack, Headbutt, False Swipe, Bug Buzz, Slash, Iron Head, Iron Defense, X-Scissor, Reversal, Swords Dance, Giga Impact

Karrablast ⇨ **Escavalier**

133

ESPEON
Sun Pokémon

REGIONS:
Alola
Johto
Kalos
(Coastal)

TYPE: PSYCHIC

Espeon doesn't have to see its opponent to sense its movements—its fine fur picks up even the slightest shift in air currents. If the orb on its forehead goes dark, that means its psychic power is temporarily depleted.

How to Say It: ESS-pee-on
Imperial Height: 2'11''
Imperial Weight: 58.4 lbs.
Metric Height: 0.9 m
Metric Weight: 26.5 kg

Possible Moves: Confusion, Helping Hand, Tackle, Tail Whip, Sand Attack, Baby-Doll Eyes, Quick Attack, Swift, Psybeam, Future Sight, Psych Up, Morning Sun, Psychic, Last Resort, Power Swap

Eevee ⇨ Espeon

ESPURR
Restraint Pokémon

REGION:
Kalos
(Central)

TYPE: PSYCHIC

Espurr emits powerful psychic energy from organs in its ears. It has to fold its ears down to keep the power contained.

How to Say It: ESS-purr
Imperial Height: 1'00''
Imperial Weight: 7.7 lbs.
Metric Height: 0.3 m
Metric Weight: 3.5 kg

Possible Moves: Scratch, Leer, Covet, Confusion, Light Screen, Psybeam, Fake Out, Disarming Voice, Psyshock

Espurr ⇨ Meowstic

EXCADRILL
Subterrene Pokémon

TYPE: GROUND-STEEL

Excadrill live several hundred feet underground, where they use their strong steel claws to dig out nests and tunnels. Sometimes that causes big trouble for subway systems.

How to Say It: EKS-kuh-dril
Imperial Height: 2'04''
Imperial Weight: 89.1 lbs.
Metric Height: 0.7 m
Metric Weight: 40.4 kg

Possible Moves: Horn Drill, Rototiller, Scratch, Mud Sport, Rapid Spin, Mud-Slap, Fury Swipes, Metal Claw, Dig, Slash, Rock Slide, Horn Drill, Earthquake, Swords Dance, Sandstorm, Drill Run, Fissure

Drilbur   Excadrill

EXEGGCUTE
Egg Pokémon

TYPE: GRASS-PSYCHIC

Exeggcute is made up of six eggs that communicate with one another using telepathy. Crabrawler sometimes seeks out this Pokémon to pick a fight, but it can't stand up to Exeggcute's psychic powers.

How to Say It: ECKS-egg-cute
Imperial Height: 1'04''
Imperial Weight: 5.5 lbs
Metric Height: 0.4 m
Metric Weight: 2.5 kg

Possible Moves: Barrage, Uproar, Hypnosis, Reflect, Leech Seed, Bullet Seed, Stun Spore, Poison Powder, Sleep Powder, Confusion, Worry Seed, Natural Gift, Solar Beam, Extrasensory, Bestow

Exeggutor

Exeggcute

Alolan
Exeggutor

135

EXEGGUTOR

Coconut Pokémon

REGIONS:
Kalos
(Coastal)
Kanto

TYPE: GRASS-PSYCHIC

Exeggutor's three heads all have minds of their own, and every decision involves a telepathic discussion. Sometimes one of the heads drops to the ground and grows into an Exeggcute.

How to Say It: ecks-EGG-u-tore
Imperial Height: 6'07''
Imperial Weight: 264.6 lbs.
Metric Height: 2.0 m
Metric Weight: 120.0 kg

Possible Moves: Seed Bomb, Barrage, Hypnosis, Confusion, Stomp, Psyshock, Egg Bomb, Wood Hammer, Leaf Storm

Exeggcute ⟹ **Exeggutor**

ALOLAN EXEGGUTOR

Coconut Pokémon

REGION:
Alola

TYPE: GRASS-DRAGON

In the tropical sun and sand, Exeggutor grows exceptionally tall, unlocking draconic powers hidden deep within. Trainers in Alola are proud of the treelike Exeggutor and consider this to be its ideal form.

How to Say It: uh-LO-luhn ecks-EGG-u-tore
Imperial Height: 35'09''
Imperial Weight: 916.2 lbs.
Metric Height: 10.9 m
Metric Weight: 415.6 kg

Possible Moves: Dragon Hammer, Seed Bomb, Barrage, Hypnosis, Confusion, Psyshock, Egg Bomb, Wood Hammer, Leaf Storm

Exeggcute ⟹ **Alolan Exeggutor**

TYPE: NORMAL

When Exploud takes a deep breath through the tubes that cover its body, watch out! It's about to unleash a thunderous bellow that will shake the ground around it.

How to Say It: ecks-PLOWD
Imperial Height: 4'11''
Imperial Weight: 185.2 lbs.
Metric Height: 1.5 m
Metric Weight: 84.0 kg

Possible Moves: Crunch, Bite, Boomburst, Ice Fang, Fire Fang, Thunder Fang, Pound, Echoed Voice, Astonish, Howl, Screech, Supersonic, Stomp, Uproar, Roar, Rest, Sleep Talk, Hyper Voice, Synchronoise, Hyper Beam

EXPLOUD
Loud Noise Pokémon

Whismur ⇨ **Loudred** ⇨ **Exploud**

FARFETCH'D
Wild Duck Pokémon

TYPE: NORMAL-FLYING

Farfetch'd always carries its trusty plant stalk. Sometimes, two of them will fight over a superior stalk.

How to Say It: FAR-fetched
Imperial Height: 2'07''
Imperial Weight: 33.1 lbs.
Metric Height: 0.8 m
Metric Weight: 15.0 kg

Possible Moves: Brave Bird, Poison Jab, Peck, Sand Attack, Leer, Fury Cutter, Fury Attack, Aerial Ace, Knock Off, Slash, Air Cutter, Swords Dance, Agility, Night Slash, Acrobatics, Feint, False Swipe, Air Slash

Does not evolve

FEAROW
Beak Pokémon

REGIONS:
Alola
Kalos
(Mountain)
Kanto

TYPE: NORMAL-FLYING

It's unclear how long Fearow has been around, but ancient artwork seems to depict this long-beaked Pokémon. Its untiring wings enable it to fly the whole day through, even when it's carrying something heavy.

How to Say It: FEER-oh
Imperial Height: 3'11''
Imperial Weight: 83.8 lbs.
Metric Height: 1.2 m
Metric Weight: 38.0 kg

Possible Moves: Drill Run, Pluck, Peck, Growl, Leer, Pursuit, Fury Attack, Aerial Ace, Mirror Move, Assurance, Agility, Focus Energy, Roost, Drill Peck

Spearow ⇨ Fearow

FEEBAS
Fish Pokémon

REGIONS:
Alola
Hoenn

TYPE: WATER

The rather shabby Feebas won't win any beauty contests, but it's a hardy Pokémon that can live happily even in dirty water. Researchers are trying to figure out what makes it so tough.

How to Say It: FEE-bass
Imperial Height: 2'00''
Imperial Weight: 16.3 lbs.
Metric Height: 0.6 m
Metric Weight: 7.4 kg

Possible Moves: Splash, Tackle, Flail

Feebas ⇨ Milotic

TYPE: FIRE

Searing heat radiates from Fennekin's large ears to keep opponents at a distance. It often snacks on twigs to gain energy.

How to Say It: FEN-ik-in
Imperial Height: 1'04''
Imperial Weight: 20.7 lbs.
Metric Height: 0.4 m
Metric Weight: 9.4 kg

Possible Moves: Scratch, Tail Whip, Ember, Howl, Flame Charge, Psybeam, Fire Spin, Lucky Chant, Light Screen, Psyshock, Flamethrower, Will-O-Wisp, Psychic, Sunny Day, Magic Room, Fire Blast

REGION:
Kalos
(Central)

FENNEKIN
Fox Pokémon

Fennekin ➡ **Braixen** ➡ **Delphox**

REGION:
Johto

FERALIGATR
Big Jaw Pokémon

TYPE: WATER

Feraligatr uses its gaping maw as an intimidation tactic. Its powerful legs propel it into a high-speed charge.

How to Say It: fer-AL-ee-gay-tur
Imperial Height: 7'07''
Imperial Weight: 195.8 lbs.
Metric Height: 2.3 m
Metric Weight: 88.8 kg

Possible Moves: Scratch, Leer, Water Gun, Rage, Bite, Scary Face, Ice Fang, Flail, Agility, Crunch, Chip Away, Slash, Screech, Thrash, Aqua Tail, Superpower, Hydro Pump

Totodile ➡ **Croconaw** ➡ **Feraligatr**

139

FERROSEED

Thorn Seed Pokémon

REGIONS:
Kalos
(Coastal)
Unova

TYPE: GRASS-STEEL

Ferroseed use their spikes to cling to cave ceilings and absorb iron. They can also shoot those spikes to cover their escape when enemies approach.

How to Say It: fer-AH-seed
Imperial Height: 2'00''
Imperial Weight: 41.4 lbs.
Metric Height: 0.6 m
Metric Weight: 18.8 kg

Possible Moves: Tackle, Harden, Rollout, Curse, Metal Claw, Pin Missile, Gyro Ball, Iron Defense, Mirror Shot, Ingrain, Self-Destruct, Iron Head, Payback, Flash Cannon, Explosion

Ferroseed ⇨ Ferrothorn

FERROTHORN

Thorn Pod Pokémon

REGIONS:
Kalos
(Coastal)
Unova

TYPE: GRASS-STEEL

Ferrothorn swings its spiked feelers to attack. It likes to hang from the ceiling of a cave and shower spikes on anyone passing below.

How to Say It: fer-AH-thorn
Imperial Height: 3'03''
Imperial Weight: 242.5 lbs.
Metric Height: 1.0 m
Metric Weight: 110.0 kg

Possible Moves: Rock Climb, Tackle, Harden, Rollout, Curse, Metal Claw, Pin Missile, Gyro Ball, Iron Defense, Mirror Shot, Ingrain, Self-Destruct, Power Whip, Iron Head, Payback, Flash Cannon, Explosion

Ferroseed ⇨ Ferrothorn

FINNEON
Wing Fish Pokémon

TYPE: WATER

With its twin tails, Finneon can leap high out of the water to absorb sunlight, making the pink markings on its body shine. Sometimes a nearby Wingull notices and swoops down to attack.

How to Say It: FINN-ee-on
Imperial Height: 1'04''
Imperial Weight: 15.4 lbs.
Metric Height: 0.4 m
Metric Weight: 7.0 kg

Possible Moves: Pound, Water Gun, Attract, Rain Dance, Gust, Water Pulse, Captivate, Safeguard, Aqua Ring, Whirlpool, U-turn, Bounce, Silver Wind, Soak

Finneon **Lumineon**

FLAAFFY
Wool Pokémon

TYPE: ELECTRIC

Flaaffy is covered in soft fleece that looks perfect for petting, but watch out—the fleece stores up electricity, and you could get a nasty shock. The bald patches of rubbery skin are much safer to touch.

How to Say It: FLAF-fee
Imperial Height: 2'07''
Imperial Weight: 29.3 lbs.
Metric Height: 0.8 m
Metric Weight: 13.3 kg

Possible Moves: Tackle, Growl, Thunder Wave, Thunder Shock, Cotton Spore, Charge, Take Down, Electro Ball, Confuse Ray, Power Gem, Discharge, Cotton Guard, Signal Beam, Light Screen, Thunder

 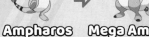

Mareep **Flaaffy** **Ampharos** **Mega Ampharos**

141

FLABÉBÉ
Single Bloom Pokémon

REGIONS:
Alola
Kalos
(Central)

TYPE: FAIRY

Flabébé relies on a flower for protection, but it's a bit picky, as it won't stop searching until it finds one with its favorite color and shape. It uses pollen from the flower to create a crown with healing powers.

How to Say It: flah-BAY-BAY
Imperial Height: 0'04''
Imperial Weight: 0.2 lbs.
Metric Height: 0.1 m
Metric Weight: 0.1 kg

Possible Moves: Tackle, Vine Whip, Fairy Wind, Lucky Chant, Razor Leaf, Wish, Magical Leaf, Grassy Terrain, Petal Blizzard, Aromatherapy, Misty Terrain, Moonblast, Petal Dance, Solar Beam

Flabébé   Floette   Florges

FLAREON
Flame Pokémon

REGIONS:
Alola
Kalos
(Coastal)
Kanto

TYPE: FIRE

Flareon prefers to roast berries with its fiery breath before chowing down. The temperature of its body averages nearly 1,500 degrees Fahrenheit—and the sac where it stores its flames is twice as hot!

How to Say It: FLAIR-ee-on
Imperial Height: 2'11''
Imperial Weight: 55.1 lbs.
Metric Height: 0.9 m
Metric Weight: 25.0 kg

Possible Moves: Ember, Helping Hand, Tackle, Tail Whip, Sand Attack, Baby-Doll Eyes, Quick Attack, Bite, Fire Fang, Fire Spin, Scary Face, Smog, Lava Plume, Last Resort, Flare Blitz

Eevee   Flareon

FLETCHINDER
Ember Pokémon

TYPE: FIRE-FLYING

Each Fletchinder jealously guards its own territory and drives intruders away. Flaming embers shoot forth from its beak to attack—or to grill its food to perfection before eating.

How to Say It: FLETCH-in-der
Imperial Height: 2'04''
Imperial Weight: 35.3 lbs.
Metric Height: 0.7 m
Metric Weight: 16.0 kg

Possible Moves: Ember, Tackle, Growl, Quick Attack, Peck, Agility, Flail, Roost, Razor Wind, Natural Gift, Flame Charge, Acrobatics, Me First, Tailwind, Steel Wing

Fletchling   Fletchinder   Talonflame

FLETCHLING
Tiny Robin Pokémon

TYPE: NORMAL-FLYING

Fletchling is generally calm and friendly, an easy partner for a beginning Trainer—but when called upon, it battles with a fierce determination. In the excitement, its body temperature spikes sharply.

How to Say It: FLETCH-ling
Imperial Height: 1'00''
Imperial Weight: 3.7 lbs.
Metric Height: 0.3 m
Metric Weight: 1.7 kg

Possible Moves: Tackle, Growl, Quick Attack, Peck, Agility, Flail, Roost, Razor Wind, Natural Gift, Flame Charge, Acrobatics, Me First, Tailwind, Steel Wing

Fletchling   Fletchinder   Talonflame

143

FLOATZEL

Sea Weasel Pokémon

REGIONS:
Kalos
(Mountain)
Sinnoh

TYPE: WATER

The flotation sac that surrounds its entire body makes Floatzel very good at rescuing people in the water. It can float them to safety like an inflatable raft.

How to Say It: FLOAT-zul
Imperial Height: 3'07''
Imperial Weight: 73.9 lbs.
Metric Height: 1.1 m
Metric Weight: 33.5 kg

Possible Moves: Ice Fang, Crunch, Sonic Boom, Growl, Water Sport, Quick Attack, Water Gun, Pursuit, Swift, Aqua Jet, Double Hit, Whirlpool, Razor Wind, Aqua Tail, Agility, Hydro Pump

Buizel ⇨ **Floatzel**

FLOETTE

Single Bloom Pokémon

REGIONS:
Alola
Kalos
(Central)

TYPE: FAIRY

Floette is a devoted flower gardener, readily lending its own power to make blooming plants even more beautiful—and as their beauty grows, their power grows as well. It uses the blossoms its raised as tools in battle.

How to Say It: floh-ET
Imperial Height: 0'08''
Imperial Weight: 2.0 lbs.
Metric Height: 0.2 m
Metric Weight: 0.9 kg

Possible Moves: Tackle, Vine Whip, Fairy Wind, Lucky Chant, Razor Leaf, Wish, Magical Leaf, Grassy Terrain, Petal Blizzard, Aromatherapy, Misty Terrain, Moonblast, Petal Dance, Solar Beam

Flabébé ⇨ **Floette** ⇨ **Florges**

FLORGES
Garden Pokémon

TYPE: FAIRY

Florges is content to spend its life among flowers, protecting them and raising them into beautiful specimens. Its attacks create breathtaking displays of fluttering petals.

How to Say It: FLORE-jess
Imperial Height: 3'07''
Imperial Weight: 22.0 lbs.
Metric Height: 1.1 m
Metric Weight: 10.0 kg

Possible Moves: Disarming Voice, Lucky Chant, Wish, Magical Leaf, Flower Shield, Grass Knot, Grassy Terrain, Petal Blizzard, Misty Terrain

Flabébé ➡ Floette ➡ Florges

TYPE: GROUND-DRAGON

Flygon is rarely seen, but can sometimes be heard in the desert—when it flaps its wings, the vibrations give off a sound like singing. It stirs up sandstorms to hide itself and confuse opponents.

How to Say It: FLY-gon
Imperial Height: 6'07''
Imperial Weight: 180.8 lbs.
Metric Height: 2.0 m
Metric Weight: 82.0 kg

Possible Moves: Dragon Claw, Dragon Breath, Dragon Dance, Sand Attack, Sonic Boom, Feint Attack, Bide, Mud-Slap, Bulldoze, Sand Tomb, Rock Slide, Supersonic, Screech, Earth Power, Dragon Tail, Earthquake, Sandstorm, Uproar, Hyper Beam, Dragon Rush

REGIONS:
Alola
Hoenn
Kalos
(Mountain)

FLYGON
Mystic Pokémon

Trapinch ➡ Vibrava ➡ Flygon

FOMANTIS
Sickle Grass Pokémon

REGION: Alola

TYPE: GRASS

Fomantis sleeps the day away, basking in the sunlight. The sweet scent it gives off sometimes attracts Cutiefly to its hiding place. During the night, it seeks out a safe place to sleep for the next day.

How to Say It: fo-MAN-tis
Imperial Height: 1'00''
Imperial Weight: 3.3 lbs.
Metric Height: 0.3 m
Metric Weight: 1.5 kg

Possible Moves: Fury Cutter, Leafage, Razor Leaf, Growth, Ingrain, Leaf Blade, Synthesis, Slash, Sweet Scent, Solar Beam, Sunny Day

Fomantis   Lurantis

FOONGUS
Mushroom Pokémon

REGIONS: Kalos (Mountain) Unova

TYPE: GRASS-POISON

Foongus uses its deceptive Poké Ball pattern to lure people or Pokémon close. Then it attacks with poison spores.

How to Say It: FOON-gus
Imperial Height: 0'08''
Imperial Weight: 2.2 lbs.
Metric Height: 1.2 m
Metric Weight: 1.0 kg

Possible Moves: Absorb, Growth, Astonish, Bide, Mega Drain, Ingrain, Feint Attack, Sweet Scent, Giga Drain, Toxic, Synthesis, Clear Smog, Solar Beam, Rage Powder, Spore

146

Foongus   Amoonguss

TYPE: BUG-STEEL

Getting too close to Forretress triggers its defensive reflex, and it shoots out parts of its steel shell in every direction. It can't control this reaction, so being around it is dangerous.

How to Say It: FOR-it-tress
Imperial Height: 3'11''
Imperial Weight: 277.3 lbs.
Metric Height: 1.2 m
Metric Weight: 125.8 kg

Possible Moves: Toxic Spikes, Tackle, Protect, Self-Destruct, Bug Bite, Take Down, Rapid Spin, Bide, Natural Gift, Spikes, Mirror Shot, Autotomize, Payback, Explosion, Iron Defense, Gyro Ball, Double-Edge, Magnet Rise, Zap Cannon, Heavy Slam

FORRETRESS
Bagworm Pokémon

Pineco **Forretress**

TYPE: DRAGON

Fraxure clash in intense battles over territory. After a battle is over, they always remember to sharpen their tusks on smooth stones so they'll be ready for the next battle.

How to Say It: FRAK-shur
Imperial Height: 3'03''
Imperial Weight: 79.4 lbs.
Metric Height: 1.0 m
Metric Weight: 36.0 kg

Possible Moves: Scratch, Leer, Assurance, Dragon Rage, Dual Chop, Scary Face, Slash, False Swipe, Dragon Claw, Dragon Dance, Taunt, Dragon Pulse, Swords Dance, Guillotine, Outrage, Giga Impact

FRAXURE
Axe Jaw Pokémon

Axew **Fraxure** **Haxorus**

FRILLISH
Floating Pokémon

REGIONS:
Alola
Unova

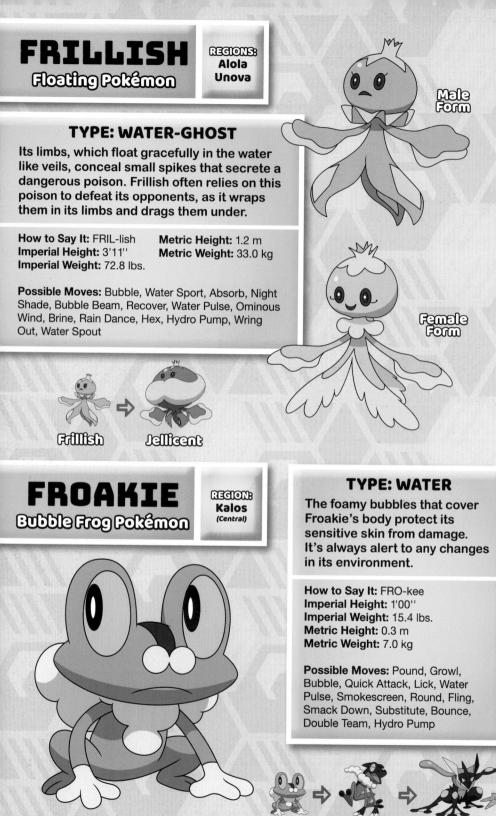

Male Form

TYPE: WATER-GHOST

Its limbs, which float gracefully in the water like veils, conceal small spikes that secrete a dangerous poison. Frillish often relies on this poison to defeat its opponents, as it wraps them in its limbs and drags them under.

How to Say It: FRIL-lish
Imperial Height: 3'11''
Imperial Weight: 72.8 lbs.
Metric Height: 1.2 m
Metric Weight: 33.0 kg

Possible Moves: Bubble, Water Sport, Absorb, Night Shade, Bubble Beam, Recover, Water Pulse, Ominous Wind, Brine, Rain Dance, Hex, Hydro Pump, Wring Out, Water Spout

Female Form

Frillish ⇨ Jellicent

FROAKIE
Bubble Frog Pokémon

REGION:
Kalos
(Central)

TYPE: WATER

The foamy bubbles that cover Froakie's body protect its sensitive skin from damage. It's always alert to any changes in its environment.

How to Say It: FRO-kee
Imperial Height: 1'00''
Imperial Weight: 15.4 lbs.
Metric Height: 0.3 m
Metric Weight: 7.0 kg

Possible Moves: Pound, Growl, Bubble, Quick Attack, Lick, Water Pulse, Smokescreen, Round, Fling, Smack Down, Substitute, Bounce, Double Team, Hydro Pump

Froakie ⇨ Frogadier ⇨ Greninja

FROGADIER
Bubble Frog Pokémon

TYPE: WATER

Swift and sure, Frogadier coats pebbles in a bubbly foam and then flings them with pinpoint accuracy. It has spectacular jumping and climbing skills.

How to Say It: FROG-uh-deer
Imperial Height: 2'00''
Imperial Weight: 24.0 lbs.
Metric Height: 0.6 m
Metric Weight: 10.9 kg

Possible Moves: Pound, Growl, Bubble, Quick Attack, Lick, Water Pulse, Smokescreen, Round, Fling, Smack Down, Substitute, Bounce, Double Team, Hydro Pump

Froakie ➡ Frogadier ➡ Greninja

FROSLASS
Snow Land Pokémon

TYPE: ICE-GHOST

Apparently, the first Froslass came into being when a woman was lost while exploring the snowy mountains. The frozen statues that decorate its icy lair may not be statues . . .

How to Say It: FROS-lass
Imperial Height: 4'03''
Imperial Weight: 58.6 lbs.
Metric Height: 1.3 m
Metric Weight: 26.6 kg

Possible Moves: Ominous Wind, Destiny Bond, Powder Snow, Leer, Double Team, Ice Shard, Icy Wind, Astonish, Draining Kiss, Will-O-Wisp, Confuse Ray, Wake-Up Slap, Captivate, Shadow Ball, Blizzard, Hail

Snorunt ➡ Froslass

149

FURFROU
Poodle Pokémon

REGIONS:
Alola
Kalos
(Central)

TYPE: NORMAL

Furfrou's long, fast-growing fur is easily trimmed into a variety of styles, but the Pokémon is picky about who wields the scissors. Rich people used to hold competitions to see whose Furfrou had the fanciest cut.

How to Say It: FUR-froo
Imperial Height: 3'11''
Imperial Weight: 61.7 lbs.
Metric Height: 1.2 m
Metric Weight: 28.0 kg

Possible Moves: Tackle, Growl, Sand Attack, Baby-Doll Eyes, Headbutt, Tail Whip, Bite, Odor Sleuth, Retaliate, Take Down, Charm, Sucker Punch, Cotton Guard

Does not evolve

FURRET
Long Body Pokémon

REGIONS:
Johto
Kalos
(Central)

TYPE: NORMAL

With its long, thin body and impressive speed, Furret has an evasive edge in battle. It can often wriggle right out of an opponent's grasp.

How to Say It: FUR-ret
Imperial Height: 5'11''
Imperial Weight: 71.6 lbs.
Metric Height: 1.8 m
Metric Weight: 32.5 kg

Possible Moves: Agility, Coil, Scratch, Foresight, Defense Curl, Quick Attack, Fury Swipes, Helping Hand, Follow Me, Slam, Rest, Sucker Punch, Amnesia, Baton Pass, Me First, Hyper Voice

Sentret ⇨ **Furret**

TYPE: DRAGON-GROUND

Gabite doesn't shed often, so its cast-off scales are hard to find, but they're a valuable ingredient in medicine. It hoards shiny things—including Carbink—in the cave where it lives.

GABITE
Cave Pokémon

How to Say It: gab-BITE
Imperial Height: 4'07''
Imperial Weight: 123.5 lbs.
Metric Height: 1.4 m
Metric Weight: 56.0 kg

Possible Moves: Dual Chop, Tackle, Sand Attack, Dragon Rage, Sandstorm, Take Down, Sand Tomb, Slash, Dragon Claw, Dig, Dragon Rush

Gible ➡ Gabite ➡ Garchomp ➡ Mega Garchomp

GALLADE
Blade Pokémon

REGIONS:
Kalos
(Central),
Sinnoh

TYPE: PSYCHIC-FIGHTING

A master of the blade, Gallade battles using the swordlike appendages that extend from its elbows.

How to Say It: guh-LADE
Imperial Height: 5'03''
Imperial Weight: 114.6 lbs.
Metric Height: 1.6 m
Metric Weight: 52.0 kg

Possible Moves: Slash, Stored Power, Close Combat, Leaf Blade, Night Slash, Leer, Confusion, Double Team, Teleport, Quick Guard, Fury Cutter, Aerial Ace, Heal Pulse, Wide Guard, Swords Dance, Psycho Cut, Helping Hand, Feint, False Swipe, Protect

MEGA GALLADE
Blade Pokémon

TYPE: PSYCHIC-FIGHTING

Imperial Height: 5'03''
Imperial Weight: 124.3 lbs.
Metric Height: 1.6 m
Metric Weight: 56.4 kg

Ralts ➡ **Kirlia** ➡ **Gallade** ➡ **Mega Gallade**

GALVANTULA
EleSpider Pokémon

TYPE: BUG-ELECTRIC

Galvantula's webs crackle with electricity, which shocks anything that blunders into them. It can also spin an electric barrier in battle.

How to Say It: gal-VAN-choo-luh
Imperial Height: 2'07''
Imperial Weight: 31.5 lbs.
Metric Height: 0.8 m
Metric Weight: 14.3 kg

Possible Moves: Sticky Web, String Shot, Absorb, Spider Web, Thunder Wave, Screech, Fury Cutter, Electroweb, Bug Bite, Gastro Acid, Slash, Electro Ball, Signal Beam, Agility, Sucker Punch, Discharge, Bug Buzz

Joltik ➡ Galvantula

TYPE: POISON

Garbodor were once a common sight in Alola, but since Grimer were brought in to deal with a pollution problem, competition for the same food source has reduced their numbers. The liquid they shoot from their arms is toxic.

REGIONS:
Alola
Kalos
(Mountain)
Unova

GARBODOR
Trash Heap Pokémon

How to Say It: gar-BOH-dur
Imperial Height: 6'03''
Imperial Weight: 236.6 lbs.
Metric Height: 1.9 m
Metric Weight: 107.3 kg

Possible Moves: Pound, Poison Gas, Recycle, Toxic Spikes, Acid Spray, Double Slap, Sludge, Stockpile, Swallow, Body Slam, Sludge Bomb, Clear Smog, Toxic, Amnesia, Belch, Gunk Shot, Explosion

Trubbish ➡ Garbodor

153

GARCHOMP
Mach Pokémon

REGIONS:
Alola
Kalos
(Mountain)
Sinnoh

TYPE: DRAGON-GROUND

Garchomp could win a race with a jet plane as it zooms through the skies. Some flying Pokémon have learned that colliding with a Garchomp moving at top speed is extremely dangerous.

How to Say It: GAR-chomp
Imperial Height: 6'03''
Imperial Weight: 209.4 lbs.
Metric Height: 1.9 m
Metric Weight: 95.0 kg

Possible Moves: Crunch, Dual Chop, Fire Fang, Tackle, Sand Attack, Dragon Rage, Sandstorm, Take Down, Sand Tomb, Slash, Dragon Claw, Dig, Dragon Rush

MEGA GARCHOMP
Mach Pokémon

TYPE: DRAGON-GROUND
Imperial Height: 6'03''
Imperial Weight: 209.4 lbs.
Metric Height: 1.9 m
Metric Weight: 95.0 kg

Gible ⇒ Gabite ⇒ Garchomp ⇒ Mega Garchomp

TYPE: PSYCHIC-FAIRY

Fiercely protective of its Trainer, Gardevoir can see into the future to detect a threat to that Trainer. It responds by unleashing the full strength of its psychic powers.

How to Say It: GAR-deh-VWAR
Imperial Height: 5'03''
Imperial Weight: 106.7 lbs.
Metric Height: 1.6 m
Metric Weight: 48.4 kg

Possible Moves: Moonblast, Stored Power, Misty Terrain, Healing Wish, Growl, Confusion, Double Team, Teleport, Disarming Voice, Wish, Magical Leaf, Heal Pulse, Draining Kiss, Calm Mind, Psychic, Imprison, Future Sight, Captivate, Hypnosis, Dream Eater

REGIONS:
Hoenn
Kalos
(Central)

GARDEVOIR
Embrace Pokémon

MEGA GARDEVOIR
Embrace Pokémon

TYPE: PSYCHIC-FAIRY

Imperial Height: 5'03''
Imperial Weight: 106.7 lbs.
Metric Height: 1.6 m
Metric Weight: 48.4 kg

Ralts ⇒ Kirlia ⇒ Gardevoir ⇒ Mega Gardevoir

155

GASTLY
Gas Pokémon

TYPE: GHOST-POISON

Gastly likes to lurk in abandoned buildings, where its presence sometimes causes strange lights to flicker. This gaseous Pokémon is hard to see, but it gives off a surprisingly delicate, sweet scent.

How to Say It: GAST-lee
Imperial Height: 4'03''
Imperial Weight: 0.2 lbs.
Metric Height: 1.3 m
Metric Weight: 0.1 kg

Possible Moves: Hypnosis, Lick, Spite, Mean Look, Curse, Night Shade, Confuse Ray, Sucker Punch, Payback, Shadow Ball, Dream Eater, Dark Pulse, Destiny Bond, Hex, Nightmare

Gastly → Haunter → Gengar → Mega Gengar

GASTRODON EAST SEA
Sea Slug Pokémon

TYPE: WATER-GROUND

Color variations between Gastrodon from different habitats have intrigued scientists for some time. Research is under way to find out what happens when a blue East Sea Gastrodon is moved to western seas.

How to Say It: GAS-stroh-don
Imperial Height: 2'11''
Imperial Weight: 65.9 lbs.
Metric Height: 0.9 m
Metric Weight: 29.9 kg

Possible Moves: Mud-Slap, Mud Sport, Harden, Water Pulse, Mud Bomb, Hidden Power, Rain Dance, Body Slam, Muddy Water, Recover

Shellos
(East Sea)

Gastrodon
(East Sea)

GASTRODON WEST SEA
Sea Slug Pokémon

TYPE: WATER-GROUND

If West Sea Gastrodon loses a part of its squishy pink body, it can regenerate. It sometimes comes forth from the seas to wander on land, and no one really knows why.

How to Say It: GAS-stroh-don
Imperial Height: 2'11''
Imperial Weight: 65.9 lbs.
Metric Height: 0.9 m
Metric Weight: 29.9 kg

Possible Moves: Mud-Slap, Mud Sport, Harden, Water Pulse, Mud Bomb, Hidden Power, Rain Dance, Body Slam, Muddy Water, Recover

Shellos
(West Sea)

Gastrodon
(West Sea)

157

GENESECT
Paleozoic Pokémon

REGION:
Unova

MYTHICAL POKÉMON

TYPE: BUG-STEEL

The powerful cannon on Genesect's back is the result of Team Plasma's meddling. This Mythical Pokémon is three hundred million years old.

How to Say It: JEN-uh-sekt
Imperial Height: 4'11''
Imperial Weight: 181.9 lbs.
Metric Height: 1.5 m
Metric Weight: 82.5 kg

Possible Moves: Fell Stinger, Techno Blast, Quick Attack, Magnet Rise, Metal Claw, Screech, Fury Cutter, Lock-On, Flame Charge, Magnet Bomb, Slash, Metal Sound, Signal Beam, Tri Attack, X-Scissor, Bug Buzz, Simple Beam, Zap Cannon, Hyper Beam, Self-Destruct

Does not evolve

GENGAR
Shadow Pokémon

TYPE: GHOST-POISON

The sudden onset of an unexplained chill might mean a Gengar is coming toward you. This Pokémon seems to have misunderstood the concept of "making friends"—it tries to create a kindred spirit by attacking humans.

How to Say It: GHEN-gar
Imperial Height: 4'11"
Imperial Weight: 89.3 lbs.
Metric Height: 1.5 m
Metric Weight: 40.5 kg

Possible Moves: Shadow Punch, Hypnosis, Lick, Spite, Mean Look, Curse, Night Shade, Confuse Ray, Sucker Punch, Payback, Shadow Ball, Dream Eater, Dark Pulse, Destiny Bond, Hex, Nightmare

MEGA GENGAR
Shadow Pokémon

TYPE: GHOST-POISON

Imperial Height: 4'07"
Imperial Weight: 89.3 lbs.
Metric Height: 1.4 m
Metric Weight: 40.5 kg

Gastly Haunter Gengar Mega Gengar

159

GEODUDE
Rock Pokémon

TYPE: ROCK-GROUND

It might be tempting to gather up Geodude found along the road and throw them around like balls, but that's a bad idea—they're very heavy, and their surface is extremely hard. Ouch!

How to Say It: JEE-oh-dude
Imperial Height: 1'04''
Imperial Weight: 44.1 lbs.
Metric Height: 0.4 m
Metric Weight: 20.0 kg

Possible Moves: Tackle, Defense Curl, Mud Sport, Rock Polish, Rollout, Magnitude, Rock Throw, Rock Blast, Smack Down, Self-Destruct, Bulldoze, Stealth Rock, Earthquake, Explosion, Double-Edge, Stone Edge

Geodude ➡ Graveler ➡ Golem

ALOLAN GEODUDE
Rock Pokémon

REGION:
Alola

TYPE: ROCK-ELECTRIC

In the Alola region, Geodude are naturally magnetic, and their bodies are often covered in iron particles they've picked up while sleeping in the sand. Stepping on one can cause a nasty shock, so beachgoers keep a sharp eye out.

How to Say It: uh-LO-luhn JEE-oh-dude
Imperial Height: 1'04''
Imperial Weight: 44.8 lbs.
Metric Height: 0.4 m
Metric Weight: 20.3 kg

Possible Moves: Tackle, Defense Curl, Charge, Rock Polish, Rollout, Spark, Rock Throw, Smack Down, Thunder Punch, Self-Destruct, Stealth Rock, Rock Blast, Discharge, Explosion, Double-Edge, Stone Edge

Alolan Geodude ➡ Alolan Graveler ➡ Alolan Golem

TYPE: DRAGON-GROUND

Gible are drawn to cozy caves that are kept warm by geothermal energy. Even in their warm caves, they tend to huddle together when the outside weather gets too cold. A passerby might get an unexpected chomping!

How to Say It: GIB-bull
Imperial Height: 2'04''
Imperial Weight: 45.2 lbs.
Metric Height: 0.7 m
Metric Weight: 20.5 kg

Possible Moves: Tackle, Sand Attack, Dragon Rage, Sandstorm, Take Down, Sand Tomb, Slash, Dragon Claw, Dig, Dragon Rush

GIBLE
Land Shark Pokémon

Gible → Gabite → Garchomp → Mega Garchomp

TYPE: ROCK

On a clear day, Gigalith can absorb sunlight and convert the energy into amazingly powerful blasts. This doesn't work in the rain or after dark, though. It often helps out around construction sites.

How to Say It: GIH-gah-lith
Imperial Height: 5'07''
Imperial Weight: 573.2 lbs.
Metric Height: 1.7 m
Metric Weight: 260.0 kg

Possible Moves: Power Gem, Tackle, Harden, Sand Attack, Headbutt, Rock Blast, Mud-Slap, Iron Defense, Smack Down, Rock Slide, Stealth Rock, Sandstorm, Stone Edge, Explosion

GIGALITH
Compressed Pokémon

Roggenrola → Boldore → Gigalith

GIRAFARIG
Long Neck Pokémon

TYPE: NORMAL-PSYCHIC

The brain that controls Girafarig's secondary head is too small to think and just reacts to its surroundings. It tends to attack anyone who approaches from behind.

How to Say It: jir-RAF-uh-rig
Imperial Height: 4'11''
Imperial Weight: 91.5 lbs.

Metric Height: 1.5 m
Metric Weight: 41.5 kg

Possible Moves: Power Swap, Guard Swap, Astonish, Tackle, Growl, Confusion, Odor Sleuth, Stomp, Agility, Psybeam, Baton Pass, Assurance, Double Hit, Psychic, Zen Headbutt, Crunch, Nasty Plot

Does not evolve

GIRATINA ALTERED FORME
Renegade Pokémon

LEGENDARY POKÉMON

TYPE: GHOST-DRAGON

As punishment, the Legendary Pokémon Giratina was banished to another dimension, where everything is distorted and reversed.

How to Say It: geer-ah-TEE-nuh
Imperial Height: 14'09"
Imperial Weight: 1,653.5 lbs.
Metric Height: 4.5 m
Metric Weight: 750.0 kg

Possible Moves: Dragon Breath, Scary Face, Ominous Wind, Ancient Power, Slash, Shadow Sneak, Destiny Bond, Dragon Claw, Earth Power, Aura Sphere, Shadow Claw, Shadow Force, Hex

Does not evolve

GIRATINA ORIGIN FORME
Renegade Pokémon

LEGENDARY POKÉMON

TYPE: GHOST-DRAGON

Imperial Height: 22'08"
Imperial Weight: 1,443.0 lbs.
Metric Height: 6.9 m
Metric Weight: 650.0 kg

Does not evolve

GLACEON
Fresh Snow Pokémon

TYPE: ICE

The icy Glaceon has amazing control over its body temperature. It can freeze its own fur and then smash into an opponent with the spiky icicles that result.

How to Say It: GLAY-cee-on
Imperial Height: 2'07''
Imperial Weight: 57.1 lbs.

Metric Height: 0.8 m
Metric Weight: 25.9 kg

Possible Moves: Icy Wind, Helping Hand, Tackle, Tail Whip, Sand Attack, Baby-Doll Eyes, Quick Attack, Bite, Ice Fang, Ice Shard, Barrier, Mirror Coat, Hail, Last Resort, Blizzard

Eevee ⇨ Glaceon

GLALIE
Face Pokémon

TYPE: ICE

When Glalie breathes icy air from its gaping mouth, it can instantly freeze its opponent. It apparently came into being from a rock on a mountainside soaking up the despair of a climber lost in the cold.

How to Say It: GLAY-lee
Imperial Height: 4'11''
Imperial Weight: 565.5 lbs.
Metric Height: 1.5 m
Metric Weight: 256.5 kg

Possible Moves: Freeze-Dry, Sheer Cold, Powder Snow, Leer, Double Team, Ice Shard, Icy Wind, Bite, Ice Fang, Headbutt, Protect, Frost Breath, Crunch, Blizzard, Hail

MEGA GLALIE
Face Pokémon

TYPE: ICE

Imperial Height: 6'11''
Imperial Weight: 772.1 lbs.
Metric Height: 2.1 m
Metric Weight: 350.2 kg

Snorunt ⇨ Glalie ⇨ Mega Glalie

165

GLAMEOW

Catty Pokémon

TYPE: NORMAL

When it's feeling happy and friendly, Glameow purrs winningly and performs a lovely dance with its spiraling tail. When it's in a bad mood, however, the claws come out.

How to Say It: GLAM-meow
Imperial Height: 1'08''
Imperial Weight: 8.6 lbs.
Metric Height: 0.5 m
Metric Weight: 3.9 kg

Possible Moves: Fake Out, Scratch, Growl, Hypnosis, Feint Attack, Fury Swipes, Charm, Assist, Captivate, Slash, Sucker Punch, Attract, Hone Claws, Play Rough

Glameow ➡ Purugly

GLIGAR

Fly Scorpion Pokémon

REGIONS: Johto Kalos (Mountain)

TYPE: GROUND-FLYING

Gliding silently through the air, Gligar can strike from above to grab onto an opponent's face with all four of its claws. The barb on its tail is poisonous.

How to Say It: GLY-gar
Imperial Height: 3'07''
Imperial Weight: 142.9 lbs.
Metric Height: 1.1 m
Metric Weight: 64.8 kg

Possible Moves: Poison Sting, Sand Attack, Harden, Knock Off, Quick Attack, Fury Cutter, Feint Attack, Acrobatics, Slash, U-turn, Screech, X-Scissor, Sky Uppercut, Swords Dance, Guillotine

Gligar ➡ Gliscor

GLISCOR
Fang Scorpion Pokémon

TYPE: GROUND-FLYING

Gliscor hangs upside down from trees, watching for its chance to attack. At the right moment, it silently swoops, with its long tail ready to seize its opponent.

How to Say It: GLY-score
Imperial Height: 6'07''
Imperial Weight: 93.7 lbs.
Metric Height: 2.0 m
Metric Weight: 42.5 kg

Possible Moves: Guillotine, Thunder Fang, Ice Fang, Fire Fang, Poison Jab, Sand Attack, Harden, Knock Off, Quick Attack, Fury Cutter, Feint Attack, Acrobatics, Night Slash, U-turn, Screech, X-Scissor, Sky Uppercut, Swords Dance

Gligar ⇨ **Gliscor**

TYPE: GRASS-POISON

Gloom doesn't always smell terrible—when it feels safe and relaxed, its aroma fades. However, its nectar usually carries an awful stench.

How to Say It: GLOOM
Imperial Height: 2'07''
Imperial Weight: 19.0 lbs.
Metric Height: 0.8 m
Metric Weight: 8.6 kg

Possible Moves: Absorb, Growth, Sweet Scent, Acid, Poison Powder, Stun Spore, Sleep Powder, Mega Drain, Lucky Chant, Natural Gift, Moonlight, Giga Drain, Petal Blizzard, Toxic, Petal Dance, Grassy Terrain

REGION:
Kalos
(Central)
Kanto

GLOOM
Weed Pokémon

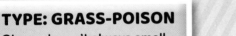

Vileplume

Oddish ⇨ **Gloom** ⇨ **Bellossom**

GOGOAT
Mount Pokémon

REGION:
Kalos
(Central)

TYPE: GRASS

This perceptive Pokémon can read its riders' feelings by paying attention to their grip on its horns. Gogoat also use their horns in battles for leadership.

How to Say It: GO-goat
Imperial Height: 5'07''
Imperial Weight: 200.6 lbs.
Metric Height: 1.7 m
Metric Weight: 91.0 kg

Possible Moves: Aerial Ace, Earthquake, Tackle, Growth, Vine Whip, Tail Whip, Leech Seed, Razor Leaf, Synthesis, Take Down, Bulldoze, Seed Bomb, Bulk Up, Double-Edge, Horn Leaf, Leaf Blade, Milk Drink

Skiddo ⇨ **Gogoat**

GOLBAT
Bat Pokémon

REGIONS:
Alola
Kalos
(Central)
Kanto

TYPE: POISON-FLYING

Golbat's fangs are hollow, which allows it to suck up blood for its meals more efficiently. This efficiency can cause problems, though—sometimes it eats so much that it has trouble flying afterward!

How to Say It: GOHL-bat
Imperial Height: 5'03''
Imperial Weight: 121.3 lbs.
Metric Height: 1.6 m
Metric Weight: 55.0 kg

Possible Moves: Screech, Absorb, Supersonic, Astonish, Bite, Wing Attack, Confuse Ray, Air Cutter, Swift, Poison Fang, Mean Look, Leech Life, Haze, Venoshock, Air Slash, Quick Guard

Zubat ⇨ **Golbat** ⇨ **Crobat**

TYPE: WATER

Seeing a school of Goldeen swimming upstream brings joy to anyone who's been pining for the return of spring. Some Trainers are such huge fans that they ignore other Pokémon and devote all their time only to Goldeen.

How to Say It: GOL-deen
Imperial Height: 2'00''
Imperial Weight: 33.1 lbs.
Metric Height: 0.6 m
Metric Weight: 15.0 kg

Possible Moves: Peck, Tail Whip, Water Sport, Supersonic, Horn Attack, Flail, Water Pulse, Aqua Ring, Fury Attack, Agility, Waterfall, Horn Drill, Soak, Megahorn

REGIONS:
Alola
Kalos
(Central)
Kanto

GOLDEEN
Goldfish Pokémon

Goldeen **Seaking**

TYPE: WATER

People used to think they could gain mysterious powers by taking the red orb from Golduck's forehead. It keeps an eye out for underwater Pokémon as it patrols near the edge of its lake home.

How to Say It: GOL-duck
Imperial Height: 5'07''
Imperial Weight: 168.9 lbs.
Metric Height: 1.7 m
Metric Weight: 76.6 kg

Possible Moves: Me First, Aqua Jet, Water Sport, Scratch, Tail Whip, Water Gun, Confusion, Fury Swipes, Water Pulse, Disable, Screech, Zen Headbutt, Aqua Tail, Soak, Psych Up, Amnesia, Hydro Pump, Wonder Room

REGIONS:
Alola
Kalos
(Central)
Kanto

GOLDUCK
Duck Pokémon

Psyduck **Golduck**

GOLEM
Megaton Pokémon

TYPE: ROCK-GROUND

Golem's annual molt leaves behind a shell that makes for good fertilizer when incorporated into the soil. This Pokémon can easily stand up to an explosion, but it really hates getting wet.

How to Say It: GO-lum
Imperial Height: 4'07''
Imperial Weight: 661.4 lbs.
Metric Height: 1.4 m
Metric Weight: 300.0 kg

Possible Moves: Heavy Slam, Tackle, Defense Curl, Mud Sport, Rock Polish, Steamroller, Magnitude, Rock Throw, Rock Blast, Smack Down, Self-Destruct, Bulldoze, Stealth Rock, Earthquake, Explosion, Double-Edge, Stone Edge

Geodude   Graveler   Golem

ALOLAN GOLEM
Megaton Pokémon

REGION:
Alola

TYPE: ROCK-ELECTRIC

The rocks Golem fires from its back carry a strong electrical charge, so even a glancing blow can deliver a powerful shock. Sometimes it grabs a Geodude to fire instead.

How to Say It: uh-LO-luhn GO-lum
Imperial Height: 5'07''
Imperial Weight: 696.7 lbs.
Metric Height: 1.7 m
Metric Weight: 316.0 kg

Possible Moves: Heavy Slam, Tackle, Defense Curl, Charge, Rock Polish, Steamroller, Spark, Rock Throw, Smack Down, Thunder Punch, Self-Destruct, Stealth Rock, Rock Blast, Discharge, Explosion, Double-Edge, Stone Edge

Alolan Geodude   Alolan Graveler   Alolan Golem

GOLETT
Automaton Pokémon

TYPE: GROUND-GHOST

Scientists haven't been able to identify the source of Golett's power, even though the Pokémon became active a long, long time ago. Its body appears to be made with sculpted clay.

How to Say It: GO-let
Imperial Height: 3'03''
Imperial Weight: 202.8 lbs.
Metric Height: 1.0 m
Metric Weight: 92.0 kg

Possible Moves: Pound, Astonish, Defense Curl, Mud-Slap, Rollout, Shadow Punch, Iron Defense, Stomping Tantrum, Mega Punch, Magnitude, Dynamic Punch, Night Shade, Curse, Earthquake, Hammer Arm, Focus Punch

Golett ⇨ Golurk

REGION:
Alola

GOLISOPOD
Hard Scale Pokémon

TYPE: BUG-WATER

When Golisopod has to battle, its six sharp-clawed arms are certainly up to the task. Most of the time, though, it lives quietly in underwater caves, where it meditates and avoids conflict.

How to Say It: go-LIE-suh-pod
Imperial Height: 6'07''
Imperial Weight: 238.1 lbs.
Metric Height: 2.0 m
Metric Weight: 108.0 kg

Possible Moves: First Impression, Struggle Bug, Sand Attack, Fury Cutter, Rock Smash, Bug Bite, Spite, Swords Dance, Slash, Razor Shell, Sucker Punch, Iron Defense, Pin Missile, Liquidation

Wimpod ⇨ Golisopod

171

GOLURK
Automaton Pokémon

REGIONS:
Alola
Kalos
(Coastal)
Unova

TYPE: GROUND-GHOST

Golurk has worked alongside people since ancient times, and it's a loyal partner to modern-day Trainers. But for some reason, it becomes indiscriminately angry when the seal on its chest is removed.

How to Say It: GO-lurk
Imperial Height: 9'02''
Imperial Weight: 727.5 lbs.
Metric Height: 2.8 m
Metric Weight: 330.0 kg

Possible Moves: Heavy Slam, High Horsepower, Pound, Astonish, Defense Curl, Mud-Slap, Rollout, Shadow Punch, Iron Defense, Stomping Tantrum, Mega Punch, Magnitude, Dynamic Punch, Night Shade, Curse, Earthquake, Hammer Arm, Focus Punch, Phantom Force

Golett ⇨ Golurk

GOODRA
Dragon Pokémon

REGIONS:
Alola
Kalos
(Mountain)

TYPE: DRAGON

Goodra loves to make friends and gets very sad when it's on its own for too long. When bullied, this apparently meek Pokémon goes into attack mode, swinging its hefty tail and horns.

How to Say It: GOO-druh
Imperial Height: 6'07''
Imperial Weight: 331.8 lbs.
Metric Height: 2.0 m
Metric Weight: 150.5 kg

Possible Moves: Aqua Tail, Outrage, Feint, Tackle, Bubble, Absorb, Protect, Bide, Dragon Breath, Rain Dance, Flail, Body Slam, Muddy Water, Dragon Pulse, Power Whip

Goomy ⇨ Sliggoo ⇨ Goodra

GOOMY
Soft Tissue Pokémon

TYPE: DRAGON

The slimy membrane that covers Goomy's body provides it with protection—partly by keeping others away, because touching it is really gross! It stays in the shade to keep itself from drying out.

How to Say It: GOO-mee
Imperial Height: 1'00''
Imperial Weight: 6.2 lbs.
Metric Height: 0.3 m
Metric Weight: 2.8 kg

Possible Moves: Tackle, Bubble, Absorb, Protect, Bide, Dragon Breath, Rain Dance, Flail, Body Slam, Muddy Water, Dragon Pulse

Goomy ➡ Sliggoo ➡ Goodra

GOREBYSS
South Sea Pokémon

TYPE: WATER

Gorebyss's skin contains special cells that change color depending on the water temperature. The warmer the water, the brighter the color, so Gorebyss in Alola are especially easy to spot from a distance.

How to Say It: GORE-a-biss
Imperial Height: 5'11''
Imperial Weight: 49.8 lbs.
Metric Height: 1.8 m
Metric Weight: 22.6 kg

Possible Moves: Whirlpool, Confusion, Water Sport, Agility, Draining Kiss, Water Pulse, Amnesia, Aqua Ring, Captivate, Dive, Baton Pass, Psychic, Aqua Tail, Coil, Hydro Pump

Clamperl ➡ Gorebyss

173

GOTHITA
Fixation Pokémon

REGIONS:
Kalos
(Mountain)
Unova

TYPE: PSYCHIC

Gothita's wide eyes are always fixed on something. It seems when they stare like that, they're seeing what others cannot.

How to Say It: GAH-THEE-tah
Imperial Height: 1'04''
Imperial Weight: 12.8 lbs.
Metric Height: 0.4 m
Metric Weight: 5.8 kg

Possible Moves: Pound, Confusion, Tickle, Play Nice, Fake Tears, Double Slap, Psybeam, Embargo, Feint Attack, Psyshock, Flatter, Future Sight, Heal Block, Psychic, Telekinesis, Charm, Magic Room

Gothita   Gothorita   Gothitelle

GOTHITELLE
Astral Body Pokémon

REGIONS:
Kalos
(Mountain)
Unova

TYPE: PSYCHIC

Gothitelle observes the stars to predict the future. It sometimes distorts the air around itself to reveal faraway constellations.

How to Say It: GAH-thih-tell
Imperial Height: 4'11''
Imperial Weight: 97.0 lbs.
Metric Height: 1.5 m
Metric Weight: 44.0 kg

Possible Moves: Pound, Confusion, Tickle, Play Nice, Fake Tears, Double Slap, Psybeam, Embargo, Feint Attack, Psyshock, Flatter, Future Sight, Heal Block, Psychic, Telekinesis, Charm, Magic Room

Gothita   Gothorita   Gothitelle

GOTHORITA
Manipulate Pokémon

TYPE: PSYCHIC

Gothorita draw their power from starlight. On starry nights, they can make stones float and control people's movements with their enhanced psychic power.

How to Say It: GAH-thoh-REE-tah
Imperial Height: 2'04''
Imperial Weight: 39.7 lbs.
Metric Height: 0.7 m
Metric Weight: 18.0 kg

Possible Moves: Pound, Confusion, Tickle, Play Nice, Fake Tears, Double Slap, Psybeam, Embargo, Feint Attack, Psyshock, Flatter, Future Sight, Heal Block, Psychic, Telekinesis, Charm, Magic Room

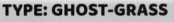

Gothita ⇨ Gothorita ⇨ Gothitelle

TYPE: GHOST-GRASS

During the new moon, the eerie song of the Gourgeist echoes through town, bringing woe to anyone who hears it.

How to Say It: GORE-guyst
Imperial Height: 2'11''
Imperial Weight: 27.6 lbs.
Metric Height: 0.9 m
Metric Weight: 12.5 kg

Possible Moves: Explosion, Phantom Force, Trick, Astonish, Confuse Ray, Scary Face, Trick-or-Treat, Worry Seed, Razor Leaf, Leech Seed, Bullet Seed, Shadow Sneak, Shadow Ball, Pain Split, Seed Bomb

GOURGEIST
Pumpkin Pokémon

Pumpkaboo ⇨ Gourgeist

175

GRANBULL
Fairy Pokémon

TYPE: FAIRY

With its massive fangs and strong jaw, Granbull looks like a fierce opponent—but it's a total sweetheart, a timid Pokémon who bites only when provoked. This amusing contrast has made it popular among young people.

How to Say It: GRAN-bull
Imperial Height: 4'07''
Imperial Weight: 107.4 lbs.

Metric Height: 1.4 m
Metric Weight: 48.7 kg

Possible Moves: Outrage, Ice Fang, Fire Fang, Thunder Fang, Tackle, Scary Face, Tail Whip, Charm, Bite, Lick, Headbutt, Roar, Rage, Play Rough, Payback, Crunch

Snubbull ⇨ Granbull

TYPE: ROCK-GROUND

Graveler can't walk very fast, but when it tucks itself into a ball, it can roll as fast as a car once it gains momentum. It loves to crunch on moss-covered rocks.

How to Say It: GRAV-el-ler
Imperial Height: 3'03''
Imperial Weight: 231.5 lbs
Metric Height: 1.0 m
Metric Weight: 105.0 kg

Possible Moves: Tackle, Defense Curl, Mud Sport, Rock Polish, Rollout, Magnitude, Rock Throw, Rock Blast, Smack Down, Self-Destruct, Bulldoze, Stealth Rock, Earthquake, Explosion, Double-Edge, Stone Edge

GRAVELER
Rock Pokémon

Geodude ➡ Graveler ➡ Golem

ALOLAN GRAVELER
Rock Pokémon

TYPE: ROCK-ELECTRIC

The crystals that appear on Graveler's body are the result of consuming dravite, a particularly tasty mineral. Graveler often fight over dravite deposits, crashing together with a sound like thunder.

How to Say It: uh-LO-luhn GRAV-el-ler
Imperial Height: 3'03''
Imperial Weight: 242.5 lbs.
Metric Height: 1.0 m
Metric Weight: 110.0 kg

Possible Moves: Tackle, Defense Curl, Charge, Rock Polish, Rollout, Spark, Rock Throw, Smack Down, Thunder Punch, Self-Destruct, Stealth Rock, Rock Blast, Discharge, Explosion, Double-Edge, Stone Edge

Alolan Geodude   Alolan Graveler   Alolan Golem

177

GRENINJA
Ninja Pokémon

REGION:
Kalos
(Central)

TYPE: WATER-DARK

Greninja can compress water into sharp-edged throwing stars. With the grace of a ninja, it slips in and out of sight to attack from the shadows.

How to Say It: greh-NIN-jah
Imperial Height: 4'11''
Imperial Weight: 88.2 lbs.

Metric Height: 1.5 m
Metric Weight: 40.0 kg

Possible Moves: Night Slash, Role Play, Mat Block, Pound, Growl, Bubble, Quick Attack, Lick, Water Pulse, Smokescreen, Shadow Sneak, Spikes, Feint Attack, Water Shuriken, Substitute, Extrasensory, Double Team, Haze, Hydro Pump

Froakie ⇨ Frogadier ⇨ Greninja

TYPE: POISON

Most people and Pokémon dislike the industrial waste created by factories, but Grimer happily feasts on the icky slime. To survive, it has to maintain a certain level of germs in its body.

How to Say It: GRY-mur
Imperial Height: 2'11''
Imperial Weight: 66.1 lbs.
Metric Height: 0.9 m
Metric Weight: 30.0 kg

Possible Moves: Poison Gas, Pound, Harden, Bite, Disable, Acid Spray, Poison Fang, Minimize, Fling, Knock Off, Crunch, Screech, Gunk Shot, Acid Armor, Belch, Memento

REGION: Kanto

GRIMER
Sludge Pokémon

Grimer → **Muk**

REGION: Alola

ALOLAN GRIMER
Sludge Pokémon

TYPE: POISON-DARK

Grimer's appearance in the Alola region developed after it was called upon to deal with a persistent garbage problem. Each crystal on its body is formed from dangerous toxins, and those toxins escape if a crystal falls off.

How to Say It: uh-LO-luhn GRY-mur
Imperial Height: 2'04''
Imperial Weight: 92.6 lbs.
Metric Height: 0.7 m
Metric Weight: 42.0 kg

Possible Moves: Pound, Poison Gas, Harden, Bite, Disable, Acid Spray, Poison Fang, Minimize, Fling, Knock Off, Crunch, Screech, Gunk Shot, Acid Armor, Belch, Memento

Alolan Grimer → **Alolan Muk**

GROTLE
Grove Pokémon

REGION: Sinnoh

TYPE: GRASS

Grotle leaves the shade of its forest home to soak up sunlight with its shell. It's good at finding clear water, and smaller Pokémon often ride on its back when they're thirsty.

How to Say It: GRAH-tul
Imperial Height: 3'07''
Imperial Weight: 213.8 lbs.
Metric Height: 1.1 m
Metric Weight: 97.0 kg

Possible Moves: Tackle, Withdraw, Absorb, Razor Leaf, Curse, Bite, Mega Drain, Leech Seed, Synthesis, Crunch, Giga Drain, Leaf Storm

Turtwig ➡ Grotle ➡ Torterra

TYPE: GROUND

Legends say that Groudon is the land personified. When it channels the full power of nature, it can expand the landmass with eruptions of magma. This Pokémon often clashes with Kyogre.

How to Say It: GRAU-don
Imperial Height: 11'06''
Imperial Weight: 2,094.4 lbs.
Metric Height: 3.5 m
Metric Weight: 950.0 kg

Possible Moves: Ancient Power, Mud Shot, Scary Face, Earth Power, Lava Plume, Rest, Earthquake, Precipice Blades, Bulk Up, Solar Beam, Fissure, Fire Blast, Hammer Armor, Eruption

REGION: Hoenn

GROUDON
Continent Pokémon

LEGENDARY POKÉMON

PRIMAL GROUDON
Continent Pokémon

TYPE: GROUND-FIRE

Imperial Height: 16'05''
Imperial Weight: 2,204.0 lbs.
Metric Height: 5.0 m
Metric Weight: 999.7 kg

Groudon ⇨ Primal Groudon

181

GROVYLE
Wood Gecko Pokémon

REGION:
Hoenn

TYPE: GRASS

Grovyle can travel so swiftly from branch to branch that it looks like it's flying through the forest. The leaves on its body are excellent camouflage.

How to Say It: GROW-vile
Imperial Height: 2'11''
Imperial Weight: 47.6 lbs.
Metric Height: 0.9 m
Metric Weight: 21.6 kg

Possible Moves: Fury Cutter, Pound, Leer, Absorb, Quick Attack, Mega Drain, Pursuit, Leaf Blade, Agility, Slam, Detect, X-Scissor, False Swipe, Quick Guard, Leaf Storm, Screech

Treecko → Grovyle → Sceptile → Mega Sceptile

GROWLITHE
Puppy Pokémon

REGIONS:
Alola
Kanto

TYPE: FIRE

If you try to pet another Trainer's Growlithe, you'll soon discover this Pokémon isn't just cute—it has a fiercely territorial side. It's known for its intelligence and loyalty.

How to Say It: GROWL-lith
Imperial Height: 2'04''
Imperial Weight: 41.9 lbs.
Metric Height: 0.7 m
Metric Weight: 19.0 kg

Possible Moves: Bite, Roar, Ember, Leer, Odor Sleuth, Helping Hand, Flame Wheel, Reversal, Fire Fang, Take Down, Flame Burst, Agility, Retaliate, Flamethrower, Crunch, Heat Wave, Outrage, Flare Blitz

Growlithe → Arcanine

TYPE: BUG

Grubbin have discovered that sticking close to Electric-type Pokémon offers some protection from the Flying types that often like to attack them! With their strong jaws, they can scrape away tree bark to get at the delicious sap underneath.

How to Say It: GRUB-bin
Imperial Height: 1'04''
Imperial Weight: 9.7 lbs.
Metric Height: 0.4 m
Metric Weight: 4.4 kg

Possible Moves: Vice Grip, String Shot, Mud-Slap, Bite, Bug Bite, Spark, Acrobatics, Crunch, X-Scissor, Dig

GRUBBIN
Larva Pokémon

Grubbin ⇨ Charjabug ⇨ Vikavolt

GRUMPIG
Manipulate Pokémon

TYPE: PSYCHIC

Grumpig breaks into a strange dance when it's using its black pearls to focus its psychic power. Many collectors consider the pearls to be priceless artwork.

How to Say It: GRUM-pig
Imperial Height: 2'11''
Imperial Weight: 157.6 lbs.
Metric Height: 0.9 m
Metric Weight: 71.5 kg

Possible Moves: Teeter Dance, Belch, Splash, Psywave, Odor Sleuth, Psybeam, Psych Up, Confuse Ray, Magic Coat, Zen Headbutt, Rest, Snore, Power Gem, Psyshock, Payback, Psychic, Bounce

Spoink ⇨ Grumpig

183

GULPIN
Stomach Pokémon

REGIONS:
**Hoenn
Kalos**
(Central)

TYPE: POISON

Gulpin's stomach takes up most of its body, so there's not much room for its other organs. Its powerful digestive enzymes make short work of anything it swallows.

How to Say It: GULL-pin
Imperial Height: 1'04''
Imperial Weight: 22.7 lbs.
Metric Height: 0.4 m
Metric Weight: 10.3 kg

Possible Moves: Pound, Yawn, Poison Gas, Sludge, Amnesia, Encore, Toxic, Acid Spray, Stockpile, Spit Up, Swallow, Belch, Sludge Bomb, Gastro Acid, Wring Out, Gunk Shot

Gulpin   Swalot

GUMSHOOS
Stakeout Pokémon

REGION:
Alola

TYPE: NORMAL

Gumshoos displays amazing patience when it's on a stakeout, waiting to ambush its prey. It's a natural enemy of Rattata, but the two rarely interact because they're awake at different times.

How to Say It: GUM-shooss
Imperial Height: 2'04''
Imperial Weight: 31.3 lbs.
Metric Height: 0.7 m
Metric Weight: 14.2 kg

Possible Moves: Tackle, Leer, Pursuit, Sand Attack, Odor Sleuth, Bide, Bite, Mud-Slap, Super Fang, Take Down, Scary Face, Crunch, Hyper Fang, Yawn, Thrash, Rest

Yungoos   Gumshoos

TYPE: FIGHTING

With its strong muscles, Gurdurr can wield its steel beam with ease in battle. It's so sturdy that a whole team of wrestlers couldn't knock it down.

How to Say It: GUR-dur
Imperial Height: 3'11''
Imperial Weight: 88.2 lbs.
Metric Height: 1.2 m
Metric Weight: 40.0 kg

Possible Moves: Pound, Leer, Focus Energy, Bide, Low Kick, Rock Throw, Wake-Up Slap, Chip Away, Bulk Up, Rock Slide, Dynamic Punch, Scary Face, Hammer Arm, Stone Edge, Focus Punch, Superpower

REGIONS:
Kalos
(Mountain)
Unova

GURDURR
Muscular Pokémon

Timburr ⇨ Gurdurr ⇨ Conkeldurr

TYPE: DARK-DRAGON

Guzzlord, one of the mysterious Ultra Beasts, seems to have an insatiable appetite for just about everything—it will even swallow buildings and mountains. This constant munching can be very destructive.

How to Say It: GUZZ-lord
Imperial Height: 18'01''
Imperial Weight: 1,957.7 lbs.
Metric Height: 5.5 m
Metric Weight: 888.0 kg

Possible Moves: Belch, Wide Guard, Swallow, Stockpile, Dragon Rage, Bite, Stomp, Brutal Swing, Steamroller, Dragon Tail, Iron Tail, Stomping Tantrum, Crunch, Hammer Arm, Thrash, Gastro Acid, Heavy Slam, Wring Out, Dragon Rush

REGION:
Alola

GUZZLORD
Junkivore Pokémon

ULTRA BEAST

Does not evolve

GYARADOS
Atrocious Pokémon

TYPE: WATER-FLYING

Gyarados is incredibly destructive, and its temper is legendary. Stories say it once burned an entire town to the ground in one night after the residents offended it in some way.

How to Say It: GARE-uh-dos
Imperial Height: 21'04''
Imperial Weight: 518.1 lbs.
Metric Height: 6.5 m
Metric Weight: 235.0 kg

Possible Moves: Bite, Thrash, Leer, Twister, Ice Fang, Aqua Tail, Scary Face, Dragon Rage, Crunch, Hydro Pump, Dragon Dance, Hurricane, Rain Dance, Hyper Beam

MEGA GYARADOS
Atrocious Pokémon

TYPE: WATER-DARK

Imperial Height: 21'04''
Imperial Weight: 672.4 lbs.
Metric Height: 6.5 m
Metric Weight: 305.0 kg

Magikarp ⇨ Gyarados ⇨ Mega Gyarados

HAKAMO-O
Scaly Pokémon

REGION: Alola

TYPE: DRAGON-FIGHTING

Hakamo-o regularly sheds its scales and grows new ones. Each set of scales is harder and sharper than the one before. It leaps at opponents with a battle cry, and the sharp scales turn its punches into a real threat.

How to Say It: HAH-kah-MOH-oh
Imperial Height: 3'11"
Imperial Weight: 103.6 lbs.
Metric Height: 1.2 m
Metric Weight: 47.0 kg

Possible Moves: Sky Uppercut, Autotomize, Tackle, Leer, Bide, Protect, Dragon Tail, Scary Face, Headbutt, Work Up, Screech, Iron Defense, Dragon Claw, Noble Roar, Dragon Dance, Outrage, Close Combat

Jangmo-o ➡ Hakamo-o ➡ Kommo-o

HAPPINY
Playhouse Pokémon

REGIONS: Alola Sinnoh

TYPE: NORMAL

In the pouch on its belly, Happiny carefully stores a round white stone that resembles an egg. It sometimes offers this stone to those it likes.

How to Say It: hap-PEE-nee
Imperial Height: 2'00"
Imperial Weight: 53.8 lbs.
Metric Height: 0.6 m
Metric Weight: 24.4 kg

Possible Moves: Pound, Charm, Copycat, Refresh, Sweet Kiss

Happiny ➡ Chansey ➡ Blissey

HARIYAMA
Arm Thrust Pokémon

REGIONS:
Alola
Hoenn
Kalos
(Coastal)

TYPE: FIGHTING

Hariyama is so strong that a single strike from its open palm can fling a truck into the air. Older Hariyama tend to channel that strength into training Makuhita instead of competing with each other.

How to Say It: HAR-ee-YAH-mah
Imperial Height: 7'07''
Imperial Weight: 559.5 lbs.
Metric Height: 2.3 m
Metric Weight: 253.8 kg

Possible Moves: Brine, Tackle, Focus Energy, Sand Attack, Arm Thrust, Fake Out, Force Palm, Whirlwind, Knock Off, Vital Throw, Belly Drum, Smelling Salts, Seismic Toss, Wake-Up Slap, Endure, Close Combat, Reversal, Heavy Slam

Makuhita ⇨ Hariyama

HAUNTER
Gas Pokémon

REGIONS:
Alola
Kalos
(Mountain)
Kanto

TYPE: GHOST-POISON

Getting licked by the cold tongue of a Haunter is more than simply unpleasant—such a lick can steal your life energy. These Pokémon live in darkness, and city lights can drive them away.

How to Say It: HAUNT-ur
Imperial Height: 5'03''
Imperial Weight: 0.2 lbs.
Metric Height: 1.6 m
Metric Weight: 0.1 kg

Possible Moves: Shadow Punch, Hypnosis, Lick, Spite, Mean Look, Curse, Night Shade, Confuse Ray, Sucker Punch, Payback, Shadow Ball, Dream Eater, Dark Pulse, Destiny Bond, Hex, Nightmare

Gastly ⇨ Haunter ⇨ Gengar ⇨ Mega Gengar

HAWLUCHA
Wrestling Pokémon

TYPE: FIGHTING-FLYING

Hawlucha is a skilled fighter and knows it—and this can sometimes get it into trouble! It enjoys showing off during a battle, often striking an intimidating pose before launching into a signature move.

How to Say It: haw-LOO-cha
Imperial Height: 2'07''
Imperial Weight: 47.4 lbs.
Metric Height: 0.8 m
Metric Weight: 21.5 kg

Possible Moves: Detect, Tackle, Hone Claws, Karate Chop, Wing Attack, Roost, Aerial Ace, Encore, Fling, Flying Press, Bounce, Endeavor, Feather Dance, High Jump Kick, Sky Attack, Sky Drop, Swords Dance

Does not evolve

HAXORUS
Axe Jaw Pokémon

TYPE: DRAGON

Haxorus can cut through steel with its mighty tusks, which stay sharp no matter what. Its body is heavily armored.

How to Say It: HAK-soar-us
Imperial Height: 5'11''
Imperial Weight: 232.6 lbs.
Metric Height: 1.8 m
Metric Weight: 105.5 kg

Possible Moves: Outrage, Scratch, Leer, Assurance, Dragon Rage, Dual Chop, Scary Face, Slash, False Swipe, Dragon Claw, Dragon Dance, Taunt, Dragon Pulse, Swords Dance, Guillotine, Giga Impact

Axew ➡ **Fraxure** ➡ **Haxorus**

HEATMOR
Anteater Pokémon

REGIONS:
Kalos
(Mountain)
Unova

TYPE: FIRE

Heatmor can control the flame from its mouth like a tongue, and the fire is so hot that it can melt through steel. Heatmor and Durant are natural enemies.

How to Say It: HEET-mohr
Imperial Height: 4'07''
Imperial Weight: 127.9 lbs.
Metric Height: 1.4 m
Metric Weight: 58.0 kg

Possible Moves: Inferno, Hone Claws, Tackle, Incinerate, Lick, Odor Sleuth, Bind, Fire Spin, Fury Swipes, Snatch, Flame Burst, Bug Bite, Slash, Amnesia, Flamethrower, Stockpile, Spit Up, Swallow, Fire Blitz

Does not evolve

HEATRAN
Lava Dome Pokémon

REGION:
Sinnoh

LEGENDARY POKÉMON

TYPE: FIRE-STEEL

Heatran makes its home in caves carved out by volcanic eruptions. This Legendary Pokémon's feet can dig into rock, allowing it to walk on walls and ceilings.

How to Say It: HEET-tran
Imperial Height: 5'07''
Imperial Weight: 948.0 lbs.
Metric Height: 1.7 m
Metric Weight: 430.0 kg

Possible Moves: Ancient Power, Leer, Fire Fang, Metal Sound, Crunch, Scary Face, Lava Plume, Fire Spin, Iron Head, Earth Power, Heat Wave, Stone Edge, Magma Storm

Does not evolve

HELIOLISK
Generator Pokémon

TYPE: ELECTRIC-NORMAL

Heliolisk generates electricity by spreading its frill out wide to soak up the sun. It uses this energy to boost its speed.

How to Say It: HEE-lee-oh-lisk
Imperial Height: 3'03''
Imperial Weight: 46.3 lbs.
Metric Height: 1.0 m
Metric Weight: 21.0 kg

Possible Moves: Eerie Impulse, Electrify, Razor Wind, Quick Attack, Thunder, Charge, Parabolic Charge

Helioptile ⇨ Heliolisk

HELIOPTILE
Generator Pokémon

TYPE: ELECTRIC-NORMAL

The frills on Helioptile's head soak up sunlight and create electricity. In this way, they can generate enough energy to keep them going without food.

How to Say It: hee-lee-AHP-tile
Imperial Height: 1'08''
Imperial Weight: 13.2 lbs.
Metric Height: 0.5 m
Metric Weight: 6.0 kg

Possible Moves: Pound, Tail Whip, Thunder Shock, Charge, Mud-Slap, Quick Attack, Razor Wind, Parabolic Charge, Thunder Wave, Bulldoze, Volt Switch, Electrify, Thunderbolt

Helioptile ⇨ Heliolisk

191

HERACROSS
Single Horn Pokémon

REGIONS:
Alola
Johto
Kalos
(Central)

TYPE: BUG-FIGHTING

Heracross loves to eat sweet nectar, which it uses as energy to clash with Vikavolt—its main rival in Alola. It's proud of its horn and is incredibly strong overall, but it's not good at flying, so it rarely uses its wings.

How to Say It: HAIR-uh-cross
Imperial Height: 4'11''
Imperial Weight: 119.0 lbs.
Metric Height: 1.5 m
Metric Weight: 54.0 kg

Possible Moves: Arm Thrust, Bullet Seed, Night Slash, Tackle, Leer, Horn Attack, Endure, Fury Attack, Aerial Ace, Chip Away, Counter, Brick Break, Take Down, Pin Missile, Close Combat, Feint, Reversal, Megahorn

MEGA HERACROSS
Single Horn Pokémon

TYPE: BUG-FIGHTING

Imperial Height: 5'07''
Imperial Weight: 137.8 lbs.
Metric Height: 1.7 m
Metric Weight: 62.5 kg

Heracross ➡ **Mega Heracross**

TYPE: NORMAL

Herdier's fur is so dense that it forms a hard, protective layer, and it grows all the time. Keeping the fur groomed can be a challenge, but many Trainers find it worthwhile because Herdier is such a loyal partner.

How to Say It: HERD-ee-er
Imperial Height: 2'11''
Imperial Weight: 32.4 lbs.
Metric Height: 0.9 m
Metric Weight: 14.7 kg

Possible Moves: Leer, Tackle, Odor Sleuth, Bite, Helping Hand, Take Down, Work Up, Crunch, Roar, Retaliate, Reversal, Last Resort, Giga Impact, Play Rough

REGIONS:
Alola
Unova

HERDIER
Loyal Dog Pokémon

Lillipup ⇨ **Herdier** ⇨ **Stoutland**

REGIONS:
Kalos
(Coastal)
Sinnoh

HIPPOPOTAS
Hippo Pokémon

TYPE: GROUND

Hippopotas lives in a dry environment. Its body gives off sand instead of sweat, and this sandy shield keeps it protected from water and germs.

How to Say It: HIP-poh-puh-TOSS
Imperial Height: 2'07''
Imperial Weight: 109.1 lbs.
Metric Height: 0.8 m
Metric Weight: 49.5 kg

Possible Moves: Tackle, Sand Attack, Bite, Yawn, Take Down, Dig, Sand Tomb, Crunch, Earthquake, Double-Edge, Fissure

Hippopotas ⇨ **Hippowdon**

HIPPOWDON
Heavyweight Pokémon

REGIONS:
Kalos
(Coastal)
Sinnoh

TYPE: GROUND

Hippowdon stores sand inside its body and expels it through the ports on its sides to create a twisting sandstorm in battle.

How to Say It: hip-POW-don
Imperial Height: 6'07"
Imperial Weight: 661.4 lbs.
Metric Height: 2.0 m
Metric Weight: 300.0 kg

Possible Moves: Ice Fang, Fire Fang, Thunder Fang, Tackle, Sand Attack, Bite, Yawn, Take Down, Dig, Sand Tomb, Crunch, Earthquake, Double-Edge, Fissure

Hippopotas   Hippowdon

HITMONCHAN
Punching Pokémon

REGION:
Kanto

TYPE: FIGHTING

Hitmonchan has the fighting spirit of a world-class boxer. It's extremely driven and never gives up.

How to Say It: HIT-mon-CHAN
Imperial Height: 4'07"
Imperial Weight: 110.7 lbs.
Metric Height: 1.4 m
Metric Weight: 50.2 kg

Possible Moves: Comet Punch, Close Combat, Counter, Focus Punch, Revenge, Agility, Pursuit, Mach Punch, Feint, Vacuum Wave, Quick Guard, Thunder Punch, Ice Punch, Fire Punch, Sky Upper, Mega Punch, Detect

Tyrogue   Hitmonchan

TYPE: FIGHTING

HITMONLEE
Kicking Pokémon

Hitmonlee can extend its legs like springs to deliver kicks with tremendous force. It's always careful to stretch and loosen up after battle.

How to Say It: HIT-mon-LEE
Imperial Height: 4'11''
Imperial Weight: 109.8 lbs.
Metric Height: 1.5 m
Metric Weight: 49.8 kg

Possible Moves: Revenge, Double Kick, Meditate, Rolling Kick, Jump Kick, Brick Break, Focus Energy, Feint, High Jump Kick, Mind Reader, Foresight, Wide Guard, Blaze Kick, Endure, Mega Kick, Close Combat, Reversal

Tyrogue ➡ Hitmonlee

TYPE: FIGHTING

HITMONTOP
Handstand Pokémon

Hitmontop's spinning kicks balance offense and defense. Walking is a less efficient mode of travel for it than spinning.

How to Say It: HIT-mon-TOP
Imperial Height: 4'07''
Imperial Weight: 105.8 lbs.
Metric Height: 1.4 m
Metric Weight: 48.0 kg

Possible Moves: Rolling Kick, Endeavor, Close Combat, Detect, Revenge, Focus Energy, Pursuit, Quick Attack, Rapid Spin, Feint, Counter, Triple Kick, Agility, Gyro Ball, Wide Guard, Quick Guard, Close Combat

Tyrogue ➡ Hitmontop

HO-OH
Rainbow Pokémon

REGION:
Johto

LEGENDARY POKÉMON

TYPE: FIRE-FLYING

When Ho-Oh's feathers catch the light at different angles, they glow in a rainbow of colors. Legend says these feathers bring joy to whoever holds one.

How to Say It: HOE-OH
Imperial Height: 12'06''
Imperial Weight: 438.7 lbs.

Metric Height: 3.8 m
Metric Weight: 199.0 kg

Possible Moves: Whirlwind, Weather Ball, Gust, Brave Bird, Extrasensory, Sunny Day, Fire Blast, Sacred Fire, Punishment, Ancient Power, Safeguard, Recover, Future Sight, Natural Gift, Calm Mind, Sky Attack

196

Does not evolve

TYPE: DARK-FLYING

Honchkrow keeps an army of Murkrow at its beck and call, ruling by intimidation. The underlings know that if they don't keep Honchkrow fed, it won't hesitate to punish them.

How to Say It: HONCH-krow
Imperial Height: 2'11''
Imperial Weight: 60.2 lbs.
Metric Height: 0.9 m
Metric Weight: 27.3 kg

Possible Moves: Night Slash, Sucker Punch, Astonish, Pursuit, Haze, Wing Attack, Swagger, Nasty Plot, Foul Play, Quash, Dark Pulse

REGIONS:
Alola
Kalos
(Mountain)
Sinnoh

HONCHKROW
Big Boss Pokémon

Murkrow ➡ **Honchkrow**

REGION:
Kalos
(Central)

HONEDGE
Sword Pokémon

TYPE: STEEL-GHOST

Beware when approaching a Honedge! Those foolish enough to wield it like a sword will quickly find themselves wrapped in its blue cloth and drained of energy.

How to Say It: HONE-ej
Imperial Height: 2'07''
Imperial Weight: 4.4 lbs.
Metric Height: 0.8 m
Metric Weight: 2.0 kg

Possible Moves: Tackle, Swords Dance, Fury Cutter, Metal Sound, Pursuit, Autotomize, Shadow Sneak, Aerial Ace, Retaliate, Slash, Iron Defense, Night Slash, Power Trick, Iron Head, Sacred Sword

Honedge ➡ **Doublade** ➡ **Aegislash**

197

HOOPA
Mischief Pokémon

MYTHICAL POKÉMON

TYPE: PSYCHIC-GHOST

According to myth, Hoopa can summon whatever it wants with the enormous power of its six rings. When that power is confined, it is much smaller and less destructive.

How to Say It: HOO-puh
Imperial Height: 1'08''
Imperial Weight: 19.8 lbs.
Metric Height: 0.5 m
Metric Weight: 9.0 kg

Possible Moves: Trick, Destiny Bond, Ally Switch, Confusion, Astonish, Magic Coat, Light Screen, Psybeam, Skill Swap, Power Split, Guard Split, Phantom Force, Zen Headbutt, Wonder Room, Trick Room, Shadow Ball, Nasty Plot, Psychic, Hyperspace Hole

HOOPA UNBOUND
Mischief Pokémon

TYPE: DARK-PSYCHIC

Imperial Height: 21'04''
Imperial Weight: 1,080.3 lbs.
Metric Height: 6.5 m
Metric Weight: 490.0 kg

Does not evolve

HOOTHOOT
Owl Pokémon

TYPE: NORMAL-FLYING

Long ago, people looked to Hoothoot to tell the time, because it moves its head in a precise rhythm and always sounds a cry at the same time of day.

How to Say It: HOOT-HOOT
Imperial Height: 2'04''
Imperial Weight: 46.7 lbs.
Metric Height: 0.7 m
Metric Weight: 21.2 kg

Possible Moves: Tackle, Growl, Foresight, Hypnosis, Peck, Uproar, Reflect, Confusion, Echoed Voice, Take Down, Air Slash, Zen Headbutt, Synchronoise, Extrasensory, Psycho Shift, Roost, Moonblast, Dream Eater

Hoothoot   Noctowl

TYPE: GRASS-FLYING

Since Hoppip floats on the wind, it must cluster together with others to withstand strong gusts. Otherwise, it might be blown away!

How to Say It: HOP-pip
Imperial Height: 1'04''
Imperial Weight: 1.1 lbs.
Metric Height: 0.4 m
Metric Weight: 0.5 kg

Possible Moves: Splash, Absorb, Synthesis, Tail Whip, Tackle, Fairy Wind, Poison Powder, Stun Spore, Sleep Powder, Bullet Seed, Leech Seed, Mega Drain, Acrobatics, Rage Powder, Cotton Spore, U-turn, Worry Seed, Giga Drain, Bounce, Memento

HOPPIP
Cottonweed Pokémon

Hoppip   Skiploom   Jumpluff

HORSEA
Dragon Pokémon

REGIONS:
Kalos
(Coastal)
Kanto

TYPE: WATER

Horsea wraps its tail around solid objects on the seafloor to avoid being swept away in a strong current. When threatened, it spits a cloud of ink to cover its escape.

How to Say It: HOR-see
Imperial Height: 1'04''
Imperial Weight: 17.6 lbs.

Metric Height: 0.4 m
Metric Weight: 8.0 kg

Possible Moves: Water Gun, Smokescreen, Leer, Bubble, Focus Energy, Bubble Beam, Agility, Twister, Brine, Hydro Pump, Dragon Dance, Dragon Pulse

Horsea ⇨ Seadra ⇨ Kingdra

TYPE: DARK-FIRE

If you hear a chorus of terrifying howls in the middle of the night, it could be a pack of Houndoom seeking out food. People long ago feared this Pokémon for its destructive potential.

How to Say It: HOWN-doom
Imperial Height: 4'07''
Imperial Weight: 77.2 lbs.
Metric Height: 1.4 m
Metric Weight: 35.0 kg

Possible Moves:
Inferno, Nasty Plot, Thunder Fang, Leer, Ember, Howl, Smog, Roar, Bite, Odor Sleuth, Beat Up, Fire Fang, Feint Attack, Embargo, Foul Play, Flamethrower, Crunch

REGIONS:
Alola
Johto
Kalos
(Coastal)

HOUNDOOM
Dark Pokémon

MEGA HOUNDOOM
Dark Pokémon

TYPE: DARK-FIRE

Imperial Height: 6'03''
Imperial Weight: 109.1 lbs.
Metric Height: 1.9 m
Metric Weight: 49.5 kg

Houndour   Houndoom   Mega Houndoom

HOUNDOUR
Dark Pokémon

TYPE: DARK-FIRE

Houndour shows extreme loyalty to its Trainer or pack, eagerly cooperating as part of a team. Its cries may sound eerie, but it's using them to communicate with friends.

How to Say It: HOWN-dowr
Imperial Height: 2'00"
Imperial Weight: 23.8 lbs.
Metric Height: 0.6 m
Metric Weight: 10.8 kg

Possible Moves: Leer, Ember, Howl, Smog, Roar, Bite, Odor Sleuth, Beat Up, Fire Fang, Feint Attack, Embargo, Foul Play, Flamethrower, Crunch, Nasty Plot, Inferno

Houndour   Houndoom   Mega Houndoom

HUNTAIL
Deep Sea Pokémon

REGIONS:
Alola
Hoenn
Kalos
(Coastal)

TYPE: WATER

Huntail live so deep in the sea that seeing them washed up on the beach is cause for alarm. They don't swim very well, instead relying on the lure at the end of their tail to bring food to them.

How to Say It: HUN-tail
Imperial Height: 5'07"
Imperial Weight: 59.5 lbs.
Metric Height: 1.7 m
Metric Weight: 27.0 kg

Possible Moves: Whirlpool, Bite, Screech, Scary Face, Feint Attack, Water Pulse, Ice Fang, Brine, Sucker Punch, Dive, Baton Pass, Crunch, Aqua Tail, Coil, Hydro Pump

Clamperl   Huntail

TYPE: DARK-DRAGON

The smaller heads on Hydreigon's arms don't have brains, but they can still eat. Any movement within its line of sight will be greeted with a frightening attack.

How to Say It: hy-DRY-guhn
Imperial Height: 5'11''
Imperial Weight: 352.7 lbs.
Metric Height: 1.8 m
Metric Weight: 160.0 kg

Possible Moves: Outrage, Hyper Voice, Tri Attack, Dragon Rage, Focus Energy, Bite, Headbutt, Dragon Breath, Roar, Crunch, Slam, Dragon Pulse, Work Up, Dragon Rush, Body Slam, Scary Face

HYDREIGON
Brutal Pokémon

Deino ⇨ **Zweilous** ⇨ **Hydreigon**

HYPNO
Hypnosis Pokémon

TYPE: PSYCHIC

Hypno's habit of sending everyone it meets to sleep so it can taste their dreams makes it a dangerous Pokémon—but if you're exhausted and having trouble sleeping, it could be a big help.

How to Say It: HIP-no
Imperial Height: 5'03''
Imperial Weight: 166.7 lbs.
Metric Height: 1.6 m
Metric Weight: 75.6 kg

Possible Moves: Future Sight, Nasty Plot, Nightmare, Switcheroo, Pound, Hypnosis, Disable, Confusion, Headbutt, Poison Gas, Meditate, Psybeam, Psych Up, Wake-Up Slap, Synchronoise, Zen Headbutt, Swagger, Psychic, Psyshock

Drowzee ⇨ **Hypno**

IGGLYBUFF
Balloon Pokémon

TYPE: NORMAL-FAIRY

Though Igglybuff is an enthusiastic singer, it's not particularly skilled yet. Its bouncing movement causes it to sweat, but fortunately this makes it smell better, not worse.

How to Say It: IG-lee-buff
Imperial Height: 1'00''
Imperial Weight: 2.2 lbs.
Metric Height: 0.3 m
Metric Weight: 1.0 kg

Possible Moves: Sing, Charm, Defense Curl, Pound, Sweet Kiss, Copycat

Igglybuff ⇨ Jigglypuff ⇨ Wigglytuff

ILLUMISE
Firefly Pokémon

REGIONS:
Hoenn
Kalos
(Central)

TYPE: BUG

Illumise gives off a sweet scent that attracts Volbeat by the dozen. Then, it directs the swarm in drawing patterns of light across the night sky.

How to Say It: EE-loom-MEE-zay
Imperial Height: 2'00''
Imperial Weight: 39.0 lbs.
Metric Height: 0.6 m
Metric Weight: 17.7 kg

Possible Moves: Play Nice, Tackle, Sweet Scent, Charm, Quick Attack, Struggle Bug, Moonlight, Wish, Encore, Flatter, Zen Buttheads, Helping Hand, Bug Buzz, Play Rough, Covet, Infestation

Does not evolve

INCINEROAR
Heel Pokémon

TYPE: FIRE-DARK

Training an Incineroar requires patience—if it's not in just the right mood, it shows complete disregard for any orders given. During battle, it throws fierce punches and kicks, then launches the flames on its belly in a final attack.

How to Say It: in-SIN-uh-roar
Imperial Height: 5'11''
Imperial Weight: 183.0 lbs.
Metric Height: 1.8 m
Metric Weight: 83.0 kg

Possible Moves: Darkest Lariat, Bulk Up, Throat Chop, Scratch, Ember, Growl, Lick, Leer, Fire Fang, Double Kick, Roar, Bite, Swagger, Fury Swipes, Thrash, Flamethrower, Scary Face, Flare Blitz, Outrage, Cross Chop

Litten ➡ **Torracat** ➡ **Incineroar**

INFERNAPE
Flame Pokémon

TYPE: FIRE-FIGHTING

Swift and agile, Infernape puts all four of its limbs to use in its distinctive fighting style. The fire on its head mirrors the fire in its spirit.

How to Say It: in-FUR-nape
Imperial Height: 3'11''
Imperial Weight: 121.3 lbs.
Metric Height: 1.2 m
Metric Weight: 55.0 kg

Possible Moves: Scratch, Leer, Ember, Taunt, Mach Punch, Fury Swipes, Flame Wheel, Feint, Punishment, Close Combat, Fire Spin, Acrobatics, Calm Mind, Flare Blitz

 Chimchar ➡ **Monferno** ➡ **Infernape**

INKAY
Revolving Pokémon

REGIONS:
Alola
Kalos
(Coastal)

TYPE: DARK-PSYCHIC

Inkay communicates with its friends by creating light patterns with the spots on its body. The lights also serve to draw foes in and mesmerize them while Inkay prepares an attack.

How to Say It: IN-kay
Imperial Height: 1'04''
Imperial Weight: 7.7 lbs.
Metric Height: 0.4 m
Metric Weight: 3.5 kg

Possible Moves: Tackle, Peck, Constrict, Reflect, Foul Play, Swagger, Psywave, Topsy-Turvy, Hypnosis, Psybeam, Switcheroo, Payback, Light Screen, Pluck, Psycho Cut, Slash, Night Slash, Superpower

Inkay ➡ **Malamar**

IVYSAUR
Seed Pokémon

REGIONS:
Kalos
(Central)
Kanto

TYPE: GRASS-POISON

Carrying the weight of the bud on its back makes Ivysaur's legs stronger. When the bud is close to blooming, the Pokémon spends more time sleeping in the sun.

How to Say It: EYE-vee-sore
Imperial Height: 3'03''
Imperial Weight: 28.7 lbs.
Metric Height: 1.0 m
Metric Weight: 13.0 kg

Possible Moves: Tackle, Growl, Leech Seed, Vine Whip, Poison Powder, Sleep Powder, Take Down, Razor Leaf, Sweet Scent, Growth, Double-Edge, Worry Seed, Synthesis, Solar Beam

Bulbasaur ➡ **Ivysaur** ➡ **Venusaur** ➡ **Mega Venusaur**

JANGMO-O
Scaly Pokémon

TYPE: DRAGON

Wild Jangmo-o live in remote mountains, far away from people. When they smack their scales together, either in battle or to communicate, the mountains ring with the metallic sound.

How to Say It: JANG-MOH-oh
Imperial Height: 2'00''
Imperial Weight: 65.5 lbs.
Metric Height: 0.6 m
Metric Weight: 29.7 kg

Possible Moves: Tackle, Leer, Bide, Protect, Dragon Tail, Scary Face, Headbutt, Work Up, Screech, Iron Defense, Dragon Claw, Noble Roar, Dragon Dance, Outrage

Jangmo-o ➡ Hakamo-o ➡ Kommo-o

207

JELLICENT

Floating Pokémon

Male Form

TYPE: WATER-GHOST

Jellicent can often be seen lurking near cruise ships and following tankers, hoping someone will fall overboard so it can drag them away. Fishermen tell scary stories about this Pokémon.

How to Say It: JEL-ih-sent
Imperial Height: 7'03''
Imperial Weight: 297.6 lbs.
Metric Height: 2.2 m
Metric Weight: 135.0 kg

Possible Moves: Bubble, Water Sport, Absorb, Night Shade, Bubble Beam, Recover, Water Pulse, Ominous Wind, Brine, Rain Dance, Hex, Hydro Pump, Wring Out, Water Spout

Female Form

Frillish → **Jellicent**

JIGGLYPUFF

Balloon Pokémon

TYPE: NORMAL-FAIRY

Because it can inflate its body like a balloon, Jigglypuff has incredible lung capacity. This allows it to sustain its mysterious song until everyone listening falls asleep.

How to Say It: JIG-lee-puff
Imperial Height: 1'08''
Imperial Weight: 12.1 lbs.
Metric Height: 0.5 m
Metric Weight: 5.5 kg

Possible Moves: Sing, Defense Curl, Pound, Play Nice, Disarming Voice, Disable, Double Slap, Rollout, Round, Stockpile, Swallow, Spit Up, Wake-Up Slap, Rest, Body Slam, Gyro Ball, Mimic, Hyper Voice, Double-Edge

Igglybuff → **Jigglypuff** → **Wigglytuff**

JIRACHI
Wish Pokémon

MYTHICAL POKÉMON

TYPE: STEEL-PSYCHIC

According to myth, if you write your wish on one of the notes attached to Jirachi's head and then sing to it in a pure voice, the Pokémon will awaken from its thousand-year slumber and grant your wish.

How to Say It: jir-AH-chi
Imperial Height: 1'00''
Imperial Weight: 2.4 lbs.

Metric Height: 0.3 m
Metric Weight: 1.1 kg

Possible Moves: Wish, Confusion, Rest, Swift, Helping Hand, Psychic, Refresh, Lucky Chant, Zen Headbutt, Double-Edge, Gravity, Healing Wish, Future Sight, Cosmic Power, Last Resort, Doom Desire

Does not evolve

JOLTEON
Lightning Pokémon

TYPE: ELECTRIC

When Jolteon's fur bristles up, don't stand too close—it might be about to call down a lightning strike! Becoming friends with this Pokémon can be difficult because of its high-strung nature.

How to Say It: JOL-tee-on
Imperial Height: 2'07''
Imperial Weight: 54.0 lbs.
Metric Height: 0.8 m
Metric Weight: 24.5 kg

Possible Moves: Thunder Shock, Helping Hand, Tackle, Tail Whip, Sand Attack, Baby-Doll Eyes, Quick Attack, Double Kick, Thunder Fang, Pin Missile, Agility, Thunder Wave, Discharge, Last Resort, Thunder

Eevee ⇒ Jolteon

JOLTIK
Attaching Pokémon

TYPE: BUG-ELECTRIC

Joltik can't produce their own electricity, so they attach to larger Pokémon and suck up the static electricity given off. They store this energy in a special pouch.

How to Say It: JOHL-tik
Imperial Height: 0'04''
Imperial Weight: 1.3 lbs.
Metric Height: 0.1 m
Metric Weight: 0.6 kg

Possible Moves: String Shot, Absorb, Spider Web, Thunder Wave, Screech, Fury Cutter, Electroweb, Bug Bite, Gastro Acid, Slash, Electro Ball, Signal Beam, Agility, Sucker Punch, Discharge, Bug Buzz

Joltik ⇒ Galvantula

JUMPLUFF
Cottonweed Pokémon

TYPE: GRASS-FLYING

If Jumpluff hits a patch of cold air while it's drifting on the wind, it will return to the ground to await a warm breeze. The winds carry its fluffy body across the sea and around the world.

How to Say It: JUM-pluff
Imperial Height: 2'07''
Imperial Weight: 6.6 lbs.
Metric Height: 0.8 m
Metric Weight: 3.0 kg

Possible Moves: Splash, Absorb, Synthesis, Tail Whip, Tackle, Fairy Wind, Poison Powder, Stun Spore, Sleep Powder, Bullet Seed, Leech Seed, Mega Drain, Acrobatics, Rage Powder, Cotton Spore, U-turn, Worry Seed, Giga Drain, Bounce, Memento

Hoppip ⟹ **Skiploom** ⟹ **Jumpluff**

TYPE: ICE-PSYCHIC

Jynx moves with its own swaying rhythm. It's right at home in Alola, where residents admire its singing voice and expert dancing techniques.

How to Say It: JINX
Imperial Height: 4'07''
Imperial Weight: 89.5 lbs.
Metric Height: 1.4 m
Metric Weight: 40.6 kg

Possible Moves: Draining Kiss, Perish Song, Pound, Lick, Lovely Kiss, Powder Snow, Double Slap, Ice Punch, Heart Stamp, Mean Look, Fake Tears, Wake-Up Slap, Avalanche, Body Slam, Wring Out, Blizzard

JYNX
Human Shape Pokémon

Smoochum ⟹ **Jynx**

211

KABUTO
Shellfish Pokémon

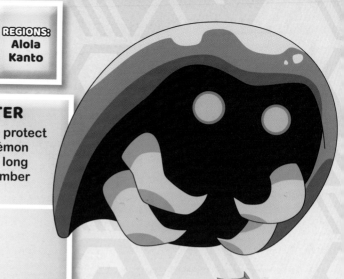

TYPE: ROCK-WATER

Kabuto uses its hard shell to protect itself from attacks. This Pokémon species was plentiful a long, long time ago, but only a small number exist in the wild today.

How to Say It: ka-BOO-toe
Imperial Height: 1'08''
Imperial Weight: 25.4 lbs.
Metric Height: 0.5 m
Metric Weight: 11.5 kg

Possible Moves: Scratch, Harden, Absorb, Leer, Mud Shot, Sand Attack, Endure, Aqua Jet, Mega Drain, Metal Sound, Ancient Power, Wring Out

Kabuto ⇒ **Kabutops**

KABUTOPS
Shellfish Pokémon

TYPE: ROCK-WATER

Kabutops is a swift swimmer and expert undersea hunter, but its body is ill-suited to life on land. The species went extinct before it could adapt to changes in its ecosystem.

How to Say It: KA-boo-tops
Imperial Height: 4'03''
Imperial Weight: 89.3 lbs.
Metric Height: 1.3 m
Metric Weight: 40.5 kg

Possible Moves: Feint, Scratch, Harden, Absorb, Leer, Mud Shot, Sand Attack, Endure, Aqua Jet, Mega Drain, Slash, Metal Sound, Ancient Power, Wring Out, Night Slash

Kabuto ⇒ **Kabutops**

KADABRA
Psi Pokémon

TYPE: PSYCHIC

When Kadabra is around, its strong psychic powers can sometimes interfere with electronics like computer monitors or televisions. Strange, creepy shadows can be seen on the screen when this happens.

How to Say It: kuh-DAB-ra
Imperial Height: 4'03''
Imperial Weight: 124.6 lbs.
Metric Height: 1.3 m
Metric Weight: 56.5 kg

Possible Moves: Kinesis, Teleport, Confusion, Disable, Psybeam, Miracle Eye, Reflect, Psycho Cut, Recover, Telekinesis, Ally Switch, Psychic, Role Play, Future Sight, Trick

Abra ➡ **Kadabra** ➡ **Alakazam** ➡ **Mega Alakazam**

KAKUNA
Cocoon Pokémon

TYPE: BUG-POISON

Kakuna appears motionless from the outside, but inside its shell, it's busily preparing to evolve. Sometimes the shell heats up from this activity.

How to Say It: kah-KOO-na
Imperial Height: 2'00''
Imperial Weight: 22.0 lbs.
Metric Height: 0.6 m
Metric Weight: 10.0 kg

Possible Move: Harden

Weedle ➡ **Kakuna** ➡ **Beedrill** ➡ **Mega Beedrill**   213

KANGASKHAN
Parent Pokémon

TYPE: NORMAL

Kangaskhan will risk everything to protect the little one in its pouch. If you hear this Pokémon crying, keep an eye out for a young Kangaskhan who's just set out on its own.

How to Say It: KANG-gas-con
Imperial Height: 7'03''
Imperial Weight: 176.4 lbs.
Metric Height: 2.2 m
Metric Weight: 80.0 kg

Possible Moves: Comet Punch, Leer, Fake Out, Tail Whip, Bite, Double Hit, Rage, Mega Punch, Chip Away, Dizzy Punch, Crunch, Endure, Outrage, Sucker Punch, Reversal

MEGA KANGASKHAN
Parent Pokémon

TYPE: NORMAL

Imperial Height: 7'03''
Imperial Weight: 220.5 lbs.
Metric Height: 2.2 m
Metric Weight: 100.0 kg

214

Kangaskhan

Mega Kangaskhan

KARRABLAST
Clamping Pokémon

TYPE: BUG

Karrablast often attack Shelmet, trying to steal their shells. When electrical energy envelops them at the same time, they both evolve.

How to Say It: KAIR-ruh-blast
Imperial Height: 1'08''
Imperial Weight: 13.0 lbs.
Metric Height: 0.5 m
Metric Weight: 5.9 kg

Possible Moves: Peck, Leer, Endure, Fury Cutter, Fury Attack, Headbutt, False Swipe, Bug Buzz, Slash, Take Down, Scary Face, X-Scissor, Flail, Swords Dance, Double-Edge

Karrablast   Escavalier

TYPE: GRASS-STEEL

Kartana, one of the mysterious Ultra Beasts, can use its entire sharp-edged body as a weapon in battle. Its blade is strong and sharp enough to slice right through a steel structure in a single stroke.

How to Say It: kar-TAH-nuh
Imperial Height: 1'00''
Imperial Weight: 0.2 lbs.
Metric Height: 0.3 m
Metric Weight: 0.1 kg

Possible Moves:
Sacred Sword, Defog, Vacuum Wave, Air Cutter, Fury Cutter, Cut, False Swipe, Razor Leaf, Synthesis, Aerial Ace, Laser Focus, Night Slash, Swords Dance, Leaf Blade, X-Scissor, Detect, Air Slash, Psycho Cut, Guillotine

KARTANA
Drawn Sword Pokémon

ULTRA BEAST

Does not evolve

KECLEON
Color Swap Pokémon

REGIONS:
Alola
Hoenn
Kalos
(Central)

TYPE: NORMAL

Kecleon is a master of camouflage—though it gets annoyed if its disguise works too well and nobody notices it! The changing color of its skin can also reflect the state of its health or mood.

How to Say It: KEH-clee-on
Imperial Height: 3'03''
Imperial Weight: 48.5 lbs.
Metric Height: 1.0 m
Metric Weight: 22.0 kg

Possible Moves: Synchronoise, Ancient Power, Thief, Tail Whip, Astonish, Lick, Scratch, Bind, Feint Attack, Fury Swipes, Feint, Psybeam, Shadow Sneak, Slash, Screech, Substitute, Sucker Punch, Shadow Claw

Does not evolve

KELDEO
Colt Pokémon

REGION:
Unova

MYTHICAL POKÉMON

TYPE: WATER-FIGHTING

Keldeo travels the world visiting beaches and riverbanks, where it can race across the water. When this Mythical Pokémon is filled with resolve, it gains a blinding speed.

How to Say It: KELL-dee-oh
Imperial Height: 4'07''
Imperial Weight: 106.9 lbs.
Metric Height: 1.4 m
Metric Weight: 48.5 kg

Possible Moves: Aqua Jet, Leer, Double Kick, Bubble Beam, Take Down, Helping Hand, Retaliate, Aqua Tail, Sacred Sword, Swords Dance, Quick Guard, Work Up, Hydro Pump, Close Combat

Ordinary Form

Resolute Form

Does not evolve

KINGDRA
Dragon Pokémon

TYPE: WATER-DRAGON

Kingdra makes its home so deep in the ocean that nothing else lives there. Some people think its yawn influences the currents.

How to Say It: KING-dra
Imperial Height: 5'11''
Imperial Weight: 335.1 lbs.
Metric Height: 1.8 m
Metric Weight: 152.0 kg

Possible Moves: Dragon Pulse, Yawn, Water Gun, Smokescreen, Leer, Bubble, Focus Energy, Bubble Beam, Agility, Twister, Brine, Hydro Pump, Dragon Dance

Horsea ➡ **Seadra** ➡ **Kingdra**

TYPE: WATER

When one Kingler waves to another with its giant claw, it's sending a message. They can't hold long conversations this way, though, because waving those heavy claws is tiring.

How to Say It: KING-lur
Imperial Height: 4'03''
Imperial Weight: 132.3 lbs.
Metric Height: 1.3 m
Metric Weight: 60.0 kg

Possible Moves: Wide Guard, Mud Sport, Bubble, Vice Grip, Leer, Harden, Bubble Beam, Mud Shot, Metal Claw, Stomp, Protect, Guillotine, Slam, Brine, Crabhammer, Flail

REGION:
Kanto

KINGLER
Pincer Pokémon

Krabby ➡ **Kingler**

217

KIRLIA

Emotion Pokémon

REGIONS: Hoenn Kalos (Central)

TYPE: PSYCHIC-FAIRY

A Kirlia whose Trainer has a positive attitude develops a shining beauty. When this Pokémon uses its psychic powers, strange mirages surround it.

How to Say It: KERL-lee-ah
Imperial Height: 2'07''
Imperial Weight: 44.5 lbs.
Metric Height: 0.8 m
Metric Weight: 20.2 kg

Possible Moves: Growl, Confusion, Double Team, Teleport, Disarming Voice, Lucky Chant, Magical Leaf, Heal Pulse, Draining Kiss, Calm Mind, Psychic, Imprison, Future Sight, Charm, Hypnosis, Dream Eater, Stored Power

Ralts ⇒ Kirlia ⇒ Gardevoir ⇒ Mega Gardevoir

Gallade ⇒ Mega Gallade

KLANG

Gear Pokémon

REGION: Unova

TYPE: STEEL

Klang's body is made up of one mini-gear and one bigger gear, which change their rotation to communicate with other Klang. It can shoot the mini-gear at an opponent in battle.

How to Say It: KLANG
Imperial Height: 2'00''
Imperial Weight: 112.4 lbs.
Metric Height: 0.6 m
Metric Weight: 51.0 kg

Possible Moves: Magnetic Flux, Gear Up, Vice Grip, Charge, Thunder Shock, Gear Grind, Bind, Charge Beam, Autotomize, Mirror Shot, Screech, Discharge, Metal Sound, Shift Gear, Lock-On, Zap Cannon, Hyper Beam

Klink ⇒ Klang ⇒ Klinklang

TYPE: STEEL-FAIRY

If you're constantly losing your keys, a Klefki might be to blame. This Pokémon loves to collect keys and sometimes even swipes them from people's homes.

How to Say It: KLEF-key
Imperial Height: 0'08''
Imperial Weight: 6.6 lbs.
Metric Height: 0.2 m
Metric Weight: 3.0 kg

Possible Moves: Fairy Lock, Tackle, Fairy Wind, Astonish, Metal Sound, Spikes, Draining Kiss, Crafty Shield, Foul Play, Torment, Mirror Shot, Imprison, Recycle, Play Rough, Magic Room, Heal Block

REGIONS:
Alola
Kalos
(Mountain)

KLEFKI
Key Ring Pokémon

Does not evolve

TYPE: STEEL

The two mini-gears that make up Klink's body are meant for each other. If they get separated, they won't mesh with any other mini-gear until they find each other again.

How to Say It: KLEENK
Imperial Height: 1'00''
Imperial Weight: 46.3 lbs.
Metric Height: 0.3 m
Metric Weight: 21.0 kg

Possible Moves: Vice Grip, Charge, Thunder Shock, Gear Grind, Bind, Charge Beam, Autotomize, Mirror Shot, Screech, Discharge, Metal Sound, Shift Gear, Lock-On, Zap Cannon, Hyper Beam

REGION:
Unova

KLINK
Gear Pokémon

Klink ➡ Klang ➡ Klinklang

KLINKLANG
Gear Pokémon

REGION: Unova

TYPE: STEEL

Klinklang stores energy in its red core and charges itself up by spinning that gear rapidly. It can shoot the energy from the spikes on its outer ring.

How to Say It: KLEENK-klang
Imperial Height: 2'00''
Imperial Weight: 178.6 lbs.
Metric Height: 0.6 m
Metric Weight: 81.0 kg

Possible Moves: Magnetic Flux, Gear Up, Vice Grip, Charge, Thunder Shock, Gear Grind, Bind, Charge Beam, Autotomize, Mirror Shot, Screech, Discharge, Metal Sound, Shift Gear, Lock-On, Zap Cannon, Hyper Beam

Klink ➡ Klang ➡ Klinklang

KOFFING
Poison Gas Pokémon

REGION: Kanto

TYPE: POISON

The gases that fill Koffing's body are extremely toxic. When it's under attack, it releases this poisonous gas from jets on its surface.

How to Say It: KOFF-ing
Imperial Height: 2'00''
Imperial Weight: 2.2 lbs.
Metric Height: 0.6 m
Metric Weight: 1.0 kg

Possible Moves: Poison Gas, Tackle, Smog, Smokescreen, Assurance, Clear Smog, Self-Destruct, Sludge, Haze, Gyro Ball, Explosion, Sludge Bomb, Destiny Bond, Memento

Koffing ➡ Weezing

KOMALA
Drowsing Pokémon

TYPE: NORMAL

Komala never wakes up—ever—although it does sometimes move around as it dreams. It lives in a permanent state of sleep, cuddling its precious log or its Trainer's arm.

How to Say It: koh-MAH-luh
Imperial Height: 1'04''
Imperial Weight: 43.9 lbs.
Metric Height: 0.4 m
Metric Weight: 19.9 kg

Possible Moves: Defense Curl, Rollout, Stockpile, Spit Up, Swallow, Rapid Spin, Yawn, Slam, Flail, Sucker Punch, Psych Up, Wood Hammer, Thrash

Does not evolve

KOMMO-O
Scaly Pokémon

REGION:
Alola

TYPE: DRAGON-FIGHTING

Long ago, Kommo-o scales were collected and turned into weapons. For this Pokémon, the scales provide offense, defense, and even a warning system—when it shakes its tail, the scales clash together in a jangle that scares off weak opponents.

How to Say It: koh-MOH-oh
Imperial Height: 5'03''
Imperial Weight: 172.4 lbs.
Metric Height: 1.6 m
Metric Weight: 78.2 kg

Possible Moves: Clanging Scales, Sky Uppercut, Belly Drum, Autotomize, Tackle, Leer, Bide, Protect, Dragon Tail, Scary Face, Headbutt, Work Up, Screech, Iron Defense, Dragon Claw, Noble Roar, Dragon Dance, Outrage, Close Combat

Jangmo-o ➡ Hakamo-o ➡ Kommo-o

KRABBY
River Crab Pokémon

REGION:
Kanto

TYPE: WATER

Krabby dig holes in sandy beaches to make their homes. When the food supply is limited, they sometimes fight over territory.

How to Say It: KRAB-ee
Imperial Height: 1'04''
Imperial Weight: 14.3 lbs.
Metric Height: 0.4 m
Metric Weight: 6.5 kg

Possible Moves: Mud Sport, Bubble, Vice Grip, Leer, Harden, Bubble Beam, Mud Shot, Metal Claw, Stomp, Protect, Guillotine, Slam, Brine, Crabhammer, Flail

Krabby ➡ Kingler

REGION: Sinnoh

KRICKETOT
Cricket Pokémon

TYPE: BUG

The sound of Kricketot's antennae knocking together resembles the sound of a xylophone. They use these sounds to communicate.

How to Say It: KRICK-eh-tot
Imperial Height: 1'00''
Imperial Weight: 4.9 lbs.
Metric Height: 0.3 m
Metric Weight: 2.2 kg

Possible Moves: Growl, Bide, Struggle Bug, Bug Bite

Kricketot   Kricketune

TYPE: BUG

Kricketune composes many different melodies that reflect its emotional state. Researchers are trying to determine whether the patterns of its music have a deeper meaning.

How to Say It: KRICK-eh-toon
Imperial Height: 3'03''
Imperial Weight: 56.2 lbs.
Metric Height: 1.0 m
Metric Weight: 25.5 kg

Possible Moves: Growl, Bide, Fury Cutter, Absorb, Sing, Focus Energy, Slash, X-Scissor, Screech, Fell Stinger, Taunt, Night Slash, Sticky Web, Bug Buzz, Perish Song

REGION: Sinnoh

KRICKETUNE
Cricket Pokémon

Kricketot   Kricketune

KROKOROK
Desert Croc Pokémon

REGIONS:
Alola
Kalos
(Coastal)
Unova

TYPE: GROUND-DARK

The membrane that covers Krokorok's eyes keeps sand out and allows it to see even on a dark night. They tend to live in small groups, often led by a female Krokorok.

How to Say It: KRAHK-oh-rahk
Imperial Height: 3'03''
Imperial Weight: 73.6 lbs.
Metric Height: 1.0 m
Metric Weight: 33.4 kg

Possible Moves: Leer, Rage, Bite, Sand Attack, Torment, Sand Tomb, Assurance, Mud-Slap, Embargo, Swagger, Crunch, Dig, Scary Face, Foul Play, Sandstorm, Earthquake, Thrash

Sandile ➡ Krokorok ➡ Krookodile

KROOKODILE
Intimidation Pokémon

REGIONS:
Alola
Kalos
(Coastal)
Unova

TYPE: GROUND-DARK

With its strong jaws, Krookodile can clamp onto its opponent. With its sharp eyes, it can spot a potential threat—or something it wants to eat—from many miles away, even in a raging sandstorm.

How to Say It: KROOK-oh-dyle
Imperial Height: 4'11''
Imperial Weight: 212.3 lbs.
Metric Height: 1.5 m
Metric Weight: 96.3 kg

Possible Moves: Power Trip, Leer, Rage, Bite, Sand Attack, Torment, Sand Tomb, Assurance, Mud-Slap, Embargo, Swagger, Crunch, Dig, Scary Face, Foul Play, Sandstorm, Earthquake, Outrage

Sandile ➡ Krokorok ➡ Krookodile

TYPE: WATER

Legends say that Kyogre is the sea personified. When it channels the full power of nature, it can raise sea levels with mighty storms. This Pokémon often clashes with Groudon.

How to Say It: kai-OH-gurr
Imperial Height: 14'09''
Imperial Weight: 776.0 lbs.
Metric Height: 4.5 m
Metric Weight: 352.0 kg

Possible Moves: Water Pulse, Scary Face, Body Slam, Muddy Water, Aqua Ring, Ice Beam, Ancient Power, Water Spout, Calm Mind, Aqua Tail, Sheer Cold, Double-Edge, Hydro Pump, Origin Pulse

REGION: Hoenn

KYOGRE
Sea Basin Pokémon

LEGENDARY POKÉMON

PRIMAL KYOGRE
Sea Basin Pokémon

TYPE: WATER

Imperial Height: 32'02''
Imperial Weight: 948.0 lbs.
Metric Height: 9.8 m
Metric Weight: 430.0 kg

Kyogre　　Primal Kyogre

KYUREM

Boundary Pokémon

LEGENDARY POKÉMON

TYPE: DRAGON-ICE

When the freezing energy inside Kyurem leaked out, its entire body froze. Legends say it will become whole with the help of a hero who will bring truth or ideals.

How to Say It: KYOO-rem
Imperial Height: 9'10''
Imperial Weight: 716.5 lbs.
Metric Height: 3.0 m
Metric Weight: 325.0 kg

Possible Moves: Icy Wind, Dragon Rage, Imprison, Ancient Power, Ice Beam, Dragon Breath, Slash, Scary Face, Glaciate, Dragon Pulse, Noble Roar, Endeavor, Blizzard, Outrage, Hyper Voice

BLACK KYUREM

Boundary Pokémon

TYPE: DRAGON-ICE

Imperial Height: 10'10''
Imperial Weight: 716.5 lbs.
Metric Height: 3.3 m
Metric Weight: 325.0 kg

WHITE KYUREM

Boundary Pokémon

TYPE: DRAGON-ICE

Imperial Height: 11'10''
Imperial Weight: 716.5 lbs.
Metric Height: 3.6 m
Metric Weight: 325.0 kg

Does not evolve

TYPE: STEEL-ROCK

Lairon lives near tasty, mineral-rich springs, where it tempers its body with iron from the water and rocks. It sometimes comes into conflict with miners going after the same iron ore it uses as a food source.

How to Say It: LAIR-ron
Imperial Height: 2'11''
Imperial Weight: 264.6 lbs.
Metric Height: 0.9 m
Metric Weight: 120.0 kg

Possible Moves: Tackle, Harden, Mud-Slap, Headbutt, Metal Claw, Rock Tomb, Protect, Roar, Iron Head, Rock Slide, Take Down, Metal Sound, Iron Tail, Iron Defense, Double-Edge, Autotomize, Heavy Slam, Metal Burst

LAIRON
Iron Armor Pokémon

Aron ⇒ Lairon ⇒ Aggron ⇒ Mega Aggron

LAMPENT
Lamp Pokémon

TYPE: GHOST-FIRE

Lampent tends to lurk grimly around hospitals, waiting for someone to take a bad turn so it can absorb the departing spirit. The stolen spirits keep its fire burning.

How to Say It: LAM-pent
Imperial Height: 2'00''
Imperial Weight: 28.7 lbs.
Metric Height: 0.6 m
Metric Weight: 13.0 kg

Possible Moves: Ember, Astonish, Minimize, Smog, Fire Spin, Confuse Ray, Night Shade, Will-O-Wisp, Flame Burst, Imprison, Hex, Memento, Inferno, Curse, Shadow Ball, Pain Split, Overheat

Litwick ⇒ Lampent ⇒ Chandelure

227

LANDORUS
Abundance Pokémon

REGION: Unova

Incarnate Forme

LEGENDARY POKÉMON

TYPE: GROUND-FLYING

Because its arrival helps crops grow, Landorus is welcomed as "The Guardian of the Fields." This Legendary Pokémon uses the energy of wind and lightning to enrich the soil.

How to Say It: LAN-duh-rus
Imperial Height: Incarnate Forme: 4'11"
Therian Forme: 4'03"
Imperial Weight: 149.9 lbs.
Metric Height: Incarnate Forme: 1.5 m
Therian Forme: 1.3 m
Metric Weight: 68.0 kg

Possible Moves: Block, Mud Shot, Rock Tomb, Imprison, Punishment, Bulldoze, Rock Throw, Extrasensory, Swords Dance, Earth Power, Rock Slide, Earthquake, Sandstorm, Fissure, Stone Edge, Hammer Arm, Outrage

Therian Forme

228   Does not evolve

TYPE: WATER-ELECTRIC

With the bright light from its antenna, Lanturn can blind and daze its opponent, then attack with electricity before it recovers. At night, the lights of many Lanturn shine through the dark ocean like stars.

How to Say It: LAN-turn
Imperial Height: 3'11''
Imperial Weight: 49.6 lbs.
Metric Height: 1.2 m
Metric Weight: 22.5 kg

Possible Moves: Stockpile, Swallow, Spit Up, Eerie Impulse, Bubble, Supersonic, Thunder Wave, Electro Ball, Water Gun, Confuse Ray, Bubble Beam, Spark, Signal Beam, Flail, Discharge, Take Down, Aqua Ring, Hydro Pump, Ion Deluge, Charge

LANTURN
Light Pokémon

Chinchou ⇨ Lanturn

TYPE: WATER-ICE

Lapras were once nearly wiped out by human activity, but thanks to legal protection, these friendly and intelligent Pokémon are now flourishing. Their lovely singing voices can often be heard near the water when they're having a good day.

How to Say It: LAP-rus
Imperial Height: 8'02''
Imperial Weight: 485.0 lbs.
Metric Height: 2.5 m
Metric Weight: 220.0 kg

Possible Moves: Sing, Growl, Water Gun, Mist, Confuse Ray, Ice Shard, Water Pulse, Body Slam, Rain Dance, Perish Song, Ice Beam, Brine, Safeguard, Hydro Pump, Sheer Cold

LAPRAS
Transport Pokémon

Does not evolve

LARVESTA
Torch Pokémon

REGIONS:
Alola
Unova

TYPE: BUG-FIRE

The flames emitted by Larvesta's horns are so intensely hot, people in ancient times assumed the Pokémon made its home on the sun. It uses fire as a defense mechanism.

How to Say It: lar-VESS-tah
Imperial Height: 3'07''
Imperial Weight: 63.5 lbs.
Metric Height: 1.1 m
Metric Weight: 28.8 kg

Possible Moves: Ember, String Shot, Absorb, Take Down, Flame Charge, Bug Bite, Double-Edge, Flame Wheel, Bug Buzz, Amnesia, Thrash, Flare Blitz

Larvesta ⇒ Volcarona

LARVITAR
Rock Skin Pokémon

REGIONS:
Alola
Johto
Kalos
(Mountain)

TYPE: ROCK-GROUND

Born underground, Larvitar works its way to the surface by tunneling through soil, which it eats as a source of nutrients. It's said that Larvitar won't evolve until it consumes a whole mountain's worth of dirt.

How to Say It: LAR-vuh-tar
Imperial Height: 2'00''
Imperial Weight: 158.7 lbs.
Metric Height: 0.6 m
Metric Weight: 72.0 kg

Possible Moves: Bite, Leer, Sandstorm, Screech, Chip Away, Rock Slide, Scary Face, Thrash, Dark Pulse, Payback, Crunch, Earthquake, Stone Edge, Hyper Beam

Larvitar ⇒ Pupitar ⇒ Tyranitar ⇒ Mega Tyranitar

LATIAS
Eon Pokémon

LEGENDARY POKÉMON

TYPE: DRAGON-PSYCHIC

Sensitive and intelligent, Latias can pick up on people's emotions and understand what they're saying. The down that covers its body can refract light to change its appearance.

How to Say It: LAT-ee-ahs
Imperial Height: 4'07''
Imperial Weight: 88.2 lbs.

Metric Height: 1.4 m
Metric Weight: 40.0 kg

Possible Moves: Psywave, Wish, Helping Hand, Safeguard, Dragon Breath, Water Sport, Refresh, Mist Ball, Zen Headbutt, Recover, Psycho Shift, Charm, Psychic, Heal Pulse, Reflect Type, Guard Split, Dragon Pulse, Healing Wish, Stored Power

MEGA LATIAS
Eon Pokémon

TYPE: DRAGON-PSYCHIC

Imperial Height: 5'11''
Imperial Weight: 114.6 lbs.
Metric Height: 1.8 m
Metric Weight: 52.0 kg

Latias ➡ **Mega Latias**

231

LATIOS
Eon Pokémon

LEGENDARY POKÉMON

TYPE: DRAGON-PSYCHIC

Latios can project images into someone else's mind to share information. When it folds its forelegs back against its body, it could beat a jet plane in a race through the sky.

How to Say It: LAT-ee-ose
Imperial Height: 6'07''
Imperial Weight: 132.3 lbs.

Metric Height: 2.0 m
Metric Weight: 60.0 kg

Possible Moves: Memento, Helping Hand, Heal Block, Psywave, Safeguard, Protect, Dragon Dance, Stored Power, Refresh, Heal Pulse, Dragon Breath, Luster Purge, Psycho Shift, Recover, Telekinesis, Zen Headbutt, Power Split, Psychic, Dragon Pulse

MEGA LATIOS
Eon Pokémon

TYPE: DRAGON-PSYCHIC

Imperial Height: 7'07''
Imperial Weight: 154.3 lbs.
Metric Height: 2.3 m
Metric Weight: 70.0 kg

Latios ⇨ Mega Latios

LEAFEON
Verdant Pokémon

TYPE: GRASS

Leafeon doesn't need to eat, because it uses photosynthesis to generate energy. A newly evolved Leafeon smells fresh and green, like spring grass, while an older one wafts the dry, crisp scent of autumn leaves.

How to Say It: LEAF-ee-on
Imperial Height: 3'03''
Imperial Weight: 56.2 lbs.
Metric Height: 1.0 m
Metric Weight: 25.5 kg

Possible Moves: Razor Leaf, Helping Hand, Tackle, Tail Whip, Sand Attack, Baby-Doll Eyes, Quick Attack, Grass Whistle, Magical Leaf, Giga Drain, Swords Dance, Synthesis, Sunny Day, Last Resort, Leaf Blade

Eevee ⇨ Leafeon

REGION:
Unova

LEAVANNY
Nurturing Pokémon

TYPE: BUG-GRASS

Leavanny loves to make warm clothes for smaller Pokémon, cutting up leaves with its arms and sewing them together with sticky silk from its mouth.

How to Say It: lee-VAN-nee
Imperial Height: 3'11''
Imperial Weight: 45.2 lbs.
Metric Height: 1.2 m
Metric Weight: 20.5 kg

Possible Moves: Slash, False Swipe, Tackle, String Shot, Bug Bite, Razor Leaf, Struggle Bug, Fell Stinger Helping Hand, Leaf Blade, X-Scissor, Entrainment, Swords Dance, Leaf Storm

Sewaddle ⇨ Swadloon ⇨ Leavanny

LEDIAN

Five Star Pokémon

TYPE: BUG-FLYING

Ledian are thought to consume starlight for food, but they're also happy to gobble down berries. They pummel their opponents with all four arms in battle, hoping to overcome the foe with a flurry of punches.

How to Say It: LEH-dee-an
Imperial Height: 4'07''
Imperial Weight: 78.5 lbs.
Metric Height: 1.4 m
Metric Weight: 35.6 kg

Possible Moves: Tackle, Supersonic, Swift, Light Screen, Reflect, Safeguard, Mach Punch, Silver Wind, Comet Punch, Baton Pass, Agility, Bug Buzz, Air Slash, Double-Edge

Ledyba   Ledian

LEDYBA

Five Star Pokémon

TYPE: BUG-FLYING

Ledyba prefer to stick together, forming brightly patterned swarms. They communicate through scent, and the aromatic fluid they give off changes according to their emotion—a swarm of angry Ledyba smells unpleasantly sour.

How to Say It: LEH-dee-bah
Imperial Height: 3'03''
Imperial Weight: 23.8 lbs.
Metric Height: 1.0 m
Metric Weight: 10.8 kg

Possible Moves: Tackle, Supersonic, Swift, Light Screen, Reflect, Safeguard, Mach Punch, Silver Wind, Comet Punch, Baton Pass, Agility, Bug Buzz, Air Slash, Double-Edge

Ledyba   Ledian

LICKILICKY
Licking Pokémon

TYPE: NORMAL

The longest Lickilicky tongue ever recorded stretched more than eighty feet. Despite its massive size, the tongue has great dexterity and can pick up small objects with ease.

How to Say It: LICK-ee-LICK-ee
Imperial Height: 5'07''
Imperial Weight: 308.6 lbs.
Metric Height: 1.7 m
Metric Weight: 140.0 kg

Possible Moves: Wring Out, Power Whip, Lick, Supersonic, Defense Curl, Knock Off, Wrap, Stomp, Disable, Slam, Rollout, Chip Away, Me First, Refresh, Screech, Gyro Ball

Lickitung Lickilicky

TYPE: NORMAL

If you don't want to get licked, stay away from Lickitung. It uses its enormous tongue to investigate its surroundings, leaving an unpleasant-smelling saliva that can cause a rash.

How to Say It: LICK-it-tung
Imperial Height: 3'11''
Imperial Weight: 144.4 lbs.
Metric Height: 1.2 m
Metric Weight: 65.5 kg

Possible Moves: Lick, Supersonic, Defense Curl, Knock Off, Wrap, Stomp, Disable, Slam, Rollout, Chip Away, Me First, Refresh, Screech, Power Whip, Wring Out

LICKITUNG
Licking Pokémon

Lickitung Lickilicky

LIEPARD

Cruel Pokémon

REGIONS:
Kalos
(Mountain)
Unova

TYPE: DARK

Elegant and swift, Liepard can move through the night without a sound. It uses this stealth to execute sneak attacks.

How to Say It: LY-purd
Imperial Height: 3'07''
Imperial Weight: 82.7 lbs.
Metric Height: 1.1 m
Metric Weight: 37.5 kg

Possible Moves: Scratch, Growl, Assist, Sand Attack, Fury Swipes, Pursuit, Torment, Fake Out, Hone Claws, Assurance, Slash, Taunt, Night Slash, Snatch, Nasty Plot, Sucker Punch, Play Rough

Purrloin ⇒ Liepard

LILEEP

Sea Lily Pokémon

REGIONS:
Alola
Hoenn

TYPE: ROCK-GRASS

Clinging to an undersea rock, Lileep waits patiently for food to drift by—then it pounces! It stays in the same place no matter how strong the water current is.

How to Say It: lil-LEEP
Imperial Height: 3'03''
Imperial Weight: 52.5 lbs.
Metric Height: 1.0 m
Metric Weight: 23.8 kg

Possible Moves: Astonish, Constrict, Acid, Ingrain, Confuse Ray, Amnesia, Brine, Giga Drain, Gastro Acid, Ancient Power, Energy Ball, Stockpile, Spit Up, Swallow, Wring Out

Lileep ⇒ Cradily

LILLIGANT
Flowering Pokémon

TYPE: GRASS

Some Trainers lavish time, attention, and money on Lilligant, attempting to cultivate its lovely flowers—but this Pokémon always blooms most beautifully when it's left alone in the wild. The showy flowers might be an attempt to attract a partner.

How to Say It: LIL-lih-gunt
Imperial Height: 3'07''
Imperial Weight: 35.9 lbs.
Metric Height: 1.1 m
Metric Weight: 16.3 kg

Possible Moves: Growth, Leech Seed, Mega Drain, Synthesis, Teeter Dance, Quiver Dance, Petal Dance, Petal Blizzard

Petilil ⇨ Lilligant

LILLIPUP
Puppy Pokémon

TYPE: NORMAL

The quiet, well-behaved Lillipup is a popular partner for Trainers who live in apartments and have to avoid disturbing their neighbors. Its fluffy facial fur acts as a sensor in battle.

How to Say It: LIL-ee-pup
Imperial Height: 1'04''
Imperial Weight: 9.0 lbs.
Metric Height: 0.4 m
Metric Weight: 4.1 kg

Possible Moves: Leer, Tackle, Odor Sleuth, Bite, Baby-Doll Eyes, Helping Hand, Take Down, Work Up, Crunch, Roar, Retaliate, Reversal, Last Resort, Giga Impact, Play Rough

Lillipup ⇨ Herdier ⇨ Stoutland

LINOONE
Rushing Pokémon

REGIONS:
Hoenn
Kalos
(Central)

TYPE: NORMAL

Because Linoone can only run in straight lines, curving roads pose quite a navigation problem. It charges ahead at top speed when hunting.

How to Say It: line-NOON
Imperial Height: 1'08''
Imperial Weight: 71.6 lbs.
Metric Height: 0.5 m
Metric Weight: 32.5 kg

Possible Moves: Play Rough, Rototiller, Switcheroo, Tackle, Growl, Tail Whip, Headbutt, Sand Attack, Odor Sleuth, Mud Sport, Fury Swipes, Covet, Bestow, Slash, Double-Edge Rest, Belly Drum, Fling

Zigzagoon   Linoone

LITLEO
Lion Cub Pokémon

REGIONS:
Alola
Kalos
(Central)

TYPE: FIRE-NORMAL

As soon as Litleo is able to battle without the help of its pride, it sets off on its own journey, filled with curiosity about what the future holds. When it gets fired up, its mane becomes hot.

How to Say It: LIT-lee-oh
Imperial Height: 2'00''
Imperial Weight: 29.8 lbs.
Metric Height: 0.6 m
Metric Weight: 13.5 kg

Possible Moves: Tackle, Leer, Ember, Work Up, Headbutt, Noble Roar, Take Down, Fire Fang, Endeavor, Echoed Voice, Flamethrower, Crunch, Hyper Voice, Incinerate, Overheat

Litleo   Pyroar

LITTEN
Fire Cat Pokémon

TYPE: FIRE

When it grooms its fur, Litten is storing up ammunition—the flaming fur is later coughed up in a fiery attack. Trainers often have a hard time getting this solitary Pokémon to trust them.

How to Say It: LIT-n
Imperial Height: 1'04''
Imperial Weight: 9.5 lbs.
Metric Height: 0.4 m
Metric Weight: 4.3 kg

Possible Moves: Scratch, Ember, Growl, Lick, Leer, Fire Fang, Double Kick, Roar, Bite, Swagger, Fury Swipes, Thrash, Flamethrower, Scary Face, Flare Blitz, Outrage

Litten   **Torracat**   **Incineroar**

REGIONS:
Kalos
(Mountain)
Unova

LITWICK
Candle Pokémon

TYPE: GHOST-FIRE

Litwick pretends to guide people and Pokémon with its light, but following it is a bad idea. The ghostly flame absorbs life energy for use as fuel.

How to Say It: LIT-wik
Imperial Height: 1'00''
Imperial Weight: 6.8 lbs.
Metric Height: 0.3 m
Metric Weight: 3.1 kg

Possible Moves: Ember, Astonish, Minimize, Smog, Fire Spin, Confuse Ray, Night Shade, Will-O-Wisp, Flame Burst, Imprison, Hex, Memento, Inferno, Curse, Shadow Ball, Pain Split, Overheat

Litwick   **Lampent**   **Chandelure**

239

LOMBRE

Jolly Pokémon

TYPE: WATER-GRASS

When the mischievous Lombre spots someone fishing, it swims up to tug on the line. The film that covers its body is unpleasantly slimy to the touch.

How to Say It: LOM-brey
Imperial Height: 3'11''
Imperial Weight: 71.6 lbs.

Metric Height: 1.2 m
Metric Weight: 32.5 kg

Possible Moves: Astonish, Growl, Absorb, Bubble, Nature Power, Fake Out, Fury Swipes, Water Sport, Bubble Beam, Zen Headbutt, Uproar, Hydro Pump, Knock Off

Lotad → Lombre → Ludicolo

LOPUNNY
Rabbit Pokémon

TYPE: NORMAL

Because Lopunny sheds its plush coat twice a year, people use its fur to craft exceptionally warm scarves and hats. It's not a fan of fighting, but its powerful kicking skills let it hold its own in battle.

How to Say It: LAH-pun-nee
Imperial Height: 3'11"
Imperial Weight: 73.4 lbs.
Metric Height: 1.2 m
Metric Weight: 33.3 kg

Possible Moves: Return, Healing Wish, Bounce, Rototiller, Mirror Coat, Magic Coat, Defense Curl, Splash, Pound, Endure, Baby-Doll Eyes, Quick Attack, Jump Kick, Baton Pass, Agility, Dizzy Punch, After You, Charm, Entertainment, High Jump Kick

MEGA LOPUNNY
Caring Pokémon

TYPE: NORMAL-FIGHTING

Imperial Height: 4'03"
Imperial Weight: 62.4 lbs.
Metric Height: 1.3 m
Metric Weight: 28.3 kg

Buneary ⇨ Lopunny ⇨ Mega Lopunny

LOTAD
Water Weed Pokémon

TYPE: WATER-GRASS

The leaf on Lotad's head is too big and heavy for it to carry on land, so it floats on the surface of the water.

How to Say It: LOW-tad
Imperial Height: 1'08''
Imperial Weight: 5.7 lbs.
Metric Height: 0.5 m
Metric Weight: 2.6 kg

Possible Moves: Astonish, Growl, Absorb, Nature Power, Mist, Natural Gift, Mega Drain, Bubble Beam, Zen Headbutt, Rain Dance, Energy Ball, Giga Drain

Lotad → Lombre → Ludicolo

LOUDRED
Big Voice Pokémon

TYPE: NORMAL

Loudred shouts at such volume that it temporarily deafens itself. The sound waves it produces can knock down a wooden house.

How to Say It: LOUD-red
Imperial Height: 3'03''
Imperial Weight: 89.3 lbs.
Metric Height: 1.0 m
Metric Weight: 40.5 kg

Possible Moves: Bite, Pound, Echoed Voice, Astonish, Howl, Screech, Supersonic, Stomp, Uproar, Roar, Rest, Sleep Talk, Hyper Voice, Synchronoise

Whismur → Loudred → Exploud

LUCARIO
Aura Pokémon

TYPE: FIGHTING-STEEL

When Lucario evolves, it gains the power not just to sense auras, but to control them. This skill is often useful in battle. If a person or Pokémon within a half-mile radius is feeling happy or sad, Lucario can tell.

How to Say It: loo-CAR-ee-oh
Imperial Height: 3'11''
Imperial Weight: 119.0 lbs.
Metric Height: 1.2 m
Metric Weight: 54.0 kg

Possible Moves: Aura Sphere, Laser Focus, Foresight, Quick Attack, Detect, Metal Claw, Counter, Feint, Power-Up Punch, Swords Dance, Metal Sound, Bone Rush, Quick Guard, Me First, Work Up, Calm Mind, Heal Pulse, Close Combat, Dragon Pulse, Extreme Speed

MEGA LUCARIO
Aura Pokémon

TYPE: FIGHTING-STEEL

Imperial Height: 4'03''
Imperial Weight: 126.8 lbs.
Metric Height: 1.3 m
Metric Weight: 57.5 kg

Riolu ➡ **Lucario** ➡ **Mega Lucario**

243

LUDICOLO

Carefree Pokémon

REGIONS:
Hoenn
Kalos
(Mountain)

TYPE: WATER-GRASS

Ludicolo just can't help leaping into a joyful dance when it hears a festive tune. Children who sing while hiking often attract its attention.

How to Say It: LOO-dee-KO-low
Imperial Height: 4'11''
Imperial Weight: 121.3 lbs.

Metric Height: 1.5 m
Metric Weight: 55.0 kg

Possible Moves: Astonish, Growl, Mega Drain, Nature Power

Lotad ⇨ Lombre ⇨ Ludicolo

LUGIA
Diving Pokémon

LEGENDARY POKÉMON

TYPE: PSYCHIC-FLYING

Lugia can knock down a house with one flutter of its enormously powerful wings. For the safety of others, this Legendary Pokémon lives at the bottom of the sea.

How to Say It: LOO-gee-uh
Imperial Height: 17'01''
Imperial Weight: 476.2 lbs.

Metric Height: 5.2 m
Metric Weight: 216.0 kg

Possible Moves: Whirlwind, Weather Ball, Gust, Dragon Rush, Extrasensory, Rain Dance, Hydro Pump, Aeroblast, Punishment, Ancient Power, Safeguard, Recover, Future Sight, Natural Gift, Calm Mind, Sky Attack

Does not evolve

LUMINEON
Neon Pokémon

TYPE: WATER

In the depths of the sea, Lumineon's body gives off light to attract food—but sometimes bigger Pokémon are attracted to the light instead, and it finds itself in an intense battle.

How to Say It: loo-MIN-ee-on
Imperial Height: 3'11''
Imperial Weight: 52.9 lbs.

Metric Height: 1.2 m
Metric Weight: 24.0 kg

Possible Moves: Soak, Gust, Pound, Water Gun, Attract, Rain Dance, Water Pulse, Captivate, Safeguard, Aqua Ring, Whirlpool, U-turn, Bounce, Silver Wind

Finneon ➡ Lumineon

LUNALA
Moone Pokémon

LEGENDARY POKÉMON

TYPE: PSYCHIC-GHOST

Lunala's wide wings soak up the light, plunging the brightest day into shadow. This Legendary Pokémon apparently makes its home in another world, and it returns there when its third eye becomes active.

How to Say It: loo-NAH-luh
Imperial Height: 13'01''
Imperial Weight: 264.6 lbs.

Metric Height: 4.0 m
Metric Weight: 120.0 kg

Possible Moves: Moongeist Beam, Cosmic Power, Hypnosis, Teleport, Confusion, Night Shade, Confuse Ray, Air Slash, Shadow Ball, Moonlight, Night Daze, Magic Coat, Moonblast, Dream Eater, Phantom Force, Wide Guard, Hyper Beam

Cosmog ⇨ Cosmoem ⇨ Lunala

LUNATONE

Meteorite Pokémon

REGIONS:
Hoenn
Kalos
(Coastal)

TYPE: ROCK-PSYCHIC

People think Lunatone came from space because it was first discovered near a meteorite. It floats to get around instead of walking, and its red eyes can freeze a foe with fear.

How to Say It: LOO-nuh-tone
Imperial Height: 3'03''
Imperial Weight: 370.4 lbs.
Metric Height: 1.0 m
Metric Weight: 168.0 kg

Possible Moves: Power Gem, Psyshock, Moonblast, Tackle, Harden, Confusion, Rock Throw, Hypnosis, Rock Polish, Psywave, Embargo, Rock Slide, Cosmic Power, Psychic, Heal Block, Stone Edge, Future Sight, Explosion, Magic Room

Does not evolve

LURANTIS

Bloom Sickle Pokémon

REGION:
Alola

TYPE: GRASS

It can be difficult to give Lurantis the proper care to keep its coloring bright and vivid, but some Trainers enthusiastically accept the challenge. The beams it shoots from its petals can pierce thick metal.

How to Say It: loor-RAN-tis
Imperial Height: 2'11''
Imperial Weight: 40.8 lbs.
Metric Height: 0.9 m
Metric Weight: 18.5 kg

Possible Moves: Petal Blizzard, X-Scissor, Fury Cutter, Leafage, Razor Leaf, Growth, Ingrain, Leaf Blade, Synthesis, Slash, Sweet Scent, Solar Blade, Sunny Day

Fomantis ⇨ **Lurantis**

TYPE: WATER

If you see many Luvdisc swimming in a hotel pool, it's likely the hotel is popular among couples on honeymoon. This Pokémon grows very sad if it's left alone, which can be a huge disadvantage in battle.

How to Say It: LOVE-disk
Imperial Height: 2'00''
Imperial Weight: 19.2 lbs.
Metric Height: 0.6 m
Metric Weight: 8.7 kg

Possible Moves: Tackle, Charm, Water Gun, Agility, Draining Kiss, Lucky Chant, Water Pulse, Attract, Heart Stamp, Flail, Sweet Kiss, Take Down, Captivate, Aqua Ring, Soak, Hydro Pump, Safeguard

REGIONS:
Alola
Hoenn
Kalos
(Coastal)

LUVDISC
Rendezvous Pokémon

Does not evolve

TYPE: ELECTRIC

A powerful electric current arcs between Luxio's claws, making it a dangerous opponent in battle. They form small groups and live together.

How to Say It: LUCKS-ee-oh
Imperial Height: 2'11''
Imperial Weight: 67.2 lbs
Metric Height: 0.9 m
Metric Weight: 30.5 kg

Possible Moves: Tackle, Leer, Charge, Spark, Bite, Roar, Swagger, Thunder Fang, Crunch, Scary Face, Discharge, Wild Charge

REGION:
Sinnoh

LUXIO
Spark Pokémon

 Shinx ➡ **Luxio** ➡ **Luxray**

249

LUXRAY
Gleam Eyes Pokémon

REGION: Sinnoh

TYPE: ELECTRIC

Luxray's gleaming golden eyes can see right through solid objects. This is very useful when it's keeping watch for approaching threats or looking for food.

How to Say It: LUCKS-ray
Imperial Height: 4'07''
Imperial Weight: 92.6 lbs.
Metric Height: 1.4 m
Metric Weight: 42.0 kg

Possible Moves: Electric Terrain, Tackle, Leer, Charge, Spark, Bite, Roar, Swagger, Thunder Fang, Crunch, Scary Face, Discharge, Wild Charge

Shinx ➡ Luxio ➡ Luxray

TYPE: ROCK

LYCANROC MIDDAY FORM: Its thick mane conceals sharp rocks that it uses in battle along with its fangs and claws. Despite its fearsome arsenal, Lycanroc displays fierce loyalty toward a Trainer who has raised it well.

LYCANROC DUSK FORM: Lycanroc's Dusk Form is a rare sight in Alola. It only appears when a Rockruff evolves at sunset, during the time between day and night. This Pokémon's calm demeanor hides a strong impulse to battle.

LYCANROC MIDNIGHT FORM: When Lycanroc faces a truly intimidating opponent, it attacks recklessly, with no concern for its own hide. The rocks in its mane contribute to the crushing power of its headbutt.

How to Say It: LIE-can-rock
Imperial Height: Midday Form: 2'07'' / Dusk Form: 2'07'' / Midnight Form: 3'07''
Imperial Weight: 55.1 lbs.
Metric Height: Midday Form: 0.8 m / Dusk Form: 0.8 m / Midnight Form: 1.1 m
Metric Weight: 25.0 kg

Possible Moves: Tackle, Leer, Sand Attack, Bite, Howl, Rock Throw, Odor Sleuth, Rock Tomb, Roar, Stealth Rock, Rock Slide, Scary Face, Crunch, Rock Climb, Stone Edge

Midday Form: Accelerock, Quick Guard, Quick Attack
Dusk Form: Thrash, Accelerock, Counter, Tackle, Leer, Sand Attack, Bite
Midnight Form: Counter, Reversal, Taunt

Dusk Form

Midday Form

Rockruff

Midnight Form

Lycanroc (Midday Form)

Lycanroc (Dusk Form)

Lycanroc (Midnight Form)

MACHAMP
Superpower Pokémon

REGIONS:
Alola
Kalos
(Coastal)
Kanto

TYPE: FIGHTING

Machamp really shines when it's called upon to perform feats of strength—with its four massive arms, it can even pick up a heavy dump truck. It's less good at tasks that require manual dexterity and precision.

How to Say It: muh-CHAMP
Imperial Height: 5'03''
Imperial Weight: 286.6 lbs.
Metric Height: 1.6 m
Metric Weight: 130.0 kg

Possible Moves: Strength, Wide Guard, Low Kick, Leer, Focus Energy, Karate Chop, Foresight, Low Sweep, Seismic Toss, Revenge, Knock Off, Vital Throw, Wake-Up Slap, Dual Chop, Submission, Bulk Up, Cross Chop, Scary Face, Dynamic Punch

Machop ➡ **Machoke** ➡ **Machamp**

MACHOKE
Superpower Pokémon

REGIONS:
Alola
Kalos
(Coastal)
Kanto

TYPE: FIGHTING

Machoke happily pitches in when people need help with a tough physical job. Moving and carrying heavy things is just one more way for it to train its muscles.

How to Say It: muh-CHOKE
Imperial Height: 4'11''
Imperial Weight: 155.4 lbs.
Metric Height: 1.5 m
Metric Weight: 70.5 kg

Possible Moves: Low Kick, Leer, Focus Energy, Karate Chop, Foresight, Low Sweep, Seismic Toss, Revenge, Knock Off, Vital Throw, Wake-Up Slap, Dual Chop, Submission, Bulk Up, Cross Chop, Scary Face, Dynamic Punch

Machop ➡ **Machoke** ➡ **Machamp**

MACHOP
Superpower Pokémon

TYPE: FIGHTING

Exercise is Machop's favorite thing in the world, and its developing muscles reinforce its devotion to working out. It's strong enough to pick up and throw the weight of a hundred people.

How to Say It: muh-CHOP
Imperial Height: 2'07''
Imperial Weight: 43.0 lbs.
Metric Height: 0.8 m
Metric Weight: 19.5 kg

Possible Moves: Low Kick, Leer, Focus Energy, Karate Chop, Foresight, Low Sweep, Seismic Toss, Revenge, Knock Off, Vital Throw, Wake-Up Slap, Dual Chop, Submission, Bulk Up, Cross Chop, Scary Face, Dynamic Punch

Machop Machoke Machamp

TYPE: FIRE

Magby thrive in volcanic areas, where they can freely spout flames. They can learn to control their flames and use them productively— for instance, one Magby serves as a gentle kiln for its Trainer, an artist famous for pottery.

How to Say It: MAG-bee
Imperial Height: 2'04''
Imperial Weight: 47.2 lbs.
Metric Height: 0.7 m
Metric Weight: 21.4 kg

Possible Moves: Smog, Leer, Ember, Smokescreen, Feint Attack, Fire Spin, Clear Smog, Flame Burst, Confuse Ray, Fire Punch, Lava Plume, Sunny Day, Flamethrower, Fire Blast

MAGBY
Live Coal Pokémon

Magby Magmar Magmortar

253

MAGCARGO

Lava Pokémon

REGIONS:
Johto
Kalos
(Mountain)

TYPE: FIRE-ROCK

Magcargo's body is so hot that it vaporizes any nearby water. When the weather turns rainy, Magcargo is surrounded by a thick cloud of steam.

How to Say It: mag-CAR-go
Imperial Height: 2'07''
Imperial Weight: 121.3 lbs.
Metric Height: 0.8 m
Metric Weight: 55.0 kg

Possible Moves: Earth Power, Yawn, Smog, Ember, Rock Throw, Harden, Recover, Flame Burst, Ancient Power, Amnesia, Lava Plume, Shell Smash, Rock Slide, Body Slam, Flamethrower, Incinerate, Clear Smog

Slugma Magcargo

MAGEARNA

Artificial Pokémon

REGION:
Alola

MYTHICAL POKÉMON

TYPE: STEEL-FAIRY

Magearna was built many centuries ago by human inventors. The rest of this Pokémon's mechanical body is just a vehicle for its true self: the Soul-Heart contained in its chest.

How to Say It: muh-GEER-nuh
Imperial Height: 3'03''
Imperial Weight: 177.5 lbs.
Metric Height: 1.0 m
Metric Weight: 80.5 kg

Possible Moves: Crafty Shield, Gear Up, Shift Gear, Iron Head, Helping Hand, Sonic Boom, Defense Curl, Psybeam, Lucky Chant, Aurora Beam, Mirror Shot, Mind Reader, Flash Cannon, Fleur Cannon, Iron Defense, Pain Split, Synchronoise, Aura Sphere, Heart Swap, Trump Card

Does not evolve

MAGIKARP
Fish Pokémon

TYPE: WATER

Magikarp splash about with abandon, leaping recklessly out of the water—which leaves them open to attack. Though extremely lacking when it comes to battle strength, they exist in huge numbers.

How to Say It: MADGE-eh-karp
Imperial Height: 2'11''
Imperial Weight: 22.0 lbs.
Metric Height: 0.9 m
Metric Weight: 10.0 kg

Possible Moves: Splash, Tackle, Flail

Magikarp ⇨ Gyarados ⇨ Mega Gyarados

TYPE: FIRE

Taking a hot bath is a great way for some people to recharge. Magmar likes to do that, too—but instead of hot water, it bathes in molten lava! Flames spout from its body in battle.

How to Say It: MAG-marr
Imperial Height: 4'03''
Imperial Weight: 98.1 lbs.
Metric Height: 1.3 m
Metric Weight: 44.5 kg

Possible Moves: Smog, Leer, Ember, Smokescreen, Feint Attack, Fire Spin, Clear Smog, Flame Burst, Confuse Ray, Fire Punch, Lava Plume, Sunny Day, Flamethrower, Fire Blast

MAGMAR
Spitfire Pokémon

Magby ⇨ Magmar ⇨ Magmortar

MAGMORTAR
Blast Pokémon

REGIONS:
Alola
Sinnoh

TYPE: FIRE

Magmortar can shoot balls of fire out of its arm, although it has to avoid firing several at once—the buildup of such intense heat can cause melting. Apparently, each pair of Magmortar claims a separate volcano as home.

How to Say It: mag-MORT-ur
Imperial Height: 5'03''
Imperial Weight: 149.9 lbs.
Metric Height: 1.6 m
Metric Weight: 68.0 kg

Possible Moves: Thunder Punch, Smog, Leer, Ember, Smokescreen, Feint Attack, Fire Spin, Clear Smog, Flame Burst, Confuse Ray, Fire Punch, Lava Plume, Sunny Day, Flamethrower, Fire Blast, Hyper Beam

Magby   Magmar   Magmortar

MAGNEMITE
Magnet Pokémon

REGIONS:
Alola
Kalos
(Mountain)
Kanto

TYPE: ELECTRIC-STEEL

Groups of Magnemite often cluster around transmission towers to suck up electricity from the power lines. They float above the ground by using electromagnetic waves.

How to Say It: MAG-ne-mite
Imperial Height: 1'00''
Imperial Weight: 13.2 lbs.
Metric Height: 0.3 m
Metric Weight: 6.0 kg

Possible Moves: Tackle, Supersonic, Thunder Shock, Magnet Bomb, Thunder Wave, Light Screen, Sonic Boom, Spark, Mirror Shot, Metal Sound, Electro Ball, Flash Cannon, Screech, Discharge, Lock-On, Magnet Rise, Gyro Ball, Zap Cannon

Magnemite   Magneton   Magnezone

TYPE: ELECTRIC-STEEL

Magneton is formed when three Magnemite link their bodies and brains together. This triples their electrical power, but their intelligence doesn't get a similar boost.

How to Say It: MAG-ne-ton
Imperial Height: 3'03"
Imperial Weight: 132.3 lbs.
Metric Height: 1.0 m
Metric Weight: 60.0 kg

Possible Moves: Tri Attack, Zap Cannon, Electric Terrain, Tackle, Supersonic, Thunder Shock, Magnet Bomb, Thunder Wave, Light Screen, Sonic Boom, Spark, Mirror Shot, Metal Sound, Electro Ball, Flash Cannon, Screech, Discharge, Lock-On, Magnet Rise, Gyro Ball

REGIONS:
Alola
Kalos
(Mountain)
Kanto

MAGNETON
Magnet Pokémon

Magnemite ⇨ Magneton ⇨ Magnezone

TYPE: ELECTRIC-STEEL

Magnezone is thought to receive and transmit signals as it flies through the air with the power of magnetism, though it's unknown where the signals come from. Sometimes a reported UFO sighting turns out to be Magnezone.

How to Say It: MAG-nuh-zone
Imperial Height: 3'11"
Imperial Weight: 396.8 lbs.
Metric Height: 1.2 m
Metric Weight: 180.0 kg

Possible Moves: Tri Attack, Zap Cannon, Magnetic Flux, Mirror Coat, Barrier, Electric Terrain, Tackle, Supersonic, Thunder Shock, Magnet Bomb, Thunder Wave, Light Screen, Sonic Boom, Spark, Mirror Shot, Metal Sound, Electro Ball, Flash Cannon, Screech, Discharge, Lock-On, Magnet Rise, Gyro Ball

REGIONS:
Alola
Kalos
(Mountain)
Sinnoh

MAGNEZONE
Magnet Area Pokémon

Magnemite ⇨ Magneton ⇨ Magnezone

257

MAKUHITA
Guts Pokémon

REGIONS:
Alola
Hoenn
Kalos
(Coastal)

TYPE: FIGHTING

Makuhita aren't native to the Alola region, but they've definitely made a name for themselves in the islands. Groups of Makuhita gather every day for training, eating, napping, and more training.

How to Say It: MAK-oo-HEE-ta
Imperial Height: 3'03''
Imperial Weight: 190.5 lbs.
Metric Height: 1.0 m
Metric Weight: 86.4 kg

Possible Moves: Tackle, Focus Energy, Sand Attack, Arm Thrust, Fake Out, Force Palm, Whirlwind, Knock Off, Vital Throw, Belly Drum, Smelling Salts, Seismic Toss, Wake-Up Slap, Endure, Close Combat, Reversal, Heavy Slam

Makuhita → Hariyama

MALAMAR
Overturning Pokémon

REGIONS:
Alola
Kalos
(Coastal)

TYPE: DARK-PSYCHIC

A master hypnotist, Malamar is popular among disreputable people who seek to take advantage of others. It controls opponents with the rhythmic flashing lights on its body, then attacks with sharp-edged fins.

How to Say It: MAL-uh-MAR
Imperial Height: 4'11''
Imperial Weight: 103.6 lbs.
Metric Height: 1.5 m
Metric Weight: 47.0 kg

Possible Moves: Superpower, Reversal, Tackle, Peck, Constrict, Reflect, Foul Play, Swagger, Psywave, Topsy-Turvy, Hypnosis, Psybeam, Switcheroo, Payback, Light Screen, Pluck, Psycho Cut, Slash, Night Slash

Inkay → Malamar

MAMOSWINE
Twin Tusk Pokémon

TYPE: ICE-GROUND

Mamoswine have been around since the last ice age, but the warmer climate reduced their population. Their huge twin tusks are formed of ice.

How to Say It: MAM-oh-swine
Imperial Height: 8'02''
Imperial Weight: 641.5 lbs.

Metric Height: 2.5 m
Metric Weight: 291.0 kg

Possible Moves: Fury Attack, Scary Face, Ancient Power, Peck, Odor Sleuth, Mud Sport, Powder Snow, Mud-Slap, Endure, Mud Bomb, Hail, Ice Fang, Take Down, Double Hit, Mist, Thrash, Earthquake, Blizzard

Swinub ➡ Piloswine ➡ Mamoswine

MANAPHY

Seafaring Pokémon

REGION: Sinnoh

MYTHICAL POKÉMON

TYPE: WATER

From its earliest days, Manaphy has possessed the power to form close bonds with any Pokémon, no matter what kind.

How to Say It: MAN-ah-fee
Imperial Height: 1'00''
Imperial Weight: 3.1 lbs.
Metric Height: 0.3 m
Metric Weight: 1.4 kg

Possible Moves: Tail Glow, Bubble, Water Sport, Charm, Supersonic, Bubble Beam, Acid Armor, Whirlpool, Water Pulse, Aqua Ring, Dive, Rain Dance, Heart Swap

Does not evolve

MANDIBUZZ

Bone Vulture Pokémon

REGIONS: Alola Unova

TYPE: DARK-FLYING

Mandibuzz weave bones into their feathers and wear them as jewelry, perhaps in an attempt to show off. They fly in circles, always keeping an eye out for a weaker opponent down below.

How to Say It: MAN-dih-buz
Imperial Height: 3'11''
Imperial Weight: 87.1 lbs.
Metric Height: 1.2 m
Metric Weight: 39.5 kg

Possible Moves: Bone Rush, Mirror Move, Brave Bird, Whirlwind, Gust, Leer, Fury Attack, Pluck, Nasty Plot, Flatter, Feint Attack, Punishment, Defog, Tailwind, Air Slash, Dark Pulse, Embargo

Vullaby ⇨ **Mandibuzz**

TYPE: ELECTRIC

According to legend, Manectric runs as fast as a bolt of lightning, powered by the electricity stored in its muscles. The same electricity enables Manectric to quickly recover from fatigue after a hard battle.

How to Say It: mane-EK-trick
Imperial Height: 4'11''
Imperial Weight: 88.6 lbs.
Metric Height: 1.5 m
Metric Weight: 40.2 kg

Possible Moves: Electric Terrain, Fire Fang, Tackle, Thunder Wave, Leer, Howl, Quick Attack, Spark, Odor Sleuth, Bite, Thunder Fang, Roar, Discharge, Charge, Wild Charge, Thunder

MANECTRIC
Discharge Pokémon

MEGA MANECTRIC
Discharge Pokémon

TYPE: ELECTRIC

Imperial Height: 5'11''
Imperial Weight: 97.0 lbs.
Metric Height: 1.8 m
Metric Weight: 44.0 kg

Electrike ⇨ **Manectric** ⇨ **Mega Manectric**

MANKEY
Pig Monkey Pokémon

TYPE: FIGHTING

Mankey's rage is so exhausting that it falls asleep, then wakes itself up by rampaging through its dreams—and waking up makes it mad! Being lonely makes it angry, but its rage drives everyone away—and then it's lonely again!

How to Say It: MANG-key
Imperial Height: 1'08''
Imperial Weight: 61.7 lbs.
Metric Height: 0.5 m
Metric Weight: 28.0 kg

Possible Moves: Covet, Scratch, Low Kick, Leer, Focus Energy, Fury Swipes, Karate Chop, Pursuit, Seismic Toss, Swagger, Cross Chop, Assurance, Punishment, Thrash, Close Combat, Screech, Stomping Tantrum, Outrage, Final Gambit

Mankey ⟹ **Primeape**

MANTINE
Kite Pokémon

TYPE: WATER-FLYING

Mantine leaping over waves is a common sight on postcards and other souvenirs in Alola. Quite a few folks have taken up surfing after being inspired by this elegant swimmer.

How to Say It: MAN-teen
Imperial Height: 6'11''
Imperial Weight: 485.0 lbs.
Metric Height: 2.1 m
Metric Weight: 220.0 kg

Possible Moves: Psybeam, Bullet Seed, Signal Beam, Roost, Tackle, Bubble, Supersonic, Bubble Beam, Confuse Ray, Wing Attack, Headbutt, Water Pulse, Wide Guard, Take Down, Agility, Air Slash, Aqua Ring, Bounce, Hydro Pump

Mantyke ⟹ **Mantine**

MANTYKE
Kite Pokémon

TYPE: WATER-FLYING

Mantyke enjoys the company of people and can often be seen swimming alongside boats. Tourists in Alola love to go swimming with this friendly Pokémon.

How to Say It: MAN-tike
Imperial Height: 3'03''
Imperial Weight: 143.3 lbs.
Metric Height: 1.0 m
Metric Weight: 65.0 kg

Possible Moves: Tackle, Bubble, Supersonic, Bubble Beam, Confuse Ray, Wing Attack, Headbutt, Water Pulse, Wide Guard, Take Down, Agility, Air Slash, Aqua Ring, Bounce, Hydro Pump

Mantyke → Mantine

MARACTUS
Cactus Pokémon

TYPE: GRASS

Maractus live in dry places, where they dance with rhythmic movements of their prickly limbs to keep others away. This motion gives off a sound like the shaking of maracas.

How to Say It: mah-RAK-tus
Imperial Height: 3'03''
Imperial Weight: 61.7 lbs.
Metric Height: 1.0 m
Metric Weight: 28.0 kg

Possible Moves: Spikey Shield, Peck, Absorb, Sweet Scent, Growth, Pin Missile, Mega Drain, Synthesis, Cotton Spore, Needle Arm, Giga Drain, Acupressure, Ingrain, Petal Dance, Sucker Punch, Sunny Day, Petal Blizzard, Solar Beam, Cotton Guard, After You

Does not evolve

MAREANIE
Brutal Star Pokémon

REGION: Alola

TYPE: POISON-WATER

Mareanie lives at the bottom of the sea or along the beach. It attacks with its head spike, which delivers poison that can weaken a foe. It's often tempted by the brightly colored coral of Corsola.

How to Say It: muh-REE-nee
Imperial Height: 1'04''
Imperial Weight: 17.6 lbs.
Metric Height: 0.4 m
Metric Weight: 8.0 kg

Possible Moves: Poison Sting, Peck, Bite, Toxic Spikes, Wide Guard, Toxic, Venoshock, Spike Cannon, Recover, Poison Jab, Venom Drench, Pin Missile, Liquidation

Mareanie ⇒ Toxapex

MAREEP
Wool Pokémon

REGIONS:
Alola
Johto
Kalos
(Coastal)

TYPE: ELECTRIC

Although Mareep looks cuddly, be careful when you pet it—its fleece is charged with static electricity that could give you a shock! Clothing made from Mareep fleece undergoes a special process to resist the charge.

How to Say It: mah-REEP
Imperial Height: 2'00''
Imperial Weight: 17.2 lbs.
Metric Height: 0.6 m
Metric Weight: 7.8 kg

Possible Moves: Tackle, Growl, Thunder Wave, Thunder Shock, Cotton Spore, Charge, Take Down, Electro Ball, Confuse Ray, Power Gem, Discharge, Cotton Guard, Signal Beam, Light Screen, Thunder

Mareep ⇒ Flaaffy ⇒ Ampharos ⇒ Mega Ampharos

MARILL
Aqua Mouse Pokémon

TYPE: WATER-FAIRY

When Marill dives underwater in search of plants to eat, its buoyant tail bobs on the surface. The tail is flexible enough to wrap around a tree as an anchor.

How to Say It: MARE-rull
Imperial Height: 1'04''
Imperial Weight: 18.7 lbs.

Metric Height: 0.4 m
Metric Weight: 8.5 kg

Possible Moves: Tackle, Water Gun, Tail Whip, Water Sport, Bubble, Defense Curl, Rollout, Bubble Beam, Helping Hand, Aqua Tail, Double-Edge, Aqua Ring, Rain Dance, Superpower, Hydro Pump, Play Rough

Azurill ⇨ Marill ⇨ Azumarill

MAROWAK
Bone Keeper Pokémon

REGIONS:
Kalos
(Coastal)
Kanto

TYPE: GROUND

Evolution has transformed this formerly weak and frightened Pokémon into a fearsome foe. Marowak uses bones as projectile weapons against those it considers enemies.

How to Say It: MARE-oh-wack
Imperial Height: 3'03''
Imperial Weight: 99.2 lbs.
Metric Height: 1.0 m
Metric Weight: 45.0 kg

Possible Moves: Growl, Tail Whip, Bone Club, Headbutt, Leer, Focus Energy, Bonemerang, Rage, False Swipe, Thrash, Fling, Stomping Tantrum, Endeavor, Double-Edge, Retaliate

Cubone   Marowak

ALOLAN MAROWAK
Bone Keeper Pokémon

REGION:
Alola

TYPE: FIRE-GHOST

The flaming bone that Marowak spins like a baton once belonged to its mother, and it's protected by its mother's spirit. It grieves for its fallen companions, visiting their graves along the roadside.

How to Say It: uh-LO-luhn MARE-oh-wack
Imperial Height: 3'03''
Imperial Weight: 75.0 lbs.
Metric Height: 1.0 m
Metric Weight: 34.0 kg

Possible Moves: Growl, Tail Whip, Bone Club, Flame Wheel, Leer, Hex, Bonemerang, Will-O-Wisp, Shadow Bone, Thrash, Fling, Stomping Tantrum, Endeavor, Flare Blitz, Retaliate, Bone Rush

Cubone   Alolan Marowak

REGION: Alola

MARSHADOW
Gloomdweller Pokémon

MYTHICAL POKÉMON

TYPE: FIGHTING-GHOST

Marshadow is a very cautious Pokémon. It sinks into the shadow and observes what is going on around it in such a way that no one else will notice it. This may be the reason why it is so rarely seen.

How to Say It: mar-SHAD-oh
Imperial Height: 2'04''
Imperial Weight: 48.9 lbs.

Metric Height: 0.7 m
Metric Weight: 22.2 kg

Possible Moves: Laser Focus, Assurance, Fire Punch, Thunder Punch, Ice Punch, Drain Punch, Counter, Pursuit, Shadow Sneak, Force Palm, Feint, Rolling Kick, Copycat, Shadow Punch, Role Play, Jump Kick, Psych Up, Spectral Thief, Close Combat, Sucker Punch, Endeavor

Zenith Marshadow

Does not evolve

267

MARSHTOMP
Mud Fish Pokémon

REGION: Hoenn

TYPE: WATER-GROUND

When the tide goes out, Marshtomp loves to play in the mud. Its well-developed hind legs offer stability, so it can travel over mud faster than it can swim.

How to Say It: MARSH-stomp
Imperial Height: 2'04''
Imperial Weight: 61.7 lbs.
Metric Height: 0.7 m
Metric Weight: 28.0 kg

Possible Moves: Mud Shot, Tackle, Growl, Water Gun, Mud-Slap, Foresight, Bide, Mud Sport, Rock Slide, Protect, Muddy Water, Take Down, Earthquake, Endeavor

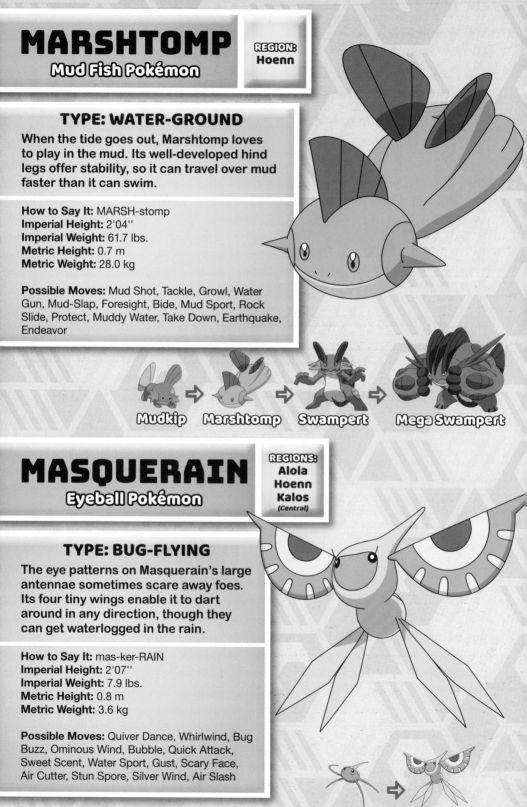

Mudkip ⇒ Marshtomp ⇒ Swampert ⇒ Mega Swampert

MASQUERAIN
Eyeball Pokémon

REGIONS: Alola Hoenn Kalos (Central)

TYPE: BUG-FLYING

The eye patterns on Masquerain's large antennae sometimes scare away foes. Its four tiny wings enable it to dart around in any direction, though they can get waterlogged in the rain.

How to Say It: mas-ker-RAIN
Imperial Height: 2'07''
Imperial Weight: 7.9 lbs.
Metric Height: 0.8 m
Metric Weight: 3.6 kg

Possible Moves: Quiver Dance, Whirlwind, Bug Buzz, Ominous Wind, Bubble, Quick Attack, Sweet Scent, Water Sport, Gust, Scary Face, Air Cutter, Stun Spore, Silver Wind, Air Slash

Surskit ⇒ Masquerain

TYPE: STEEL-FAIRY

Don't be fooled by Mawile's cute appearance. It distracts foes with a smile, then attacks using the massive jaws on the back of its head. Because the jaws don't have any taste buds, Mawile also uses them to eat foods that it dislikes.

How to Say It: MAW-while
Imperial Height: 2'00''
Imperial Weight: 25.4 lbs.
Metric Height: 0.6 m
Metric Weight: 11.5 kg

Possible Moves: Play Rough, Iron Head, Taunt, Growl, Fairy Wind, Astonish, Fake Tears, Bite, Sweet Scent, Vice Grip, Feint Attack, Baton Pass, Crunch, Iron Defense, Sucker Punch, Stockpile, Swallow, Spit Up

MAWILE
Deceiver Pokémon

MEGA MAWILE
Deceiver Pokémon

TYPE: STEEL-FAIRY

Imperial Height: 3'03''
Imperial Weight: 51.8 lbs.
Metric Height: 1.0 m
Metric Weight: 23.5 kg

Mawile   Mega Mawile

MEDICHAM

Meditate Pokémon

TYPE: FIGHTING-PSYCHIC

Medicham has developed a sixth sense and psychic powers through long meditation training. It can disappear into its mountain home if danger approaches.

How to Say It: MED-uh-cham
Imperial Height: 4'03''
Imperial Weight: 69.4 lbs.
Metric Height: 1.3 m
Metric Weight: 31.5 kg

Possible Moves: Zen Headbutt, Fire Punch, Thunder Punch, Ice Punch, Bide, Meditate, Confusion, Detect, Endure, Hidden Power, Mind Reader, Feint, Calm Mind, Force Palm, High Jump Kick, Psych Up, Acupressure, Power Trick, Reversal, Recover, Counter

MEGA MEDICHAM

Meditate Pokémon

TYPE: FIGHTING-PSYCHIC

Imperial Height: 4'03''
Imperial Weight: 69.4 lbs.
Metric Height: 1.3 m
Metric Weight: 31.5 kg

Meditite ⇨ **Medicham** ⇨ **Mega Medicham**

MEDITITE
Meditate Pokémon

TYPE:
FIGHTING-PSYCHIC

Through intense meditation and extreme hunger, Meditite works hard to train its mental powers.

How to Say It: MED-uh-tite
Imperial Height: 2'00''
Imperial Weight: 24.7 lbs.
Metric Height: 0.6 m
Metric Weight: 11.2 kg

Possible Moves: Bide, Meditate, Confusion, Detect, Endure, Feint, Force Palm, Hidden Power, Calm Mind, Mind Readers, High Jump Kick, Psyche Up, Acupressure, Power Trick, Reversal, Recover, Counter

Meditite ⇨ **Medicham** ⇨ **Mega Medicham**

MEGANIUM
Herb Pokémon

TYPE: GRASS

Meganium's flower wafts a soothing aroma. During a battle, the fragrance grows stronger as this Pokémon attempts to calm its enemies.

How to Say It: meg-GAY-nee-um
Imperial Height: 5'11''
Imperial Weight: 221.6 lbs.
Metric Height: 1.8 m
Metric Weight: 100.5 kg

Possible Moves: Petal Dance, Petal Blizzard, Tackle, Growl, Razor Leaf, Poison Powder, Synthesis, Reflect, Magical Leaf, Natural Gift, Petal Dance, Sweet Scent, Light Screen, Body Slam, Safeguard, Aromatherapy, Solar Beam

 Chikorita ⇨ **Bayleef** ⇨ **Meganium**

271

MELOETTA
Melody Pokémon

REGION: Unova

MYTHICAL POKÉMON

TYPE: NORMAL-PSYCHIC

When Meloetta sings, its voice can control the emotions of people or Pokémon. The beautiful melodies of this Mythical Pokémon can bring aching sadness or radiant joy.

How to Say It: mell-oh-ET-tuh
Imperial Height: 2'00''
Imperial Weight: 14.3 lbs.
Metric Height: 0.6 m
Metric Weight: 6.5 kg

Possible Moves: Round, Quick Attack, Confusion, Sing, Teeter Dance, Acrobatics, Psybeam, Echoed Voice, U-turn, Wake-Up Slap, Psychic, Hyper Voice, Role Play, Close Combat, Perish Song

Aria Forme

Pirouette Forme

Does not evolve

MEOWSTIC
Constraint Pokémon

TYPE: PSYCHIC

When Meowstic unfolds its ears, the psychic blast created by the eyeball patterns inside can pulverize heavy machinery. It keeps its ears tightly folded unless it's in danger.

How to Say It: MYOW-stik
Imperial Height: 2'00''
Imperial Weight: 18.7 lbs.
Metric Height: 0.6 m
Metric Weight: 8.5 kg

Possible Moves (male): Quick Guard, Mean Look, Helping Hand, Scratch, Leer, Covet, Confusion, Light Screen, Psybeam, Fake Out, Disarming Voice, Psyshock, Charm, Miracle Eye, Reflect, Psychic, Role Play, Imprison, Sucker Punch, Misty Terrain

Possible Moves (female): Stored Power, Me First, Magical Leaf, Scratch, Leer, Covet, Confusion, Light Screen, Psybeam, Fake Out, Disarming Voice, Psyshock, Charge Beam, Shadow Ball, Extrasensory, Psychic, Role Play, Signal Beam, Sucker Punch, Future Sight

Male Form

Female Form

Espurr → Meowstic (Male Form)

Espurr → Meowstic (Female Form)

273

MEOWTH
Scratch Cat Pokémon

REGION: Kanto

TYPE: NORMAL

Meowth lazes about during the day and becomes active at night, when it roams city streets looking for coins and other shiny objects. It has developed a rivalry with Murkrow.

How to Say It: mee-OWTH
Imperial Height: 1'04''
Imperial Weight: 9.3 lbs.
Metric Height: 0.4 m
Metric Weight: 4.2 kg

Possible Moves: Scratch, Growl, Bite, Fake Out, Fury Swipes, Screech, Feint Attack, Taunt, Pay Day, Slash, Nasty Plot, Assurance, Captivate, Night Slash, Feint

Meowth   Persian

ALOLAN MEOWTH
Scratch Cat Pokémon

REGION: Alola

TYPE: DARK

Meowth is very vain about the golden Charm on its forehead, becoming enraged if any dirt dulls its bright surface. These crafty Pokémon are not native to Alola, but thanks to human interference, their population has surged.

How to Say It: uh-LO-luhn mee-OWTH
Imperial Height: 1'04''
Imperial Weight: 9.3 lbs.
Metric Height: 0.4 m
Metric Weight: 4.2 kg

Possible Moves: Scratch, Growl, Bite, Fake Out, Fury Swipes, Screech, Feint Attack, Taunt, Pay Day, Slash, Nasty Plot, Assurance, Captivate, Night Slash, Feint, Dark Pulse

Alolan Meowth   Alolan Persian

TYPE: PSYCHIC

According to legend, Mesprit brought the first taste of joy and sorrow to people's hearts. It is known as "The Being of Emotion."

How to Say It: MESS-prit
Imperial Height: 1'00''
Imperial Weight: 0.7 lbs.
Metric Height: 0.3 m
Metric Weight: 0.3 kg

Possible Moves: Rest, Confusion, Imprison, Protect, Swift, Lucky Chant, Future Sight, Charm, Extrasensory, Copycat, Natural Gift, Healing Wish

REGION: Sinnoh

MESPRIT
Emotion Pokémon

LEGENDARY POKÉMON

Does not evolve

METAGROSS

Iron Leg Pokémon

REGIONS:
Alola
Hoenn

TYPE: STEEL-PSYCHIC

Metagross is formed when two Metang combine. It is intimidating both physically and mentally—it can easily pin a foe underneath its massive steel body, and its four brains perform complicated calculations in the blink of an eye.

How to Say It: MET-uh-gross
Imperial Height: 5'03''
Imperial Weight: 1,212.5 lbs.
Metric Height: 1.6 m
Metric Weight: 550.0 kg

Possible Moves: Hammer Arm, Confusion, Metal Claw, Magnet Rise, Take Down, Pursuit, Bullet Punch, Miracle Eye, Zen Headbutt, Scary Face, Psychic, Agility, Meteor Mash, Iron Defense, Hyper Beam

MEGA METAGROSS

Iron Leg Pokémon

TYPE: STEEL-PSYCHIC
Imperial Height: 8'02''
Imperial Weight: 2,078.7 lbs.
Metric Height: 2.5 m
Metric Weight: 942.9 kg

Beldum ⇨ Metang ⇨ Metagross ⇨ Mega Metagross

TYPE: STEEL-PSYCHIC

Metang is formed when two Beldum combine. This doubles their psychic power but does not boost their intelligence. Metang is always seeking magnetic minerals and is particularly drawn to Nosepass.

How to Say It: met-TANG
Imperial Height: 3'11''
Imperial Weight: 446.4 lbs.
Metric Height: 1.2 m
Metric Weight: 202.5 kg

Possible Moves: Confusion, Metal Claw, Magnet Rise, Take Down, Pursuit, Bullet Punch, Miracle Eye, Zen Headbutt, Scary Face, Psychic, Agility, Meteor Mash, Iron Defense, Hyper Beam

REGIONS:
Alola
Hoenn

METANG
Iron Claw Pokémon

Beldum ⇨ Metang ⇨ Metagross ⇨ Mega Metagross

REGIONS:
Alola
Kalos
(Central)
Kanto

METAPOD
Cocoon Pokémon

TYPE: BUG

Inside Metapod's hard shell, its body is soft and vulnerable. It takes care not to move around too much or get into serious battles for fear of breaking the shell.

How to Say It: MET-uh-pod
Imperial Height: 2'04''
Imperial Weight: 21.8 lbs.
Metric Height: 0.7 m
Metric Weight: 9.9 kg

Possible Move: Harden

Caterpie ⇨ Metapod ⇨ Butterfree

MEW
New Species Pokémon

REGION:
Kanto

MYTHICAL POKÉMON

TYPE: PSYCHIC

It is said that within Mew's cells rests the entirety of the Pokémon genetic code. This Mythical Pokémon can turn invisible to keep others from noticing it.

How to Say It: MUE
Imperial Height: 1'04''
Imperial Weight: 8.8 lbs.

Metric Height: 0.4 m
Metric Weight: 4.0 kg

Possible Moves: Pound, Reflect Type, Transform, Mega Punch, Metronome, Psychic, Barrier, Ancient Power, Amnesia, Me First, Baton Pass, Nasty Plot, Aura Sphere

Does not evolve

MEWTWO
Genetic Pokémon

LEGENDARY POKÉMON

TYPE: PSYCHIC

Scientists created Mewtwo by manipulating its genes. If only they could have given it a sense of compassion . . .

How to Say It: MUE-TOO
Imperial Height: 6'07''
Imperial Weight: 269.0 lbs.

Metric Height: 2.0 m
Metric Weight: 122.0 kg

Possible Moves: Laser Focus, Psywave, Confusion, Disable, Safeguard, Swift, Future Sight, Psych Up, Miracle Eye, Psycho Cut, Power Swap, Guard Swap, Recover, Psychic, Barrier, Aura Sphere, Amnesia, Mist, Me First, Psystrike

MEGA MEWTWO X
Genetic Pokémon

TYPE: PSYCHIC-FIGHTING

Imperial Height: 7'07''
Imperial Weight: 280.0 lbs.
Metric Height: 2.3 m
Metric Weight: 127.0 kg

MEGA MEWTWO Y
Genetic Pokémon

TYPE: PSYCHIC

Imperial Height: 4'11''
Imperial Weight: 72.8 lbs.
Metric Height: 1.5 m
Metric Weight: 33.0 kg

Mega
Mewtwo X

Mewtwo

Mega
Mewtwo Y

MIENFOO

Martial Arts Pokémon

REGIONS:
Alola
Kalos
(Coastal)
Unova

TYPE: FIGHTING

As the sun climbs in the sky, Mienfoo gather to train, moving in slow unison as they practice flowing through their battle poses. Different packs of Mienfoo use different poses.

How to Say It: MEEN-FOO
Imperial Height: 2'11''
Imperial Weight: 44.1 lbs.
Metric Height: 0.9 m
Metric Weight: 20.0 kg

Possible Moves: Pound, Meditate, Detect, Fake Out, Double Slap, Swift, Calm Mind, Force Palm, Drain Punch, Jump Kick, U-turn, Quick Guard, Bounce, High Jump Kick, Reversal, Aura Sphere

Mienfoo   Mienshao

MIENSHAO

Martial Arts Pokémon

REGIONS:
Alola
Kalos
(Coastal)
Unova

TYPE: FIGHTING

Mienshao signals its entry into battle with a strange cry. As it wears down its opponent with an onslaught of lightning-fast kicks and arm chops, it carefully builds up its own power to prepare for its finishing move.

How to Say It: MEEN-SHAU
Imperial Height: 4'07''
Imperial Weight: 78.3 lbs.
Metric Height: 1.4 m
Metric Weight: 35.5 kg

Possible Moves: Aura Sphere, Reversal, Pound, Meditate, Detect, Fake Out, Double Slap, Swift, Calm Mind, Force Palm, Drain Punch, Jump Kick, U-turn, Wide Guard, Bounce, High Jump Kick

Mienfoo   Mienshao

TYPE: DARK

Mightyena sounds a deep growl before attacking. In the wild, these Pokémon live together in packs.

How to Say It: MY-tee-EH-nah
Imperial Height: 3'03''
Imperial Weight: 81.6 lbs.
Metric Height: 1.0 m
Metric Weight: 37.0 kg

Possible Moves: Snarl, Fire Fang, Thunder Fang, Ice Fang Crunch, Tackle, Howl, Sand Attack, Bite, Odor Sleuth, Roar, Swagger, Assurance, Scary Face, Taunt, Yawn, Embargo, Take Down, Sucker Punch, Play Rough

MIGHTYENA
Bite Pokémon

Poochyena **Mightyena**

TYPE: WATER

Milotic sometimes serves as a muse to artists who wish to capture its astounding beauty in their work. Just looking at this lovely Pokémon can be enough to calm one's nerves or stop a fight.

How to Say It: MY-low-tic
Imperial Height: 20'04''
Imperial Weight: 357.1 lbs.
Metric Height: 6.2 m
Metric Weight: 162.0 kg

Possible Moves: Water Pulse, Wrap, Water Gun, Water Sport, Refresh, Disarming Voice, Twister, Aqua Ring, Captivate, Dragon Tail, Recover, Aqua Tail, Attract, Safeguard, Coil, Hydro Pump, Rain Dance

MILOTIC
Tender Pokémon

Feebas **Milotic**

MILTANK

Milk Cow Pokémon

REGIONS:
Alola
Johto
Kalos
(Coastal)

TYPE: NORMAL

The milk that Miltank produces is calorie-dense and highly nutritious. Although it's best known for this milk, it can also hold its own in battle thanks to its strength and toughness.

How to Say It: MILL-tank
Imperial Height: 3'11''
Imperial Weight: 166.4 lbs.
Metric Height: 1.2 m
Metric Weight: 75.5 kg

Possible Moves: Tackle, Growl, Defense Curl, Stomp, Milk Drink, Bide, Rollout, Body Slam, Zen Headbutt, Captivate, Gyro Ball, Heal Bell, Wake-Up Slap

Does not evolve

MIME JR.

Mime Pokémon

REGIONS:
Alola
Kalos
(Coastal)
Sinnoh

TYPE: PSYCHIC-FAIRY

Mime Jr. is constantly working to perfect its mimicry skills, but it tends to become overly excited when it's doing well. As a result, it forgets that it was even imitating something in the first place.

How to Say It: mime JOO-nyur
Imperial Height: 2'00''
Imperial Weight: 28.7 lbs.
Metric Height: 0.6 m
Metric Weight: 13.0 kg

Possible Moves: Tickle, Barrier, Pound, Confusion, Copycat, Meditate, Double Slap, Mimic, Encore, Light Screen, Reflect, Psybeam, Substitute, Recycle, Trick, Psychic, Role Play, Baton Pass, Safeguard

Mime Jr.   Mr. Mime

TYPE: GHOST-FAIRY

What does Mimikyu look like? No one really knows, but apparently it's terrifying—it always hides underneath an old rag so it doesn't scare anyone while it's trying to make friends.

How to Say It: MEE-mee-kyoo
Imperial Height: 0'08''
Imperial Weight: 1.5 lbs.
Metric Height: 0.2 m
Metric Weight: 0.7 kg

Possible Moves: Wood Hammer, Splash, Scratch, Astonish, Copycat, Double Team, Baby-Doll Eyes, Shadow Sneak, Mimic, Feint Attack, Charm, Slash, Shadow Claw, Hone Claws, Play Rough, Pain Split

REGION:
Alola

MIMIKYU
Disguise Pokémon

Does not evolve

REGIONS:
Alola
Unova

MINCCINO
Chinchilla Pokémon

TYPE: NORMAL

Minccino is fussy about keeping its habitat clean. It sweeps away dust and dirt with its fluffy tail, and when its tail gets too dirty for its taste, it seeks out a clear spring for a very long bath.

How to Say It: min-CHEE-noh
Imperial Height: 1'04''
Imperial Weight: 12.8 lbs.
Metric Height: 0.4 m
Metric Weight: 5.8 kg

Possible Moves: Pound, Baby-Doll Eyes, Helping Hand, Tickle, Double Slap, Encore, Swift, Sing, Tail Slap, Charm, Wake-Up Slap, Echoed Voice, Slam, Captivate, Hyper Voice, Last Resort, After You

Minccino ⇨ **Cinccino**

MINIOR
Meteor Pokémon

REGION: Alola

Meteor Form

TYPE: ROCK-FLYING

Minior came into being when tiny particles in the ozone layer underwent mutation. When its shell becomes too heavy, it falls to the ground, and the impact can knock its shell clean off.

How to Say It: MIN-ee-or
Imperial Height: 1'00'' (both forms)
Imperial Weight: Meteor Form: 88.2 lbs.
                    Red Core Form: 0.7 lbs.
Metric Height: 0.3 m (both forms)
Metric Weight: Meteor Form: 40.0 kg
                   Red Core Form: 0.3 kg

Possible Moves: Tackle, Defense Curl, Rollout, Confuse Ray, Swift, Ancient Power, Self-Destruct, Stealth Rock, Take Down, Autotomize, Cosmic Power, Power Gem, Double-Edge, Shell Smash, Explosion

Red Core Form

Does not evolve

MINUN
Cheering Pokémon

REGIONS: Hoenn Kalos *(Central)*

TYPE: ELECTRIC

Minun shoots out sparks when cheering on its teammates. If the battle isn't going well, the spark showers get more intense.

How to Say It: MY-nun
Imperial Height: 1'04''
Imperial Weight: 9.3 lbs.
Metric Height: 0.4 m
Metric Weight: 4.2 kg

Possible Moves: Nuzzle, Play Nice, Growl, Thunder Wave, Quick Attack, Helping Hand, Spark, Encore, Switcheroo, Swift, Electro Ball, Copycat, Fake Tears, Charge, Discharge, Baton Pass, Agility, Trump Card, Thunder, Nasty Plot, Entrainment

Does not evolve

MISDREAVUS
Screech Pokémon

TYPE: GHOST

Misdreavus gets its energy from scaring people and soaking up their fear. One of its favorite tricks is hiding in an otherwise empty room and making a noise that sounds like someone weeping.

How to Say It: mis-DREE-vuss
Imperial Height: 2'04''
Imperial Weight: 2.2 lbs.
Metric Height: 0.7 m
Metric Weight: 1.0 kg

Possible Moves: Growl, Psywave, Spite, Astonish, Confuse Ray, Mean Look, Hex, Psybeam, Pain Split, Payback, Shadow Ball, Perish Song, Grudge, Power Gem

Misdreavus ⇨ Mismagius

MISMAGIUS
Magical Pokémon

TYPE: GHOST

Mismagius wields an impressive arsenal of tricks to torment people—launching curses, creating visions of terror, and casting love spells. Some people have been fooled into thinking the last one is harmless fun.

How to Say It: miss-MAG-ee-us
Imperial Height: 2'11''
Imperial Weight: 9.7 lbs.
Metric Height: 0.9 m
Metric Weight: 4.4 kg

Possible Moves: Mystical Fire, Power Gem, Phantom Force, Lucky Chant, Magical Leaf, Growl, Psywave, Spite, Astonish

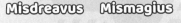

Misdreavus ⇨ Mismagius

285

MOLTRES
Flame Pokémon

LEGENDARY POKÉMON

TYPE: FIRE-FLYING

When Moltres gets hurt, some say it dives into an active volcano and heals itself by bathing in lava. This Legendary Pokémon can give off flames and control fire.

How to Say It: MOHL-trace
Imperial Height: 6'07''
Imperial Weight: 132.3 lbs.
Metric Height: 2.0 m
Metric Weight: 60.0 kg

Possible Moves: Roost, Hurricane, Sky Attack, Heat Wave, Wing Attack, Ember, Fire Spin, Agility, Endure, Ancient Power, Flamethrower, Safeguard, Air Slash, Sunny Day, Solar Beam, Burn Up

Does not evolve

MONFERNO
Playful Pokémon

TYPE: FIRE-FIGHTING

An excellent climber, Monferno can strike from above. It can flare up its tail flame to keep enemies at bay.

How to Say It: mon-FUR-no
Imperial Height: 2'11''
Imperial Weight: 48.5 lbs.
Metric Height: 0.9 m
Metric Weight: 22.0 kg

Possible Moves: Scratch, Leer, Ember, Taunt, Mach Punch, Fury Swipes, Flame Wheel, Feint, Torment, Close Combat, Fire Spin, Acrobatics, Slack Off, Flare Blitz

Chimchar ⇨ Monferno ⇨ Infernape

MORELULL
Illuminating Pokémon

TYPE: GRASS-FAIRY

The spores that Morelull gives off flicker with a hypnotic light that sends viewers to sleep. During the day, it plants itself beside a tree to absorb nutrients from the roots while it naps.

How to Say It: MORE-eh-lull
Imperial Height: 0'08''
Imperial Weight: 3.3 lbs.
Metric Height: 0.2 m
Metric Weight: 1.5 kg

Possible Moves: Absorb, Astonish, Flash, Moonlight, Mega Drain, Sleep Powder, Ingrain, Confuse Ray, Giga Drain, Strength Sap, Spore, Moonblast, Dream Eater, Spotlight

Morelull ⇨ Shiinotic

287

MOTHIM
Moth Pokémon

REGIONS:
Kalos
(Central)
Sinnoh

TYPE: BUG-FLYING

Mothim loves the taste of Combee's honey. Sometimes it will raid a hive at night to steal the sweet substance.

How to Say It: MOTH-im
Imperial Height: 2'11''
Imperial Weight: 51.4 lbs.
Metric Height: 0.9 m
Metric Weight: 23.3 kg

Possible Moves: Tackle, Protect, Bug Bite, Hidden Power, Confusion, Gust, Poison Powder, Psybeam, Camouflage, Silver Wind, Air Slash, Psychic, Lunge, Bug Buzz, Quiver Dance

Burmy
(Male Form)   **Mothim**

MR. MIME
Barrier Pokémon

REGIONS:
Alola
Kalos
(Coastal)
Kanto

TYPE: PSYCHIC-FAIRY

Mr. Mime often pretends to be trapped behind an invisible wall. It's a common pantomime trick, but Mr. Mime can make those walls real, and it's been known to attack those who aren't impressed.

How to Say It: MIS-ter MIME
Imperial Height: 4'03''
Imperial Weight: 120.1 lbs.
Metric Height: 1.3 m
Metric Weight: 54.5 kg

Possible Moves: Misty Terrain, Magical Leaf, Quick Guard, Wide Guard, Power Swap, Guard Swap, Barrier, Confusion, Copycat, Meditate, Double Slap, Mimic, Psywave, Encore, Light Screen, Reflect, Psybeam, Substitute, Recycle, Trick, Psychic, Role Play, Baton Pass, Safeguard

Mime Jr.   Mr. Mime

TYPE: GROUND

MUDBRAY
Donkey Pokémon

Mudbray just loves to get dirty, but it isn't just for fun. Playing in the mud actually gives it better traction for running—when its hooves are covered in dirt, they're less likely to slip, and it can run faster.

How to Say It: MUD-bray
Imperial Height: 3'03''
Imperial Weight: 242.5 lbs.
Metric Height: 1.0 m
Metric Weight: 110.0 kg

Possible Moves: Mud-Slap, Mud Sport, Rototiller, Bulldoze, Double Kick, Stomp, Bide, High Horsepower, Iron Defense, Heavy Slam, Counter, Earthquake, Mega Kick, Superpower

Mudbray ⇨ Mudsdale

TYPE: WATER

MUDKIP
Mud Fish Pokémon

Because its fin is so sensitive to the motion of air and water, Mudkip knows what's going on nearby without opening its eyes. The flared gills on its cheeks allow it to breathe underwater.

How to Say It: MUD-kip
Imperial Height: 1'04''
Imperial Weight: 16.8 lbs.
Metric Height: 0.4 m
Metric Weight: 7.6 kg

Possible Moves: Tackle, Growl, Mud-Slap, Water Gun, Bide, Foresight, Mud Sport, Take Down, Whirlpool, Protect, Hydro Pump, Endeavor, Rock Throw

Mudkip ⇨ Marshtomp ⇨ Swampert ⇨ Mega Swampert

MUDSDALE
Draft Horse Pokémon

REGION:
Alola

TYPE: GROUND

With the help of the mud that coats its hooves, Mudsdale can deliver heavy kicks powerful enough to demolish a big truck. The mud it produces is weather-resistant, and people used to use it to shore up their houses.

How to Say It: MUDZ-dale
Imperial Height: 8'02''
Imperial Weight: 2,028.3 lbs.
Metric Height: 2.5 m
Metric Weight: 920.0 kg

Possible Moves: Mud-Slap, Mud Sport, Rototiller, Bulldoze, Double Kick, Stomp, Bide, High Horsepower, Iron Defense, Heavy Slam, Counter, Earthquake, Mega Kick, Superpower

Mudbray ⇒ Mudsdale

MUK
Sludge Pokémon

TYPE: POISON

Muk really stinks, but some Trainers are fond of it, terrible smell and all. Recent efforts to reduce pollution and clean up the environment have also reduced this Pokémon's numbers.

How to Say It: MUCK
Imperial Height: 3'11''
Imperial Weight: 66.1 lbs.
Metric Height: 1.2 m
Metric Weight: 30.0 kg

Possible Moves: Venom Drench, Pound, Poison Gas, Harden, Mud-Slap, Disable, Mud Bomb, Minimize, Fling, Sludge Bomb, Sludge Wave, Screech, Gunk Shot, Acid Armor, Memento

Grimer ⇒ Muk

REGION:
Alola

ALOLAN MUK
Sludge Pokémon

TYPE: POISON-DARK

Muk's bright and colorful markings are the result of chemical changes in its body, caused by its diet of all sorts of garbage. It's generally a pleasant and friendly companion, but if it gets hungry, it can turn destructive.

How to Say It: uh-LO-luhn MUCK
Imperial Height: 3'03''
Imperial Weight: 114.6 lbs.
Metric Height: 1.0 m
Metric Weight: 52.0 kg

Possible Moves: Venom Drench, Pound, Poison Gas, Harden, Bite, Disable, Acid Spray, Poison Fang, Minimize, Fling, Knock Off, Crunch, Screech, Gunk Shot, Acid Armor, Belch, Memento

Alolan Grimer ⇒ Alolan Muk

MUNCHLAX
Big Eater Pokémon

TYPE: NORMAL

Munchlax has an insatiable appetite, and it isn't too picky about flavors. To sustain itself, it has to keep eating, swallowing just about anything that looks edible.

How to Say It: MUNCH-lax
Imperial Height: 2'00''
Imperial Weight: 231.5 lbs.
Metric Height: 0.6 m
Metric Weight: 105.0 kg

Possible Moves: Last Resort, Recycle, Lick, Metronome, Odor Sleuth, Tackle, Defense Curl, Amnesia, Chip Away, Screech, Body Slam, Stockpile, Swallow, Rollout, Fling, Belly Drum, Natural Gift, Snatch

Munchlax   Snorlax

MUNNA
Dream Eater Pokémon

REGION:
Unova

TYPE: PSYCHIC

When people and Pokémon sleep, Munna appears to eat their dreams and nightmares. After eating a happy dream, it gives off pink mist.

How to Say It: MOON-nuh
Imperial Height: 2'00''
Imperial Weight: 51.4 lbs.
Metric Height: 0.6 m
Metric Weight: 23.3 kg

Possible Moves: Psywave, Defense Curl, Lucky Chant, Yawn, Psybeam, Imprison, Moonlight, Hypnosis, Zen Headbutt, Synchronoise, Nightmare, Future Sight, Calm Mind, Psychic, Dream Eater, Telekinesis, Stored Power

Munna   Musharna

TYPE: DARK-FLYING

It's unusual to see a Murkrow flying around during the day—they generally sleep until dusk and do their flying at night. They keep an eye out for sparkly objects, which they sometimes offer as a gift to a Trainer.

How to Say It: MUR-crow
Imperial Height: 1'08''
Imperial Weight: 4.6 lbs.
Metric Height: 0.5 m
Metric Weight: 2.1 kg

Possible Moves: Peck, Astonish, Pursuit, Haze, Wing Attack, Night Shade, Assurance, Taunt, Feint Attack, Mean Look, Foul Play, Tailwind, Sucker Punch, Torment, Quash

REGIONS:
Alola
Johto
Kalos
(Mountain)

MURKROW
Darkness Pokémon

Murkrow ➡ Honchkrow

TYPE: PSYCHIC

The dream mist that rises from Musharna's forehead is influenced by the dreams it eats. It can take on many different colors.

How to Say It: moo-SHAHR-nuh
Imperial Height: 3'07''
Imperial Weight: 133.4 lbs.
Metric Height: 1.1 m
Metric Weight: 60.5 kg

Possible Moves: Psychic Terrain, Defense Curl, Lucky Chant, Psybeam, Hypnosis

REGION:
Unova

MUSHARNA
Drowsing Pokémon

Munna ➡ Musharna

NAGANADEL
Poison Pin Pokémon

ULTRA BEAST

TYPE:
POISON-DRAGON

Naganadel, one of the mysterious Ultra Beasts, stores a poisonous liquid in vast quantities inside its body. The poison, which gives off an eerie glow and adheres to anything it touches, can be fired from its needles.

How to Say It: NAW-guh-NAW-duhl
Imperial Height: 11'10''
Imperial Weight: 330.7 lbs.
Metric Height: 3.6 m
Metric Weight: 150.0 kg

Possible Moves: Air Cutter, Dragon Pulse, Peck, Growl, Helping Hand, Acid, Fury Attack, Venoshock, Charm, Venom Drench, Nasty Plot, Poison Jab, Toxic, Fell Stinger, Air Slash, Dragon Pulse

Poipole **Naganadel**

NATU
Tiny Bird Pokémon

TYPE: PSYCHIC-FLYING

Natu's wings aren't developed enough for flight, but it can jump high into the air, which allows it to nibble on buds growing from high branches. It has a watchful expression.

How to Say It: NAH-too
Imperial Height: 0'08''
Imperial Weight: 4.4 lbs.
Metric Height: 0.2 m
Metric Weight: 2.0 kg

Possible Moves: Peck, Leer, Night Shade, Teleport, Lucky Chant, Miracle Eye, Me First, Confuse Ray, Wish, Psycho Shift, Future Sight, Stored Power, Ominous Wind, Power Swap, Guard Swap, Psychic

Natu **Xatu**

TYPE: PSYCHIC

Some think Necrozma arrived from another world many eons ago. When it emerges from its underground slumber, it seems to absorb light for use as energy to power its laser-like blasts.

How to Say It: neh-KROHZ-muh
Imperial Height: 7'10''
Imperial Weight: 507.1 lbs.
Metric Height: 2.4 m
Metric Weight: 230.0 kg

Possible Moves: Moonlight, Morning Sun, Charge Beam, Mirror Shot, Metal Claw, Confusion, Slash, Stored Power, Rock Blast, Night Slash, Gravity, Psycho Cut, Power Gem, Autotomize, Stealth Rock, Iron Defense, Wring Out, Prismatic Laser

REGION: Alola

NECROZMA
Prism Pokémon

LEGENDARY POKÉMON

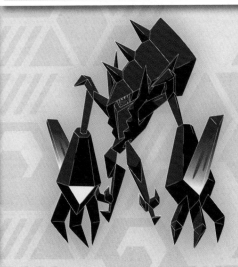

Does not evolve

TYPE: ROCK-POISON

Nihilego, one of the mysterious Ultra Beasts, can apparently infest other beings and incite them to violence. Research is inconclusive as to whether this Pokémon can think for itself, but it sometimes exhibits the behavior of a young girl.

How to Say It: NIE-uh-LEE-go
Imperial Height: 3'11''
Imperial Weight: 122.4 lbs.
Metric Height: 1.2 m
Metric Weight: 55.5 kg

Possible Moves: Power Split, Guard Split, Tickle, Acid, Constrict, Pound, Clear Smog, Psywave, Headbutt, Venoshock, Toxic Spikes, Safeguard, Power Gem, Mirror Coat, Acid Spray, Venom Drench, Stealth Rock, Wonder Room, Head Smash

REGION: Alola

NIHILEGO
Parasite Pokémon

ULTRA BEAST

Does not evolve

NIDOKING
Drill Pokémon

REGIONS:
Kalos
(Coastal)
Kanto

TYPE: POISON-GROUND

When Nidoking swings its massive tail, it can knock down a radio tower. Nothing can stand in the way of its furious rampage.

How to Say It: NEE-do-king
Imperial Height: 4'07''
Imperial Weight: 136.7 lbs.
Metric Height: 1.4 m
Metric Weight: 62.0 kg

Possible Moves: Megahorn, Peck, Focus Energy, Double Kick, Poison Sting, Chip Away, Thrash, Earth Power

Nidoran ♂ ➡ Nidorino ➡ Nidoking

NIDOQUEEN
Drill Pokémon

REGIONS:
Kalos
(Coastal)
Kanto

TYPE: POISON-GROUND

When defending its nest, Nidoqueen hurls its hard-scaled body at an intruder. The impact is often enough to send the enemy flying through the air.

How to Say It: NEE-do-kween
Imperial Height: 4'03''
Imperial Weight: 132.3 lbs.
Metric Height: 1.3 m
Metric Weight: 60.0 kg

Possible Moves: Superpower, Scratch, Tail Whip, Double Kick, Poison Sting, Chip Away, Body Slam, Earth Power

Nidoran ♀ ➡ Nidorina ➡ Nidoqueen

NIDORAN ♀
Poison Pin Pokémon

TYPE: POISON

Though Nidoran ♀ is small, it's quite dangerous. The barbs in its fur and the horn on its head are both extremely poisonous.

How to Say It: NEE-do-ran
Imperial Height: 1'04''
Imperial Weight: 15.4 lbs.
Metric Height: 0.4 m
Metric Weight: 7.0 kg

Possible Moves: Growl, Scratch, Tail Whip, Double Kick, Poison Sting, Fury Swipes, Bite, Helping Hand, Toxic Spikes, Flatter, Crunch, Captivate, Poison Fang

Nidoran ♀ → Nidorina → Nidoqueen

NIDORAN ♂
Poison Pin Pokémon

TYPE: POISON

Nidoran♂ has excellent hearing and, thanks to specialized muscles, it can move and rotate its ears to pick up the slightest sound.

How to Say It: NEE-do-ran
Imperial Height: 1'08''
Imperial Weight: 19.8 lbs.
Metric Height: 0.5 m
Metric Weight: 9.0 kg

Possible Moves: Leer, Peck, Focus Energy, Double Kick, Poison Sting, Fury Attack, Horn Attack, Helping Hand, Toxic Spikes, Flatter, Poison Jab, Captivate, Horn Drill

Nidoran ♂ → Nidorino → Nidoking

297

NIDORINA
Poison Pin Pokémon

REGIONS:
Kalos
(Coastal)
Kanto

TYPE: POISON

Nidorina are very social and become nervous on their own. When among friends, their poisonous barbs retract so they don't hurt anyone.

How to Say It: NEE-do-REE-na
Imperial Height: 2'07"
Imperial Weight: 44.1 lbs.
Metric Height: 0.8 m
Metric Weight: 20.0 kg

Possible Moves: Growl, Scratch, Tail Whip, Double Kick, Poison Sting, Fury Swipes, Bite, Helping Hand, Toxic Spikes, Flatter, Crunch, Captivate, Poison Fang

Nidoran ♀ → Nidorina → Nidoqueen

NIDORINO
Poison Pin Pokémon

REGIONS:
Kalos
(Coastal)
Kanto

TYPE: POISON

The horn on Nidorino's forehead is made of an extremely hard substance. When challenged, its body bristles with poisonous barbs.

How to Say It: NEE-do-REE-no
Imperial Height: 2'11"
Imperial Weight: 43.0 lbs.
Metric Height: 0.9 m
Metric Weight: 19.5 kg

Possible Moves: Leer, Peck, Focus Energy, Double Kick, Poison Sting, Fury Attack, Horn Attack, Helping Hand, Toxic Spikes, Flatter, Poison Jab, Captivate, Horn Drill

Nidoran ♂ → Nidorino → Nidoking

NINCADA
Trainee Pokémon

REGIONS:
Hoenn
Kalos
(Central)

TYPE: BUG-GROUND

Nincada prefers to stay out of the sun, living underground and feeding on tree roots. When Evolution approaches, it stops moving altogether.

How to Say It: nin-KAH-da
Imperial Height: 1'08''
Imperial Weight: 12.1 lbs.
Metric Height: 0.5 m
Metric Weight: 5.5 kg

Possible Moves: Scratch, Harden, Absorb, Sand Attack. Fury Swipes, Mud-Slap, Metal Claw, Mind Reader, Bide, False Swipe, Dig

Ninjask

Nincada

Shedinja

NINETALES

Fox Pokémon

TYPE: FIRE

Ninetales is capable of bending fire to its will. It can live for a thousand years and was created when nine saints merged into a single being, according to legend.

How to Say It: NINE-tails
Imperial Height: 3'07''
Imperial Weight: 43.9 lbs.
Metric Height: 1.1 m
Metric Weight: 19.9 kg

Possible Moves: Imprison, Nasty Plot, Flamethrower, Quick Attack, Confuse Ray, Safeguard

Vulpix ➡ **Ninetales**

ALOLAN NINETALES

Fox Pokémon

TYPE: ICE-FAIRY

In its frosty coat, Ninetales creates ice droplets that can be used to shower over opponents. It's generally calm and collected, but if it becomes angry, it can freeze the offenders in their tracks.

How to Say It: uh-LO-luhn NINE-tails
Imperial Height: 3'07''
Imperial Weight: 43.9 lbs.
Metric Height: 1.1 m
Metric Weight: 19.9 kg

Possible Moves: Dazzling Gleam, Imprison, Nasty Plot, Ice Beam, Ice Shard, Confuse Ray, Safeguard

Alolan Vulpix ➡ **Alolan Ninetales**

TYPE: BUG-FLYING

Ninjask moves so fast that it's hard to see, although its cry is quite audible. Proper training is a must to keep its defiant nature in check.

How to Say It: NIN-jask
Imperial Height: 2'07''
Imperial Weight: 26.5 lbs.
Metric Height: 0.8 m
Metric Weight: 12.0 kg

Possible Moves: Bug Bite, Scratch, Harden, Leech Life, Sand Attack, Fury Swipes, Mind Reader, Double Team, Fury Cutter, Screech, Swords Dance, Slash, Agility, Baton Pass, X-Scissor, Absorb

REGIONS:
Hoenn
Kalos
(Central)

NINJASK
Ninja Pokémon

Nincada

Ninjask

Shedinja

TYPE: NORMAL-FLYING

Noctowl can see through even the darkest night, so hiding in the shadows is not an option for an opponent trying to escape. A Noctowl that has swiveled its head upside down is an unhappy Noctowl—keep your distance.

How to Say It: NAHK-towl
Imperial Height: 5'03''
Imperial Weight: 89.9 lbs.
Metric Height: 1.6 m
Metric Weight: 40.8 kg

Possible Moves: Dream Eater, Sky Attack, Tackle, Growl, Foresight, Hypnosis, Peck, Uproar, Reflect, Confusion, Echoed Voice, Take Down, Air Slash, Zen Headbutt, Synchronoise, Extrasensory, Psycho Shift, Roost

REGIONS:
Alola
Johto
Kalos
(Mountain)

NOCTOWL
Owl Pokémon

Hoothoot

Noctowl

NOIBAT
Sound Wave Pokémon

REGIONS:
Alola
Kalos
(Mountain)

TYPE: FLYING-DRAGON

Noibat loves to eat different kinds of fruit, but it's a little picky about the flavor and texture. It uses its sonar to pick out only the ones that are perfectly ripe.

How to Say It: NOY-bat
Imperial Height: 1'08''
Imperial Weight: 17.6 lbs.
Metric Height: 0.5 m
Metric Weight: 8.0 kg

Possible Moves: Screech, Supersonic, Tackle, Absorb, Gust, Bite, Wing Attack, Agility, Air Cutter, Roost, Razor Wind, Tailwind, Whirlwind, Super Fang, Air Slash, Hurricane

Noibat   Noivern

NOIVERN
Sound Wave Pokémon

REGIONS:
Alola
Kalos
(Mountain)

TYPE: FLYING-DRAGON

Noivern has a reputation for being wild and uncontrollable, but some Trainers have found that offering a particularly tasty fruit is a good way to get this Pokémon on your team.

How to Say It: NOY-vurn
Imperial Height: 4'11''
Imperial Weight: 187.4 lbs.
Metric Height: 1.5 m
Metric Weight: 85.0 kg

Possible Moves: Moonlight, Boomburst, Dragon Pulse, Hurricane, Screech, Supersonic, Tackle, Absorb, Gust, Bite, Wing Attack, Agility, Air Cutter, Roost, Razor Wind, Tailwind, Whirlwind, Super Fang, Air Slash

Noibat   Noivern

TYPE: ROCK

Some Trainers bring along a Nosepass for navigation on their journey, since its magnetic nose serves as a foolproof compass. If the nose attracts metal objects, Nosepass collects them and uses them as a shield.

How to Say It: NOSE-pass
Imperial Height: 3'03''
Imperial Weight: 213.8 lbs.
Metric Height: 1.0 m
Metric Weight: 97.0 kg

Possible Moves: Tackle, Harden, Block, Rock Throw, Thunder Wave, Rest, Spark, Rock Slide, Power Gem, Rock Blast, Discharge, Sandstorm, Earth Power, Stone Edge, Lock-On, Zap Cannon

NOSEPASS
Compass Pokémon

Nosepass ⇨ **Probopass**

NUMEL
Numb Pokémon

TYPE: FIRE-GROUND

The rather dull Numel sometimes doesn't notice when it's being attacked. Its body is full of magma, so Numel takes care to stay dry. Rain can make the magma cool and harden.

How to Say It: NUM-mull
Imperial Height: 2'04''
Imperial Weight: 52.9 lbs.
Metric Height: 0.7 m
Metric Weight: 24.0 kg

Possible Moves: Growl, Tackle, Ember, Magnitude, Focus Energy, Flame Burst, Take Down, Amnesia, Lava Plume, Earth Power, Curse, Yawn, Earthquake, Flamethrower, Double-Edge

Numel ⇨ **Camerupt** ⇨ **Mega Camerupt**

NUZLEAF
Wily Pokémon

REGION:
Hoenn

TYPE: GRASS-DARK

Nuzleaf can play the leaf on its head like a flute, and the music makes listeners nervous. It lives in dense forests and doesn't like visitors.

How to Say It: NUHZ-leaf
Imperial Height: 3'03''
Imperial Weight: 61.7 lbs.
Metric Height: 1.0 m
Metric Weight: 28.0 kg

Possible Moves: Razor Leaf, Pound, Harden, Growth, Nature Power, Fake Out, Torment, Feint Attack, Razor Wind, Swagger, Extrasensory, Leaf Blade

Seedot ⇨ Nuzleaf ⇨ Shiftry

OCTILLERY
Jet Pokémon

REGIONS:
Alola
Johto
Kalos
(Coastal)

TYPE: WATER

Octillery likes to sleep in dark, isolated caves. When it's disturbed, it sprays a special kind of ink that dulls the opponent's sense of smell, giving Octillery an opportunity to flee.

How to Say It: ock-TILL-er-ree
Imperial Height: 2'11''
Imperial Weight: 62.8 lbs.
Metric Height: 0.9 m
Metric Weight: 28.5 kg

Possible Moves: Gunk Shot, Rock Blast, Water Gun, Constrict, Psybeam, Aurora Beam, Bubble Beam, Focus Energy, Octazooka, Wring Out, Signal Beam, Ice Beam, Bullet Seed, Hydro Pump, Hyper Beam, Soak

Remoraid ⇨ Octillery

TYPE: GRASS-POISON

Oddish seeks out fertile ground where it can absorb nutrients from the soil. When it finds the perfect spot, it buries itself, and its feet apparently become like tree roots.

REGIONS:
Kalos
(Central)
Kanto

ODDISH
Weed Pokémon

How to Say It: ODD-ish
Imperial Height: 1'08''
Imperial Weight: 11.9 lbs.
Metric Height: 0.5 m
Metric Weight: 5.4 kg

Possible Moves: Absorb, Growth, Sweet Scent, Acid, Poison Powder, Stun Spore, Sleep Powder, Mega Drain, Lucky Chant, Natural Gift, Moonlight, Giga Drain, Toxic, Natural Gift, Moonblast, Petal Dance, Grassy Terrain

Vileplume

Bellossom

Oddish → **Gloom**

REGIONS:
Alola
Kanto

OMANYTE
Spiral Pokémon

TYPE: ROCK-WATER

Omanyte's sturdy shell protects it from enemy attacks. This ancient Pokémon was restored from a fossil found at the site of an ocean that no longer exists.

How to Say It: AH-man-ite
Imperial Height: 1'04''
Imperial Weight: 16.5 lbs.
Metric Height: 0.4 m
Metric Weight: 7.5 kg

Possible Moves: Constrict, Withdraw, Bite, Water Gun, Rollout, Leer, Mud Shot, Brine, Protect, Ancient Power, Tickle, Rock Blast, Shell Smash, Hydro Pump

Omanyte → **Omastar**

OMASTAR
Spiral Pokémon

TYPE: ROCK-WATER

Omastar grasps food with its tentacles, leading some to believe it could be a distant ancestor of Octillery. Its heavy, cumbersome shell prevented it from thriving in the ancient past.

How to Say It: AH-mah-star
Imperial Height: 3'03''
Imperial Weight: 77.2 lbs.
Metric Height: 1.0 m
Metric Weight: 35.0 kg

Possible Moves: Constrict, Withdraw, Bite, Water Gun, Rollout, Leer, Mud Shot, Brine, Protect, Ancient Power, Spike Cannon, Tickle, Rock Blast, Shell Smash, Hydro Pump

Omanyte ⇨ **Omastar**

ONIX
Rock Snake Pokémon

TYPE: ROCK-GROUND

Thanks to its internal magnet, Onix never loses its way while boring through the ground. Its body grows smoother with age as the rough edges wear away.

How to Say It: ON-icks
Imperial Height: 28'10''
Imperial Weight: 463.0 lbs.
Metric Height: 8.8 m
Metric Weight: 210.0 kg

Possible Moves: Mud Sport, Tackle, Harden, Bind, Curse, Rock Throw, Rock Tomb, Rage, Stealth Rock, Rock Polish, Gyro Ball, Smack Down, Dragon Breath, Slam, Screech, Rock Slide, Sand Tomb, Iron Tail, Dig, Stone Edge, Double-Edge, Sandstorm

Onix ⇨ **Steelix** ⇨ **Mega Steelix**

TYPE: NORMAL-PSYCHIC

ORANGURU
Sage Pokémon

Extremely intelligent and somewhat particular, Oranguru can be a bad fit for Trainers who lack experience. In the wild, it spends most of its time in the jungle canopy, though it sometimes emerges in search of an intellectual challenge.

How to Say It: or-RANG-goo-roo
Imperial Height: 4'11''
Imperial Weight: 167.6 lbs.
Metric Height: 1.5 m
Metric Weight: 76.0 kg

Possible Moves: Confusion, After You, Taunt, Quash, Stored Power, Psych Up, Feint Attack, Nasty Plot, Zen Headbutt, Instruct, Foul Play, Calm Mind, Psychic, Future Sight, Trick Room

Does not evolve

ORICORIO (BAILE STYLE)
Dancing Pokémon

TYPE: FIRE-FLYING

Drinking red nectar gives Oricorio a fiery style when it dances. It's best to enjoy this beautiful performance from a distance, because its beating wings give off scorching flames.

How to Say It: or-ih-KOR-ee-oh
Imperial Height: 2'00''
Imperial Weight: 7.5 lbs.
Metric Height: 0.6 m
Metric Weight: 3.4 kg

Possible Moves: Pound, Growl, Peck, Helping Hand, Air Cutter, Baton Pass, Feather Dance, Double Slap, Teeter Dance, Roost, Captivate, Air Slash, Revelation Dance, Mirror Move, Agility, Hurricane

Does not evolve

ORICORIO (PA'U STYLE)
Dancing Pokémon

TYPE: PSYCHIC-FLYING

Drinking pink nectar transforms Oricorio into a hypnotically swaying dancer. As its opponents watch, entranced, the swaying movement relaxes Oricorio's mind so it can build up psychic energy for attacks.

How to Say It: or-ih-KOR-ee-oh
Imperial Height: 2'00''
Imperial Weight: 7.5 lbs.
Metric Height: 0.6 m
Metric Weight: 3.4 kg

Possible Moves: Pound, Growl, Peck, Helping Hand, Air Cutter, Baton Pass, Feather Dance, Double Slap, Teeter Dance, Roost, Captivate, Air Slash, Revelation Dance, Mirror Move, Agility, Hurricane

Does not evolve

ORICORIO (POM-POM STYLE)
Dancing Pokémon

TYPE: ELECTRIC-FLYING

Drinking yellow nectar makes Oricorio's dance style truly electric. The charge generated by the rubbing of its feathers allows it to land shocking punches in battle as it performs a cheerful dance.

How to Say It: or-ih-KOR-ee-oh
Imperial Height: 2'00''
Imperial Weight: 7.5 lbs.
Metric Height: 0.6 m
Metric Weight: 3.4 kg

Possible Moves: Pound, Growl, Peck, Helping Hand, Air Cutter, Baton Pass, Feather Dance, Double Slap, Teeter Dance, Roost, Captivate, Air Slash, Revelation Dance, Mirror Move, Agility, Hurricane

Does not evolve

REGION: Alola

ORICORIO (SENSU STYLE)
Dancing Pokémon

TYPE: GHOST-FLYING

Drinking purple nectar inspires Oricorio to perform a dreamy and elegant dance. The spirits of the departed are drawn to this beautiful performance, and Oricorio channels their power into its attacks.

How to Say It: or-ih-KOR-ee-oh
Imperial Height: 2'00''
Imperial Weight: 7.5 lbs.
Metric Height: 0.6 m
Metric Weight: 3.4 kg

Possible Moves: Pound, Growl, Peck, Helping Hand, Air Cutter, Baton Pass, Feather Dance, Double Slap, Teeter Dance, Roost, Captivate, Air Slash, Revelation Dance, Mirror Move, Agility, Hurricane

Does not evolve

REGION: Unova

OSHAWOTT
Sea Otter Pokémon

TYPE: WATER

Oshawott can detach the scalchop on its belly and use it as a weapon in battle or as a tool for cutting up food and other things.

How to Say It: AH-shah-wot
Imperial Height: 1'08''
Imperial Weight: 13.0 lbs.
Metric Height: 0.5 m
Metric Weight: 5.9 kg

Possible Moves: Tackle, Tail Whip, Water Gun, Water Sport, Focus Energy, Razor Shell, Fury Cutter, Water Pulse, Revenge, Aqua Jet, Encore, Aqua Tail, Retaliate, Swords Dance, Hydro Pump

Oshawott → Dewott → Samurott

PACHIRISU
EleSquirrel Pokémon

REGIONS:
Kalos
(Coastal)
Sinnoh

TYPE: ELECTRIC

When Pachirisu affectionately rub their cheeks together, they're sharing electric energy with each other. The balls of fur they shed crackle with static.

How to Say It: patch-ee-REE-sue
Imperial Height: 1'04''
Imperial Weight: 8.6 lbs.
Metric Height: 0.4 m
Metric Weight: 3.9 kg

Possible Moves: Growl, Bide, Quick Attack, Charm, Spark, Endure, Nuzzle, Swift, Electro Ball, Sweet Kiss, Thunder Wave, Super Fang, Discharge, Last Resort, Hyper Fang

Does not evolve

PALKIA
Spatial Pokémon

REGION:
Sinnoh

LEGENDARY POKÉMON

TYPE: WATER-DRAGON

It is said Palkia can cause rents and distortions in space. In ancient times, it was revered as a legend.

How to Say It: PALL-kee-ah
Imperial Height: 13'09''
Imperial Weight: 740.8 lbs.
Metric Height: 4.2 m
Metric Weight: 336.0 kg

Possible Moves: Dragon Breath, Scary Face, Water Pulse, Ancient Power, Slash, Power Gem, Aqua Tail, Dragon Claw, Earth Power, Aura Sphere, Spacial Rend, Hydro Pump

Does not evolve

TYPE: GHOST-GROUND

In order to evolve, this Pokémon took control of people playing in the sand to build up its body into a sand castle. Those who disappear can sometimes be found buried underneath Palossand, drained of their vitality.

How to Say It: PAL-uh-sand
Imperial Height: 4'03''
Imperial Weight: 551.2 lbs.
Metric Height: 1.3 m
Metric Weight: 250.0 kg

Possible Moves: Harden, Absorb, Astonish, Sand Attack, Sand Tomb, Mega Drain, Bulldoze, Hypnosis, Iron Defense, Giga Drain, Shadow Ball, Earth Power, Shore Up, Sandstorm

REGION: Alola

PALOSSAND
Sand Castle Pokémon

Sandygast ⇨ Palossand

REGION: Unova

PALPITOAD
Vibration Pokémon

TYPE: WATER-GROUND

With the vibrations of its head bumps, Palpitoad can make ripples in the water or cause seismic activity. Its long tongue is coated in a sticky substance.

How to Say It: PAL-pih-tohd
Imperial Height: 2'07''
Imperial Weight: 37.5 lbs.
Metric Height: 0.8 m
Metric Weight: 17.0 kg

Possible Moves: Bubble, Growl, Supersonic, Round, Bubble Beam, Mud Shot, Aqua Ring, Uproar, Muddy Water, Rain Dance, Flail, Echoed Voice, Hydro Pump, Hyper Voice

Tympole ⇨ Palpitoad ⇨ Seismitoad

PANCHAM
Playful Pokémon

REGIONS:
Alola
Kalos
(Central)

TYPE: FIGHTING

The leaf Pancham holds in its mouth serves no purpose—it's just imitating its hero, Pangoro. Trainers who are beginning their journey could have some trouble handling this mischievous Pokémon.

How to Say It: PAN-chum
Imperial Height: 2'00''
Imperial Weight: 17.6 lbs.
Metric Height: 0.6 m
Metric Weight: 8.0 kg

Possible Moves: Tackle, Leer, Arm Thrust, Work Up, Karate Chop, Comet Punch, Slash, Circle Throw, Vital Throw, Body Slam, Crunch, Entrainment, Parting Shot, Sky Uppercut

Pancham Pangoro

PANGORO
Daunting Pokémon

REGIONS:
Alola
Kalos
(Central)

TYPE: FIGHTING-DARK

The bamboo leaf Pangoro keeps in its mouth helps it track its opponent's movements. Its respect for authority is based on battle prowess—a Trainer might have to engage in a test of physical strength before this Pokémon will listen.

How to Say It: PAN-go-roh
Imperial Height: 6'11''
Imperial Weight: 299.8 lbs.
Metric Height: 2.1 m
Metric Weight: 136.0 kg

Possible Moves: Bullet Punch, Hammer Arm, Low Sweep, Entrainment, Tackle, Leer, Arm Thrust, Work Up, Karate Chop, Comet Punch, Slash, Circle Throw, Vital Throw, Body Slam, Crunch, Parting Shot, Sky Uppercut, Taunt

Pancham Pangoro

PANPOUR
Spray Pokémon

TYPE: WATER

Panpour's head tuft is full of nutrient-rich water. It uses its tail to water plants, which then grow big and healthy.

How to Say It: PAN-por
Imperial Height: 2'00''
Imperial Weight: 29.8 lbs.
Metric Height: 0.6 m
Metric Weight: 13.5 kg

Possible Moves: Scratch, Play Nice, Leer, Lick, Water Gun, Fury Swipes, Water Sport, Bite, Scald, Taunt, Fling, Acrobatics, Brine, Recycle, Natural Gift, Crunch

Panpour ➡ **Simipour**

PANSAGE
Grass Monkey Pokémon

TYPE: GRASS

Chewing the leaf from Pansage's head is a known method of stress relief. It willingly shares its leaf—along with any berries it's collected—with those who need it.

How to Say It: PAN-sayj
Imperial Height: 2'00''
Imperial Weight: 23.1 lbs.
Metric Height: 0.6 m
Metric Weight: 10.5 kg

Possible Moves: Scratch, Play Nice, Leer, Lick, Vine Whip, Fury Swipes, Leech Seed, Bite, Seed Bomb, Torment, Fling, Acrobatics, Grass Knot, Recycle, Natural Gift, Crunch

Pansage ➡ **Simisage**

PANSEAR
High Temp Pokémon

REGIONS:
Kalos
(Central)
Unova

TYPE: FIRE

Clever and helpful, Pansear prefers to cook its berries rather than eating them raw. Its natural habitat is volcanic caves, so it's no surprise that its fiery tuft burns at six hundred degrees Fahrenheit.

How to Say It: PAN-seer
Imperial Height: 2'00''
Imperial Weight: 24.3 lbs.
Metric Height: 0.6 m
Metric Weight: 11.0 kg

Possible Moves: Scratch, Play Nice, Leer, Lick, Incinerate, Fury Swipes, Yawn, Bite, Flame Burst, Amnesia, Fling, Acrobatics, Fire Blast, Recycle, Natural Gift, Crunch

Pansear   Simisear

PARAS
Mushroom Pokémon

REGIONS:
Alola
Kanto

TYPE: BUG-GRASS

When Paras eats, it's mostly just feeding the mushrooms that grow on its back. These mushrooms, known as tochukaso, can be picked, dried, and ground into a powder for use in medicine.

How to Say It: PAIR-us (sounds like *Paris*)
Imperial Height: 1'00''
Imperial Weight: 11.9 lbs.
Metric Height: 0.3 m
Metric Weight: 5.4 kg

Possible Moves: Scratch, Stun Spore, Poison Powder, Absorb, Fury Cutter, Spore, Slash, Growth, Giga Drain, Aromatherapy, Rage Powder, X-Scissor

Paras   Parasect

TYPE: BUG-GRASS

Parasect is just a pawn of the giant mushroom that controls it. The mushroom's spores are toxic, but they do have medicinal properties for those careful enough to harvest them safely.

How to Say It: PARA-sekt
Imperial Height: 3'03''
Imperial Weight: 65.0 lbs.
Metric Height: 1.0 m
Metric Weight: 29.5 kg

Possible Moves: Cross Poison, Scratch, Stun Spore, Poison Powder, Absorb, Fury Cutter, Spore, Slash, Growth, Giga Drain, Aromatherapy, Rage Powder, X-Scissor

PARASECT
Mushroom Pokémon

Paras ➡ Parasect

TYPE: FIGHTING

Passimian are real team players—they learn from each other and work together for the benefit of the group. Each group, composed of about twenty Passimian, shares a remarkably strong bond.

How to Say It: pass-SIM-ee-uhn
Imperial Height: 6'07''
Imperial Weight: 182.5 lbs.
Metric Height: 2.0 m
Metric Weight: 82.8 kg

Possible Moves: Tackle, Leer, Rock Smash, Focus Energy, Beat Up, Scary Face, Take Down, Bestow, Thrash, Bulk Up, Double-Edge, Fling, Close Combat, Reversal, Giga Impact

REGION:
Alola

PASSIMIAN
Teamwork Pokémon

Does not evolve

PATRAT

Scout Pokémon

TYPE: NORMAL

Wary and cautious, Patrat are very serious about their job as lookouts. They store food in their cheeks so they don't have to leave their posts.

How to Say It: pat-RAT
Imperial Height: 1'08''
Imperial Weight: 25.6 lbs.
Metric Height: 0.5 m
Metric Weight: 11.6 kg

Possible Moves: Tackle, Leer, Bite, Bide, Detect, Sand Attack, Crunch, Hypnosis, Super Fang, After You, Work Up, Hyper Fang, Mean Look, Baton Pass, Slam

Patrat   Watchog

PAWNIARD

Sharp Blade Pokémon

TYPE: DARK-STEEL

Pawniard celebrates a victory by clanging its arm blades together, then keeps the blades sharp by repeatedly scraping them against a stone from a riverbed. It prefers to return to the same stone after each battle.

How to Say It: PAWN-yard
Imperial Height: 1'08''
Imperial Weight: 22.5 lbs.
Metric Height: 0.5 m
Metric Weight: 10.2 kg

Possible Moves: Scratch, Leer, Fury Cutter, Torment, Feint Attack, Scary Face, Metal Claw, Slash, Assurance, Metal Sound, Embargo, Iron Defense, Night Slash, Iron Head, Swords Dance, Guillotine

Pawniard   Bisharp

PELIPPER
Water Bird Pokémon

TYPE: WATER-FLYING

Young male Pelipper have the task of gathering food while the others guard the nest. With their impressively roomy beaks, they can easily carry enough food for everyone.

How to Say It: PEL-ip-purr
Imperial Height: 3'11''
Imperial Weight: 61.7 lbs.

Metric Height: 1.2 m
Metric Weight: 28.0 kg

Possible Moves: Protect, Hurricane, Hydro Pump, Tailwind, Soak, Growl, Water Gun, Water Sport, Wing Attack, Supersonic, Mist, Water Pulse, Payback, Brine, Fling, Stockpile, Swallow, Spit Up, Roost

Wingull ➡ Pelipper

PERSIAN
Classy Cat Pokémon

TYPE: NORMAL

It's tough to become friends with this Pokémon. Persian is vain and violent, and anyone who meets its gaze will feel the pain of its sharp claws.

How to Say It: PER-zhun
Imperial Height: 3'03''
Imperial Weight: 70.5 lbs.
Metric Height: 1.0 m
Metric Weight: 32.0 kg

Possible Moves: Swift, Play Rough, Switcheroo, Scratch, Growl, Bite, Fake Out, Fury Swipes, Screech, Feint Attack, Taunt, Power Gem, Slash, Nasty Plot, Assurance, Captivate, Night Slash, Feint

Meowth ⇨ Persian

ALOLAN PERSIAN
Classy Cat Pokémon

TYPE: DARK

Trainers in Alola adore Persian for its coat, which is very smooth and has a velvety texture. This Pokémon has developed a haughty attitude and prefers to fight dirty when it gets into battle.

How to Say It: uh-LO-luhn PER-zhun
Imperial Height: 3'07''
Imperial Weight: 72.8 lbs.
Metric Height: 1.1 m
Metric Weight: 33.0 kg

Possible Moves: Swift, Quash, Play Rough, Switcheroo, Scratch, Growl, Bite, Fake Out, Fury Swipes, Screech, Feint Attack, Taunt, Power Gem, Slash, Nasty Plot, Assurance, Captivate, Night Slash, Feint, Dark Pulse

Alolan Meowth ⇨ Alolan Persian

PETILIL
Bulb Pokémon

TYPE: GRASS

Petilil benefits from regular pruning. The leaves that sprout from its head can be brewed into a tea that perks up a weary mind—that is, if you're hardy enough to drink the incredibly bitter concoction!

How to Say It: PEH-tuh-LIL
Imperial Height: 1'08''
Imperial Weight: 14.6 lbs.
Metric Height: 0.5 m
Metric Weight: 6.6 kg

Possible Moves: Absorb, Growth, Leech Seed, Sleep Powder, Mega Drain, Synthesis, Magical Leaf, Stun Spore, Giga Drain, Aromatherapy, Helping Hand, Energy Ball, Entrainment, Sunny Day, After You, Leaf Storm

Petilil ⇒ **Lilligant**

TYPE: GROUND

Phanpy sucks up water with its long trunk to spray itself for a bath, or to playfully squirt others. It makes its nest by digging into a riverbank.

How to Say It: FAN-pee
Imperial Height: 1'08''
Imperial Weight: 73.9 lbs.
Metric Height: 0.5 m
Metric Weight: 33.5 kg

Possible Moves: Odor Sleuth, Tackle, Growl, Defense Curl, Flail, Take Down, Rollout, Natural Gift, Slam, Endure, Charm, Last Resort, Double-Edge

REGION:
Johto

PHANPY
Long Nose Pokémon

Phanpy ⇒ **Donphan**

PHANTUMP

Stump Pokémon

REGIONS:
Alola
Kalos
(Mountain)

TYPE: GHOST-GRASS

The eerie cry of a Phantump is a reminder of its origin—an old tree stump inhabited by the spirit of a lost child. The leaves on its head are said to possess medicinal qualities.

How to Say It: FAN-tump
Imperial Height: 1'04''
Imperial Weight: 15.4 lbs.
Metric Height: 0.4 m
Metric Weight: 7.0 kg

Possible Moves: Tackle, Confuse Ray, Astonish, Growth, Ingrain, Feint Attack, Leech Seed, Curse, Will-O-Wisp, Forest's Curse, Destiny Bond, Phantom Force, Wood Hammer, Horn Leech

Phantump   Trevenant

PHEROMOSA

Lissome Pokémon

ULTRA BEAST

TYPE: BUG-FIGHTING

Pheromosa, one of the mysterious Ultra Beasts, seems to be extremely wary of germs and won't touch anything willingly. Witnesses have seen it charging through the region at amazing speeds.

How to Say It: fair-uh-MO-suh
Imperial Height: 5'11''
Imperial Weight: 55.1 lbs.
Metric Height: 1.8 m
Metric Weight: 25.0 kg

Possible Moves: Quiver Dance, Quick Guard, Low Kick, Rapid Spin, Leer, Double Kick, Swift, Stomp, Feint, Silver Wind, Bounce, Jump Kick, Agility, Triple Kick, Lunge, Bug Buzz, Me First, High Jump Kick, Speed Swap

REGION:
Alola

Does not evolve

REGION: Sinnoh

PHIONE
Sea Drifter Pokémon

MYTHICAL POKÉMON

TYPE: WATER

Phione gather in large groups as they drift with the current through warm seas. After floating for a time, they always return home, no matter how far they have traveled.

How to Say It: fee-OH-nay
Imperial Height: 1'04''
Imperial Weight: 6.8 lbs.
Metric Height: 0.4 m
Metric Weight: 3.1 kg

Possible Moves: Bubble, Water Sport, Charm, Supersonic, Bubble Beam, Acid Armor, Whirlpool, Water Pulse, Aqua Ring, Dive, Rain Dance

Does not evolve

PICHU
Tiny Mouse Pokémon

REGIONS:
Alola
Johto
Kalos
(Central)

TYPE: ELECTRIC

Pichu is so adorable, but that doesn't mean it's harmless! Its Trainer has to watch out, because this little Pokémon isn't very good at controlling its own electricity and sometimes shocks itself and others.

How to Say It: PEE-choo
Imperial Height: 1'00''
Imperial Weight: 4.4 lbs.
Metric Height: 0.3 m
Metric Weight: 2.0 kg

Possible Moves: Thunder Shock, Charm, Tail Whip, Sweet Kiss, Nasty Plot, Thunder Wave

Pichu   Pikachu   Raichu

Alolan Raichu

PIDGEOT
Bird Pokémon

TYPE: NORMAL-FLYING

Many Trainers are drawn to Pidgeot because of its lovely feathers. The beautiful colors of its crest are particularly striking.

How to Say It: PIDG-ee-ott
Imperial Height: 4'11"
Imperial Weight: 87.1 lbs.
Metric Height: 1.5 m
Metric Weight: 39.5 kg

Possible Moves: Hurricane, Tackle, Sand Attack, Gust, Quick Attack, Whirlwind, Twister, Feather Dance, Agility, Wing Attack, Roost, Tailwind, Mirror Move, Air Slash

MEGA PIDGEOT
Bird Pokémon

TYPE: NORMAL-FLYING

Imperial Height: 7'03"
Imperial Weight: 111.3 lbs.
Metric Height: 2.2 m
Metric Weight: 50.5 kg

Pidgey ⇨ Pidgeotto ⇨ Pidgeot ⇨ Mega Pidgeot

PIDGEOTTO
Bird Pokémon

REGIONS:
Kalos
(Central)
Kanto

TYPE: NORMAL-FLYING

Very territorial, Pidgeotto keeps up a steady patrol of the large area it claims as its own. Any intruder will be driven off with merciless attacks from its sharp claws.

How to Say It: PIDG-ee-OH-toe
Imperial Height: 3'07''
Imperial Weight: 66.1 lbs.
Metric Height: 1.1 m
Metric Weight: 30.0 kg

Possible Moves: Tackle, Sand Attack, Gust, Quick Attack, Whirlwind, Twister, Feather Dance, Agility, Wing Attack, Roost, Tailwind, Mirror Move, Air Slash, Hurricane

Pidgey ➡ Pidgeotto ➡ Pidgeot ➡ Mega Pidgeot

PIDGEY
Tiny Bird Pokémon

REGIONS:
Kalos
(Central)
Kanto

TYPE: NORMAL-FLYING

Thanks to Pidgey's excellent sense of direction, it can always find its way home, no matter how far it has traveled.

How to Say It: PIDG-ee
Imperial Height: 1'00''
Imperial Weight: 4.0 lbs.
Metric Height: 0.3 m
Metric Weight: 1.8 kg

Possible Moves: Tackle, Sand Attack, Gust, Quick Attack, Whirlwind, Twister, Feather Dance, Agility, Wing Attack, Roost, Tailwind, Mirror Move, Air Slash, Hurricane

Pidgey ➡ Pidgeotto ➡ Pidgeot ➡ Mega Pidgeot

PIDOVE
Tiny Pigeon Pokémon

TYPE: NORMAL-FLYING

Even wild Pidove are used to having people around. They live in cities and often flock to places where people spend time, like plazas and parks.

How to Say It: pih-DUV
Imperial Height: 1'00''
Imperial Weight: 4.6 lbs.
Metric Height: 0.3 m
Metric Weight: 2.1 kg

Possible Moves: Gust, Growl, Leer, Quick Attack, Air Cutter, Roost, Detect, Taunt, Air Slash, Razor Wind, Feather Dance, Swagger, Facade, Tailwind, Sky Attack

Pidove ➡ **Tranquill** ➡ **Unfezant**

PIGNITE
Fire Pig Pokémon

TYPE: FIRE-FIGHTING

"Food is fuel"—for Pignite, that common phrase is a bit more literal. When it eats, its internal fire is stoked, which increases its power and speed.

How to Say It: pig-NYTE
Imperial Height: 3'03''
Imperial Weight: 122.4 lbs.
Metric Height: 1.0 m
Metric Weight: 55.5 kg

Possible Moves: Tackle, Tail Whip, Ember, Odor Sleuth, Defense Curl, Flame Charge, Arm Thrust, Smog, Rollout, Take Down, Heat Crash, Assurance, Flamethrower, Head Smash, Roar, Flare Blitz

Tepig ➡ **Pignite** ➡ **Emboar**

PIKACHU
Mouse Pokémon

REGIONS:
Alola
Kalos
(Central)
Kanto

TYPE: ELECTRIC

Pikachu naturally stores up electricity in its body, and it needs to discharge that energy on a regular basis to maintain good health. To take advantage of this, some have suggested creating a Pikachu-fueled power plant.

How to Say It: PEE-ka-choo
Imperial Height: 1'04''
Imperial Weight: 13.2 lbs.
Metric Height: 0.4 m
Metric Weight: 6.0 kg

Possible Moves: Tail Whip, Thunder Shock, Growl, Play Nice, Quick Attack, Electro Ball, Thunder Wave, Feint, Double Team, Spark, Nuzzle, Discharge, Slam, Thunderbolt, Agility, Wild Charge, Light Screen, Thunder

Pichu → Pikachu → Raichu

Alolan Raichu

REGION:
Kanto

Pikachu Libre
Special Move:
Flying Press

Pikachu Belle
Special Move:
Icicle Crash

Pikachu PhD
Special Move:
Electric Terrain

Pikachu Pop Star
Special Move:
Draining Kiss

Pikachu Rock Star
Special Move:
Meteor Mash

Does not evolve

PIKIPEK
Woodpecker Pokémon

TYPE: NORMAL-FLYING

Pikipek can drill into the side of a tree at the rate of sixteen pecks per second! It uses the resulting hole as a place to nest and to store berries—both for food and for ammunition.

How to Say It: PICK-kee-peck
Imperial Height: 1'00''
Imperial Weight: 2.6 lbs.
Metric Height: 0.3 m
Metric Weight: 1.2 kg

Possible Moves: Peck, Growl, Echoed Voice, Rock Smash, Supersonic, Pluck, Roost, Fury Attack, Screech, Drill Peck, Bullet Seed, Feather Dance, Hyper Voice

Pikipek → Trumbeak → Toucannon

PILOSWINE
Swine Pokémon

TYPE: ICE-GROUND

Piloswine's long, thick hair helps protect it from the intense cold of its surroundings. Its tusks can dig through the ice to find buried food.

How to Say It: PILE-oh-swine
Imperial Height: 3'07''
Imperial Weight: 123.0 lbs.
Metric Height: 1.1 m
Metric Weight: 55.8 kg

Possible Moves: Ancient Power, Peck, Odor Sleuth, Mud Sport, Powder Snow, Mud-Slap, Endure, Mud Bomb, Icy Wind, Ice Fang, Take Down, Fury Attack, Mist, Thrash, Earthquake, Blizzard, Amnesia

Swinub → Piloswine → Mamoswine

PINECO
Bagworm Pokémon

REGIONS:
Alola
Johto

TYPE: BUG

Pineco gets bigger and more durable as it grows, using saliva to adhere tree bark to its body. It hangs motionless from a tree, watching carefully until it sees its favorite foods.

How to Say It: PINE-co
Imperial Height: 2'00''
Imperial Weight: 15.9 lbs.
Metric Height: 0.6 m
Metric Weight: 7.2 kg

Possible Moves: Tackle, Protect, Self-Destruct, Bug Bite, Take Down, Rapid Spin, Bide, Natural Gift, Spikes, Payback, Explosion, Iron Defense, Gyro Ball, Double-Edge

Pineco ⇒ Forretress

PINSIR
Stag Beetle Pokémon

TYPE: BUG

Though Pinsir is incredibly tough, it can't cope with cold weather, so it's right at home in Alola—though it does find itself competing with the native Vikavolt. Its horns can lift a much larger foe or topple a tree.

How to Say It: PIN-sir
Imperial Height: 4'11''
Imperial Weight: 121.3 lbs.
Metric Height: 1.5 m
Metric Weight: 55.0 kg

Possible Moves: Vice Grip, Focus Energy, Bind, Seismic Toss, Harden, Revenge, Vital Throw, Double Hit, Brick Break, X-Scissor, Submission, Storm Throw, Swords Dance, Thrash, Superpower, Guillotine

MEGA PINSIR
Stag Beetle Pokémon

TYPE: BUG-FLYING

Imperial Height: 5'07''
Imperial Weight: 130.1 lbs.
Metric Height: 1.7 m
Metric Weight: 59.0 kg

Pinsir

Mega Pinsir

PIPLUP
Penguin Pokémon

REGION:
Sinnoh

TYPE: WATER

Proud and stubborn, Piplup can be a challenge to train. It's quite independent, preferring to take care of itself and find its own food.

How to Say It: PIP-lup
Imperial Height: 1'04''
Imperial Weight: 11.5 lbs.
Metric Height: 0.4 m
Metric Weight: 5.2 kg

Possible Moves: Pound, Growl, Bubble, Water Sport, Peck, Bubble Beam, Bide, Fury Attack, Brine, Whirlpool, Mist, Drill Peck, Hydro Pump

Piplup ⇨ Prinplup ⇨ Empoleon

PLUSLE
Cheering Pokémon

REGIONS:
Hoenn
Kalos
(Central)

TYPE: ELECTRIC

Plusle can short out the electricity in its body to create a crackling shower of sparks! It always cheers on its friends in battle.

How to Say It: PLUS-ull
Imperial Height: 1'04''
Imperial Weight: 9.3 lbs.
Metric Height: 0.4 m
Metric Weight: 4.2 kg

Possible Moves: Nuzzle, Play Nice, Growl, Thunder Wave, Quick Attack, Helping Hand, Spark, Encore, Bestow, Swift, Electro Ball, Copycat, Charm, Charge, Discharge, Baton Pass, Agility, Last Resort, Thunder

Does not evolve

POIPOLE
Poison Pin Pokémon

ULTRA BEAST

TYPE: POISON

Poipole, one of the mysterious Ultra Beasts, is crowned with needles that spray a dangerous poison. This creature lives in another world, where it is popular enough that it could be a first partner.

How to Say It: POY-pull
Imperial Height: 2'00"
Imperial Weight: 4.0 lbs.
Metric Height: 0.6 m
Metric Weight: 1.8 kg

Possible Moves: Dragon Pulse, Peck, Growl, Helping Hand, Acid, Fury Attack, Venoshock, Charm, Venom Drench, Nasty Plot, Poison Jab, Toxic, Fell Stinger

Poipole   Naganadel

REGIONS:
Alola
Johto
Kalos
(Mountain)

POLITOED
Frog Pokémon

TYPE: WATER

When several Politoed gather together to sing under the moon, the angry quality of their cries makes it sound like they're having a heated argument. Poliwag and Poliwhirl regard this Pokémon as a leader.

How to Say It: PAUL-lee-TOED
Imperial Height: 3'07"
Imperial Weight: 74.7 lbs.
Metric Height: 1.1 m
Metric Weight: 33.9 kg

Possible Moves: Bubble Beam, Hypnosis, Double Slap, Perish Song, Swagger, Bounce, Hyper Voice

Poliwag   Poliwhirl   Politoed

POLIWAG

Tadpole Pokémon

TYPE: WATER

Poliwag's skin is so thin that you can see right through it to the Pokémon's spiral-shaped insides. It's not very skilled at walking on land, but a Trainer can help it get better.

How to Say It: PAUL-lee-wag
Imperial Height: 2'00''
Imperial Weight: 27.3 lbs.
Metric Height: 0.6 m
Metric Weight: 12.4 kg

Possible Moves: Water Sport, Water Gun, Hypnosis, Bubble, Double Slap, Rain Dance, Body Slam, Bubble Beam, Mud Shot, Belly Drum, Wake-Up Slap, Hydro Pump, Mud Bomb

Poliwag ➡ Poliwhirl ➡ Poliwrath
Politoed

POLIWHIRL

Tadpole Pokémon

TYPE: WATER

Poliwhirl is amphibious, equally at home on land or in the water. It weighs the options carefully—there's more food to be found on land, but it's also more likely to be attacked by dangerous Pokémon.

How to Say It: PAUL-lee-wirl
Imperial Height: 3'03''
Imperial Weight: 44.1 lbs.
Metric Height: 1.0 m
Metric Weight: 20.0 kg

Possible Moves: Water Sport, Water Gun, Hypnosis, Bubble, Double Slap, Rain Dance, Body Slam, Bubble Beam, Mud Shot, Belly Drum, Wake-Up Slap, Hydro Pump, Mud Bomb

Poliwag ➡ Poliwhirl ➡ Poliwrath
Politoed

POLIWRATH
Tadpole Pokémon

TYPE: WATER-FIGHTING

Kids in Alola often learn to swim by watching local Poliwrath cut through the waves with a powerful breaststroke. This Pokémon's body is dense with muscles, so it has to swim instead of floating.

How to Say It: PAUL-lee-rath
Imperial Height: 4'03''
Imperial Weight: 119.0 lbs.
Metric Height: 1.3 m
Metric Weight: 54.0 kg

Possible Moves: Submission, Circle Throw, Bubble Beam, Hypnosis, Double Slap, Dynamic Punch, Mind Reader

Poliwag → **Poliwhirl** → **Poliwrath**

TYPE: FIRE

At the beginning of its life, Ponyta's legs are too weak to hold it up. It quickly learns to run by chasing after its elders.

How to Say It: POH-nee-tah
Imperial Height: 3'03''
Imperial Weight: 66.1 lbs.
Metric Height: 1.0 m
Metric Weight: 30.0 kg

Possible Moves: Growl, Tackle, Tail Whip, Ember, Flame Wheel, Stomp, Flame Charge, Fire Spin, Take Down, Inferno, Agility, Fire Blast, Bounce, Flare Blitz

REGION:
Kanto

PONYTA
Fire Horse Pokémon

Ponyta → **Rapidash**

POOCHYENA
Bite Pokémon

TYPE: DARK

Poochyena tries to look bigger than it is by bristling up its tail. It tends to react to unexpected movement by biting, and it easily chases prey to exhaustion.

How to Say It: POO-chee-EH-nah
Imperial Height: 1'08''
Imperial Weight: 30.0 lbs.
Metric Height: 0.5 m
Metric Weight: 13.6 kg

Possible Moves: Tackle, Howl, Sand Attack, Bite, Odor Sleuth, Roar, Swagger, Assurance, Scary Face, Taunt, Embargo, Take Down, Sucker Punch, Crunch, Yawn, Play Rough

Poochyena ⇨ Mightyena

POPPLIO
Sea Lion Pokémon

REGION:
Alola

TYPE: WATER

Popplio uses the water balloons it blows from its nose as weapons in battle. It's a hard worker and puts in lots of practice creating and controlling these balloons.

How to Say It: POP-lee-oh
Imperial Height: 1'04''
Imperial Weight: 16.5 lbs.
Metric Height: 0.4 m
Metric Weight: 7.5 kg

Possible Moves: Pound, Water Gun, Growl, Disarming Voice, Baby-Doll Eyes, Aqua Jet, Icy Wind, Encore, Bubble Beam, Sing, Double Slap, Hyper Voice, Moonblast, Captivate, Hydro Pump, Misty Terrain

Popplio ⇨ Brionne ⇨ Primarina

TYPE: NORMAL

Porygon were first created about twenty years ago, and at the time, they were made with cutting-edge technology. By converting itself into data, this Pokémon can travel through cyberspace.

How to Say It: PORE-ee-gon
Imperial Height: 2'07''
Imperial Weight: 80.5 lbs.
Metric Height: 0.8 m
Metric Weight: 36.5 kg

Possible Moves: Conversion 2, Tackle, Conversion, Sharpen, Psybeam, Agility, Recover, Magnet Rise, Signal Beam, Recycle, Discharge, Lock-On, Tri Attack, Magic Coat, Zap Cannon

PORYGON
Virtual Pokémon

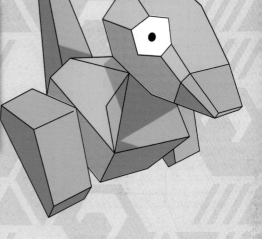

Porygon ➡ Porygon2 ➡ Porygon-Z

TYPE: NORMAL

Porygon2 came into being when programmers updated the original Porygon with the latest technology. Their goal was to create new developments on other planets, but it hasn't happened yet.

How to Say It: PORE-ee-gon TOO
Imperial Height: 2'00''
Imperial Weight: 71.6 lbs.
Metric Height: 0.6 m
Metric Weight: 32.5 kg

Possible Moves: Zap Cannon, Magic Coat, Conversion 2, Tackle, Conversion, Defense Curl, Psybeam, Agility, Recover, Magnet Rise, Signal Beam, Recycle, Discharge, Lock-On, Tri Attack, Magic Coat, Hyper Beam

REGIONS:
Alola
Johto

PORYGON2
Virtual Pokémon

Porygon ➡ Porygon2 ➡ Porygon-Z

PORYGON-Z
Virtual Pokémon

TYPE: NORMAL

Porygon-Z underwent a programming upgrade that was supposed to enable travel between dimensions. Afterward, though, it started to exhibit odd behavior due to an apparent glitch in the new program.

How to Say It: PORE-ee-gon ZEE
Imperial Height: 2'11''
Imperial Weight: 75.0 lbs.
Metric Height: 0.9 m
Metric Weight: 34.0 kg

Possible Moves: Trick Room, Zap Cannon, Magic Coat, Conversion 2, Tackle, Conversion, Nasty Plot, Psybeam, Agility, Recover, Magnet Rise, Signal Beam, Embargo, Discharge, Lock-On, Tri Attack, Hyper Beam

Porygon   Porygon2   Porygon-Z

PRIMARINA
Soloist Pokémon

REGION:
Alola

TYPE: WATER-FAIRY

This Pokémon's singing voice is a delicate and powerful weapon, used to attack its foes and to control the water balloons it creates. Groups of Primarina teach these battle songs to the next generation.

How to Say It: PREE-muh-REE-nuh
Imperial Height: 5'11''
Imperial Weight: 97.0 lbs.
Metric Height: 1.8 m
Metric Weight: 44.0 kg

Possible Moves: Sparkling Aria, Pound, Water Gun, Growl, Disarming Voice, Baby-Doll Eyes, Aqua Jet, Icy Wind, Encore, Bubble Beam, Sing, Double Slap, Hyper Voice, Moonblast, Captivate, Hydro Pump, Misty Terrain

Popplio   Brionne   Primarina

TYPE: FIGHTING

Primeape's rage can be so intense that the wild emotions coursing through its body put its own health at risk. Even returning it to its Poké Ball might not be enough to calm it down.

How to Say It: PRIME-ape
Imperial Height: 3'03''
Imperial Weight: 70.5 lbs.
Metric Height: 1.0 m
Metric Weight: 32.0 kg

Possible Moves: Rage, Final Gambit, Fling, Scratch, Low Kick, Leer, Focus Energy, Fury Swipes, Karate Chop, Pursuit, Seismic Toss, Swagger, Cross Chop, Assurance, Punishment, Thrash, Close Combat, Screech, Stomping Tantrum, Outrage

REGIONS:
Alola
Kanto

PRIMEAPE
Pig Monkey Pokémon

Mankey ➡ **Primeape**

REGION:
Sinnoh

PRINPLUP
Penguin Pokémon

TYPE: WATER

Because Prinplup have a strong sense of self-importance, they tend to live alone. They can topple trees by striking with their wings.

How to Say It: PRIN-plup
Imperial Height: 2'07''
Imperial Weight: 50.7 lbs.
Metric Height: 0.8 m
Metric Weight: 23.0 kg

Possible Moves: Tackle, Growl, Bubble, Water Sport, Peck, Metal Claw, Bubble Beam, Bide, Fury Attack, Brine, Whirlpool, Mist, Drill Peck, Hydro Pump

Piplup ➡ **Prinplup** ➡ **Empoleon**

PROBOPASS
Compass Pokémon

REGIONS:
Alola
Kalos
(Coastal)
Sinnoh

TYPE: ROCK-STEEL

Probopass sends forth its three small Mini-Noses in strategic maneuvers to outflank an opponent in battle. The magnetic field that surrounds this Pokémon can disrupt or disable electrical devices in the area.

How to Say It: PRO-bow-pass
Imperial Height: 4'07"
Imperial Weight: 749.6 lbs.
Metric Height: 1.4 m
Metric Weight: 340.0 kg

Possible Moves: Tri Attack, Magnetic Flux, Magnet Rise, Gravity, Wide Guard, Tackle, Iron Defense, Block, Magnet Bomb, Thunder Wave, Rest, Spark, Rock Slide, Power Gem, Rock Blast, Discharge, Sandstorm, Earth Power, Stone Edge, Lock-On, Zap Cannon

Nosepass ⇨ Probopass

PSYDUCK
Duck Pokémon

REGIONS:
Alola
Kalos
(Central)
Kanto

TYPE: WATER

Poor Psyduck suffers from terrible headaches, which somehow enhance its psychic powers—but it's often too miserable to control those powers. The pain can be intense enough to make it cry.

How to Say It: SY-duck
Imperial Height: 2'07"
Imperial Weight: 43.2 lbs.
Metric Height: 0.8 m
Metric Weight: 19.6 kg

Possible Moves: Water Sport, Scratch, Tail Whip, Water Gun, Confusion, Fury Swipes, Water Pulse, Disable, Screech, Zen Headbutt, Aqua Tail, Soak, Psych Up, Amnesia, Hydro Pump, Wonder Room

Psyduck ⇨ Golduck

PUMPKABOO
Pumpkin Pokémon

TYPE: GHOST-GRASS

The nocturnal Pumpkaboo tends to get restless as darkness falls. Stories say it serves as a guide for wandering spirits, leading them through the night to find their true home.

How to Say It: PUMP-kuh-boo
Imperial Height: 1'04''
Imperial Weight: 11.0 lbs.
Metric Height: 0.4 m
Metric Weight: 5.0 kg

Possible Moves: Trick, Astonish, Confuse Ray, Scary Face, Trick-or-Treat, Worry Seed, Razor Leaf, Leech Seed, Bullet Seed, Shadow Sneak, Shadow Ball, Pain Split, Seed Bomb

Pumpkaboo ⇨ **Gourgeist**

REGIONS:
Alola
Johto
Kalos
(Mountain)

PUPITAR
Hard Shell Pokémon

TYPE: ROCK-GROUND

A rock-solid shell protects Pupitar's body as it impatiently waits to evolve. It expresses this frustration by causing trouble and wildly thrashing about.

How to Say It: PUE-puh-tar
Imperial Height: 3'11''
Imperial Weight: 335.1 lbs.
Metric Height: 1.2 m
Metric Weight: 152.0 kg

Possible Moves: Bite, Leer, Sandstorm, Screech, Chip Away, Rock Slide, Scary Face, Thrash, Dark Pulse, Payback, Crunch, Earthquake, Stone Edge, Hyper Beam

Larvitar ⇨ **Pupitar** ⇨ **Tyranitar** ⇨ **Mega Tyranitar**

PURRLOIN

Devious Pokémon

TYPE: DARK

Purrloin acts cute and innocent to trick people into trusting it. Then it steals their stuff.

How to Say It: PUR-loyn
Imperial Height: 1'04''
Imperial Weight: 22.3 lbs.
Metric Height: 0.4 m
Metric Weight: 10.1 kg

Possible Moves: Scratch, Growl, Assist, Sand Attack, Fury Swipes, Pursuit, Torment, Fake Out, Hone Claws, Assurance, Slash, Captivate, Night Slash, Snatch, Nasty Plot, Sucker Punch, Play Rough

Purrloin   Liepard

PURUGLY

Tiger Cat Pokémon

REGION:
Sinnoh

TYPE: NORMAL

Purugly wraps its two tails around its waist to make itself look bigger. It's been known to kick other Pokémon out of their comfortable nests and take over.

How to Say It: pur-UGG-lee
Imperial Height: 3'03''
Imperial Weight: 96.6 lbs.
Metric Height: 1.0 m
Metric Weight: 43.8 kg

Possible Moves: Fake Out, Scratch, Growl, Hypnosis, Feint Attack, Fury Swipes, Charm, Assist, Captivate, Slash, Swagger, Body Slam, Attract, Hone Claws

Glameow   Purugly

Male Form

PYROAR
Royal Pokémon

TYPE: FIRE-NORMAL

Ablaze with loyalty, Pyroar protects its pride at all costs—even if that means putting itself in harm's way. It uses its scorching-hot breath to repel foes.

How to Say It: PIE-roar
Imperial Height: 4'11''
Imperial Weight: 179.7 lbs.

Metric Height: 1.5 m
Metric Weight: 81.5 kg

Possible Moves: Hyper Beam, Tackle, Leer, Ember, Work Up, Headbutt, Noble Roar, Take Down, Fire Fang, Endeavor, Echoed Voice, Flamethrower, Crunch, Hyper Voice, Incinerate, Overheat

Female Form

Litleo ⇨ Pyroar

PYUKUMUKU
Sea Cucumber Pokémon

TYPE: WATER

Pyukumuku has a remarkable and revolting weapon in battle: It can spew out its innards to strike at its opponent. It's covered in a sticky slime that beachgoers use to soothe their skin after a sunburn.

How to Say It: PYOO-koo-MOO-koo
Imperial Height: 1'00''
Imperial Weight: 2.6 lbs.
Metric Height: 0.3 m
Metric Weight: 1.2 kg

Possible Moves: Baton Pass, Water Sport, Mud Sport, Harden, Bide, Helping Hand, Taunt, Safeguard, Counter, Purify, Curse, Gastro Acid, Pain Split, Recover, Soak, Toxic, Memento

Does not evolve

QUAGSIRE
Water Fish Pokémon

REGIONS:
Johto
Kalos
(Mountain)

TYPE: WATER-GROUND

Quagsire doesn't exactly hunt for food—it hangs out in the water with its mouth open and waits for something to drift in. Fortunately, this lack of movement means it doesn't need to eat much.

How to Say It: KWAG-sire
Imperial Height: 4'07''
Imperial Weight: 165.3 lbs.
Metric Height: 1.4 m
Metric Weight: 75.0 kg

Possible Moves: Water Gun, Tail Whip, Mud Sport, Mud Shot, Slam, Mud Bomb, Amnesia, Yawn, Earthquake, Rain Dance, Mist, Haze, Muddy Water

Wooper ➡ Quagsire

QUILAVA
Volcano Pokémon

REGION:
Johto

TYPE: FIRE

To keep opponents from getting too close, Quilava heats up the air around it by flaring the flames on its body. It's extremely nimble and good at dodging.

How to Say It: kwi-LAH-va
Imperial Height: 2'11''
Imperial Weight: 41.9 lbs.
Metric Height: 0.9 m
Metric Weight: 19.0 kg

Possible Moves: Tackle, Leer, Smokescreen, Ember, Quick Attack, Flame Wheel, Defense Curl, Swift, Flame Charge, Lava Plume, Flamethrower, Inferno, Rollout, Double-Edge, Burn Up, Eruption

Cyndaquil ➡ Quilava ➡ Typhlosion

TYPE: GRASS

Quilladin often train for battle by charging forcefully into each other. Despite their spiky appearance, they have a gentle nature and don't like confrontation.

How to Say It: QUILL-uh-din
Imperial Height: 2'04''
Imperial Weight: 63.9 lbs.
Metric Height: 0.7 m
Metric Weight: 29.0 kg

Possible Moves: Growl, Vine Whip, Rollout, Bite, Leech Seed, Pin Missile, Needle Arm, Take Down, Seed Bomb, Mud Shot, Bulk Up, Body Slam, Pain Split, Wood Hammer

REGION:
Kalos
(Central)

QUILLADIN
Spiny Armor Pokémon

Chespin ⇨ **Quilladin** ⇨ **Chesnaught**

REGIONS:
Johto
Kalos
(Coastal)

QWILFISH
Balloon Pokémon

TYPE: WATER-POISON

Qwilfish puffs up its body by sucking in water, then uses that water pressure to send the poisonous spikes that cover it shooting outward at an opponent.

How to Say It: KWILL-fish
Imperial Height: 1'08''
Imperial Weight: 8.6 lbs.
Metric Height: 0.5 m
Metric Weight: 3.9 kg

Possible Moves: Fell Stinger, Hydro Pump, Destiny Bond, Water Gun, Spikes, Tackle, Poison Sting, Harden, Minimize, Bubble, Rollout, Toxic Spikes, Stockpile, Spit Up, Revenge, Brine, Pin Missile, Take Down, Aqua Tail, Poison Jab

Does not evolve

343

RAICHU
Mouse Pokémon

REGIONS:
Kalos
(Central)
Kanto

TYPE: ELECTRIC

Raichu can unleash enough electricity to defeat a much larger Pokémon in a single devastating shock. When it's all charged up, it will attack just about anything—including its Trainer!

How to Say It: RYE-choo
Imperial Height: 2'07''
Imperial Weight: 66.1 lbs.
Metric Height: 0.8 m
Metric Weight: 30.0 kg

Possible Moves: Thunder Shock, Tail Whip, Quick Attack, Thunderbolt

Pichu → Pikachu → Raichu

ALOLAN RAICHU
Mouse Pokémon

REGION:
Alola

TYPE: ELECTRIC-PSYCHIC

Researchers speculate that Raichu looks different in the Alola region because of what it eats. It can "surf" on its own tail, standing on the flat surface and using psychic power to raise itself off the ground.

How to Say It: uh-LO-luhn RYE-choo
Imperial Height: 2'04''
Imperial Weight: 46.3 lbs.
Metric Height: 0.7 m
Metric Weight: 21.0 kg

Possible Moves: Psychic, Speed Swap, Thunder Shock, Tail Whip, Quick Attack, Thunderbolt

Pichu → Pikachu → Alolan Raichu

TYPE: ELECTRIC

When Raikou roars, the air and land shudder. This Legendary Pokémon moves with lightning speed.

How to Say It: RYE-coo
Imperial Height: 6'03''
Imperial Weight: 392.4 lbs.
Metric Height: 1.9 m
Metric Weight: 178.0 kg

Possible Moves: Bite, Leer, Thunder Shock, Roar, Quick Attack, Spark, Reflect, Crunch, Thunder Fang, Discharge, Extrasensory, Rain Dance, Calm Mind, Thunder

REGION: Johto

RAIKOU
Thunder Pokémon

LEGENDARY POKÉMON

Does not evolve

RALTS
Feeling Pokémon

TYPE: PSYCHIC-FAIRY

With its horns, Ralts can sense people's emotions. Its own mood tends to reflect what it senses, and it's drawn to people with a positive attitude.

How to Say It: RALTS
Imperial Height: 1'04''
Imperial Weight: 14.6 lbs.
Metric Height: 0.4 m
Metric Weight: 6.6 kg

Possible Moves: Growl, Confusion, Double Team, Teleport, Disarming Voice, Lucky Chant, Magical Leaf, Heal Pulse, Draining Kiss, Calm Mind, Psychic, Imprison, Future Sight, Charm, Hypnosis, Dream Eater, Stored Power

Ralts → Kirlia → Gardevoir → Mega Gardevoir

Kirlia → Gallade → Mega Gallade

RAMPARDOS
Head Butt Pokémon

TYPE: ROCK

A headbutt from Rampardos is powerful enough to knock down a tall building. To adapt to this rough treatment, its skull has grown thick and hard—which unfortunately doesn't leave much room for brains.

How to Say It: ram-PAR-dose
Imperial Height: 5'03"
Imperial Weight: 226.0 lbs.
Metric Height: 1.6 m
Metric Weight: 102.5 kg

Possible Moves: Endeavor, Headbutt, Leer, Focus Energy, Pursuit, Take Down, Scary Face, Assurance, Chip Away, Ancient Power, Zen Headbutt, Screech, Head Smash

Cranidos ⇨ Rampardos

REGION:
Kanto

RAPIDASH
Fire Horse Pokémon

TYPE: FIRE

Most of the time, Rapidash travels at a casual canter across the flat lands where it lives. When it breaks into a gallop, its mane blazes brightly.

How to Say It: RAP-id-dash
Imperial Height: 5'07"
Imperial Weight: 209.4 lbs.
Metric Height: 1.7 m
Metric Weight: 95.0 kg

Possible Moves: Poison Jab, Megahorn, Growl, Quick Attack, Tail Whip, Ember, Flame Wheel, Stomp, Flame Charge, Fire Spin, Take Down, Inferno, Agility, Fury Attack, Fire Blast, Bounce, Flare Blitz

Ponyta ⇨ Rapidash

RATICATE

Mouse Pokémon

REGION: Kanto

TYPE: NORMAL

The webbing on its hind feet makes Raticate a good swimmer. Approach with caution—this Pokémon has a nasty temper and will bite with little provocation.

How to Say It: RAT-ih-kate
Imperial Height: 2'04''
Imperial Weight: 40.8 lbs.
Metric Height: 0.7 m
Metric Weight: 18.5 kg

Possible Moves: Scary Face, Swords Dance, Tackle, Tail Whip, Quick Attack, Focus Energy, Bite, Pursuit, Hyper Fang, Assurance, Crunch, Sucker Punch, Super Fang, Double-Edge, Endeavor

Rattata ⇨ Raticate

ALOLAN RATICATE

Mouse Pokémon

REGION: Alola

TYPE: DARK-NORMAL

Each Raticate leads a group of Rattata, and the groups regularly scuffle over food. This Pokémon is rather picky about what it eats, so a restaurant where a Raticate lives is likely to be a good one.

How to Say It: uh-LO-luhn RAT-ih-kate
Imperial Height: 2'04''
Imperial Weight: 56.2 lbs.
Metric Height: 0.7 m
Metric Weight: 25.5 kg

Possible Moves: Scary Face, Swords Dance, Tackle, Tail Whip, Quick Attack, Focus Energy, Bite, Pursuit, Hyper Fang, Assurance, Crunch, Sucker Punch, Super Fang, Double-Edge, Endeavor

  Alolan Rattata ⇨ Alolan Raticate

REGION: Kanto

RATTATA
Mouse Pokémon

TYPE: NORMAL

Rattata's teeth keep growing throughout its life, so it has to chew on hard objects to keep them whittled down. They can live happily even in filthy conditions, which sometimes leads to overpopulation.

How to Say It: RA-TAT-ta
Imperial Height: 1'00''
Imperial Weight: 7.7 lbs.
Metric Height: 0.3 m
Metric Weight: 3.5 kg

Possible Moves: Tackle, Tail Whip, Quick Attack, Focus Energy, Bite, Pursuit, Hyper Fang, Assurance, Crunch, Sucker Punch, Super Fang, Double-Edge, Endeavor

Rattata → Raticate

REGION: Alola

ALOLAN RATTATA
Mouse Pokémon

TYPE: DARK-NORMAL

Rattata sleep during the day and spend their nights searching for the best food to bring back to the Raticate who leads them. They use their strong teeth to gnaw their way into people's kitchens.

How to Say It: uh-LO-luhn RA-TAT-ta
Imperial Height: 1'00''
Imperial Weight: 8.4 lbs.
Metric Height: 0.3 m
Metric Weight: 3.8 kg

Possible Moves: Tackle, Tail Whip, Quick Attack, Focus Energy, Bite, Pursuit, Hyper Fang, Assurance, Crunch, Sucker Punch, Super Fang, Double-Edge, Endeavor

Alolan Rattata → Alolan Raticate

RAYQUAZA
Sky High Pokémon

REGION:
Hoenn

LEGENDARY POKÉMON

TYPE: DRAGON-FLYING

Legends say the ancient Pokémon Rayquaza flies through the upper atmosphere and feeds on meteoroids. It's known for stopping the endless battles between Kyogre and Groudon.

How to Say It: ray-KWAY-zuh
Imperial Height: 23'00''
Imperial Weight: 455.2 lbs.
Metric Height: 7.0 m
Metric Weight: 206.5 kg

Possible Moves: Twister, Scary Face, Crunch, Hyper Voice, Rest, Air Slash, Ancient Power, Outrage, Dragon Dance, Fly, Extreme Speed, Hyper Beam, Dragon Pulse, Rest

MEGA RAYQUAZA
Sky High Pokémon

TYPE: DRAGON-FLYING

Imperial Height: 35'05''
Imperial Weight: 864.2 lbs.
Metric Height: 10.8 m
Metric Weight: 392.0 kg

Rayquaza

Mega Rayquaza

TYPE: ICE

Created during an ice age, Regice's body is frozen solid, and even lava can't melt it. It can lower the temperature of the air around it by several hundred degrees.

How to Say It: REDGE-ice
Imperial Height: 5'11"
Imperial Weight: 385.8 lbs.
Metric Height: 1.8 m
Metric Weight: 175.0 kg

Possible Moves: Explosion, Stomp, Icy Wind, Curse, Superpower, Ancient Power, Amnesia, Charge Beam, Lock-On, Zap Cannon, Ice Beam, Hammer Arm, Hyper Beam, Bulldoze

Does not evolve

REGION: Hoenn

REGICE
Iceberg Pokémon

LEGENDARY POKÉMON

TYPE: NORMAL

According to legend, Regigigas built smaller models of itself out of rock, ice, and magma. It's so enormous that it could tow an entire continent behind it.

How to Say It: rej-jee-GIG-us
Imperial Height: 12'02"
Imperial Weight: 925.9 lbs.
Metric Height: 3.7 m
Metric Weight: 420.0 kg

Possible Moves: Fire Punch, Ice Punch, Thunder Punch, Dizzy Punch, Knock Off, Confuse Ray, Foresight, Revenge, Wide Guard, Zen Headbutt, Payback, Crush Grip, Heavy Slam, Giga Impact

Does not evolve

REGION: Sinnoh

REGIGIGAS
Colossal Pokémon

LEGENDARY POKÉMON

REGIROCK
Rock Peak Pokémon

LEGENDARY POKÉMON

TYPE: ROCK

Regirock's body is made entirely of rocks, and these rocks were recently discovered to be from all around the world. It repairs itself after battle by seeking out new rocks.

How to Say It: REDGE-ee-rock
Imperial Height: 5'07''
Imperial Weight: 507.1 lbs.
Metric Height: 1.7 m
Metric Weight: 230.0 kg

Possible Moves: Explosion, Stomp, Rock Throw, Curse, Superpower, Ancient Power, Iron Defense, Charge Beam, Lock-On, Zap Cannon, Stone Edge, Hammer Arm, Hyper Beam, Bulldoze

Does not evolve

REGISTEEL
Iron Pokémon

REGION: Hoenn

LEGENDARY POKÉMON

TYPE: STEEL

Registeel isn't actually made of steel—it's a strange substance harder than any known metal. Ancient people sealed it away in a prison.

How to Say It: REDGE-ee-steel
Imperial Height: 6'03''
Imperial Weight: 451.9 lbs.
Metric Height: 1.9 m
Metric Weight: 205.0 kg

Possible Moves: Explosion, Stomp, Metal Claw, Curse, Superpower, Ancient Power, Iron Defense, Amnesia, Charge Beam, Lock-On, Zap Cannon, Iron Head, Flash Cannon, Hammer Arm, Hyper Beam, Bulldoze

Does not evolve

TYPE: WATER-ROCK

Relicanth today look much the same as they did 100 million years ago. The abundant fat within their bodies helps them survive the pressure and cold of their deep-sea home.

How to Say It: REL-uh-canth
Imperial Height: 3'03''
Imperial Weight: 51.6 lbs.
Metric Height: 1.0 m
Metric Weight: 23.4 kg

Possible Moves: Flail, Head Smash, Tackle, Harden, Mud Sport, Water Gun, Rock Tomb, Ancient Power, Dive, Take Down, Yawn, Rest, Hydro Pump, Double-Edge

REGIONS:
Alola
Hoenn
Kalos
(Coastal)

RELICANTH
Longevity Pokémon

Does not evolve

REGIONS:
Alola
Johto
Kalos
(Coastal)

REMORAID
Jet Pokémon

TYPE: WATER

Remoraid often lives alongside Mantine, gobbling up the larger Pokémon's leftover food scraps. In exchange, Remoraid helps defend Mantine by attacking foes with a high-velocity jet of water.

How to Say It: REM-oh-raid
Imperial Height: 2'00''
Imperial Weight: 26.5 lbs.
Metric Height: 0.6 m
Metric Weight: 12.0 kg

Possible Moves: Water Gun, Lock-On, Psybeam, Aurora Beam, Bubble Beam, Focus Energy, Water Pulse, Signal Beam, Ice Beam, Bullet Seed, Hydro Pump, Hyper Beam, Soak

Remoraid ⇨ **Octillery**

RESHIRAM
Vast White Pokémon

REGION: Unova

LEGENDARY POKÉMON

TYPE: DRAGON-FIRE

Legends say Reshiram is drawn to those who value the truth. The flare of its fiery tail can disrupt the atmosphere and cause strange weather patterns.

How to Say It: RESH-i-ram
Imperial Height: 10'06''
Imperial Weight: 727.5 lbs.

Metric Height: 3.2 m
Metric Weight: 330.0 kg

Possible Moves: Fire Fang, Dragon Rage, Imprison, Ancient Power, Flamethrower, Dragon Breath, Slash, Extrasensory, Fusion Flare, Dragon Pulse, Noble Roar, Crunch, Fire Blast, Outrage, Hyper Voice, Blue Flare

Overdrive Mode

Does not evolve

TYPE: PSYCHIC

Reuniclus shake hands with each other to create a network between their brains. Working together boosts their psychic power, and they can crush huge rocks with their minds.

How to Say It: ree-yoo-NIH-klus
Imperial Height: 3'03''
Imperial Weight: 44.3 lbs.
Metric Height: 1.0 m
Metric Weight: 20.1 kg

Possible Moves: Psywave, Reflect, Rollout, Snatch, Hidden Power, Light Screen, Charm, Recover, Psyshock, Endeavor, Future Sight, Pain Split, Psychic, Dizzy Punch, Skill Swap, Heal Block, Wonder Room

REGIONS:
Kalos
(Coastal)
Unova

REUNICLUS
Multiplying Pokémon

Solosis ⇒ Duosion ⇒ Reuniclus

REGIONS:
Kalos
(Coastal)
Kanto

RHYDON
Drill Pokémon

TYPE: GROUND-ROCK

Rhydon's horn, which it uses as a drill, is hard enough to crush diamonds. Its hide is like armor, and it can run right through molten lava without feeling a thing.

How to Say It: RYE-don
Imperial Height: 6'03''
Imperial Weight: 264.6 lbs.
Metric Height: 1.9 m
Metric Weight: 120.0 kg

Possible Moves: Megahorn, Horn Drill, Horn Attack, Tail Whip, Stomp, Fury Attack, Scary Face, Rock Blast, Bulldoze, Chip Away, Take Down, Hammer Arm, Drill Run, Stone Edge, Earthquake, Smack Down

Rhyhorn ⇒ Rhydon ⇒ Rhyperior

RHYHORN
Spikes Pokémon

REGIONS:
Kalos
(Coastal)
Kanto

TYPE: GROUND-ROCK

A charging Rhyhorn is so single-minded that it doesn't think about anything else until it demolishes its target.

How to Say It: RYE-horn
Imperial Height: 3'03"
Imperial Weight: 253.5 lbs.
Metric Height: 1.0 m
Metric Weight: 115.0 kg

Possible Moves: Horn Attack, Tail Whip, Stomp, Fury Attack, Scary Face, Rock Blast, Bulldoze, Chip Away, Take Down, Drill Run, Stone Edge, Earthquake, Horn Drill, Megahorn, Rock Blast

Rhyhorn ⇒ Rhydon ⇒ Rhyperior

RHYPERIOR
Drill Pokémon

REGIONS:
Kalos
(Coastal)
Sinnoh

TYPE: GROUND-ROCK

Rhyperior uses the holes in its hands to bombard its opponents with rocks. Sometimes it even hurls a Geodude! Rhyperior's rocky hide is thick enough to protect it from molten lava.

How to Say It: rye-PEER-ee-or
Imperial Height: 7'10"
Imperial Weight: 623.5 lbs.
Metric Height: 2.4 m
Metric Weight: 282.8 kg

Possible Moves: Hammer Arm, Rock Wrecker, Horn Drill, Poison Jab, Horn Attack, Tail Whip, Fury Attack, Scary Face, Scary Face, Smack Down, Stomp, Bulldoze, Chip Away, Rock Blast, Drill Run, Take Down, Stone Edge, Earthquake, Megahorn

Rhyhorn ⇒ Rhydon ⇒ Rhyperior

TYPE: BUG-FAIRY

Ribombee gathers up pollen and forms it into a variety of puffs with different effects. Some enhance battle skills and can be used as supplements, while others deliver excellent nutrition.

How to Say It: rih-BOMB-bee
Imperial Height: 0'08''
Imperial Weight: 1.1 lbs.
Metric Height: 0.2 m
Metric Weight: 0.5 kg

Possible Moves: Pollen Puff, Absorb, Fairy Wind, Stun Spore, Struggle Bug, Silver Wind, Draining Kiss, Sweet Scent, Bug Buzz, Dazzling Gleam, Aromatherapy, Quiver Dance

REGION: Alola

RIBOMBEE
Bee Fly Pokémon

Cutiefly ➡ **Ribombee**

REGIONS: Alola Kalos *(Central)* Sinnoh

RIOLU
Emanation Pokémon

TYPE: FIGHTING

Riolu has a reputation as a hard worker with great stamina. It can sense the auras of others, whether people or Pokémon, and uses this sense to determine how they're doing physically and emotionally.

How to Say It: ree-OH-loo
Imperial Height: 2'04''
Imperial Weight: 44.5 lbs.
Metric Height: 0.7 m
Metric Weight: 20.2 kg

Possible Moves: Foresight, Quick Attack, Endure, Counter, Feint, Force Palm, Copycat, Screech, Reversal, Nasty Plot, Final Gambit

Riolu ➡ **Lucario** ➡ **Mega Lucario**

ROCKRUFF

Puppy Pokémon

REGION: Alola

TYPE: ROCK

Rockruff has a long history of living in harmony with people. This friendly Pokémon is often recommended for Trainers just starting their journey, although it tends to develop a bit of a wild side as it grows.

How to Say It: ROCK-ruff
Imperial Height: 1'08''
Imperial Weight: 20.3 lbs.
Metric Height: 0.5 m
Metric Weight: 9.2 kg

Possible Moves: Tackle, Leer, Sand Attack, Bite, Howl, Rock Throw, Odor Sleuth, Rock Tomb, Roar, Stealth Rock, Rock Slide, Scary Face, Crunch, Rock Climb, Stone Edge

Rockruff

Lycanroc
(Midday Form)

Lycanroc
(Dusk Form)

Lycanroc
(Midnight Form)

ROGGENROLA

Mantle Pokémon

REGIONS: Alola Kalos *(Coastal)* Unova

TYPE: ROCK

The cavity that takes up much of a Roggenrola's body is an ear, which allows it to track sounds through the darkness of its underground home. These Pokémon compete with Carbink and Geodude to see who has the hardest surface.

How to Say It: rah-gen-ROH-lah
Imperial Height: 1'04''
Imperial Weight: 39.7 lbs.
Metric Height: 0.4 m
Metric Weight: 18.0 kg

Possible Moves: Tackle, Harden, Sand Attack, Headbutt, Rock Blast, Mud-Slap, Iron Defense, Smack Down, Rock Slide, Stealth Rock, Sandstorm, Stone Edge, Explosion

Roggenrola   Boldore   Gigalith

TYPE: GRASS-POISON

Thieves sometimes try to swipe the lovely blossoms Roselia grows. It responds with a shower of sharp, poisonous thorns.

REGIONS:
Hoenn
Kalos
(Central)

ROSELIA
Thorn Pokémon

How to Say It: roh-ZEH-lee-uh
Imperial Height: 1'00''
Imperial Weight: 4.4 lbs.
Metric Height: 0.3 m
Metric Weight: 2.0 kg

Possible Moves: Absorb, Growth, Poison Sting, Stun Spore, Mega Drain, Leech Seed, Magical Leaf, Grass Whistle, Giga Drain, Toxic Spikes, Sweet Scent, Ingrain, Petal Dance, Toxic, Aromatherapy, Synthesis, Petal Blizzard

Budew   **Roselia**   **Roserade**

REGIONS:
Kalos
(Central)
Sinnoh

ROSERADE
Bouquet Pokémon

TYPE: GRASS-POISON

With its beautiful blooms, enticing aroma, and graceful movements, Roserade is quite enchanting—but watch out! Its arms conceal thorny whips, and the thorns carry poison.

How to Say It: ROSE-raid
Imperial Height: 2'11''
Imperial Weight: 32.0 lbs.
Metric Height: 0.9 m
Metric Weight: 14.5 kg

Possible Moves: Venom Drench, Grassy Terrain, Weather Ball, Poison Sting, Mega Drain, Magical Leaf, Sweet Scent

Budew   **Roselia**   **Roserade**   359

ROTOM
Plasma Pokémon

REGIONS:
Kalos
(Mountain)
Sinnoh

TYPE: ELECTRIC-GHOST

Scientists are conducting ongoing research on Rotom, which shows potential as a power source. Sometimes it sneaks into electrical appliances and causes trouble.

How to Say It: ROW-tom
Imperial Height: 1'00''
Imperial Weight: 0.7 lbs.
Metric Height: 0.3 m
Metric Weight: 0.3 kg

Possible Moves: Discharge, Charge, Trick, Astonish, Thunder Wave, Thunder Shock, Confuse Ray, Uproar, Double Team, Shock Wave, Ominous Wind, Substitute, Electro Ball, Hex

Does not evolve

TYPE: GRASS-FLYING

During the day, Rowlet rests and generates energy via photosynthesis. In the night, it flies silently to sneak up on foes and launch a flurry of kicking attacks.

How to Say It: ROW-let
Imperial Height: 1'00''
Imperial Weight: 3.3 lbs.
Metric Height: 0.3 m
Metric Weight: 1.5 kg

Possible Moves: Tackle, Leafage, Ominous Wind, Growl, Peck, Astonish, Razor Leaf, Foresight, Pluck, Synthesis, Fury Attack, Sucker Punch, Leaf Blade, Feather Dance, Brave Bird, Nasty Plot

ROWLET
Grass Quill Pokémon

Rowlet → Dartrix → Decidueye

RUFFLET
Eaglet Pokémon

TYPE: NORMAL-FLYING

Rufflet hasn't yet learned to control its aggressive impulses, and it will pick a fight with just about any opponent. Every defeat makes it stronger, which reinforces its reckless behavior.

How to Say It: RUF-lit
Imperial Height: 1'08''
Imperial Weight: 23.1 lbs.
Metric Height: 0.5 m
Metric Weight: 10.5 kg

Possible Moves: Peck, Leer, Fury Attack, Wing Attack, Hone Claws, Scary Face, Aerial Ace, Slash, Defog, Tailwind, Air Slash, Crush Claw, Sky Drop, Whirlwind, Brave Bird, Thrash

Rufflet → Braviary

SABLEYE
Darkness Pokémon

REGIONS:
Alola
Hoenn
Kalos
(Coastal)

DARK-GHOST

Sableye can often be found pursuing Carbink to satisfy their love of shiny gemstones. Stories say this gem-eyed Pokémon can make off with your spirit, so many people avoid them.

How to Say It: SAY-bull-eye
Imperial Height: 1'08''
Imperial Weight: 24.3 lbs.
Metric Height: 0.5 m
Metric Weight: 11.0 kg

Possible Moves: Leer, Scratch, Foresight, Night Shade, Astonish, Fury Swipes, Detect, Shadow Sneak, Feint Attack, Fake Out, Punishment, Knock Off, Shadow Claw, Confuse Ray, Zen Headbutt, Power Gem, Shadow Ball, Foul Play, Quash, Mean Look

MEGA SABLEYE
Darkness Pokémon

TYPE: DARK-GHOST

Imperial Height: 1'08''
Imperial Weight: 354.9 lbs.
Metric Height: 0.5 m
Metric Weight: 161.0 kg

Sableye   **Mega Sableye**

TYPE: DRAGON-FLYING

In its delight at finally being able to fly, Salamence sometimes gets a little rowdy. Its fiery celebration can be hazardous to nearby fields and property. It's also inclined to destructive fits of temper.

How to Say It: SAL-uh-mence
Imperial Height: 4'11''
Imperial Weight: 226.2 lbs.
Metric Height: 1.5 m
Metric Weight: 102.6 kg

Possible Moves: Fly, Protect, Dragon Tail, Fire Fang, Thunder Fang, Rage, Ember, Leer, Bite, Dragon Breath, Headbutt, Focus Energy, Crunch, Dragon Claw, Zen Headbutt, Scary Face, Flamethrower, Double-Edge

SALAMENCE
Dragon Pokémon

MEGA SALAMENCE
Dragon Pokémon

TYPE: DRAGON-FLYING

Imperial Height: 5'11''
Imperial Weight: 248.2 lbs.
Metric Height: 1.8 m
Metric Weight: 112.6 kg

Bagon → **Shelgon** →

Salamence →

Mega Salamence

SALANDIT
Toxic Lizard Pokémon

**REGION:
Alola**

TYPE: POISON-FIRE

Salandit gives off a toxic gas that causes dizziness and confusion when inhaled. It uses this gas to distract opponents before attacking. These Pokémon can often be found living on the slopes of volcanoes.

How to Say It: suh-LAN-dit
Imperial Height: 2'00''
Imperial Weight: 10.6 lbs.
Metric Height: 0.6 m
Metric Weight: 4.8 kg

Possible Moves: Scratch, Poison Gas, Ember, Sweet Scent, Dragon Rage, Smog, Double Slap, Flame Burst, Toxic, Nasty Plot, Venoshock, Flamethrower, Venom Drench, Dragon Pulse

Salandit ➡ Salazzle

SALAZZLE
Toxic Lizard Pokémon

**REGION:
Alola**

TYPE: POISON-FIRE

Apparently, all Salazzle are female. They tend to attract several male Salandit and live together in a group. The poisonous gas they give off contains powerful pheromones and is sometimes used as a perfume ingredient.

How to Say It: suh-LAZ-zuhl
Imperial Height: 3'11''
Imperial Weight: 48.9 lbs.
Metric Height: 1.2 m
Metric Weight: 22.2 kg

Possible Moves: Captivate, Disable, Encore, Torment, Swagger, Pound, Poison Gas, Ember, Sweet Scent, Dragon Rage, Smog, Double Slap, Flame Burst, Toxic, Nasty Plot, Venoshock, Flamethrower, Venom Drench, Dragon Pulse

Salandit ➡ Salazzle

TYPE: WATER

From the armor on its front legs, Samurott can draw its swordlike seamitars in a heartbeat. Its glare can make everyone behave.

How to Say It: SAM-uh-rot
Imperial Height: 4'11''
Imperial Weight: 208.6 lbs.
Metric Height: 1.5 m
Metric Weight: 94.6 kg

Possible Moves: Megahorn, Tackle, Tail Whip, Water Gun, Water Sport, Focus Energy, Razor Shell, Fury Cutter, Water Pulse, Revenge, Aqua Jet, Slash, Encore, Aqua Tail, Retaliate, Swords Dance, Hydro Pump

SAMUROTT
Formidable Pokémon

Oshawott ⇨ **Dewott** ⇨ **Samurott**

TYPE: GROUND-DARK

Keep a sharp eye out if you're walking through the desert. Sandile like to bury themselves in the sand, where they stay hidden and protected from the sun—and if you step on them, you might get chomped!

How to Say It: SAN-dyle
Imperial Height: 2'04''
Imperial Weight: 33.5 lbs.
Metric Height: 0.7 m
Metric Weight: 15.2 kg

Possible Moves: Leer, Rage, Bite, Sand Attack, Torment, Sand Tomb, Assurance, Mud-Slap, Embargo, Swagger, Crunch, Dig, Scary Face, Foul Play, Sandstorm, Earthquake, Thrash

SANDILE
Desert Croc Pokémon

Sandile ⇨ **Krokorok** ⇨ **Krookodile**

SANDSHREW
Mouse Pokémon

REGIONS:
Kalos
(Mountain)
Kanto

TYPE: GROUND

Sandshrew often lives in the desert and other dry places, so it's accustomed to life with very little rainfall. It can move quickly by curling itself into a ball and rolling across the sand.

How to Say It: SAND-shroo
Imperial Height: 2'00''
Imperial Weight: 26.5 lbs.
Metric Height: 0.6 m
Metric Weight: 12.0 kg

Possible Moves: Scratch, Defense Curl, Sand Attack, Poison Sting, Rollout, Rapid Spin, Swift, Fury Cutter, Magnitude, Fury Swipes, Sand Tomb, Slash, Dig, Gyro Ball, Swords Dance, Sandstorm, Earthquake

Sandshrew ⇨ Sandslash

ALOLAN SANDSHREW
Mouse Pokémon

REGION:
Alola

TYPE: ICE-STEEL

Sandshrew lives high in the snowy mountains of Alola, where it has developed a shell of thick steel. It's very good at sliding across the ice—whether it does so under its own power or as part of a Sandshrew-sliding contest!

How to Say It: uh-LO-luhn SAND-shroo
Imperial Height: 2'04''
Imperial Weight: 88.2 lbs.
Metric Height: 0.7 m
Metric Weight: 40.0 kg

Possible Moves: Scratch, Defense Curl, Bide, Powder Snow, Ice Ball, Rapid Spin, Fury Cutter, Metal Claw, Swift, Fury Swipes, Iron Defense, Slash, Iron Head, Gyro Ball, Swords Dance, Hail, Blizzard

Alolan Sandshrew ⇨ Alolan Sandslash

TYPE: GROUND

The spikes that cover Sandslash are sharp but brittle, easily broken on impact. Fortunately, they grow back very quickly. It sometimes ambushes foes by rolling up into a spiny ball and dropping from above.

How to Say It: SAND-slash
Imperial Height: 3'03''
Imperial Weight: 65.0 lbs.
Metric Height: 1.0 m
Metric Weight: 29.5 kg

Possible Moves: Scratch, Defense Curl, Sand Attack, Poison Sting, Rollout, Rapid Spin, Swift, Fury Cutter, Magnitude, Fury Swipes, Crush Claw, Sand Tomb, Slash, Dig, Gyro Ball, Swords Dance, Sandstorm, Earthquake

REGIONS:
Kalos
(Mountain)
Kanto

SANDSLASH
Mouse Pokémon

Sandshrew ⇨ Sandslash

REGION:
Alola

ALOLAN SANDSLASH
Mouse Pokémon

TYPE: ICE-STEEL

Sandslash is covered in spikes of tough steel, and in the cold mountains where it lives, each spike develops a thick coating of ice. A plume of snow flies up behind it as it dashes across the snowfield.

How to Say It: uh-LO-luhn SAND-slash
Imperial Height: 3'11''
Imperial Weight: 121.3 lbs.
Metric Height: 1.2 m
Metric Weight: 55.0 kg

Possible Moves: Icicle Spear, Metal Burst, Icicle Crash, Slash, Defense Curl, Ice Ball, Metal Claw

Alolan Sandshrew ⇨ Alolan Sandslash

SANDYGAST
Sand Heap Pokémon

REGION:
Alola

TYPE: GHOST-GROUND

A child created a mound of sand while playing on the beach, and it became a Sandygast. Putting your hand in its mouth is a sure way to fall prey to its mind control.

How to Say It: SAN-dee-GAST
Imperial Height: 1'08''
Imperial Weight: 154.3 lbs.
Metric Height: 0.5 m
Metric Weight: 70.0 kg

Possible Moves: Harden, Absorb, Astonish, Sand Attack, Sand Tomb, Mega Drain, Bulldoze, Hypnosis, Iron Defense, Giga Drain, Shadow Ball, Earth Power, Shore Up, Sandstorm

Sandygast   Palossand

SAWK
Karate Pokémon

REGIONS:
Kalos
(Coastal)
Unova

TYPE: FIGHTING

Sawk go deep into the mountains to train their fighting skills relentlessly. If they are disturbed during this training, they become very angry.

How to Say It: SAWK
Imperial Height: 4'07''
Imperial Weight: 112.4 lbs.
Metric Height: 1.4 m
Metric Weight: 51.0 kg

Possible Moves: Rock Smash, Leer, Bide, Focus Energy, Double Kick, Low Sweep, Counter, Karate Chop, Brick Break, Bulk Up, Retaliate, Endure, Quick Guard, Close Combat, Reversal

Does not evolve

TYPE: NORMAL-GRASS

As the seasons change, their horns display different kinds of plant growth. Because of their seasonal migration, some people regard Sawsbuck's appearance as a sign of spring.

How to Say It: SAWZ-buk
Imperial Height: 6'03''
Imperial Weight: 203.9 lbs.
Metric Height: 1.9 m
Metric Weight: 92.5 kg

Possible Moves: Megahorn, Tackle, Camouflage, Growl, Sand Attack, Double Kick, Leech Seed, Feint Attack, Take Down, Jump Kick, Aromatherapy, Energy Ball, Charm, Horn Leech, Nature Power, Double-Edge, Solar Beam

REGION: Unova

SAWSBUCK
Season Pokémon

Autumn Form

Winter Form

Summer Form

Spring Form

Deerling ⇨ Sawsbuck

REGION: Kalos *(Coastal)*

SCATTERBUG
Scatterdust Pokémon

TYPE: BUG

When threatened, Scatterbug protects itself with a cloud of black powder that can paralyze its attacker. This powder also serves as protection from the elements.

How to Say It: SCAT-ter-BUG
Imperial Height: 1'00''
Imperial Weight: 5.5 lbs.

Metric Height: 0.3 m
Metric Weight: 2.5 kg

Possible Moves: Tackle, String Shot, Stun Spore, Bug Bite

 ⇨ ⇨

Scatterbug ⇨ Spewpa ⇨ Vivillon

369

SCEPTILE
Forest Pokémon

REGION: Hoenn

TYPE: GRASS

Razor-edged leaves and nutritious seeds sprout from Sceptile's back. It wields the leaves in battle, and cares for trees by planting its seeds nearby to enrich the soil.

How to Say It: SEP-tile
Imperial Height: 5'07''
Imperial Weight: 115.1 lbs.
Metric Height: 1.7 m
Metric Weight: 52.2 kg

Possible Moves: Dual Chop, Fury Cutter, Leaf Storm, Night Slash, Pound, Leer, Absorb, Quick Attack, Mega Drain, Pursuit, Leaf Blade, Agility, Slam, Detect, X-Scissor, False Swipe, Quick Guard, Screech

MEGA SCEPTILE
Forest Pokémon

TYPE: GRASS-DRAGON
Imperial Height: 6'03''
Imperial Weight: 121.7 lbs.
Metric Height: 1.9 m
Metric Weight: 55.2 kg

Treecko ⇨ Grovyle ⇨ Sceptile ⇨ Mega Sceptile

SCIZOR
Pincer Pokémon

TYPE: BUG-STEEL

When the hot sun beats down, or when a battle gets really fired up, Scizor can release heat through its wings to keep its metal body from melting. Its steel-hard pincers deliver merciless blows.

How to Say It: SIH-zor
Imperial Height: 5'11''
Imperial Weight: 260.1 lbs.
Metric Height: 1.8 m
Metric Weight: 118.0 kg

Possible Moves: Feint, Bullet Punch, Quick Attack, Leer, Focus Energy, Pursuit, False Swipe, Agility, Metal Claw, Fury Cutter, Slash, Razor Wind, Iron Defense, X-Scissor, Night Slash, Double Hit, Iron Head, Swords Dance

MEGA SCIZOR
Pincer Pokémon

TYPE: BUG-STEEL

Imperial Height: 6'07''
Imperial Weight: 275.6 lbs.
Metric Height: 2.0 m
Metric Weight: 125.0 kg

Scyther ➡ **Scizor** ➡ **Mega Scizor**

371

SCOLIPEDE
Megapede Pokémon

REGIONS:
Kalos
(Central)
Unova

TYPE: BUG-POISON

The claws near Scolipede's head can be used to grab, immobilize, and poison its opponent. It moves quickly when chasing down enemies.

How to Say It: SKOH-lih-peed
Imperial Height: 8'02''
Imperial Weight: 442.0 lbs.
Metric Height: 2.5 m
Metric Weight: 200.5 kg

Possible Moves: Iron Defense, Megahorn, Defense Curl, Rollout, Poison Sting, Screech, Pursuit, Protect, Poison Tail, Bug Bite, Venoshock, Baton Pass, Agility, Steamroller, Toxic, Venom Drench, Rock Climb, Double-Edge

Venipede ⇒ Whirlipede ⇒ Scolipede

SCRAFTY
Hoodlum Pokémon

REGIONS:
Alola
Kalos
(Central)
Unova

TYPE: DARK-FIGHTING

Scrafty don't venture outside their territory. They stay close to home so they can defend their turf—and their friends and families—from any encroaching threat.

How to Say It: SKRAF-tee
Imperial Height: 3'07''
Imperial Weight: 66.1 lbs.
Metric Height: 1.1 m
Metric Weight: 30.0 kg

Possible Moves: Leer, Headbutt, Sand Attack, Feint Attack, Sand Attack, Swagger, Low Kick, Payback, Brick Break, Chip Away, High Jump Kick, Scary Face, Crunch, Facade, Rock Climb, Focus Punch, Head Smash

Scraggy ⇒ Scrafty

SCRAGGY
Shedding Pokémon

TYPE: DARK-FIGHTING

The saggy skin that covers Scraggy's lower half can be pulled up to its neck as a shield against attacks. These Pokémon tend to travel in small groups, aiming headbutts at anyone who dares to meet their eyes.

How to Say It: SKRAG-ee
Imperial Height: 2'00''
Imperial Weight: 26.0 lbs.

Metric Height: 0.6 m
Metric Weight: 11.8 kg

Possible Moves: Leer, Headbutt, Sand Attack, Feint Attack, Swagger, Low Kick, Payback, Brick Break, Chip Away, High Jump Kick, Scary Face, Crunch, Facade, Rock Climb, Focus Punch, Head Smash

Scraggy ⇨ Scrafty

TYPE: BUG-FLYING

Scyther's impressive speed in battle leaves its opponents' heads spinning, which gives it an opening to slash in with its sharp scythes. Young Scyther live in the mountains, where they form groups to train these skills.

SCYTHER
Mantis Pokémon

How to Say It: SY-thur
Imperial Height: 4'11''
Imperial Weight: 123.5 lbs.
Metric Height: 1.5 m
Metric Weight: 56.0 kg

Possible Moves: Vacuum Wave, Quick Attack, Leer, Focus Energy, Pursuit, False Swipe, Agility, Wing Attack, Fury Cutter, Slash, Razor Wind, Double Team, X-Scissor, Night Slash, Double Hit, Air Slash, Swords Dance, Feint

Scyther ⇨ Scizor ⇨ Mega Scizor

SEADRA
Dragon Pokémon

REGIONS:
Kalos
(Coastal)
Kanto

TYPE: WATER

When Seadra spins around in the water, it can cause a whirlpool with enough force to capsize a small boat. It sleeps among coral branches.

How to Say It: SEE-dra
Imperial Height: 3'11''
Imperial Weight: 55.1 lbs.
Metric Height: 1.2 m
Metric Weight: 25.0 kg

Possible Moves: Water Gun, Smokescreen, Leer, Bubble, Focus Energy, Bubble Beam, Agility, Twister, Brine, Hydro Pump, Dragon Dance, Dragon Pulse

Horsea → Seadra → Kingdra

SEAKING
Goldfish Pokémon

REGIONS:
Alola
Kalos
(Coastal)
Kanto

TYPE: WATER

When autumn arrives, Seaking turns a deep red, just like the leaves on the trees. Fans of this Pokémon tend to argue about which of its features is more admirable: the fins or the horn.

How to Say It: SEE-king
Imperial Height: 4'03''
Imperial Weight: 86.0 lbs.
Metric Height: 1.3 m
Metric Weight: 39.0 kg

Possible Moves: Megahorn, Poison Jab, Peck, Tail Whip, Water Sport, Supersonic, Horn Attack, Flail, Water Pulse, Aqua Ring, Fury Attack, Agility, Waterfall, Horn Drill, Soak

Goldeen → Seaking

SEALEO
Ball Roll Pokémon

TYPE: ICE-WATER

Sealeo learns about new things by exploring them with its nose, examining the fragrance and texture. It particularly enjoys spinning round objects on its nose.

How to Say It: SEEL-ee-oh
Imperial Height: 3'07''
Imperial Weight: 193.1 lbs.
Metric Height: 1.1 m
Metric Weight: 87.6 kg

Possible Moves: Powder Snow, Growl, Water Gun, Encore, Ice Ball, Body Slam, Aurora Beam, Hail, Swagger, Rest, Snore, Blizzard, Sheer Cold, Defense Curl, Rollout, Brine

Spheal ➡ **Sealeo** ➡ **Walrein**

REGION: Hoenn

SEEDOT
Acorn Pokémon

TYPE: GRASS

Because Seedot hangs from branches by the top of its head, it looks just like an acorn when it isn't moving. For a glossy finish, it drinks plenty of water and polishes itself with leaves.

How to Say It: SEE-dot
Imperial Height: 1'08''
Imperial Weight: 8.8 lbs.
Metric Height: 0.5 m
Metric Weight: 4.0 kg

Possible Moves: Bide, Harden, Growth, Nature Power, Synthesis, Sunny Day, Explosion

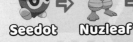

Seedot ➡ **Nuzleaf** ➡ **Shiftry**

375

SEEL
Seal Lion Pokémon

REGIONS:
Alola
Kanto

TYPE: WATER

Researchers aren't sure why Seel have shown up in Alola. They thrive in cold water thanks to a thick layer of blubber, but swimming in warm seas can tire them out quickly.

How to Say It: SEEL
Imperial Height: 3'07"
Imperial Weight: 198.4 lbs.
Metric Height: 1.1 m
Metric Weight: 90.0 kg

Possible Moves: Headbutt, Growl, Water Sport, Icy Wind, Encore, Ice Shard, Rest, Aqua Ring, Aurora Beam, Aqua Jet, Brine, Take Down, Dive, Aqua Tail, Ice Beam, Safeguard, Hail

Seel → Dewgong

SEISMITOAD
Vibration Pokémon

REGION:
Unova

TYPE: WATER-GROUND

When Seismitoad vibrates the bumps on its hands, its punches get a serious power boost—enough to pulverize a boulder with a single hit.

How to Say It: SYZ-mih-tohd
Imperial Height: 4'11"
Imperial Weight: 136.7 lbs.
Metric Height: 1.5 m
Metric Weight: 62.0 kg

Possible Moves: Bubble, Growl, Supersonic, Round, Bubble Beam, Mud Shot, Aqua Ring, Uproar, Muddy Water, Rain Dance, Acid, Flail, Drain Punch, Echoed Voice, Hydro Pump, Hyper Voice

Tympole → Palpitoad → Seismitoad

SENTRET
Scout Pokémon

TYPE: NORMAL

Sentret always sleep in groups of two or more so one of them can keep watch and alert its friends if danger threatens. When alone, they're too nervous to sleep.

How to Say It: SEN-tret
Imperial Height: 2'07''
Imperial Weight: 13.2 lbs.
Metric Height: 0.8 m
Metric Weight: 6.0 kg

Possible Moves: Scratch, Foresight, Defense Curl, Quick Attack, Fury Swipes, Helping Hand, Follow Me, Slam, Rest, Sucker Punch, Amnesia, Baton Pass, Me First, Hyper Voice

Sentret ⇒ **Furret**

SERPERIOR
Regal Pokémon

TYPE: GRASS

A single glare from Serperior can stop most opponents in their tracks. The energy it absorbs from the sun gets a boost inside its body.

How to Say It: sur-PEER-ee-ur
Imperial Height: 10'10''
Imperial Weight: 138.9 lbs.
Metric Height: 3.3 m
Metric Weight: 63.0 kg

Possible Moves: Tackle, Leer, Vine Whip, Wrap, Growth, Leaf Tornado, Leech Seed, Mega Drain, Slam, Leaf Blade, Coil, Giga Drain, Wring Out, Gastro Acid, Leaf Storm

Snivy ⇒ **Servine** ⇒ **Serperior**

377

SERVINE
Grass Snake Pokémon

REGION: Unova

TYPE: GRASS

Dirt on its leaves blocks its photosynthesis, so Servine is fussy about staying clean. It confounds its enemies with quick movements before it strikes with its whiplike vines.

How to Say It: SUR-vine
Imperial Height: 2'07''
Imperial Weight: 35.3 lbs.
Metric Height: 0.8 m
Metric Weight: 16.0 kg

Possible Moves: Tackle, Leer, Vine Whip, Wrap, Growth, Leaf Tornado, Leech Seed, Mega Drain, Slam, Leaf Blade, Coil, Giga Drain, Wring Out, Gastro Acid, Leaf Storm

Snivy   Servine   Serperior

SEVIPER
Fang Snake Pokémon

REGIONS: Hoenn Kalos *(Coastal)*

TYPE: POISON

The sharp blade on Seviper's tail also gives off a powerful poison. These Pokémon constantly feud with Zangoose.

How to Say It: seh-VY-per
Imperial Height: 8'10''
Imperial Weight: 115.7 lbs.
Metric Height: 2.7 m
Metric Weight: 52.5 kg

Possible Moves: Wrap, Swagger, Bite, Lick, Poison Tail, Feint, Screech, Venoshock, Glare, Poison Fang, Venom Drench, Night Slash, Gastro Acid, Haze, Poison Jab, Crunch, Belch, Coil, Wring Out, Swords Dance

Does not evolve

TYPE: BUG-GRASS

Sewaddle makes clothing for itself by sewing leaves together with the sticky thread it produces from its mouth. Fashion designers often use it as a mascot.

How to Say It: seh-WAH-dul
Imperial Height: 1'00''
Imperial Weight: 5.5 lbs.
Metric Height: 0.3 m
Metric Weight: 2.5 kg

Possible Moves: Tackle, String Shot, Bug Bite, Razor Leaf, Struggle Bug, Endure, Sticky Web, Bug Buzz, Flail

SEWADDLE
Sewing Pokémon

Sewaddle ⇨ Swadloon ⇨ Leavanny

379

SHARPEDO
Brutal Pokémon

TYPE: WATER-DARK

Sharpedo can shoot forward at 75 mph when chasing an enemy. This bully of the sea has teeth that are strong enough to crush iron, and the fin on its back is prized by fishermen.

How to Say It: shar-PEE-do
Imperial Height: 5'11''
Imperial Weight: 195.8 lbs.
Metric Height: 1.8 m
Metric Weight: 88.8 kg

Possible Moves: Slash, Night Slash, Feint, Leer, Bite, Rage, Focus Energy, Aqua Jet, Assurance, Screech, Swagger, Ice Fang, Scary Face, Poison Fang, Crunch, Agility, Skull Bash, Taunt

MEGA SHARPEDO
Brutal Pokémon

TYPE: WATER-DARK
Imperial Height: 8'02''
Imperial Weight: 287.3 lbs.
Metric Height: 2.5 m
Metric Weight: 130.3 kg

Carvanha ⇨ Sharpedo ⇨ Mega Sharpedo

SHAYMIN (LAND FORME)
Gratitude Pokémon

MYTHICAL POKÉMON

TYPE: GRASS

When the Gracidea flower blooms, Shaymin gains the power of flight. Wherever it goes, it clears the air of toxins and brings feelings of gratitude.

How to Say It: SHAY-min
Imperial Height: 0'08''
Imperial Weight: 4.6 lbs.
Metric Height: 0.2 m
Metric Weight: 2.1 kg

Possible Moves: Growth, Magical Leaf, Leech Seed, Synthesis, Sweet Scent, Natural Gift, Worry Seed, Aromatherapy, Energy Ball, Sweet Kiss, Healing Wish, Seed Flare

Does not evolve

SHAYMIN (SKY FORME)
Gratitude Pokémon

MYTHICAL POKÉMON

TYPE: GRASS-FLYING

Shaymin has the power to clean the environment in this Forme, too. Once it has transformed, Shaymin Sky Forme flies off to find a new home.

How to Say It: SHAY-min
Imperial Height: 1'04''
Imperial Weight: 11.5 lbs.
Metric Height: 0.4 m
Metric Weight: 5.2 kg

Possible Moves: Growth, Magical Leaf, Leech Seed, Quick Attack, Sweet Scent, Natural Gift, Worry Seed, Air Slash, Energy Ball, Sweet Kiss, Leaf Storm, Seed Flare

Does not evolve

SHEDINJA

Shed Pokémon

REGIONS:
**Hoenn
Kalos**
(Central)

TYPE: BUG-GHOST

Shedinja is a strange Pokémon. It doesn't move, it doesn't breathe, and no one really knows where it came from. Its body seems to be nothing more than a hollow shell.

How to Say It: sheh-DIN-ja
Imperial Height: 2'07''
Imperial Weight: 2.6 lbs.
Metric Height: 0.8 m
Metric Weight: 1.2 kg

Possible Moves: Scratch, Harden, Absorb, Sand Attack, Fury Swipes, Mind Reader, Spite, Confuse Ray, Shadow Sneak, Grudge, Phantom Force, Heal Block, Shadow Ball

Nincada ➡ Ninjask
Nincada ➡ Shedinja

SHELGON

Endurance Pokémon

REGIONS:
**Alola
Hoenn
Kalos**
(Coastal)

TYPE: DRAGON

From the outside, Shelgon appears completely motionless as it awaits Evolution—but within its shell, it's undergoing rapid changes on a cellular level. During this period, it hides in a cave and consumes no food or water.

How to Say It: SHELL-gon
Imperial Height: 3'07''
Imperial Weight: 243.6 lbs.
Metric Height: 1.1 m
Metric Weight: 110.5 kg

Possible Moves: Protect, Rage, Ember, Leer, Bite, Dragon Breath, Headbutt, Focus Energy, Crunch, Dragon Claw, Zen Headbutt, Scary Face, Flamethrower, Double-Edge

Bagon ➡ Shelgon ➡ Salamence ➡ Mega Salamence

TYPE: WATER

Shellder shells are so tough and sturdy that they've been used to make shields in the past. If the Pokémon would just pull its tongue in, nothing could ever get to it.

How to Say It: SHELL-der
Imperial Height: 1'00''
Imperial Weight: 8.8 lbs.
Metric Height: 0.3 m
Metric Weight: 4.0 kg

Possible Moves: Tackle, Water Gun, Withdraw, Supersonic, Icicle Spear, Protect, Leer, Clamp, Ice Shard, Razor Shell, Aurora Beam, Whirlpool, Brine, Iron Defense, Ice Beam, Shell Smash, Hydro Pump

SHELLDER
Bivalve Pokémon

Shellder ⇨ **Cloyster**

SHELLOS (EAST SEA)
Sea Slug Pokémon

TYPE: WATER

East Sea Shellos are bright blue, reflecting the color of their ocean home. Although the two variants of Shellos look quite different from each other, they have the same battle skills and behaviors.

How to Say It: SHELL-loss
Imperial Height: 1'00''
Imperial Weight: 13.9 lbs.
Metric Height: 0.3 m
Metric Weight: 6.3 kg

Possible Moves: Mud-Slap, Mud Sport, Harden, Water Pulse, Mud Bomb, Hidden Power, Rain Dance, Body Slam, Muddy Water, Recover

Shellos
(East Sea)

⇨

Gastrodon
(East Sea)

SHELLOS (WEST SEA)
Sea Slug Pokémon

REGIONS:
Alola
Sinnoh

TYPE: WATER

The seashore-dwelling Shellos have varied coloration depending on where they live and what they eat. West Sea Shellos are bright pink.

How to Say It: SHELL-loss
Imperial Height: 1'00''
Imperial Weight: 13.9 lbs.
Metric Height: 0.3 m
Metric Weight: 6.3 kg

Possible Moves: Mud-Slap, Mud Sport, Harden, Water Pulse, Mud Bomb, Hidden Power, Rain Dance, Body Slam, Muddy Water, Recover

Shellos
(West Sea) ⇨ **Gastrodon**
(West Sea)

SHELMET
Snail Pokémon

REGIONS:
Kalos
(Mountain)
Unova

TYPE: BUG

Shelmet evolves when exposed to electricity, but only if Karrablast is nearby. It's unclear why this is the case.

How to Say It: SHELL-meht
Imperial Height: 1'04''
Imperial Weight: 17.0 lbs.
Metric Height: 0.4 m
Metric Weight: 7.7 kg

Possible Moves: Absorb, Acid, Bide, Curse, Struggle Bug, Mega Drain, Yawn, Protect, Acid Armor, Giga Drain, Body Slam, Bug Buzz, Recover, Guard Swap, Final Gambit

Shelmet ⇨ **Accelgor**

TYPE: ROCK-STEEL

In its own time, this ancient Pokémon lived in the jungle. Many Shieldon fossils have been found, and the heavy armor that protected this Pokémon's face is generally well preserved.

How to Say It: SHEEL-don
Imperial Height: 1'08''
Imperial Weight: 125.7 lbs.
Metric Height: 0.5 m
Metric Weight: 57.0 kg

Possible Moves: Tackle, Protect, Taunt, Metal Sound, Take Down, Iron Defense, Swagger, Ancient Power, Endure, Metal Burst, Iron Head, Heavy Slam

REGIONS:
Alola
Sinnoh

SHIELDON
Shield Pokémon

Shieldon ➡ Bastiodon

REGION:
Hoenn

SHIFTRY
Wicked Pokémon

TYPE: GRASS-DARK

Shiftry makes its home in the tops of ancient trees. Its leafy fans can stir up powerful gusts of wind.

How to Say It: SHIFF-tree
Imperial Height: 4'03''
Imperial Weight: 131.4 lbs.
Metric Height: 1.3 m
Metric Weight: 59.6 kg

Possible Moves: Feint Attack, Whirlwind, Nasty Plot, Razor Leaf, Leaf Tornado, Leaf Storm, Hurricane

Seedot ➡ Nuzleaf ➡ Shiftry

385

SHIINOTIC

Illuminating Pokémon

TYPE: GRASS-FAIRY

It's a bad idea to wander in Shiinotic's forest home at night. The strange, flickering lights given off by this Pokémon's spores can confuse travelers and cause them to lose their way.

How to Say It: shee-NAH-tick
Imperial Height: 3'03"
Imperial Weight: 25.4 lbs.
Metric Height: 1.0 m
Metric Weight: 11.5 kg

Possible Moves: Absorb, Astonish, Ingrain, Flash, Moonlight, Mega Drain, Sleep Powder, Confuse Ray, Giga Drain, Strength Sap, Spore, Moonblast, Dream Eater, Spotlight

Morelull ⇨ **Shiinotic**

SHINX

Flash Pokémon

REGION: Sinnoh

TYPE: ELECTRIC

When Shinx senses danger, its fur gives off a bright flash. This brilliant light blinds its attacker so Shinx can make a hasty escape.

How to Say It: SHINKS
Imperial Height: 1'08"
Imperial Weight: 20.9 lbs.
Metric Height: 0.5 m
Metric Weight: 9.5 kg

Possible Moves: Tackle, Leer, Charge, Spark, Baby-Doll Eyes, Bite, Roar, Swagger, Thunder Fang, Crunch, Scary Face, Discharge, Wild Charge

Shinx ⇨ **Luxio** ⇨ **Luxray**

SHROOMISH
Mushroom Pokémon

TYPE: GRASS

Shroomish live deep in the forest and make their home in moist soil, using rotted plant material as food. The spores it shakes from its cap are poisonous.

How to Say It: SHROOM-ish
Imperial Height: 1'04"
Imperial Weight: 9.9 lbs.
Metric Height: 0.4 m
Metric Weight: 4.5 kg

Possible Moves: Absorb, Tackle, Stun Spore, Leech Seed, Mega Drain, Headbutt, Poison Powder, Worry Seed, Growth, Giga Drain, Seed Bomb, Spore, Toxic

Shroomish ⇨ Breloom

SHUCKLE
Mold Pokémon

TYPE: BUG-ROCK

Shuckle stores berries in its shell so it always has a food supply. This comes in handy when it hides away under the rocks.

How to Say It: SHUCK-kull
Imperial Height: 2'00"
Imperial Weight: 45.2 lbs.
Metric Height: 0.6 m
Metric Weight: 20.5 kg

Possible Moves: Sticky Web, Withdraw, Constrict, Bide, Rollout, Encore, Wrap, Struggle Bug, Safeguard, Rest, Rock Throw, Gastro Acid, Power Trick, Shell Smash, Rock Slide, Bug Bite, Power Split, Guard Split, Stone Edge

Does not evolve

SHUPPET

Puppet Pokémon

TYPE: GHOST

Shuppet feeds on negative emotions, so having one around to suck up all the bad feelings can be beneficial. On the other hand, if you notice Shuppet gathering around a house, you might do well to stay away.

How to Say It: SHUP-pett
Imperial Height: 2'00''
Imperial Weight: 5.1 lbs.
Metric Height: 0.6 m
Metric Weight: 2.3 kg

Possible Moves: Knock Off, Screech, Night Shade, Spite, Will-O-Wisp, Shadow Sneak, Curse, Feint Attack, Hex, Shadow Ball, Sucker Punch, Embargo, Snatch, Grudge, Trick, Phantom Force

Shuppet ⇨ Banette ⇨ Mega Banette

SIGILYPH

Avianoid Pokémon

TYPE: PSYCHIC-FLYING

Sigilyph were appointed to keep watch over an ancient city. Their patrol route never varies.

How to Say It: SIH-jih-liff
Imperial Height: 4'07''
Imperial Weight: 30.9 lbs.
Metric Height: 1.4 m
Metric Weight: 14.0 kg

Possible Moves: Gust, Miracle Eye, Hypnosis, Psywave, Tailwind, Whirlwind, Psybeam, Air Cutter, Light Screen, Reflect, Synchronoise, Mirror Move, Gravity, Air Slash, Psychic, Cosmic Power, Sky Attack

Does not evolve

SILCOON
Cocoon Pokémon

TYPE: BUG

While waiting to evolve, Silcoon wraps its body in silk and attaches itself to a branch. It leaves a tiny hole so it can see. The cocoon protects the Pokémon and collects rainwater so it can drink.

How to Say It: sill-COON
Imperial Height: 2'00''
Imperial Weight: 22.0 lbs.

Metric Height: 0.6 m
Metric Weight: 10.0 kg

Possible Move: Harden

Wurmple ➡ Silcoon ➡ Beautifly

SILVALLY
Synthetic Pokémon

REGION: Alola

LEGENDARY POKÉMON

TYPE: NORMAL

Learning to trust its Trainer caused this Pokémon to evolve and discard the mask that kept its power tightly controlled. Silvally can change its type in battle, making it a formidable opponent.

How to Say It: sill-VAL-lie
Imperial Height: 7'07''
Imperial Weight: 221.6 lbs.
Metric Height: 2.3 m
Metric Weight: 100.5 kg

Possible Moves: Multi-Attack, Heal Block, Imprison, Iron Head, Poison Fang, Fire Fang, Ice Fang, Thunder Fang, Tackle, Rage, Pursuit, Bite, Aerial Ace, Crush Claw, Scary Face, X-Scissor, Take Down, Metal Sound, Crunch, Double Hit, Air Slash, Punishment, Razor Wind, Tri Attack, Double-Edge, Parting Shot

Type: Null ⇒ Silvally

SIMIPOUR
Geyser Pokémon

TYPE: WATER

Simipour can shoot water out of its tail with such force that it can punch right through a concrete wall. When its stores run low, it dips its tail into clean water to suck up a refill.

How to Say It: SIH-mee-por
Imperial Height: 3'03''
Imperial Weight: 63.9 lbs.
Metric Height: 1.0 m
Metric Weight: 29.0 kg

Possible Moves: Leer, Lick, Fury Swipes, Scald

Panpour ⇨ Simipour

TYPE: GRASS

Simisage's tail is covered in thorns, and it uses the tail like a whip to lash out at opponents. It always seems to be in a bad mood.

How to Say It: SIH-mee-sayj
Imperial Height: 3'07''
Imperial Weight: 67.2 lbs.
Metric Height: 1.1 m
Metric Weight: 30.5 kg

Possible Moves: Leer, Lick, Fury Swipes, Seed Bomb

SIMISAGE
Thorn Monkey Pokémon

Pansage ⇨ Simisage

SIMISEAR

Ember Pokémon

TYPE: FIRE

Simisear's head and tail give off embers in the heat of battle . . . or any time it's excited. It has quite a sweet tooth.

How to Say It: SIH-mee-seer
Imperial Height: 3'03"
Imperial Weight: 67.1 lbs.
Metric Height: 1.0 m
Metric Weight: 28.0 kg

Possible Moves: Leer, Lick, Fury Swipes, Flame Burst

Pansear ➡ **Simisear**

SKARMORY

Armor Bird Pokémon

TYPE: STEEL-FLYING

Skarmory sheds its sharp-edged feathers as it grows, and warriors of old would collect them for use as weapons. When it rains, Skarmory stays in its nest so its metal doesn't rust.

How to Say It: SKAR-more-ree
Imperial Height: 5'07"
Imperial Weight: 111.3 lbs.
Metric Height: 1.7 m
Metric Weight: 50.5 kg

Possible Moves: Leer, Peck, Sand Attack, Metal Claw, Air Cutter, Fury Attack, Feint, Swift, Spikes, Agility, Steel Wing, Slash, Metal Sound, Air Slash, Autotomize, Night Slash

Does not evolve

TYPE: GRASS

Calm and gentle, Skiddo have been living side by side with people for many generations. They can create energy via photosynthesis.

How to Say It: skid-OO
Imperial Height: 2'11''
Imperial Weight: 68.3 lbs.
Metric Height: 0.9 m
Metric Weight: 31.0 kg

Possible Moves: Tackle, Growth, Vine Whip, Tail Whip, Leech Seed, Razor Leaf, Worry Seed, Synthesis, Take Down, Bulldoze, Seed Bomb, Bulk Up, Double-Edge, Horn Leech, Leaf Blade, Milk Drink

REGION:
Kalos
(Central)

SKIDDO
Mount Pokémon

Skiddo ⇨ Gogoat

TYPE: GRASS-FLYING

In mild temperatures, the flower on Skiploom's head begins to bloom. The petals start to open at just above sixty-four degrees Fahrenheit, and warmer temperatures coax them into full blossom.

How to Say It: SKIP-loom
Imperial Height: 2'00''
Imperial Weight: 2.2 lbs.
Metric Height: 0.6 m
Metric Weight: 1.0 kg

Possible Moves: Splash, Absorb, Synthesis, Tail Whip, Tackle, Fairy Wind, Poison Powder, Stun Spore, Sleep Powder, Bullet Seed, Leech Seed, Mega Drain, Acrobatics, Rage Powder, Cotton Spore, U-turn, Worry Seed, Giga Drain, Bounce, Memento

REGIONS:
Johto
Kalos
(Central)

SKIPLOOM
Cottonweed Pokémon

Hoppip ⇨ Skiploom ⇨ Jumpluff

SKITTY
Kitten Pokémon

REGIONS:
Hoenn
Kalos
(Central)

TYPE: NORMAL

Anything that moves, including its own tail, draws Skitty's attention and starts a playful game of chase. Wild Skitty live in trees.

How to Say It: SKIT-tee
Imperial Height: 2'00''
Imperial Weight: 24.3 lbs.
Metric Height: 0.6 m
Metric Weight: 11.0 kg

Possible Moves: Fake Out, Growl, Tail Whip, Tackle, Foresight, Attract, Sing, Disarming Voice, Double Slap, Copycat, Assist, Charm, Feint Attack, Wake-Up Slap, Covet, Heal Bell, Double-Edge, Captivate, Play Rough

Skitty   Delcatty

SKORUPI
Scorpion Pokémon

REGIONS:
Kalos
(Mountain)
Sinnoh

TYPE: POISON-BUG

After burying itself in the sand, Skorupi lurks in hiding. If an intruder gets too close, it latches on with the poisonous claws on its tail.

How to Say It: skor-ROOP-ee
Imperial Height: 2'07''
Imperial Weight: 26.5 lbs.
Metric Height: 0.8 m
Metric Weight: 12.0 kg

Possible Moves: Bite, Poison Sting, Leer, Knock Off, Pin Missile, Acupressure, Pursuit, Bug Bite, Poison Fang, Venoshock, Hone Claws, Toxic Spikes, Night Slash, Scary Face, Crunch, Fell Stinger, Cross Poison

Skorupi   Drapion

SKRELP
Mock Kelp Pokémon

TYPE: POISON-WATER

Skrelp is a weak swimmer, so it spends much of its time hidden among seaweed in an effort to avoid attacks. If you see a Dhelmise in Alolan waters, there's a good chance you'll find Skrelp nearby.

How to Say It: SKRELP
Imperial Height: 1'08''
Imperial Weight: 16.1 lbs.
Metric Height: 0.5 m
Metric Weight: 7.3 kg

Possible Moves: Tackle, Smokescreen, Water Gun, Feint Attack, Tail Whip, Bubble, Acid, Camouflage, Poison Tail, Water Pulse, Double Team, Toxic, Aqua Tail, Sludge Bomb, Hydro Pump, Dragon Pulse

Skrelp ⇨ **Dragalge**

TYPE: POISON-DARK

From the end of its tail, Skuntank can shoot a noxious fluid more than 160 feet. This fluid smells awful, and the stench only gets worse if it's not cleaned up immediately.

How to Say It: SKUN-tank
Imperial Height: 3'03''
Imperial Weight: 83.8 lbs.
Metric Height: 1.0 m
Metric Weight: 38.0 kg

Possible Moves: Scratch, Focus Energy, Poison Gas, Screech, Fury Swipes, Smokescreen, Feint, Slash, Toxic, Acid Spray, Night Slash, Memento, Belch, Explosion, Venom Drench, Sucker Punch

REGIONS:
Kalos
(Coastal)
Sinnoh

SKUNTANK
Skunk Pokémon

Stunky ⇨ **Skuntank**

SLAKING

Lazy Pokémon

REGION: Hoenn

TYPE: NORMAL

Slaking lies in one place and pulls up grass to eat. Circular bare spots in a meadow might be a sign that a Slaking lives nearby. After eating everything within reach, it moves to another spot, but it's not happy about that.

How to Say It: SLACK-ing
Imperial Height: 6'07''
Imperial Weight: 287.7 lbs.
Metric Height: 2.0 m
Metric Weight: 130.5 kg

Possible Moves: Scratch, Yawn, Encore, Slack Off, Feint Attack, Amnesia, Covet, Swagger, Chip Away, Counter, Flail, Fling, Punishment, Hammer Arm

Slakoth　**Vigoroth**　**Slaking**

SLAKOTH

Slacker Pokémon

REGION: Hoenn

TYPE: NORMAL

It's rare to see a Slakoth move. It's awake for only a few hours per day, its heart beats extremely slowly, and it doesn't require much food.

How to Say It: SLACK-oth
Imperial Height: 2'07''
Imperial Weight: 52.9 lbs.
Metric Height: 0.8 m
Metric Weight: 24.0 kg

Possible Moves: Scratch, Yawn, Encore, Slack Off, Feint Attack, Amnesia, Covet, Chip Away, Counter, Flail, Play Rough

Slakoth　**Vigoroth**　**Slaking**

TYPE: DRAGON

Sliggoo doesn't have teeth, so it has to dissolve its food before eating. The mucus it sprays can cause just about anything to melt, given enough time.

How to Say It: SLIH-goo
Imperial Height: 2'07''
Imperial Weight: 38.6 lbs.
Metric Height: 0.8 m
Metric Weight: 17.5 kg

Possible Moves:
Tackle, Bubble, Absorb, Protect, Bide, Dragon Breath, Rain Dance, Flail, Body Slam, Muddy Water, Dragon Pulse

SLIGGOO
Soft Tissue Pokémon

Goomy ⇨ Sliggoo ⇨ Goodra

397

SLOWBRO
Hermit Crab Pokémon

REGIONS:
Alola
Kalos
(Coastal)
Kanto

TYPE: WATER-PSYCHIC

Thanks to Shellder's poisonous bite, Slowbro has grown even more scatterbrained, content to stare at the sea and let its mind wander. It's occasionally startled into a moment of insight—but that moment passes just as quickly.

How to Say It: SLOW-bro
Imperial Height: 5'03''
Imperial Weight: 173.1 lbs.
Metric Height: 1.6 m
Metric Weight: 78.5 kg

Possible Moves: Withdraw, Heal Pulse, Curse, Yawn, Tackle, Growl, Water Gun, Confusion, Disable, Headbutt, Water Pulse, Zen Headbutt, Slack Off, Amnesia, Psychic, Rain Dance, Psych Up

MEGA SLOWBRO
Hermit Crab Pokémon

TYPE: WATER-PSYCHIC

Imperial Height: 6'07''
Imperial Weight: 264.6 lbs.
Metric Height: 2.0 m
Metric Weight: 120.0 kg

Slowpoke ➡ Slowbro ➡ Mega Slowbro

SLOWKING
Royal Pokémon

TYPE: WATER-PSYCHIC

When Slowking was bitten on the head, the poisons that were released interacted with its system in a mysterious way, enhancing its brainpower to the point of genius.

How to Say It: SLOW-king
Imperial Height: 6'07''
Imperial Weight: 175.3 lbs.
Metric Height: 2.0 m
Metric Weight: 79.5 kg

Possible Moves: Heal Pulse, Power Gem, Hidden Power, Curse, Yawn, Tackle, Growl, Water Gun, Confusion, Disable, Headbutt, Water Pulse, Zen Headbutt, Nasty Plot, Swagger, Psychic, Trump Card, Psych Up

Slowpoke ⇒ Slowking

SLOWPOKE
Dopey Pokémon

TYPE: WATER-PSYCHIC

If Slowpoke's tail breaks off as it goes about its business, it probably won't even notice, and a new one will grow in quickly. The discarded tail can be dried for use in cooking.

How to Say It: SLOW-poke
Imperial Height: 3'11''
Imperial Weight: 79.4 lbs.
Metric Height: 1.2 m
Metric Weight: 36.0 kg

Possible Moves: Curse, Yawn, Tackle, Growl, Water Gun, Confusion, Disable, Headbutt, Water Pulse, Zen Headbutt, Slack Off, Amnesia, Psychic, Rain Dance, Psych Up, Heal Pulse

Slowking

Slowpoke ⇒ Slowbro ⇒ Mega Slowbro

399

SLUGMA

Lava Pokémon

TYPE: FIRE

The magma that circulates within Slugma's body serves as its blood, supplying its organs with oxygen and nutrients. It has to stay warm, or the magma will harden.

How to Say It: SLUG-ma
Imperial Height: 2'04''
Imperial Weight: 77.2 lbs.
Metric Height: 0.7 m
Metric Weight: 35.0 kg

Possible Moves: Yawn, Smog, Ember, Rock Throw, Harden, Recover, Flame Burst, Ancient Power, Amnesia, Lava Plume, Rock Slide, Body Slam, Flamethrower, Earth Power

Slugma   Magcargo

SLURPUFF

Meringue Pokémon

TYPE: FAIRY

Pastry chefs love having a Slurpuff in the kitchen. With its incredibly sensitive nose, it can tell exactly when a dessert is baked to perfection.

How to Say It: SLUR-puff
Imperial Height: 2'07''
Imperial Weight: 11.0 lbs.
Metric Height: 0.8 m
Metric Weight: 5.0 kg

Possible Moves: Sweet Scent, Tackle, Fairy Wind, Play Nice, Fake Tears, Round, Cotton Spore, Endeavor, Aromatherapy, Draining Kiss, Energy Ball, Cotton Guard, Wish, Play Rough, Light Screen, Safeguard

Swirlix   Slurpuff

REGIONS:
Alola
Johto
Kalos
(Central)

SMEARGLE
Painter Pokémon

TYPE: NORMAL

Smeargle's tail tip produces a fluid that it uses like paint—it literally marks its territory, using many different symbols. Towns with an apparent graffiti problem might just be home to lots of Smeargle.

How to Say It: SMEAR-gull
Imperial Height: 3'11''
Imperial Weight: 127.9 lbs.
Metric Height: 1.2 m
Metric Weight: 58.0 kg

Possible Move: Sketch

Does not evolve

REGIONS:
Alola
Johto
Kalos
(Mountain)

SMOOCHUM
Kiss Pokémon

TYPE: ICE-PSYCHIC

Smoochum's lips are filled with highly sensitive touch receptors, so it uses them to inspect unfamiliar objects. It can't stand being dirty, though, so it immediately licks away any grime left on its lips.

How to Say It: SMOO-chum
Imperial Height: 1'04''
Imperial Weight: 13.2 lbs.
Metric Height: 0.4 m
Metric Weight: 6.0 kg

Possible Moves: Pound, Lick, Sweet Kiss, Powder Snow, Confusion, Sing, Heart Stamp, Mean Look, Fake Tears, Lucky Chant, Avalanche, Psychic, Copycat, Perish Song, Blizzard

Smoochum ⇨ Jynx

SNEASEL
Sharp Claw Pokémon

REGIONS:
Alola
Johto
Kalos
(Mountain)

TYPE: DARK-ICE

Sneasel has a reputation as a crafty, vicious egg thief. It lies in wait until a nest is left unguarded, then strikes quickly and stealthily with its sharp claws.

How to Say It: SNEE-zul
Imperial Height: 2'11''
Imperial Weight: 61.7 lbs.
Metric Height: 0.9 m
Metric Weight: 28.0 kg

Possible Moves: Scratch, Leer, Taunt, Quick Attack, Feint Attack, Icy Wind, Fury Swipes, Agility, Metal Claw, Hone Claws, Beat Up, Screech, Slash, Snatch, Punishment, Ice Shard

Sneasel ⇨ Weavile

SNIVY
Grass Snake Pokémon

REGION:
Unova

TYPE: GRASS

Soaking up sunlight with its tail increases Snivy's speed. Though it has hands, it generally uses the vines that extend from its neck instead.

How to Say It: SNY-vee
Imperial Height: 2'00''
Imperial Weight: 17.9 lbs.
Metric Height: 0.6 m
Metric Weight: 8.1 kg

Possible Moves: Tackle, Leer, Vine Whip, Wrap, Growth, Leaf Tornado, Leech Seed, Mega Drain, Slam, Leaf Blade, Coil, Giga Drain, Wring Out, Gastro Acid, Leaf Storm

Snivy ⇨ Servine ⇨ Serperior

TYPE: NORMAL

The stomach of a Snorlax can handle just about anything—which is fortunate, because its massive body requires nearly 900 pounds of food every day. If it dozes off during a meal, it can keep eating in its sleep.

How to Say It: SNOR-lacks
Imperial Height: 6'11''
Imperial Weight: 1,014.1 lbs.
Metric Height: 2.1 m
Metric Weight: 460.0 kg

Possible Moves: Tackle, Defense Curl, Amnesia, Lick, Chip Away, Yawn, Body Slam, Rest, Snore, Sleep Talk, Giga Impact, Rollout, Block, Belly Drum, Crunch, Heavy Slam, High Horsepower

REGIONS:
Alola
Kalos
(Central)
Kanto

SNORLAX
Sleeping Pokémon

Munchlax ⇨ Snorlax

TYPE: ICE

If a Snorunt comes to visit, don't shoo it away! According to tradition, having a Snorunt living in your house guarantees prosperity for many years. This Pokémon is quite happy in the bitter cold.

How to Say It: SNOW-runt
Imperial Height: 2'04''
Imperial Weight: 37.0 lbs.
Metric Height: 0.7 m
Metric Weight: 16.8 kg

Possible Moves: Powder Snow, Leer, Double Team, Ice Shard, Icy Wind, Bite, Ice Fang, Headbutt, Protect, Frost Breath, Crunch, Blizzard, Hail

REGIONS:
Alola
Hoenn

SNORUNT
Snow Hat Pokémon

Froslass

Snorunt ⇨ Glalie ⇨ Mega Glalie

SNOVER
Frost Tree Pokémon

REGIONS:
Kalos
(Mountain)
Sinnoh

TYPE: GRASS-ICE

Snover live high in the mountains most of the year, but in the winter, they migrate to lower elevations.

How to Say It: SNOW-vur
Imperial Height: 3'03''
Imperial Weight: 111.3 lbs.
Metric Height: 1.0 m
Metric Weight: 50.5 kg

Possible Moves: Powder Snow, Leer, Razor Leaf, Icy Wind, Grass Whistle, Swagger, Mist, Ice Shard, Ingrain, Wood Hammer, Blizzard, Sheer Cold

Snover ⇨ **Abomasnow** ⇨ **Mega Abomasnow**

SNUBBULL
Fairy Pokémon

REGIONS:
Alola
Johto
Kalos
(Coastal)

TYPE: FAIRY

Snubbull might look scary, but it's a big wimp, often too cowardly or too lazy to pick a fight. It attempts to drive off a would-be opponent with a growl—but many people find this adorable.

How to Say It: SNUB-bull
Imperial Height: 2'00''
Imperial Weight: 17.2 lbs.
Metric Height: 0.6 m
Metric Weight: 7.8 kg

Possible Moves: Ice Fang, Fire Fang, Thunder Fang, Tackle, Scary Face, Tail Whip, Charm, Bite, Lick, Headbutt, Roar, Rage, Play Rough, Payback, Crunch

Snubbull ⇨ **Granbull**

SOLGALEO
Sunne Pokémon

LEGENDARY POKÉMON

TYPE: PSYCHIC-STEEL

Solgaleo's entire body radiates a bright light that can wipe away the darkness of night. This Legendary Pokémon apparently makes its home in another world, and it returns there when its third eye becomes active.

How to Say It: SOUL-gah-LAY-oh
Imperial Height: 11'02''
Imperial Weight: 507.1 lbs.
Metric Height: 3.4 m
Metric Weight: 230.0 kg

Possible Moves: Sunsteel Strike, Cosmic Power, Wake-Up Slap, Teleport, Metal Claw, Iron Head, Metal Sound, Zen Headbutt, Flash Cannon, Morning Sun, Crunch, Metal Burst, Solar Beam, Noble Roar, Flare Blitz, Wide Guard, Giga Impact

Cosmog ➡ Cosmoem ➡ Solgaleo

SOLOSIS
Cell Pokémon

REGION:
Kalos
(Coastal)
Unova

TYPE: PSYCHIC

The special liquid that surrounds Solosis protects it from any harsh conditions. They communicate with telepathy.

How to Say It: soh-LOH-sis
Imperial Height: 1'00''
Imperial Weight: 2.2 lbs.
Metric Height: 0.3 m
Metric Weight: 1.0 kg

Possible Moves: Psywave, Reflect, Rollout, Snatch, Hidden Power, Light Screen, Charm, Recover, Psyshock, Endeavor, Future Sight, Pain Split, Psychic, Skill Swap, Heal Block, Wonder Room

Solosis   Duosion   Reuniclus

SOLROCK
Meteorite Pokémon

REGIONS:
Hoenn
Kalos
(Coastal)

TYPE: ROCK-PSYCHIC

When Solrock spins, it gives off heat and light. It uses sunlight for energy and can apparently pick up on others' emotions.

How to Say It: SOLE-rock
Imperial Height: 3'11''
Imperial Weight: 339.5 lbs.
Metric Height: 1.2 m
Metric Weight: 154.0 kg

Possible Moves: Flare Blitz, Tackle, Harden, Confusion, Rock Throw, Fire Spin, Rock Polish, Psywave, Embargo, Rock Slide, Cosmic Power, Psychic, Heal Block, Stone Edge, Solar Beam, Explosion, Wonder Room

Does not evolve

TYPE: NORMAL-FLYING

Spearow's wings are too short for effective flying, so they stay on the ground and move about with rapid hops. They drive off so many Bug types that farmers really like having them around.

How to Say It: SPEER-oh
Imperial Height: 1'00''
Imperial Weight: 4.4 lbs.
Metric Height: 0.3 m
Metric Weight: 2.0 kg

Possible Moves: Peck, Growl, Leer, Pursuit, Fury Attack, Aerial Ace, Mirror Move, Assurance, Agility, Focus Energy, Roost, Drill Peck

REGIONS:
Alola
Kalos
(Mountain)
Kanto

SPEAROW
Tiny Bird Pokémon

Spearow ⇨ Fearow

REGION:
Kalos
(Central)

SPEWPA
Scatterdust Pokémon

TYPE: BUG

Like Scatterbug, Spewpa releases a protective cloud of powder when attacked. It can also bristle up its thick fur in an attempt to scare off any aggressors.

How to Say It: SPEW-puh
Imperial Height: 1'00''
Imperial Weight: 18.5 lbs.
Metric Height: 0.3 m
Metric Weight: 8.4 kg

Possible Moves: Harden, Protect

Scatterbug ⇨ Spewpa ⇨ Vivillon

407

SPHEAL

Clap Pokémon

TYPE: ICE-WATER

Spheal can roll across the ice faster than it can walk. When it's happy, it bursts into applause by clapping its fins together, so a group of joyful Spheal is rather noisy.

How to Say It: SFEEL
Imperial Height: 2'07''
Imperial Weight: 87.1 lbs.
Metric Height: 0.8 m
Metric Weight: 39.5 kg

Possible Moves: Defense Curl, Powder Snow, Growl, Water Gun, Rollout, Encore, Ice Ball, Body Slam, Aurora Beam, Hail, Rest, Snore, Blizzard, Sheer Cold, Brine

Spheal → Sealeo → Walrein

SPINARAK

String Spit Pokémon

TYPE: BUG-POISON

The threads Spinarak uses to spin its web are so sturdy that they're sometimes used to reinforce fishing nets. Rather than go out hunting for food, this patient Pokémon waits for something to blunder into its web.

How to Say It: SPIN-uh-rack
Imperial Height: 1'08''
Imperial Weight: 18.7 lbs.
Metric Height: 0.5 m
Metric Weight: 8.5 kg

Possible Moves: Poison Sting, String Shot, Constrict, Absorb, Infestation, Scary Face, Night Shade, Shadow Sneak, Fury Swipes, Sucker Punch, Spider Web, Agility, Pin Missile, Psychic, Poison Jab, Cross Poison, Sticky Web, Toxic Thread

Spinarak → Ariados

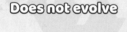

REGIONS:
Alola
Hoenn
Kalos
(Mountain)

SPINDA
Spot Panda Pokémon

TYPE: NORMAL

As Spinda staggers and totters about, it has the mistaken impression that it's walking straight. Each Spinda's spot pattern is slightly different, and collectors appreciate the variety.

How to Say It: SPIN-dah
Imperial Height: 3'07''
Imperial Weight: 11.0 lbs.
Metric Height: 1.1 m
Metric Weight: 5.0 kg

Possible Moves: Tackle, Copycat, Feint Attack, Psybeam, Hypnosis, Dizzy Punch, Sucker Punch, Teeter Dance, Uproar, Psych Up, Double-Edge, Flail, Thrash

Does not evolve

REGION:
Sinnoh

SPIRITOMB
Forbidden Pokémon

TYPE: GHOST-DARK

Long ago, Spiritomb was bound to an odd keystone as punishment for bad behavior. Its body is formed of more than a hundred spirits.

How to Say It: SPIR-it-tomb
Imperial Height: 3'03''
Imperial Weight: 238.1 lbs.
Metric Height: 1.0 m
Metric Weight: 108.0 kg

Possible Moves: Curse, Pursuit, Confuse Ray, Spite, Shadow Sneak, Feint Attack, Hypnosis, Dream Eater, Ominous Wind, Sucker Punch, Nasty Plot, Memento, Dark Pulse

Does not evolve

SPOINK

Bounce Pokémon

TYPE: PSYCHIC

The constant bouncing motion of Spoink's springy tail regulates its heartbeat. It's always looking for a bigger pearl for its head, because the jewel focuses its psychic powers.

How to Say It: SPOINK
Imperial Height: 2'04''
Imperial Weight: 67.5 lbs.
Metric Height: 0.7 m
Metric Weight: 30.6 kg

Possible Moves: Splash, Psywave, Odor Sleuth, Psybeam, Psych Up, Confuse Ray, Magic Coat, Zen Headbutt, Rest, Snore, Power Gem, Psyshock, Payback, Psychic, Bounce

Spoink ⇨ Grumpig

SPRITZEE

Perfume Pokémon

REGION:
Kalos
(Central)

TYPE: FAIRY

Long ago, this Pokémon was popular among the nobility for its lovely scent. Instead of spraying perfume, ladies would keep a Spritzee close at hand.

How to Say It: SPRIT-zee
Imperial Height: 0'08''
Imperial Weight: 1.1 lbs.
Metric Height: 0.2 m
Metric Weight: 0.5 kg

Possible Moves: Sweet Scent, Fairy Wind, Sweet Kiss, Odor Sleuth, Echoed Voice, Calm Mind, Draining Kiss, Aromatherapy, Attract, Moonblast, Charm, Flail, Misty Terrain, Skill Swap, Psychic, Disarming Voice

Spritzee ⇨ Aromatisse

TYPE: WATER

With its aerodynamic shape and grooved surface, Squirtle's shell helps it cut through the water very quickly. It also offers protection in battle.

How to Say It: SKWIR-tul
Imperial Height: 1'08''
Imperial Weight: 19.8 lbs.
Metric Height: 0.5 m
Metric Weight: 9.0 kg

Possible Moves: Tackle, Tail Whip, Water Gun, Withdraw, Bubble, Bite, Rapid Spin, Protect, Water Pulse, Aqua Tail, Skull Bash, Iron Defense, Rain Dance, Hydro Pump

SQUIRTLE
Tiny Turtle Pokémon

 ⇨ ⇨ Blastoise ⇨ Mega Blastoise

Squirtle   **Wartortle**   **Blastoise**   **Mega Blastoise**

REGION:
Alola

STAKATAKA
Rampart Pokémon

ULTRA BEAST

TYPE: ROCK-STEEL

It's thought that Stakataka, one of the mysterious Ultra Beasts, is made up of several life-forms stacked on top of one another. This creature resembles a stone wall covered with markings that look like blue eyes.

How to Say It: STACK-uh-TACK-uh
Imperial Height: 18'01''
Imperial Weight: 1,807.8 lbs.
Metric Height: 5.5 m
Metric Weight: 820.0 kg

Possible Moves: Protect, Tackle, Rock Slide, Stealth Rock, Bide, Take Down, Rock Throw, Autotomize, Iron Defense, Iron Head, Rock Blast, Wide Guard, Double-Edge

Does not evolve

STANTLER
Big Horn Pokémon

REGION: Johto

TYPE: NORMAL

The intricately curved antlers that grow from Stantler's head have been regarded as priceless works of art by collectors.

How to Say It: STAN-tler
Imperial Height: 4'07''
Imperial Weight: 157.0 lbs.
Metric Height: 1.4 m
Metric Weight: 71.2 kg

Possible Moves: Tackle, Leer, Astonish, Hypnosis, Stomp, Sand Attack, Take Down, Confuse Ray, Calm Mind, Role Play, Zen Headbutt, Jump Kick, Imprison, Captivate, Me First

Does not evolve

STARAPTOR
Predator Pokémon

REGIONS: Kalos *(Coastal)* Sinnoh

TYPE: NORMAL-FLYING

After evolving, Staraptor go off on their own, leaving their flocks behind. With their strong wings, they can fly with ease, even when carrying a burden.

How to Say It: star-RAP-tor
Imperial Height: 3'11''
Imperial Weight: 54.9 lbs.
Metric Height: 1.2 m
Metric Weight: 24.9 kg

Possible Moves: Tackle, Growl, Quick Attack, Wing Attack, Double Team, Endeavor, Whirlwind, Aerial Ace, Take Down, Close Combat, Agility, Brave Bird, Final Gambit

Starly ⇨ Staravia ⇨ Staraptor

TYPE: NORMAL-FLYING

Staravia travel in large flocks that can be very territorial. Battles sometimes break out between two competing flocks.

How to Say It: star-EY-vee-a
Imperial Height: 2'00''
Imperial Weight: 34.2 lbs.
Metric Height: 0.6 m
Metric Weight: 15.5 kg

Possible Moves: Tackle, Growl, Quick Attack, Wing Attack, Double Team, Endeavor, Whirlwind, Aerial Ace, Take Down, Agility, Brave Bird, Final Gambit

REGIONS:
Kalos
(Coastal)
Sinnoh

STARAVIA
Starling Pokémon

Starly ⇨ Staravia ⇨ Staraptor

TYPE: NORMAL-FLYING

Huge flocks of Starly gather in fields and mountains. In such large numbers, their wings flap with impressive power . . . and their noisy singing is quite a nuisance!

How to Say It: STAR-lee
Imperial Height: 1'00''
Imperial Weight: 4.4 lbs.
Metric Height: 0.3 m
Metric Weight: 2.0 kg

Possible Moves: Tackle, Growl, Quick Attack, Wing Attack, Double Team, Endeavor, Whirlwind, Aerial Ace, Take Down, Agility, Brave Bird, Final Gambit

REGIONS:
Kalos
(Coastal)
Sinnoh

STARLY
Starling Pokémon

Starly ⇨ Staravia ⇨ Staraptor

413

STARMIE
Mysterious Pokémon

REGIONS:
Alola
Kalos
(Coastal)
Kanto

TYPE: WATER-PSYCHIC

Getting close to a Starmie could give you a headache, possibly because of mysterious signals transmitted by its glowing core. With a shape like a many-pointed star, could this Pokémon have fallen from outer space?

How to Say It: STAR-mee
Imperial Height: 3'07''
Imperial Weight: 176.4 lbs.
Metric Height: 1.1 m
Metric Weight: 80.0 kg

Possible Moves: Hydro Pump, Spotlight, Water Gun, Rapid Spin, Recover, Swift, Confuse Ray

Staryu ⇨ Starmie

STARYU
Star Shape Pokémon

REGIONS:
Alola
Kalos
(Coastal)
Kanto

TYPE: WATER

A cluster of red lights glowing on the beach at night is probably a Staryu colony. Its red core glows at night, and as long as the core is whole, this Pokémon can regenerate from almost any injury.

How to Say It: STAR-you
Imperial Height: 2'07''
Imperial Weight: 76.1 lbs.
Metric Height: 0.8 m
Metric Weight: 34.5 kg

Possible Moves: Tackle, Harden, Water Gun, Rapid Spin, Recover, Psywave, Swift, Bubble Beam, Camouflage, Gyro Ball, Brine, Minimize, Reflect Type, Power Gem, Confuse Ray, Psychic, Light Screen, Cosmic Power, Hydro Pump

Staryu ⇨ Starmie

TYPE: STEEL-GROUND

Steelix lives deep underground and can tunnel straight down more than half a mile below the surface.

STEELIX
Iron Snake Pokémon

How to Say It: STEE-licks
Imperial Height: 30'02''
Imperial Weight: 881.8 lbs.
Metric Height: 9.2 m
Metric Weight: 400.0 kg

Possible Moves: Thunder Fang, Ice Fang, Fire Fang, Mud Sport, Tackle, Harden, Bind, Curse, Rock Throw, Rock Tomb, Rage, Stealth Rock, Autotomize, Gyro Ball, Smack Down, Dragon Breath, Slam, Screech, Rock Slide, Crunch, Iron Tail, Dig, Stone Edge, Double-Edge, Sandstorm

MEGA STEELIX
Iron Snake Pokémon

TYPE: STEEL-GROUND

Imperial Height: 34'05''
Imperial Weight: 1,631.4 lbs.
Metric Height: 10.5 m
Metric Weight: 740.0 kg

Onix ➡ **Steelix** ➡ **Mega Steelix**

STEENEE
Fruit Pokémon

REGION:
Alola

TYPE: GRASS

Lively and cheerful, Steenee often attracts a crowd of other Pokémon drawn to its energy and its lovely scent. Its sepals have evolved into a hard shell to protect its head and body from attackers.

How to Say It: STEE-nee
Imperial Height: 2'04''
Imperial Weight: 18.1 lbs.
Metric Height: 0.7 m
Metric Weight: 8.2 kg

Possible Moves: Double Slap, Splash, Play Nice, Rapid Spin, Razor Leaf, Sweet Scent, Magical Leaf, Teeter Dance, Stomp, Aromatic Mist, Captivate, Aromatherapy, Leaf Storm

Bounsweet ⇨ Steenee ⇨ Tsareena

STOUTLAND
Big-Hearted Pokémon

REGIONS:
Alola
Unova

TYPE: NORMAL

Stoutland's bravery and intelligence make it an excellent partner. Many Trainers put their trust in this Pokémon to help rescue explorers stranded in the mountains—or to keep an eye on the kids.

How to Say It: STOWT-lund
Imperial Height: 3'11''
Imperial Weight: 134.5 lbs.
Metric Height: 1.2 m
Metric Weight: 61.0 kg

Possible Moves: Ice Fang, Fire Fang, Thunder Fang, Leer, Tackle, Odor Sleuth, Bite, Helping Hand, Take Down, Work Up, Crunch, Roar, Retaliate, Reversal, Last Resort, Giga Impact, Play Rough

416 Lillipup ⇨ Herdier ⇨ Stoutland

STUFFUL
Flailing Pokémon

TYPE: NORMAL-FIGHTING

Petting an unfamiliar Stufful is a bad idea, even though it's really cute—it dislikes being touched by anyone it doesn't consider a friend, and responds with a flailing of limbs that can knock over a strong fighter.

How to Say It: STUFF-fuhl
Imperial Height: 1'08''
Imperial Weight: 15.0 lbs.
Metric Height: 0.5 m
Metric Weight: 6.8 kg

Possible Moves: Tackle, Leer, Bide, Baby-Doll Eyes, Brutal Swing, Flail, Payback, Take Down, Hammer Arm, Thrash, Pain Split, Double-Edge, Superpower

Stufful → Bewear

TYPE: GROUND-ELECTRIC

Stunfisk buries its flat body in mud, so it's hard to see and often gets stepped on. When that happens, its thick skin keeps it from being hurt, and it zaps the offender with a cheery smile.

How to Say It: STUN-fisk
Imperial Height: 2'04''
Imperial Weight: 24.3 lbs.
Metric Height: 0.7 m
Metric Weight: 11.0 kg

Possible Moves: Fissure, Flail, Tackle, Water Gun, Mud-Slap, Mud Sport, Bide, Thunder Shock, Mud Shot, Camouflage, Mud Bomb, Discharge, Endure, Bounce, Muddy Water, Thunderbolt, Revenge

STUNFISK
Trap Pokémon

Does not evolve

STUNKY

Skunk Pokémon

TYPE: POISON-DARK

The terrible-smelling fluid that Stunky sprays from its rear can keep others far away from it for a whole day.

How to Say It: STUNK-ee
Imperial Height: 1'04''
Imperial Weight: 42.3 lbs.
Metric Height: 0.4 m
Metric Weight: 19.2 kg

Possible Moves: Scratch, Focus Energy, Poison Gas, Screech, Fury Swipes, Smokescreen, Feint, Slash, Toxic, Acid Spray, Night Slash, Memento, Belch, Explosion, Bite, Venom Drench, Sucker Punch

Stunky ⇨ Skuntank

SUDOWOODO

Imitation Pokémon

TYPE: ROCK

Sudowoodo may look like a tree, but if you try to water it, it will run away! This Pokémon is favored by elderly Trainers and is sometimes sought after by collectors, who prefer Sudowoodo with bigger patches of green.

How to Say It: SOO-doe-WOO-doe
Imperial Height: 3'11''
Imperial Weight: 83.8 lbs.
Metric Height: 1.2 m
Metric Weight: 38.0 kg

Possible Moves: Slam, Wood Hammer, Copycat, Flail, Low Kick, Rock Throw, Mimic, Feint Attack, Tearful Look, Rock Tomb, Block, Rock Slide, Counter, Sucker Punch, Double-Edge, Stone Edge, Hammer Arm, Head Smash

Bonsly ⇨ Sudowoodo

SUICUNE
Aurora Pokémon

LEGENDARY POKÉMON

TYPE: WATER

Suicune can clear pollution from lakes and rivers. This Legendary Pokémon's heart is as pure as clear water.

How to Say It: SWEE-koon
Imperial Height: 6'07''
Imperial Weight: 412.3 lbs.
Metric Height: 2.0 m
Metric Weight: 187.0 kg

Possible Moves: Sheer Cold, Bite, Leer, Bubble Beam, Rain Dance, Gust, Aurora Beam, Mist, Mirror Coat, Ice Fang, Tailwind, Extrasensory, Hydro Pump, Calm Mind, Blizzard

Does not evolve

SUNFLORA
Sun Pokémon

TYPE: GRASS

Sunflora soaks up the sun's rays and transforms that energy into nutrients. It's very active during the warmth of the day, but when sunset arrives, it stops moving.

How to Say It: sun-FLOR-uh
Imperial Height: 2'07''
Imperial Weight: 18.7 lbs.
Metric Height: 0.8 m
Metric Weight: 8.5 kg

Possible Moves: Flower Shield, Absorb, Pound, Growth, Ingrain, Grass Whistle, Mega Drain, Leech Seed, Razor Leaf, Worry Seed, Giga Drain, Bullet Seed, Petal Dance, Natural Gift, Solar Beam, Double-Edge, Sunny Day, Leaf Storm, Petal Blizzard

Sunkern ➡ Sunflora

SUNKERN
Seed Pokémon

TYPE: GRASS

Sunkern doesn't consume food but lives entirely on dewdrops. It avoids movement as much as possible so it doesn't use up its stored energy.

How to Say It: SUN-kurn
Imperial Height: 1'00''
Imperial Weight: 4.0 lbs.
Metric Height: 0.3 m
Metric Weight: 1.8 kg

Possible Moves: Absorb, Growth, Mega Drain, Ingrain, Grass Whistle, Leech Seed, Endeavor, Worry Seed, Razor Leaf, Synthesis, Sunny Day, Giga Drain, Seed Bomb, Natural Gift, Double-Edge

Sunkern ➡ Sunflora

TYPE: BUG-WATER

When threatened, Surskit produces a fluid from the point on its head. The fluid tastes very unpleasant to flying Pokémon, so they stay away. It can move across the water's surface as if it's skating.

How to Say It: SUR-skit
Imperial Height: 1'08''
Imperial Weight: 3.7 lbs.
Metric Height: 0.5 m
Metric Weight: 1.7 kg

Possible Moves: Bubble, Quick Attack, Sweet Scent, Water Sport, Bubble Beam, Agility, Mist, Haze, Aqua Jet, Baton Pass, Sticky Web

SURSKIT
Pond Skater Pokémon

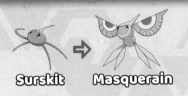

Surskit   **Masquerain**

TYPE: NORMAL-FLYING

Swablu uses its cottony wings to polish everything around it. It also likes to land on people's heads, so a woman walking down the sidewalk could suddenly discover she's wearing a fluffy Swablu hat.

How to Say It: swah-BLUE
Imperial Height: 1'04''
Imperial Weight: 2.6 lbs.
Metric Height: 0.4 m
Metric Weight: 1.2 kg

Possible Moves: Peck, Growl, Astonish, Sing, Fury Attack, Safeguard, Disarming Voice, Mist, Round, Natural Gift, Take Down, Refresh, Mirror Move, Cotton Guard, Dragon Pulse, Perish Song, Moonblast

SWABLU
Cotton Bird Pokémon

Swablu   **Altaria**   **Mega Altaria**   421

SWADLOON
Leaf-Wrapped Pokémon

REGION:
Unova

TYPE: BUG-GRASS

When many Swadloon live in a forest, the plants grow strong and healthy. These Pokémon eat fallen leaves and give off nutrients that enrich the soil.

How to Say It: SWAHD-loon
Imperial Height: 1'08''
Imperial Weight: 16.1 lbs.
Metric Height: 0.5 m
Metric Weight: 7.3 kg

Possible Moves: Grass Whistle, Tackle, String Shot, Bug Bite, Razor Leaf, Protect

Sewaddle ⇨ Swadloon ⇨ Leavanny

SWALOT
Poison Bag Pokémon

REGIONS:
Hoenn
Kalos
(Coastal)

TYPE: POISON

Swalot's mouth can open wide enough to swallow a car tire easily. It defends itself by secreting a poisonous fluid.

How to Say It: SWAH-lot
Imperial Height: 5'07''
Imperial Weight: 176.4 lbs.
Metric Height: 1.7 m
Metric Weight: 80.0 kg

Possible Moves: Body Slam, Venom Drench, Gunk Shot, Wring Out, Pound, Yawn, Poison Gas, Sludge, Amnesia, Acid Spray, Encore, Toxic, Stockpile, Spit Up, Swallow, Sludge Bomb, Gastro Acid, Belch

Gulpin ⇨ Swalot

SWAMPERT
Mud Fish Pokémon

TYPE: WATER-GROUND

Swampert can tell when a storm is coming by shifts in the winds and waves. It's strong enough to drag and lift heavy boulders, so it builds a fort to take shelter.

How to Say It: SWAM-pert
Imperial Height: 4'11''
Imperial Weight: 180.6 lbs.
Metric Height: 1.5 m
Metric Weight: 81.9 kg

Possible Moves: Mud Shot, Hammer Arm, Tackle, Growl, Water Gun, Mud-Slap, Foresight, Bide, Mud Bomb, Rock Slide, Protect, Muddy Water, Take Down, Earthquake, Endeavor

MEGA SWAMPERT
Mud Fish Pokémon

TYPE: WATER-GROUND

Imperial Height: 6'03''
Imperial Weight: 224.9 lbs.
Metric Height: 1.9 m
Metric Weight: 102.0 kg

Mudkip ⇨ Marshtomp ⇨ Swampert ⇨ Mega Swampert

SWANNA
White Bird Pokémon

REGIONS:
Kalos *(Central)*
Unova

TYPE: WATER-FLYING

In the evening, a flock of Swanna performs an elegant dance around its leader. Their exceptional stamina and wing strength allow them to fly thousands of miles at a time.

How to Say It: SWAH-nuh
Imperial Height: 4'03''
Imperial Weight: 53.4 lbs.
Metric Height: 1.3 m
Metric Weight: 24.2 kg

Possible Moves: Water Gun, Water Sport, Defog, Wing Attack, Water Pulse, Aerial Ace, Bubble Beam, Feather Dance, Aqua Ring, Air Slash, Roost, Rain Dance, Tailwind, Brave Bird, Hurricane

Ducklett ⇨ Swanna

SWELLOW
Swallow Pokémon

REGIONS:
Hoenn
Kalos *(Coastal)*

TYPE: NORMAL-FLYING

Soaring gracefully through the sky, Swellow will go into a steep dive if it spots food on the ground. It's very vain about keeping its wings properly groomed.

How to Say It: SWELL-low
Imperial Height: 2'04''
Imperial Weight: 43.7 lbs.
Metric Height: 0.7 m
Metric Weight: 19.8 kg

Possible Moves: Air Slash, Pluck, Peck, Growl, Focus Energy, Quick Attack, Wing Attack, Double Team, Endeavor, Aerial Ace, Agility, Quick Guard, Brave Bird, Reversal

Taillow ⇨ Swellow

TYPE: ICE-GROUND

Swinub keeps its nose to the ground in search of food. Its favorite thing to eat is a certain kind of mushroom found under dead grass. Sometimes, it finds a hot spring while it's sniffing about.

How to Say It: SWY-nub
Imperial Height: 1'04''
Imperial Weight: 14.3 lbs.
Metric Height: 0.4 m
Metric Weight: 6.5 kg

Possible Moves: Tackle, Odor Sleuth, Mud Sport, Powder Snow, Mud-Slap, Endure, Mud Bomb, Icy Wind, Ice Shard, Take Down, Mist, Earthquake, Flail, Blizzard, Amnesia

SWINUB
Pig Pokémon

Swinub ➡ Piloswine ➡ Mamoswine

SWIRLIX
Cotton Candy Pokémon

TYPE: FAIRY

Swirlix loves to snack on sweets. Its sugary eating habits have made its white fur sweet and sticky, just like cotton candy.

How to Say It: SWUR-licks
Imperial Height: 1'04''
Imperial Weight: 7.7 lbs.
Metric Height: 0.4 m
Metric Weight: 3.5 kg

Possible Moves: Sweet Scent, Tackle, Fairy Wind, Play Nice, Fake Tears, Round, Cotton Spore, Endeavor, Aromatherapy, Draining Kiss, Energy Ball, Cotton Guard, Wish, Play Rough, Light Screen, Safeguard

Swirlix ➡ Slurpuff

425

SWOOBAT
Courting Pokémon

REGIONS:
Kalos
(Coastal)
Unova

TYPE: PSYCHIC-FLYING

When a male Swoobat is trying to impress a female, it gives off ultrasonic waves that put everyone in a good mood. Under other circumstances, Swoobat's waves can pulverize concrete.

How to Say It: SWOO-bat
Imperial Height: 2'11''
Imperial Weight: 23.1 lbs.
Metric Height: 0.9 m
Metric Weight: 10.5 kg

Possible Moves: Confusion, Odor Sleuth, Gust, Assurance, Heart Stamp, Imprison, Air Cutter, Attract, Amnesia, Calm Mind, Air Slash, Future Sight, Psychic, Endeavor

Woobat ⇨ Swoobat

SYLVEON
Intertwining Pokémon

REGIONS:
Alola
Kalos
(Coastal)

TYPE: FAIRY

Sylveon projects a calming aura from its feelers, which look like flowing ribbons. It sometimes uses this aura in battle to trick its opponents into dropping their defenses.

How to Say It: SIL-vee-on
Imperial Height: 3'03''
Imperial Weight: 51.8 lbs.
Metric Height: 1.0 m
Metric Weight: 23.5 kg

Possible Moves: Fairy Wind, Disarming Voice, Helping Hand, Tackle, Tail Whip, Sand Attack, Baby-Doll Eyes, Quick Attack, Swift, Draining Kiss, Skill Swap, Misty Terrain, Light Screen, Moonblast, Last Resort, Psych Up

Eevee ⇨ Sylveon

TYPE: NORMAL-FLYING

Although Taillow is fierce and courageous in battle, even against stronger foes, hunger or loneliness sometimes makes it cry.

How to Say It: TAY-low
Imperial Height: 1'00''
Imperial Weight: 5.1 lbs.
Metric Height: 0.3 m
Metric Weight: 2.3 kg

Possible Moves: Peck, Growl, Focus Energy, Quick Attack, Wing Attack, Double Team, Endeavor, Aerial Ace, Agility, Air Slash, Brave Bird, Reversal

REGIONS:
Hoenn
Kalos
(Coastal)

TAILLOW
Tiny Swallow Pokémon

Taillow ⇨ Swellow

TYPE: FIRE-FLYING

Talonflame can swoop at incredible speeds when attacking, which enhances the already impressive power of its kick. Its wings give off showers of embers as it flies.

How to Say It: TAL-un-flame
Imperial Height: 3'11''
Imperial Weight: 54.0 lbs.
Metric Height: 1.2 m
Metric Weight: 24.5 kg

Possible Moves: Ember, Brave Bird, Flare Blitz, Tackle, Growl, Quick Attack, Peck, Agility, Flail, Roost, Razor Wind, Natural Gift, Flame Charge, Acrobatics, Me First, Tailwind, Steel Wing

REGIONS:
Alola
Kalos
(Central)

TALONFLAME
Scorching Pokémon

Fletchling ⇨ Fletchinder ⇨ Talonflame

427

TANGELA

Vine Pokémon

REGION: Kanto

TYPE: GRASS

If grabbed by an attacker, Tangela can break away and leave the foe with a handful of vines. The vines grow back within a day.

How to Say It: TANG-ghel-a
Imperial Height: 3'03"
Imperial Weight: 77.2 lbs.
Metric Height: 1.0 m
Metric Weight: 35.0 kg

Possible Moves: Ingrain, Constrict, Sleep Powder, Absorb, Growth, Poison Powder, Vine Whip, Bind, Mega Drain, Stun Spore, Knock Off, Ancient Power, Natural Gift, Slam, Tickle, Wring Out, Power Whip, Grassy Terrain, Giga Drain

Tangela → Tangrowth

TANGROWTH

Vine Pokémon

REGION: Sinnoh

TYPE: GRASS

During warmer times of the year, Tangrowth's vines grow so rapidly that they cover its eyes. It can control its vines like arms.

How to Say It: TANG-growth
Imperial Height: 6'07"
Imperial Weight: 283.5 lbs.
Metric Height: 2.0 m
Metric Weight: 128.6 kg

Possible Moves: Block, Ingrain, Constrict, Sleep Powder, Vine Whip, Absorb, Poison Powder, Bind, Growth, Mega Drain, Knock Off, Stun Spore, Natural Gift, Giga Drain, Ancient Power, Slam, Tickle, Wring Out, Grassy Terrain, Power Whip

Tangela → Tangrowth

REGION: Alola

TAPU BULU
Land Spirit Pokémon

LEGENDARY POKÉMON

TYPE: GRASS-FAIRY

Tapu Bulu has a reputation for laziness—rather than battling directly, it commands vines to pin down its foes. The plants that grow abundantly in its wake give it energy. It's known as the guardian deity of Ula'ula Island.

How to Say It: TAH-poo BOO-loo
Imperial Height: 6'03''
Imperial Weight: 100.3 lbs.
Metric Height: 1.9 m
Metric Weight: 45.5 kg

Possible Moves: Grassy Terrain, Wood Hammer, Superpower, Mean Look, Disable, Whirlwind, Withdraw, Leafage, Horn Attack, Giga Drain, Scary Face, Leech Seed, Horn Leech, Rototiller, Nature's Madness, Zen Headbutt, Megahorn, Skull Bash

Does not evolve

REGION: Alola

TAPU FINI
Land Spirit Pokémon

LEGENDARY POKÉMON

TYPE: WATER-FAIRY

Tapu Fini can control and cleanse water, washing away impurities. When threatened, it summons a dense fog to confuse its enemies. This Pokémon draws energy from ocean currents. It's known as the guardian deity of Poni Island.

How to Say It: TAH-poo FEE-nee
Imperial Height: 4'03''
Imperial Weight: 46.7 lbs.
Metric Height: 1.3 m
Metric Weight: 21.2 kg

Possible Moves: Misty Terrain, Moonblast, Heal Pulse, Mean Look, Haze, Mist, Withdraw, Water Gun, Water Pulse, Whirlpool, Soak, Refresh, Brine, Defog, Nature's Madness, Muddy Water, Aqua Ring, Hydro Pump

Does not evolve

TAPU KOKO
Land Spirit Pokémon

LEGENDARY POKÉMON

TYPE: ELECTRIC-FAIRY

Somewhat lacking in attention span, Tapu Koko is quick to anger but just as quickly forgets why it's angry. Calling thunderclouds lets it store up lightning as energy. It's known as the guardian deity of Melemele Island.

How to Say It: TAH-poo KO-ko
Imperial Height: 5'11''
Imperial Weight: 45.2 lbs.

Metric Height: 1.8 m
Metric Weight: 20.5 kg

Possible Moves: Electric Terrain, Brave Bird, Power Swap, Mean Look, Quick Attack, False Swipe, Withdraw, Thunder Shock, Spark, Shock Wave, Screech, Charge, Wild Charge, Mirror Move, Nature's Madness, Discharge, Agility, Electro Ball

Does not evolve

TAPU LELE
Land Spirit Pokémon

LEGENDARY POKÉMON

TYPE: PSYCHIC-FAIRY

As Tapu Lele flutters through the air, people in search of good health gather up the glowing scales that fall from its body. It draws energy from the scent of flowers. It's known as the guardian deity of Akala Island.

How to Say It: TAH-poo LEH-leh **Metric Height:** 1.2 m
Imperial Height: 3'11'' **Metric Weight:** 18.6 kg
Imperial Weight: 41.0 lbs.

Possible Moves: Psychic Terrain, Aromatic Mist, Aromatherapy, Mean Look, Draining Kiss, Astonish, Withdraw, Confusion, Psywave, Psybeam, Sweet Scent, Skill Swap, Psyshock, Tickle, Nature's Madness, Extrasensory, Flatter, Moonblast

Does not evolve

**REGIONS:
Alola
Kalos
(Coastal)
Kanto**

TAUROS
Wild Bull Pokémon

TYPE: NORMAL

Although Tauros in other regions are known for their fierce love of battle, the Tauros in Alola are calm enough that many people can ride them without fear. The practice of Tauros riding can apparently be traced to this region.

How to Say It: TORE-ros **Metric Height:** 1.4 m
Imperial Height: 4'07'' **Metric Weight:** 88.4 kg
Imperial Weight: 194.9 lbs.

Possible Moves: Tackle, Tail Whip, Rage, Horn Attack, Scary Face, Pursuit, Rest, Payback, Work Up, Zen Headbutt, Take Down, Swagger, Thrash, Giga Impact, Double-Edge

Does not evolve

TEDDIURSA
Little Bear Pokémon

REGIONS:
Johto
Kalos
(Mountain)

TYPE: NORMAL

Teddiursa changes the flavor of its honey-soaked paws by incorporating different kinds of berries and pollen.

How to Say It: TED-dy-UR-sa
Imperial Height: 2'00''
Imperial Weight: 19.4 lbs.
Metric Height: 0.6 m
Metric Weight: 8.8 kg

Possible Moves: Fling, Covet, Scratch, Baby-Doll Eyes, Lick, Fake Tears, Fury Swipes, Feint Attack, Sweet Scent, Play Nice, Slash, Charm, Rest, Snore, Thrash

Teddiursa ⇨ Ursaring

TENTACOOL
Jellyfish Pokémon

REGIONS:
Alola
Kalos
(Coastal)
Kanto

TYPE: WATER-POISON

If you find a dried-out Tentacool on the beach, you could try soaking it in water to restore it to good health. Watch out, though—its tentacles carry a poison that could send you to the hospital.

How to Say It: TEN-ta-cool
Imperial Height: 2'11''
Imperial Weight: 100.3 lbs.
Metric Height: 0.9 m
Metric Weight: 45.5 kg

Possible Moves: Poison Sting, Supersonic, Constrict, Acid, Toxic Spikes, Water Pulse, Wrap, Acid Spray, Bubble Beam, Barrier, Poison Jab, Brine, Screech, Hex, Sludge Wave, Hydro Pump, Wring Out

Tentacool ⇨ Tentacruel

TENTACRUEL
Jellyfish Pokémon

TYPE: WATER-POISON

Tentacruel starts out with 80 tentacles, all packed with nasty poison. As it grows older, some of its tentacles are damaged or broken off in battle. When many Tentacruel gather, other Pokémon flee the area.

How to Say It: TEN-ta-crool
Imperial Height: 5'03''
Imperial Weight: 121.3 lbs.
Metric Height: 1.6 m
Metric Weight: 55.0 kg

Possible Moves: Reflect Type, Wring Out, Poison Sting, Supersonic, Constrict, Acid, Toxic Spikes, Water Pulse, Wrap, Acid Spray, Bubble Beam, Barrier, Poison Jab, Brine, Screech, Hex, Sludge Wave, Hydro Pump, Wring Out

Tentacool ⇨ **Tentacruel**

TYPE: FIRE

Tepig uses the fireballs from its nose in battle—and in cooking! It likes to roast berries rather than eating them raw, though sometimes they get a little overdone.

How to Say It: TEH-pig
Imperial Height: 1'08''
Imperial Weight: 21.8 lbs.
Metric Height: 0.5 m
Metric Weight: 9.9 kg

Possible Moves: Tackle, Tail Whip, Ember, Odor Sleuth, Defense Curl, Flame Charge, Smog, Rollout, Take Down, Heat Crash, Assurance, Flamethrower, Head Smash, Roar, Flare Blitz

TEPIG
Fire Pig Pokémon

Tepig ⇨ **Pignite** ⇨ **Emboar**

TERRAKION

Cavern Pokémon

REGION: **Unova**

LEGENDARY POKÉMON

TYPE: ROCK-FIGHTING

Legends tell of a time when Terrakion attacked a mighty castle to protect its Pokémon friends. They say it knocked down a giant wall with the force of its charge.

How to Say It: tur-RAK-ee-un
Imperial Height: 6'03''
Imperial Weight: 573.2 lbs.
Metric Height: 1.9 m
Metric Weight: 260.0 kg

Possible Moves: Quick Attack, Leer, Double Kick, Smack Down, Take Down, Helping Hand, Retaliate, Rock Slide, Sacred Sword, Swords Dance, Quick Guard, Work Up, Stone Edge, Close Combat

Does not evolve

THROH

Judo Pokémon

REGIONS: **Kalos** *(Coastal)* **Unova**

TYPE: FIGHTING

Throh make belts for themselves out of vines and pull those belts tight to power up their muscles. They can't resist the challenge of throwing a bigger opponent.

How to Say It: THROH
Imperial Height: 4'03''
Imperial Weight: 122.4 lbs.
Metric Height: 1.3 m
Metric Weight: 55.5 kg

Possible Moves: Mat Block, Bind, Leer, Bide, Focus Energy, Seismic Toss, Vital Throw, Revenge, Storm Throw, Body Slam, Bulk Up, Circle Throw, Endure, Wide Guard, Superpower, Reversal

Does not evolve

THUNDURUS
Bolt Strike Pokémon

LEGENDARY POKÉMON

TYPE: ELECTRIC-FLYING

Thundurus can discharge powerful electric bolts from the spikes on its tail. This Legendary Pokémon causes terrible lightning storms, which often result in forest fires.

How to Say It: THUN-duh-rus
Imperial Height: Incarnate Forme: 4'11''
Therian Forme: 9'10''
Imperial Weight: 134.5 lbs.
Metric Height: Incarnate Forme: 1.5 m
Therian Forme: 3.0 m
Metric Weight: 61.0 kg

Possible Moves: Uproar, Astonish, Thunder Shock, Swagger, Bite, Revenge, Shock Wave, Heal Block, Agility, Discharge, Crunch, Charge, Nasty Plot, Thunder, Dark Pulse, Hammer Arm, Thrash

Incarnate Forme

Therian Forme

TIMBURR

Muscular Pokémon

REGIONS:
Kalos
(Mountain)
Unova

TYPE: FIGHTING

Timburr always carries a wooden beam, which it trades for bigger ones as it grows. These Pokémon can be a big help to construction workers.

How to Say It: TIM-bur
Imperial Height: 2'00''
Imperial Weight: 27.6 lbs.
Metric Height: 0.6 m
Metric Weight: 12.5 kg

Possible Moves: Pound, Leer, Focus Energy, Bide, Low Kick, Rock Throw, Wake-Up Slap, Chip Away, Bulk Up, Rock Slide, Dynamic Punch, Scary Face, Hammer Arm, Stone Edge, Focus Punch, Superpower

Timburr   Gurdurr   Conkeldurr

TIRTOUGA

Prototurtle Pokémon

REGIONS:
Alola
Unova

TYPE: WATER-ROCK

Studies of Tirtouga's fossilized skeleton indicate that it could reach depths of half a mile when diving in the warm oceans of its ancient home. It originally lived 100 million years ago.

How to Say It: teer-TOO-gah
Imperial Height: 2'04''
Imperial Weight: 36.4 lbs.
Metric Height: 0.7 m
Metric Weight: 16.5 kg

Possible Moves: Bide, Withdraw, Water Gun, Rollout, Bite, Protect, Aqua Jet, Ancient Power, Crunch, Wide Guard, Brine, Smack Down, Curse, Shell Smash, Aqua Tail, Rock Slide, Rain Dance, Hydro Pump

Tirtouga   Carracosta

TOGEDEMARU
Roly-Poly Pokémon

TYPE: ELECTRIC-STEEL

Its back is covered with long, spiny fur that usually lies flat. Togedemaru can bristle up the fur during battle for use as a weapon, or during storms to attract lightning, which it stores as electricity in its body.

How to Say It: TOH-geh-deh-MAH-roo
Imperial Height: 1'00''
Imperial Weight: 7.3 lbs.
Metric Height: 0.3 m
Metric Weight: 3.3 kg

Possible Moves: Tackle, Thunder Shock, Defense Curl, Rollout, Charge, Spark, Nuzzle, Magnet Rise, Discharge, Zing Zap, Electric Terrain, Wild Charge, Pin Missile, Spiky Shield, Fell Stinger

Does not evolve

REGION: Sinnoh

TOGEKISS
Jubilee Pokémon

TYPE: FAIRY-FLYING

Togekiss flies around the world to seek out places of peace, bringing gifts and blessings to those who practice respect and harmony toward one another.

How to Say It: TOE-geh-kiss
Imperial Height: 4'11''
Imperial Weight: 83.8 lbs.
Metric Height: 1.5 m
Metric Weight: 38.0 kg

Possible Moves: After You, Sky Attack, Extreme Speed, Aura Sphere, Air Slash

Togepi ➡ Togetic ➡ Togekiss

TOGEPI
Spike Ball Pokémon

REGION: Johto

TYPE: FAIRY

Togepi soaks up good vibes from other beings for use as energy. Its shell is filled with happy feelings and warm fuzzies.

How to Say It: TOE-ghep-pee
Imperial Height: 1'00''
Imperial Weight: 3.3 lbs.
Metric Height: 0.3 m
Metric Weight: 1.5 kg

Possible Moves: Growl, Charm, Metronome, Sweet Kiss, Yawn, Encore, Follow Me, Bestow, Wish, Ancient Power, Safeguard, Baton Pass, Double-Edge, Last Resort, After You

Togepi ➡ Togetic ➡ Togekiss

TOGETIC
Happiness Pokémon

REGION: Johto

TYPE: FAIRY-FLYING

Widely regarded as a bringer of good luck, Togetic seeks out people with pure hearts and showers happiness upon them.

How to Say It: TOE-ghet-tic
Imperial Height: 2'00''
Imperial Weight: 7.1 lbs.
Metric Height: 0.6 m
Metric Weight: 3.2 kg

Possible Moves: Magical Leaf, Growl, Charm, Metronome, Sweet Kiss, Yawn, Fairy Wind, Encore, Follow Me, Bestow, Wish, Ancient Power, Safeguard, Baton Pass, Double-Edge, Last Resort, After You

Togepi ➡ Togetic ➡ Togekiss

TORCHIC
Chick Pokémon

TYPE: FIRE

Torchic's internal fire and soft feathers make it a perfect cuddle buddy. In battle, it can breathe flames and shoot fireballs!

How to Say It: TOR-chick
Imperial Height: 1'04''
Imperial Weight: 5.5 lbs.
Metric Height: 0.4 m
Metric Weight: 2.5 kg

Possible Moves: Scratch, Growl, Focus Energy, Ember, Peck, Sand Attack, Fire Spin, Quick Attack, Slash, Mirror Move, Flamethrower, Flame Burst

Torchic ⇨ Combusken ⇨ Blaziken ⇨ Mega Blaziken

TYPE: FIRE

Because wild Torkoal get their energy by burning coal within their shells, they tend to live near large coal deposits in the mountains. A Trainer who has Torkoal as a partner must keep a steady source of fuel on hand.

How to Say It: TOR-coal
Imperial Height: 1'08''
Imperial Weight: 177.2 lbs.
Metric Height: 0.5 m
Metric Weight: 80.4 kg

Possible Moves: Ember, Smog, Withdraw, Rapid Spin, Fire Spin, Smokescreen, Flame Wheel, Curse, Lava Plume, Body Slam, Protect, Flamethrower, Iron Defense, Amnesia, Flail, Heat Wave, Shell Smash, Inferno

TORKOAL
Coal Pokémon

Does not evolve

TORNADUS
Cyclone Pokémon

LEGENDARY POKÉMON

TYPE: FLYING

Wrapped in its cloud, Tornadus flies at two hundred mph. This Legendary Pokémon causes fierce windstorms with gales that can knock down houses.

How to Say It: tohr-NAY-dus
Imperial Height: Incarnate Forme: 4'11''
          Therian Forme: 4'07''
Imperial Weight: 138.9 lbs.
Metric Height: Incarnate Forme: 1.5 m
          Therian Forme: 1.4 m
Metric Weight: 63.0 kg

Possible Moves: Uproar, Astonish, Gust, Swagger, Bite, Revenge, Air Cutter, Extrasensory, Agility, Air Slash, Crunch, Tailwind, Rain Dance, Hurricane, Dark Pulse, Hammer Arm, Thrash

Incarnate Forme

Therian Forme

440   **Does not evolve**

TYPE: FIRE

Torracat attacks with powerful punches from its front legs, which are strong enough to bend iron. When it spits flames, the fiery bell at its throat starts to ring.

How to Say It: TOR-ruh-cat
Imperial Height: 2'04''
Imperial Weight: 55.1 lbs.
Metric Height: 0.7 m
Metric Weight: 25.0 kg

Possible Moves: Scratch, Ember, Growl, Lick, Leer, Fire Fang, Roar, Bite, Swagger, Fury Swipes, Thrash, Flamethrower, Scary Face, Flare Blitz, Outrage, Double Kick

REGION: Alola

TORRACAT
Fire Cat Pokémon

Litten → Torracat → Incineroar

REGION: Sinnoh

TORTERRA
Continent Pokémon

TYPE: GRASS-GROUND

There's enough room on Torterra's enormous back for several small Pokémon to make their nests. According to ancient folklore, a particularly large Torterra lived under the ground.

How to Say It: tor-TER-ra
Imperial Height: 7'03''
Imperial Weight: 683.4 lbs.
Metric Height: 2.2 m
Metric Weight: 310.0 kg

Possible Moves: Wood Hammer, Tackle, Withdraw, Absorb, Razor Leaf, Curse, Bite, Mega Drain, Earthquake, Leech Seed, Synthesis, Crunch, Giga Drain, Leaf Storm

Turtwig → Grotle → Torterra

TOTODILE
Big Jaw Pokémon

REGION: Johto

TYPE: WATER

Be careful around a playful Totodile! It tends to nibble on friends as a sign of affection, but its jaws are strong enough to cause serious harm.

How to Say It: TOE-toe-dyle
Imperial Height: 2'00''
Imperial Weight: 20.9 lbs.
Metric Height: 0.6 m
Metric Weight: 9.5 kg

Possible Moves: Scratch, Leer, Water Gun, Rage, Bite, Scary Face, Ice Fang, Flail, Crunch, Chip Away, Slash, Screech, Thrash, Aqua Tail, Superpower, Hydro Pump

Totodile　➡　Croconaw　➡　Feraligatr

TOUCANNON
Cannon Pokémon

REGION: Alola

TYPE: NORMAL-FLYING

The inside of Toucannon's beak gets very hot during a battle—over 200 degrees Fahrenheit. The heat fuels its explosive seed-shooting and can also cause serious burns to its opponent.

How to Say It: too-CAN-nun
Imperial Height: 3'07''
Imperial Weight: 57.3 lbs.
Metric Height: 1.1 m
Metric Weight: 26.0 kg

Possible Moves: Beak Blast, Rock Blast, Peck, Growl, Echoed Voice, Rock Smash, Supersonic, Pluck, Roost, Fury Attack, Screech, Drill Peck, Bullet Seed, Feather Dance, Hyper Voice

Pikipek　➡　Trumbeak　➡　Toucannon

TYPE: POISON-WATER

It's a good thing Toxapex lives at the bottom of the ocean, because its poison is very dangerous. Those who fall prey to it can expect three very painful days before they recover, and the effects can linger.

How to Say It: TOX-uh-pex
Imperial Height: 2'04''
Imperial Weight: 32.0 lbs.
Metric Height: 0.7 m
Metric Weight: 14.5 kg

Possible Moves: Baneful Bunker, Poison Sting, Peck, Bite, Toxic Spikes, Wide Guard, Toxic, Venoshock, Spike Cannon, Recover, Poison Jab, Venom Drench, Pin Missile, Liquidation

TOXAPEX
Brutal Star Pokémon

Mareanie ⇨ **Toxapex**

TOXICROAK
Toxic Mouth Pokémon

TYPE: POISON-FIGHTING

Toxicroak's dangerous poison is stored in its throat sac and delivered through the claws on its knuckles.

How to Say It: TOX-uh-croak
Imperial Height: 4'03''
Imperial Weight: 97.9 lbs.
Metric Height: 1.3 m
Metric Weight: 44.4 kg

Possible Moves: Astonish, Mud-Slap, Poison Sting, Taunt, Pursuit, Feint Attack, Revenge, Swagger, Mud Bomb, Sucker Punch, Venoshock, Nasty Plot, Poison Jab, Sludge Bomb, Belch, Flatter

Croagunk ⇨ **Toxicroak**

443

TRANQUILL
Wild Pidgeon Pokémon

TYPE: NORMAL-FLYING

Tranquill can always find its way back home, whether to its nest deep in the forest or to its Trainer's side. It's said that when these Pokémon nest together, peace surrounds the area.

How to Say It: TRAN-kwil
Imperial Height: 2'00''
Imperial Weight: 33.1 lbs.
Metric Height: 0.6 m
Metric Weight: 15.0 kg

Possible Moves: Gust, Growl, Leer, Quick Attack, Air Cutter, Roost, Detect, Taunt, Air Slash, Razor Wind, Feather Dance, Swagger, Facade, Tailwind, Sky Attack

Pidove ⇒ Tranquill ⇒ Unfezant

TRAPINCH
Ant Pit Pokémon

REGIONS:
Alola
Hoenn
Kalos
(Mountain)

TYPE: GROUND

Trapinch's huge jaws can easily crush rocks while it's digging through the sand to create its nest. This patient Pokémon waits for something edible to fall into its nest, which looks like a funnel.

How to Say It: TRAP-inch
Imperial Height: 2'04''
Imperial Weight: 33.1 lbs.
Metric Height: 0.7 m
Metric Weight: 15.0 kg

Possible Moves: Sand Attack, Bite, Feint Attack, Bide, Mud-Slap, Bulldoze, Sand Tomb, Rock Slide, Dig, Crunch, Earth Power, Feint, Earthquake, Sandstorm, Superpower, Hyper Beam, Fissure

Trapinch ⇒ Vibrava ⇒ Flygon

TREECKO
Wood Gecko Pokémon

TYPE: GRASS

The tiny hooks on Treecko's feet allow it to climb straight up walls. With its calm attitude, it coolly stands up to bigger opponents.

How to Say It: TREE-ko
Imperial Height: 1'08''
Imperial Weight: 11.0 lbs.

Metric Height: 0.5 m
Metric Weight: 5.0 kg

Possible Moves: Pound, Leer, Absorb, Quick Attack, Pursuit, Screech, Mega Drain, Agility, Slam, Detect, Giga Drain, Energy Ball, Quick Guard, Endeavor

Treecko → Grovyle → Sceptile → Mega Sceptile

TREVENANT
Elder Tree Pokémon

TYPE: GHOST-GRASS

Trevenant serves as a guardian to its forest home and protects the creatures who live there. Anyone who tries to harm the forest will surely face its wrath.

How to Say It: TREV-uh-nunt
Imperial Height: 4'11''
Imperial Weight: 156.5 lbs.
Metric Height: 1.5 m
Metric Weight: 71.0 kg

Possible Moves: Shadow Claw, Horn Leech, Tackle, Confuse Ray, Astonish, Growth, Ingrain, Feint Attack, Leech Seed, Curse, Will-O-Wisp, Forest's Curse, Destiny Bond, Phantom Force, Wood Hammer, Horn Leech

Phantump → Trevenant

TROPIUS

Fruit Pokémon

TYPE: GRASS-FLYING

Ranchers who live in warm, tropical areas often raise Tropius so they can harvest the sweet fruit that grows around their necks. In Alola, the fruit is extra delicious.

How to Say It: TROP-ee-us
Imperial Height: 6'07''
Imperial Weight: 220.5 lbs.
Metric Height: 2.0 m
Metric Weight: 100.0 kg

Possible Moves: Leer, Gust, Growth, Razor Leaf, Stomp, Sweet Scent, Whirlwind, Magical Leaf, Body Slam, Synthesis, Leaf Tornado, Air Slash, Bestow, Solar Beam, Natural Gift, Leaf Storm

Does not evolve

TRUBBISH

REGIONS: Alola Kalos (Mountain) Unova

Trash Bag Pokémon

TYPE: POISON

When Trubbish encounters tasty trash, it will munch until it's completely full, and the gases it gives off afterward can be toxic. In Alola, Trubbish and Grimer often battle over sources of delicious garbage.

How to Say It: TRUB-bish
Imperial Height: 2'00''
Imperial Weight: 68.3 lbs.
Metric Height: 0.6 m
Metric Weight: 31.0 kg

Possible Moves: Pound, Poison Gas, Recycle, Toxic Spikes, Acid Spray, Double Slap, Sludge, Stockpile, Swallow, Take Down, Sludge Bomb, Clear Smog, Toxic, Amnesia, Belch, Gunk Shot, Explosion

Trubbish ⇨ Garbodor

TYPE: NORMAL-FLYING

Trumbeak stores berry seeds in its beak to use as ammunition. It attacks opponents with a rapid-fire burst of seeds. Its beak is also very good at making lots of noise!

How to Say It: TRUM-beak
Imperial Height: 2'00''
Imperial Weight: 32.6 lbs.
Metric Height: 0.6 m
Metric Weight: 14.8 kg

Possible Moves: Rock Blast, Peck, Growl, Echoed Voice, Rock Smash, Supersonic, Pluck, Roost, Fury Attack, Screech, Drill Peck, Bullet Seed, Feather Dance, Hyper Voice

TRUMBEAK
Bugle Beak Pokémon

Pikipek ⇨ **Trumbeak** ⇨ **Toucannon**

TSAREENA
Fruit Pokémon

TYPE: GRASS

Beauty salons sometimes use images of the lovely Tsareena in their advertising. It can be a fierce fighter, using its long legs to deliver skillful kicks as it mocks its defeated opponent.

How to Say It: zar-EE-nuh
Imperial Height: 3'11''
Imperial Weight: 47.2 lbs.
Metric Height: 1.2 m
Metric Weight: 21.4 kg

Possible Moves: Trop Kick, Punishment, Double Slap, Splash, Swagger, Rapid Spin, Razor Leaf, Sweet Scent, Magical Leaf, Teeter Dance, Stomp, Aromatic Mist, Captivate, Aromatherapy, Leaf Storm, High Jump Kick, Power Whip

Bounsweet ⇨ **Steenee** ⇨ **Tsareena**

TURTONATOR
Blast Turtle Pokémon

REGION:
Alola

TYPE: FIRE-DRAGON

Poisonous gases and flames spew from Turtonator's nostrils. Its shell is made of unstable material that might explode upon impact, so opponents are advised to aim for its stomach instead.

How to Say It: TURT-nay-ter
Imperial Height: 6'07''
Imperial Weight: 467.4 lbs.
Metric Height: 2.0 m
Metric Weight: 212.0 kg

Possible Moves: Ember, Tackle, Smog, Protect, Incinerate, Flail, Endure, Iron Defense, Flamethrower, Body Slam, Shell Smash, Dragon Pulse, Shell Trap, Overheat, Explosion

Does not evolve

TURTWIG
Tiny Leaf Pokémon

TYPE: GRASS

Turtwig's shell is made of soil, and its whole body can produce energy via photosynthesis. If it goes too long without water, its leaf wilts.

How to Say It: TUR-twig
Imperial Height: 1'04"
Imperial Weight: 22.5 lbs.
Metric Height: 0.4 m
Metric Weight: 10.2 kg

Possible Moves: Tackle, Withdraw, Absorb, Razor Leaf, Curse, Bite, Mega Drain, Leech Seed, Synthesis, Crunch, Giga Drain, Leaf Storm

Turtwig ➡ Grotle ➡ Torterra

TYMPOLE
Tadpole Pokémon

TYPE: WATER

Tympole creates sound waves with the vibrations of its cheeks. People can't hear these sounds, so it can communicate with others undetected.

How to Say It: TIM-pohl
Imperial Height: 1'08"
Imperial Weight: 9.9 lbs.
Metric Height: 0.5 m
Metric Weight: 4.5 kg

Possible Moves: Bubble, Growl, Supersonic, Round, Bubble Beam, Mud Shot, Aqua Ring, Uproar, Muddy Water, Rain Dance, Flail, Echoed Voice, Hydro Pump, Hyper Voice

Tympole ➡ Palpitoad ➡ Seismitoad

TYNAMO

EleFish Pokémon

REGION: Unova

TYPE: ELECTRIC

A single Tynamo can't generate much power, but when several of them join forces, they can unleash an electric shock with the force of a lightning strike.

How to Say It: TIE-nah-moh
Imperial Height: 0'08''
Imperial Weight: 0.7 lbs.
Metric Height: 0.2 m
Metric Weight: 0.3 kg

Possible Moves: Tackle, Thunder Wave, Spark, Charge Beam

Tynamo ⇨ Eelektrik ⇨ Eelektross

TYPHLOSION

Volcano Pokémon

REGION: Johto

TYPE: FIRE

The heat shimmer given off by Typhlosion's flames serves to conceal the Pokémon's movements. It can unleash a fiery explosion to scorch everything around it.

How to Say It: tie-FLOW-zhun
Imperial Height: 5'07''
Imperial Weight: 175.3 lbs.
Metric Height: 1.7 m
Metric Weight: 79.5 kg

Possible Moves: Gyro Ball, Tackle, Leer, Smokescreen, Ember, Quick Attack, Flame Wheel, Defense Curl, Swift, Flame Charge, Lava Plume, Flamethrower, Inferno, Rollout, Double-Edge, Eruption, Burn Up

Cyndaquil ⇨ Quilava ⇨ Typhlosion

TYPE: NORMAL

The synthetic Pokémon known as Type: Null wears a heavy mask to keep its power in check. Some fear that without the mask, it would lose control of its powers and go on a destructive rampage.

How to Say It: TYPE NULL
Imperial Height: 6'03''
Imperial Weight: 265.7 lbs.
Metric Height: 1.9 m
Metric Weight: 120.5 kg

Possible Moves: Tackle, Rage, Pursuit, Imprison, Aerial Ace, Crush Claw, Scary Face, X-Scissor, Take Down, Metal Sound, Iron Head, Double Hit, Air Slash, Punishment, Razor Wind, Tri Attack, Double-Edge, Heal Block

TYPE: NULL
Synthetic Pokémon

LEGENDARY POKÉMON

Type: Null ➡ Silvally

TYRANITAR
Armor Pokémon

TYPE: ROCK-DARK

Tyranitar doesn't waste time challenging weak opponents. It possesses enough power to obliterate a mountain, so consider the bright side if you encounter one and it ignores you.

How to Say It: tie-RAN-uh-tar
Imperial Height: 6'07''
Imperial Weight: 445.3 lbs.
Metric Height: 2.0 m
Metric Weight: 202.0 kg

Possible Moves: Thunder Fang, Ice Fang, Fire Fang, Bite, Leer, Sandstorm, Screech, Chip Away, Rock Slide, Scary Face, Thrash, Dark Pulse, Payback, Crunch, Earthquake, Stone Edge, Hyper Beam, Giga Impact

MEGA TYRANITAR
Armor Pokémon

TYPE: ROCK-DARK
Imperial Height: 8'02''
Imperial Weight: 562.2 lbs.
Metric Height: 2.5 m
Metric Weight: 255.0 kg

452

Larvitar ➡ **Pupitar** ➡ **Tyranitar** ➡ **Mega Tyranitar**

TYPE: ROCK-DRAGON

Because fossil restoration is not a perfect science, some researchers have speculated that the Tyrantrum who lived in ancient times were covered in feathers. In the modern world, this restored Pokémon can crush a car in its jaws.

How to Say It: tie-RAN-trum
Imperial Height: 8'02''
Imperial Weight: 595.2 lbs.
Metric Height: 2.5 m
Metric Weight: 270.0 kg

Possible Moves: Head Smash, Tail Whip, Tackle, Roar, Stomp, Bide, Stealth Rock, Bite, Charm, Ancient Power, Dragon Tail, Crunch, Dragon Claw, Thrash, Earthquake, Horn Drill, Rock Slide, Giga Impact

REGIONS: Alola Kalos *(Coastal)*

TYRANTRUM
Despot Pokémon

Tyrunt ⇨ Tyrantrum

REGION: Johto

TYROGUE
Scuffle Pokémon

TYPE: FIGHTING

Training and working out every day is a must for keeping Tyrogue's stress levels under control. Its Trainer must take a disciplined approach.

How to Say It: tie-ROHG
Imperial Height: 2'04''
Imperial Weight: 46.3 lbs.
Metric Height: 0.7 m
Metric Weight: 21.0 kg

Possible Moves: Tackle, Helping Hand, Fake Out, Foresight

Tyrogue

Hitmonlee   Hitmontop

Hitmonchan

453

TYRUNT
Royal Heir Pokémon

REGIONS:
Alola
Kalos
(Coastal)

TYPE: ROCK-DRAGON

Its amazing jaw strength and its lack of concern for others make for a dangerous combination. Tyrunt has been known to injure its companions by accident while trying to be playful.

How to Say It: TIE-runt
Imperial Height: 2'07''
Imperial Weight: 57.3 lbs.
Metric Height: 0.8 m
Metric Weight: 26.0 kg

Possible Moves: Tail Whip, Tackle, Roar, Stomp, Bide, Stealth Rock, Bite, Charm, Ancient Power, Dragon Tail, Crunch, Dragon Claw, Thrash, Earthquake, Horn Drill

Tyrunt ⇨ Tyrantrum

TYPE: DARK

Umbreon's black fur makes it well suited for battles in the dark. It can rely on this camouflage to keep it hidden until it's ready to strike. When it's angry, its sweat turns toxic.

How to Say It: UM-bree-on
Imperial Height: 3'03''
Imperial Weight: 59.5 lbs.
Metric Height: 1.0 m
Metric Weight: 27.0 kg

Possible Moves: Pursuit, Helping Hand, Tackle, Tail Whip, Sand Attack, Baby-Doll Eyes, Quick Attack, Confuse Ray, Feint Attack, Assurance, Screech, Moonlight, Mean Look, Last Resort, Guard Swap

REGIONS:
Alola
Johto
Kalos
(Coastal)

UMBREON
Moonlight Pokémon

Eevee ⇨ Umbreon

Male Form

Female Form

REGION:
Unova

UNFEZANT
Proud Pokémon

TYPE: NORMAL-FLYING

Unfezant has a prickly personality and rarely bonds with anyone other than its Trainer. The males have impressive head plumage, and the females are better at flying.

How to Say It: un-FEZ-ent
Imperial Height: 3'11''
Imperial Weight: 63.9 lbs.
Metric Height: 1.2 m
Metric Weight: 29.0 kg

Possible Moves: Gust, Growl, Leer, Quick Attack, Air Cutter, Roost, Detect, Taunt, Air Slash, Razor Wind, Feather Dance, Swagger, Facade, Tailwind, Sky Attack

Pidove ⇨ Tranquill ⇨ Unfezant

455

UNOWN
Symbol Pokémon

REGION:
Johto

TYPE: PSYCHIC

Unown can be found in many different shapes that resemble ancient writing. It's not known which came first.

How to Say It: un-KNOWN
Imperial Height: 1'08''
Imperial Weight: 11.0 lbs.
Metric Height: 0.5 m
Metric Weight: 5.0 kg

Possible Moves: Hidden Power

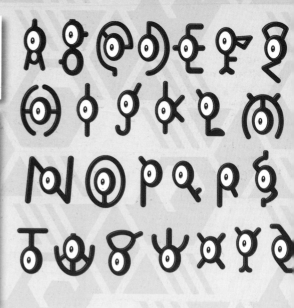

Does not evolve

URSARING
Hibernator Pokémon

REGIONS:
Johto
Kalos
(Mountain)

TYPE: NORMAL

Ursaring makes daily rounds through the forest where it lives, climbing high into the trees and splashing through the streams to find food.

How to Say It: UR-sa-ring
Imperial Height: 5'11''
Imperial Weight: 277.3 lbs.
Metric Height: 1.8 m
Metric Weight: 125.8 kg

Possible Moves: Hammer Arm, Covet, Scratch, Leer, Lick, Fake Tears, Fury Swipes, Feint Attack, Sweet Scent, Play Nice, Slash, Scary Face, Rest, Snore, Thrash

Teddiursa   Ursaring

TYPE: PSYCHIC

According to legend, Uxie brought the gift of intelligence to humankind. It is known as "The Being of Knowledge."

How to Say It: YOOK-zee
Imperial Height: 1'00''
Imperial Weight: 0.7 lbs.
Metric Height: 0.3 m
Metric Weight: 0.3 kg

Possible Moves: Rest, Confusion, Imprison, Endure, Swift, Yawn, Future Sight, Amnesia, Extrasensory, Flail, Natural Gift, Memento

REGION: Sinnoh

UXIE
Knowledge Pokémon

LEGENDARY POKÉMON

Does not evolve

VANILLISH
Icy Snow Pokémon

REGIONS:
Alola
Kalos
(Mountain)
Unova

TYPE: ICE

Vanillish can control ice particles to surround its opponents and freeze them solid. In hot weather, its icy body is in danger of melting, although this Pokémon can be frozen again to restore it to health.

How to Say It: vuh-NIHL-lish
Imperial Height: 3'07''
Imperial Weight: 90.4 lbs.
Metric Height: 1.1 m
Metric Weight: 41.0 kg

Possible Moves: Icicle Spear, Harden, Astonish, Uproar, Icy Wind, Mist, Avalanche, Taunt, Mirror Shot, Acid Armor, Ice Beam, Hail, Mirror Coat, Blizzard, Sheer Cold

Vanillite ➡ Vanillish ➡ Vanilluxe

VANILLITE
Fresh Snow Pokémon

REGIONS:
Alola
Kalos
(Mountain)
Unova

TYPE: ICE

Vanillite is particularly popular in Alola and other warm places, because hugging this icy Pokémon is a lovely way to cool off. It can breathe out tiny crystals of ice to create a snow flurry around itself.

How to Say It: vuh-NIHL-lyte
Imperial Height: 1'04''
Imperial Weight: 12.6 lbs.
Metric Height: 0.4 m
Metric Weight: 5.7 kg

Possible Moves: Icicle Spear, Harden, Astonish, Uproar, Icy Wind, Mist, Avalanche, Taunt, Mirror Shot, Acid Armor, Ice Beam, Hail, Mirror Coat, Blizzard, Sheer Cold

Vanillite ➡ Vanillish ➡ Vanilluxe

VANILLUXE
Snowstorm Pokémon

TYPE: ICE

Vanilluxe has two heads, each with a mind of its own, and they don't always agree. When they decide to work together, this Pokémon can create impressive blizzards with the snow clouds it forms inside its body.

How to Say It: vuh-NIHL-lux
Imperial Height: 4'03''
Imperial Weight: 126.8 lbs.
Metric Height: 1.3 m
Metric Weight: 57.5 kg

Possible Moves: Sheer Cold, Freeze-Dry, Weather Ball, Icicle Spear, Harden, Astonish, Uproar, Icy Wind, Mist, Avalanche, Taunt, Mirror Shot, Acid Armor, Ice Beam, Hail, Mirror Coat, Blizzard

Vanillite ➡ **Vanillish** ➡ **Vanilluxe**

TYPE: WATER

Vaporeon lives near water, and some who see it wandering the shore think it's a mermaid! When submerged, its camouflage is perfect—it can disappear entirely in order to launch a sneak attack.

How to Say It: vay-POUR-ree-on
Imperial Height: 3'03''
Imperial Weight: 63.9 lbs.
Metric Height: 1.0 m
Metric Weight: 29.0 kg

Possible Moves: Water Gun, Helping Hand, Tackle, Tail Whip, Sand Attack, Baby-Doll Eyes, Quick Attack, Water Pulse, Aurora Beam, Aqua Ring, Acid Armor, Haze, Muddy Water, Last Resort, Hydro Pump

VAPOREON
Bubble Jet Pokémon

Eevee ➡ **Vaporeon**

VENIPEDE
Centipede Pokémon

REGIONS:
Kalos
(Central)
Unova

TYPE: BUG-POISON

Venipede uses the feelers at both ends of its body to explore its surroundings. It's extremely aggressive, and its bite is poisonous.

How to Say It: VEHN-ih-peed
Imperial Height: 1'04''
Imperial Weight: 11.7 lbs.

Metric Height: 0.4 m
Metric Weight: 5.3 kg

Possible Moves: Defense Curl, Rollout, Poison Sting, Screech, Pursuit, Protect, Poison Tail, Bug Bite, Venoshock, Agility, Steamroller, Toxic, Venom Drench, Rock Climb, Double-Edge

Venipede ⇒ Whirlipede ⇒ Scolipede

TYPE: BUG-POISON

When they become active after dark, Venomoth are often drawn to street-lamps. It isn't the light that attracts them, but the promise of food.

How to Say It: VEH-no-moth
Imperial Height: 4'11''
Imperial Weight: 27.6 lbs.
Metric Height: 1.5 m
Metric Weight: 12.5 kg

Possible Moves: Silver Wind, Tackle, Disable, Foresight, Supersonic, Confusion, Poison Powder, Leech Life, Stun Spore, Psybeam, Sleep Powder, Gust, Signal Beam, Zen Headbutt, Poison Fang, Psychic, Bug Buzz, Quiver Dance

REGION: Kanto

VENOMOTH
Poison Moth Pokémon

Venonat → Venomoth

REGION: Kanto

VENONAT
Insect Pokémon

TYPE: BUG-POISON

Venonat's large, sensitive eyes pick up even the tiniest movement. The stiff hair that covers its body protects it from harm.

How to Say It: VEH-no-nat
Imperial Height: 3'03''
Imperial Weight: 66.1 lbs.
Metric Height: 1.0 m
Metric Weight: 30.0 kg

Possible Moves: Tackle, Disable, Foresight, Supersonic, Confusion, Poison Powder, Leech Life, Stun Spore, Psybeam, Sleep Powder, Signal Beam, Zen Headbutt, Poison Fang, Psychic

Venonat → Venomoth

461

VENUSAUR
Seed Pokémon

REGIONS:
Kalos
(Central)
Kanto

TYPE: GRASS-POISON

When Venusaur is well nourished and spends enough time in the sun, the flower on its back is brightly colored. The blossom gives off a soothing scent.

How to Say It: VEE-nuh-sore
Imperial Height: 6'07''
Imperial Weight: 220.5 lbs.
Metric Height: 2.0 m
Metric Weight: 100.0 kg

Possible Moves: Tackle, Growl, Vine Whip, Leech Seed, Poison Powder, Sleep Powder, Take Down, Razor Leaf, Sweet Scent, Growth, Double-Edge, Petal Dance, Worry Seed, Synthesis, Petal Blizzard, Solar Beam

MEGA VENUSAUR
Seed Pokémon

TYPE: GRASS-POISON

Imperial Height: 7'10''
Imperial Weight: 342.8 lbs.
Metric Height: 2.4 m
Metric Weight: 155.5 kg

 Bulbasaur ⇨ **Ivysaur** ⇨ **Venusaur** ⇨  **Mega Venusaur**

VESPIQUEN
Beehive Pokémon

TYPE: BUG-FLYING

Vespiquen controls the colony that lives in its honeycomb body by releasing pheromones. It feeds the colony with honey provided by Combee.

How to Say It: VES-pih-kwen
Imperial Height: 3'11''
Imperial Weight: 84.9 lbs.
Metric Height: 1.2 m
Metric Weight: 38.5 kg

Possible Moves: Fell Stinger, Destiny Bond, Sweet Scent, Gust, Poison Sting, Confuse Ray, Fury Cutter, Pursuit, Fury Swipes, Defend Order, Slash, Power Gem, Heal Order, Toxic, Air Slash, Captivate, Attack Order, Swagger

Combee ➡ **Vespiquen**

TYPE: GROUND-DRAGON

Vibrava has to eat a lot to fuel the growth of its underdeveloped wings. Instead of flying, it vibrates its wings together, creating ultrasonic waves that it uses in battle.

How to Say It: VY-BRAH-va
Imperial Height: 3'07''
Imperial Weight: 33.7 lbs.
Metric Height: 1.1 m
Metric Weight: 15.3 kg

Possible Moves: Dragon Breath, Sand Attack, Sonic Boom, Feint Attack, Bide, Mud-Slap, Bulldoze, Sand Tomb, Rock Slide, Supersonic, Screech, Earth Power, Bug Buzz, Earthquake, Sandstorm, Uproar, Hyper Beam, Boomburst

VIBRAVA
Vibration Pokémon

Trapinch ➡ **Vibrava** ➡ **Flygon**

VICTINI
Victory Pokémon

REGION: Unova

MYTHICAL POKÉMON

TYPE: PSYCHIC-FIRE

According to myth, Victini can bring victory in any kind of competition. Because it creates unlimited energy, it can share the overflow with others.

How to Say It: vik-TEE-nee
Imperial Height: 1'04''
Imperial Weight: 8.8 lbs.

Metric Height: 0.4 m
Metric Weight: 4.0 kg

Possible Moves: Searing Shot, Focus Energy, Confusion, Incinerate, Quick Attack, Endure, Headbutt, Flame Charge, Reversal, Flame Burst, Zen Headbutt, Inferno, Double-Edge, Flare Blitz, Final Gambit, Stored Power, Overheat

464

Does not evolve

VICTREEBEL
Flycatcher Pokémon

TYPE: GRASS-POISON

Victreebel uses its long vine like a fishing lure, swishing and flicking it to draw prey closer to its gaping mouth.

How to Say It: VICK-tree-bell
Imperial Height: 5'07''
Imperial Weight: 34.2 lbs.
Metric Height: 1.7 m
Metric Weight: 15.5 kg

Possible Moves: Stockpile, Swallow, Spit Up, Vine Whip, Sleep Powder, Sweet Scent, Razor Leaf, Leaf Tornado, Leaf Storm, Leaf Blade

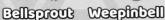

Bellsprout ⇨ **Weepinbell** ⇨ **Victreebel**

REGION:
Hoenn

VIGOROTH
Wild Monkey Pokémon

TYPE: NORMAL

Vigoroth just can't sit still! If it spends too much time inactive, it gets stressed out and goes on a rampage. It doesn't sleep very well.

How to Say It: VIG-er-roth
Imperial Height: 4'07''
Imperial Weight: 102.5 lbs.
Metric Height: 1.4 m
Metric Weight: 46.5 kg

Possible Moves: Scratch, Focus Energy, Encore, Uproar, Fury Swipes, Endure, Slash, Counter, Chip Away, Focus Punch, Reversal

Slakoth ⇨ **Vigoroth** ⇨ **Slaking**

VIKAVOLT
Levitate Pokémon

TYPE: BUG-ELECTRIC

Vikavolt uses its large jaws to focus the electricity it produces inside its body, then unleashes a powerful zap to stun its opponents. Flying-type Pokémon that once posed a threat are no match for its shocking attacks.

How to Say It: VIE-kuh-volt
Imperial Height: 4'11''
Imperial Weight: 99.2 lbs.
Metric Height: 1.5 m
Metric Weight: 45.0 kg

Possible Moves: Thunderbolt, Air Slash, Charge, Vice Grip, String Shot, Mud-Slap, Bite, Bug Bite, Spark, Acrobatics, Guillotine, Bug Buzz, Dig, Zap Cannon, Agility

Grubbin ⇨ Charjabug ⇨ Vikavolt

VILEPLUME
Flower Pokémon

REGIONS:
Kalos
(Central)
Kanto

TYPE: GRASS-POISON

Many people are terribly allergic to the poisonous pollen Vileplume gives off. The petals of its flower are truly enormous.

How to Say It: VILE-ploom
Imperial Height: 3'11''
Imperial Weight: 41.0 lbs.
Metric Height: 1.2 m
Metric Weight: 18.6 kg

Possible Moves: Mega Drain, Aromatherapy, Stun Spore, Poison Powder, Petal Blizzard, Petal Dance, Solar Beam

Oddish ⇨ Gloom ⇨ Vileplume

VIRIZION
Grassland Pokémon

LEGENDARY POKÉMON

TYPE: GRASS-FIGHTING

According to legend, Virizion can move so swiftly that its opponents are left bewildered. Its horns are lovely and graceful—and as sharp as blades.

How to Say It: vih-RY-zee-un
Imperial Height: 6'07''
Imperial Weight: 440.9 lbs.

Metric Height: 2.0 m
Metric Weight: 200.0 kg

Possible Moves: Quick Attack, Leer, Double Kick, Magical Leaf, Take Down, Helping Hand, Retaliate, Giga Drain, Sacred Sword, Swords Dance, Quick Guard, Work Up, Leaf Blade, Close Combat

Does not evolve

VIVILLON

Scale Pokémon

REGION:
Kalos
(Central)

TYPE: BUG-FLYING

The colorful patterns on Vivillon's wings are determined by the Pokémon's habitat. Vivillon from different parts of the world have different wing patterns.

How to Say It: VIH-vee-yon
Imperial Height: 3'11"
Imperial Weight: 37.5 lbs.
Metric Height: 1.2 m
Metric Weight: 17.0 kg

Possible Moves: Powder, Sleep Powder, Poison Powder, Stun Spore, Gust, Light Screen, Struggle Bug, Psybeam, Supersonic, Draining Kiss, Aromatherapy, Bug Buzz, Safeguard, Quiver Dance, Hurricane

Scatterbug ⇨ Spewpa ⇨ Vivillon

VOLBEAT

Firefly Pokémon

REGIONS:
Hoenn
Kalos
(Central)

TYPE: BUG

When night falls, Volbeat flashes the light on its tail in different patterns to send messages to others. It follows the sweet scent of Illumise.

How to Say It: VOLL-beat
Imperial Height: 2'04"
Imperial Weight: 39.0 lbs.
Metric Height: 0.7 m
Metric Weight: 17.7 kg

Possible Moves: Flash, Tackle, Double Team, Confuse Ray, Moonlight, Quick Attack, Tail Glow, Signal Beam, Protect, Helping Hand, Zen Headbutt, Bug Buzz, Double-Edge, Struggle Bug, Play Rough, Infestation

Does not evolve

VOLCANION
Steam Pokémon

MYTHICAL POKÉMON

TYPE: FIRE-WATER

The Mythical Pokémon Volcanion lives in the mountains and stays far away from humans. The arms on its back can shoot out steam with incredibly destructive force, though it often uses these steam clouds to cover its escape.

How to Say It: vol-KAY-nee-un
Imperial Height: 5'07''
Imperial Weight: 429.9 lbs.
Metric Height: 1.7 m
Metric Weight: 195.0 kg

Possible Moves: Steam Eruption, Flare Blitz, Take Down

Does not evolve

REGIONS:
Alola
Unova

VOLCARONA
Sun Pokémon

TYPE: BUG-FIRE

Ancient people held fearful respect for Volcarona, whose flaming scales reminded them of a raging sun. Legend says it emerged from a burning cocoon to provide warmth to people and Pokémon stuck in the cold.

How to Say It: vol-kah-ROH-nah
Imperial Height: 5'03''
Imperial Weight: 101.4 lbs.
Metric Height: 1.6 m
Metric Weight: 46.0 kg

Possible Moves: Gust, Fire Spin, Whirlwind, Silver Wind, Quiver Dance, Heat Wave, Bug Buzz, Rage Powder, Hurricane, Fiery Dance, Flare Blitz, Thrash, Amnesia, Absorb

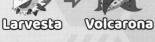

Larvesta ➡ Volcarona

VOLTORB
Ball Pokémon

REGIONS:
Kalos
(Mountain)
Kanto

TYPE: ELECTRIC

Voltorb looks a lot like a Poké Ball, and it was first spotted at a Poké Ball factory. What's the connection? Nobody knows.

How to Say It: VOLT-orb
Imperial Height: 1'08''
Imperial Weight: 22.9 lbs.
Metric Height: 0.5 m
Metric Weight: 10.4 kg

Possible Moves: Charge, Tackle, Sonic Boom, Eerie Impulse, Spark, Rollout, Screech, Charge Beam, Light Screen, Electro Ball, Self-Destruct, Swift, Magnet Rise, Gyro Ball, Explosion, Mirror Coat, Discharge

Voltorb → Electrode

VULLABY
Diapered Pokémon

REGIONS:
Alola
Unova

TYPE: DARK-FLYING

Vullaby wears bones around its lower half as a shield, and it replaces the bones as it outgrows them. Its wings aren't yet big enough to carry it through the air.

How to Say It: VUL-luh-bye
Imperial Height: 1'08''
Imperial Weight: 19.8 lbs.
Metric Height: 0.5 m
Metric Weight: 9.0 kg

Possible Moves: Gust, Leer, Fury Attack, Pluck, Nasty Plot, Flatter, Feint Attack, Punishment, Defog, Tailwind, Air Slash, Dark Pulse, Embargo, Whirlwind, Brave Bird, Mirror Move

Vullaby → Mandibuzz

VULPIX
Fox Pokémon

TYPE: FIRE

Vulpix is prized for its lovely fur and multiple tails, which keep splitting as it grows. Some people think the ghostly fire from its mouth is a departed spirit.

How to Say It: VULL-picks
Imperial Height: 2'00''
Imperial Weight: 21.8 lbs.
Metric Height: 0.6 m
Metric Weight: 9.9 kg

Possible Moves: Ember, Tail Whip, Roar, Quick Attack, Fire Spin, Confuse Ray, Imprison, Flame Burst, Safeguard, Will-O-Wisp, Payback, Flamethrower, Captivate, Inferno, Grudge, Extrasensory, Fire Blast, Baby-Doll Eyes, Feint Attack, Hex

Vulpix ➡ **Ninetales**

ALOLAN VULPIX
Fox Pokémon

TYPE: ICE

Vulpix in the Alola region were once known as Keokeo, and some older folks still use that name. Its six tails can create a spray of ice crystals to cool itself off when it gets too hot.

How to Say It: uh-LO-luhn VULL-picks
Imperial Height: 2'00''
Imperial Weight: 21.8 lbs.
Metric Height: 0.6 m
Metric Weight: 9.9 kg

Possible Moves: Powder Snow, Tail Whip, Roar, Baby-Doll Eyes, Ice Shard, Confuse Ray, Icy Wind, Payback, Mist, Feint Attack, Hex, Aurora Beam, Extrasensory, Safeguard, Ice Beam, Imprison, Blizzard, Grudge, Captivate, Sheer Cold

Alolan Vulpix ➡ **Alolan Ninetales**

WAILMER

Ball Whale Pokémon

REGIONS:
Alola
Hoenn
Kalos
(Coastal)

TYPE: WATER

When Wailmer is feeling playful, it inflates its round body by sucking in seawater, then bounces joyfully around. It releases the water in a showy way by shooting impressive spouts from its nostrils.

How to Say It: WAIL-murr
Imperial Height: 6'07''
Imperial Weight: 286.6 lbs.
Metric Height: 2.0 m
Metric Weight: 130.0 kg

Possible Moves: Splash, Growl, Water Gun, Rollout, Whirlpool, Astonish, Water Pulse, Mist, Brine, Rest, Water Spout, Amnesia, Dive, Bounce, Hydro Pump, Heavy Slam

Wailmer   Wailord

WAILORD

Float Whale Pokémon

REGIONS:
Alola
Hoenn
Kalos
(Coastal)

TYPE: WATER

Wailord swim with their mouths open to gather food. In some places, pods of these enormous Pokémon become a tourist attraction of sorts, as visitors go out in boats to see if they can spot one.

How to Say It: WAIL-ord
Imperial Height: 47'07''
Imperial Weight: 877.4 lbs.
Metric Height: 14.5 m
Metric Weight: 398.0 kg

Possible Moves: Soak, Noble Roar, Heavy Slam, Splash, Growl, Water Gun, Rollout, Whirlpool, Astonish, Water Pulse, Mist, Brine, Rest, Water Spout, Amnesia, Dive, Bounce, Hydro Pump, Heavy Slam

Wailmer   Wailord

TYPE: ICE-WATER

Walrein's giant tusks are capable of smashing through icebergs. Its thick blubber keeps it warm in frigid seas and is great for fending off hits in battle.

How to Say It: WAL-rain
Imperial Height: 4'07''
Imperial Weight: 332.0 lbs.
Metric Height: 1.4 m
Metric Weight: 150.6 kg

Possible Moves: Crunch, Powder Snow, Growl, Water Gun, Encore, Ice Ball, Body Slam, Aurora Beam, Hail, Swagger, Rest, Snore, Ice Fang, Blizzard, Sheer Cold, Defense Curl, Rollout, Brine

WALREIN
Ice Break Pokémon

Spheal ➡ **Sealeo** ➡ **Walrein**

WARTORTLE
Turtle Pokémon

TYPE: WATER

The fur on Wartortle's tail darkens with age. Its shell bears the scratches of many battles.

How to Say It: WOR-TORE-tul
Imperial Height: 3'03''
Imperial Weight: 49.6 lbs.
Metric Height: 1.0 m
Metric Weight: 22.5 kg

Possible Moves: Tackle, Tail Whip, Water Gun, Withdraw, Bubble, Bite, Rapid Spin, Protect, Water Pulse, Aqua Tail, Skull Bash, Iron Defense, Rain Dance, Hydro Pump

Squirtle ➡ **Wartortle** ➡ **Blastoise** ➡ **Mega Blastoise**

WATCHOG
Lookout Pokémon

REGIONS:
Kalos
(Mountain)
Unova

TYPE: NORMAL

Watchog can make its stripes and eyes glow in the dark. Its tail stands straight up to alert others when it spots an intruder.

How to Say It: WAH-chawg
Imperial Height: 3'07''
Imperial Weight: 59.5 lbs.
Metric Height: 1.1 m
Metric Weight: 27.0 kg

Possible Moves: Rototiller, Tackle, Leer, Bite, Low Kick, Bide, Detect, Sand Attack, Crunch, Hypnosis, Confuse Ray, Super Fang, After You, Psych Up, Hyper Fang, Mean Look, Baton Pass, Slam, Nasty Plot, Focus Energy

Patrat ⇨ Watchog

WEAVILE
Sharp Claw Pokémon

REGIONS:
Alola
Kalos
(Mountain)
Sinnoh

TYPE: DARK-ICE

In the cold places where they live, Weavile communicate with others in their group by carving up rocks and trees with their sharp claws. In the Alola region, they often battle with the cold-dwelling Sandshrew and Vulpix.

How to Say It: WEE-vile
Imperial Height: 3'07''
Imperial Weight: 75.0 lbs.
Metric Height: 1.1 m
Metric Weight: 34.0 kg

Possible Moves: Embargo, Revenge, Assurance, Scratch, Leer, Taunt, Quick Attack, Feint Attack, Icy Wind, Fury Swipes, Nasty Plot, Metal Claw, Hone Claws, Fling, Screech, Night Slash, Snatch, Punishment, Dark Pulse

Sneasel ⇨ Weavile

WEEDLE
Hairy Bug Pokémon

TYPE: BUG-POISON

Weedle's sense of smell is excellent. With its large red nose, it can sniff out the leaves it likes best.

How to Say It: WEE-dull
Imperial Height: 1'00''
Imperial Weight: 7.1 lbs.

Metric Height: 0.3 m
Metric Weight: 3.2 kg

Possible Moves: Poison Sting, String Shot, Bug Bite

Weedle　**Kakuna**　**Beedrill**　**Mega Beedrill**

WEEPINBELL
Flycatcher Pokémon

TYPE: GRASS-POISON

The hooked stem behind its head lets Weepinbell hang from a tree branch to sleep. Sometimes it falls to the ground during the night.

How to Say It: WEE-pin-bell
Imperial Height: 3'03''
Imperial Weight: 14.1 lbs.
Metric Height: 1.0 m
Metric Weight: 6.4 kg

Possible Moves: Vine Whip, Growth, Wrap, Sleep Powder, Poison Powder, Stun Spore, Acid, Knock Off, Sweet Scent, Gastro Acid, Razor Leaf, Poison Jab, Slam, Wring Out

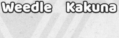

Bellsprout　**Weepinbell**　**Victreebel**

WEEZING
Poison Gas Pokémon

REGION:
Kanto

TYPE: POISON

Rotting food gives off a noxious gas that attracts Weezing. Its twin bodies take turns inflating and deflating to keep its poisonous gases churning.

How to Say It: WEEZ-ing
Imperial Height: 3'11''
Imperial Weight: 20.9 lbs.
Metric Height: 1.2 m
Metric Weight: 9.5 kg

Possible Moves: Poison Gas, Tackle, Smog, Smokescreen, Assurance, Clear Smog, Self-Destruct, Sludge, Haze, Double Hit, Explosion, Sludge Bomb, Destiny Bond, Memento, Gyro Ball, Belch

Koffing   Weezing

WHIMSICOTT
Windveiled Pokémon

REGIONS:
Alola
Unova

TYPE: GRASS-FAIRY

Whimsicott is so light and fluffy that it drifts on the wind. The cotton that covers its body is easily shed, whether Whimsicott is making a mess in someone's home or being blown about by a strong wind.

How to Say It: WHIM-sih-kot
Imperial Height: 2'04''
Imperial Weight: 14.6 lbs.
Metric Height: 0.7 m
Metric Weight: 6.6 kg

Possible Moves: Growth, Leech Seed, Mega Drain, Cotton Spore, Gust, Tailwind, Hurricane, Moonblast

Cottonee   Whimsicott

TYPE: BUG-POISON

Covered in a sturdy shell, Whirlipede doesn't move much unless it's attacked. Then it leaps into action, spinning at high velocity and smashing into the attacker.

How to Say It: WHIR-lih-peed
Imperial Height: 3'11''
Imperial Weight: 129.0 lbs.
Metric Height: 1.2 m
Metric Weight: 58.5 kg

Possible Moves: Defense Curl, Rollout, Poison Sting, Screech, Pursuit, Protect, Poison Tail, Iron Defense, Bug Bite, Venoshock, Agility, Steamroller, Toxic, Venom Drench, Rock Climb, Double-Edge

REGIONS:
Kalos
(Central)
Unova

WHIRLIPEDE
Curlipede Pokémon

Venipede ⇨ Whirlipede ⇨ Scolipede

TYPE: WATER-GROUND

Whiscash lives in the swamp, where it rests on the murky bottom most of the time, waiting for food to float by. If you see one leaping energetically out of the water, it might mean an earthquake is threatening.

How to Say It: WISS-cash
Imperial Height: 2'11''
Imperial Weight: 52.0 lbs.
Metric Height: 0.9 m
Metric Weight: 23.6 kg

Possible Moves: Thrash, Belch, Zen Headbutt, Tickle, Mud-Slap, Mud Sport, Water Sport, Water Gun, Mud Bomb, Amnesia, Water Pulse, Magnitude, Rest, Snore, Aqua Tail, Earthquake, Muddy Water, Future Sight, Fissure

REGIONS:
Alola
Hoenn
Kalos
(Mountain)

WHISCASH
Whiskers Pokémon

Barboach ⇨ Whiscash

477

WHISMUR
Whisper Pokémon

REGIONS:
Hoenn
Kalos
(Coastal)

TYPE: NORMAL

When Whismur isn't in trouble, the noises it makes are very quiet. As soon as danger approaches, it sounds an earsplitting wail.

How to Say It: WHIS-mur
Imperial Height: 2'00''
Imperial Weight: 35.9 lbs.
Metric Height: 0.6 m
Metric Weight: 16.3 kg

Possible Moves: Pound, Uproar, Astonish, Howl, Supersonic, Stomp, Screech, Roar, Synchronoise, Rest, Sleep Talk, Hyper Voice, Echoed Voice

Whismur ➡ Loudred ➡ Exploud

WIGGLYTUFF
Balloon Pokémon

REGIONS:
Alola
Kalos
(Mountain)
Kanto

TYPE: NORMAL-FAIRY

When the weather gets warm, Wigglytuff shed their fur, which can be spun into delightfully soft yarn. As these Pokémon breathe in, their bodies expand to hold more air—sometimes they make a game of how much they can inflate.

How to Say It: WIG-lee-tuff
Imperial Height: 3'03''
Imperial Weight: 26.5 lbs.
Metric Height: 1.0 m
Metric Weight: 12.0 kg

Possible Moves: Double-Edge, Play Rough, Sing, Defense Curl, Disable, Double Slap

Igglybuff ➡ Jigglypuff ➡ Wigglytuff

TYPE: BUG-WATER

When the cowardly Wimpod flees from battle, it leaves a path swept clean by the passing of its many legs. It helps keep the beaches and seabeds clean, too, scavenging just about anything edible.

How to Say It: WIM-pod
Imperial Height: 1'08''
Imperial Weight: 26.5 lbs.
Metric Height: 0.5 m
Metric Weight: 12.0 kg

Possible Moves: Struggle Bug, Sand Attack

REGION: Alola

WIMPOD
Turn Tail Pokémon

Wimpod   **Golisopod**

REGIONS: Alola Hoenn Kalos *(Coastal)*

WINGULL
Seagull Pokémon

TYPE: WATER-FLYING

Wingull's bones are hollow, allowing it to soar effortlessly. If several Wingull are circling in one spot above the sea, fishermen take note and cast their lines in that area for a good catch.

How to Say It: WING-gull
Imperial Height: 2'00''
Imperial Weight: 20.9 lbs.
Metric Height: 0.6 m
Metric Weight: 9.5 kg

Possible Moves: Growl, Water Gun, Supersonic, Wing Attack, Mist, Water Pulse, Quick Attack, Air Cutter, Pursuit, Aerial Ace, Roost, Agility, Air Slash, Hurricane

Wingull   **Pelipper**

WISHIWASHI

Small Fry Pokémon

Solo Form

TYPE: WATER

If a Wishiwashi looks like it's about to cry, watch out! The light that shines from its watering eyes draws the entire school, and they band together to fight off their opponent by sheer strength of numbers.

How to Say It: WISH-ee-WASH-ee
Imperial Height: Solo Form: 0'08'' / School Form: 26'11''
Imperial Weight: Solo Form: 0.7 lbs. / School Form: 173.3 lbs.
Metric Height: Solo Form: 0.2 m / School Form: 8.2 m
Metric Weight: Solo Form: 0.3 kg / School Form: 78.6 kg

Possible Moves: Water Gun, Growl, Helping Hand, Feint Attack, Brine, Aqua Ring, Tearful Look, Take Down, Dive, Beat Up, Aqua Tail, Double-Edge, Soak, Endeavor, Hydro Pump

School Form

Does not evolve

WOBBUFFET

Patient Pokémon

REGIONS:
Johto
Kalos
(Coastal)

TYPE: PSYCHIC

Relying on its powers of endurance, Wobbuffet prefers not to attack—unless a foe goes after its tail. Then, it unleashes a powerful counterstrike.

How to Say It: WAH-buf-fett
Imperial Height: 4' 03''
Imperial Weight: 62.8 lbs.
Metric Height: 1.3 m
Metric Weight: 28.5 kg

Possible Moves: Counter, Mirror Coat, Safeguard, Destiny Bond

Wynaut ⇨ Wobbuffet

TYPE: PSYCHIC-FLYING

When Woobat attaches itself to something, it leaves a heart-shaped mark with its nose. The nose is also the source of its echolocation signals.

How to Say It: WOO-bat
Imperial Height: 1'04''
Imperial Weight: 4.6 lbs.
Metric Height: 0.4 m
Metric Weight: 2.1 kg

Possible Moves:
Confusion, Odor Sleuth, Gust, Assurance, Heart Stamp, Imprison, Air Cutter, Attract, Amnesia, Calm Mind, Air Slash, Future Sight, Psychic, Endeavor

WOOBAT
Bat Pokémon

Woobat ⇨ Swoobat

TYPE: WATER-GROUND

Though Wooper usually live in the water, they sometimes come ashore to look for food. To protect their bodies, they cover themselves with a sticky substance that is poisonous to the touch.

How to Say It: WOOP-pur
Imperial Height: 1'04''
Imperial Weight: 18.7 lbs.
Metric Height: 0.4 m
Metric Weight: 8.5 kg

Possible Moves: Water Gun, Tail Whip, Mud Sport, Mud Shot, Slam, Mud Bomb, Amnesia, Yawn, Earthquake, Rain Dance, Mist, Haze, Muddy Water

WOOPER
Water Fish Pokémon

Wooper ⇨ Quagsire

WORMADAM (PLANT CLOAK)
Bagworm Pokémon

TYPE: BUG-GRASS

The cloak it wore as Burmy becomes a permanent part of Wormadam's body. Its appearance is determined by its surroundings at the time of Evolution.

How to Say It: WUR-muh-dam
Imperial Height: 1'08''
Imperial Weight: 14.3 lbs.

Metric Height: 0.5 m
Metric Weight: 6.5 kg

Possible Moves: Quiver Dance, Sucker Punch, Tackle, Protect, Bug Bite, Hidden Power, Confusion, Razor Leaf, Growth, Psybeam, Captivate, Flail, Attract, Psychic, Leaf Storm, Bug Buzz

Burmy
(Female Form)

Wormadam
(Plant Cloak)

WORMADAM (SANDY CLOAK)
Bagworm Pokémon

REGIONS:
Kalos
(Central)
Sinnoh

TYPE: BUG-GROUND

If you want a Bug- and Ground-type Wormadam, make sure your Burmy has a Sandy Cloak! Once Burmy evolves, there's no turning back.

How to Say It: WUR-muh-dam
Imperial Height: 1'08''
Imperial Weight: 14.3 lbs.

Metric Height: 0.5 m
Metric Weight: 6.5 kg

Possible Moves: Quiver Dance, Sucker Punch Tackle, Protect, Bug Bite, Hidden Power, Confusion, Rock Blast, Harden, Psybeam, Captivate, Flail, Attract, Psychic, Fissure , Bug Buzz

Burmy
(Female Form)

Wormadam
(Sandy Cloak)

WORMADAM (TRASH CLOAK)
Bagworm Pokémon

TYPE: BUG-STEEL

Looking for a Wormadam with awesome Steel-type moves? You'll need to evolve a Burmy with a Trash Cloak.

How to Say It: WUR-muh-dam
Imperial Height: 1'08''
Imperial Weight: 14.3 lbs.

Metric Height: 0.5 m
Metric Weight: 6.5 kg

Possible Moves: Quiver Dance, Metal Burst, Sucker Punch, Tackle, Protect, Bug Bite, Hidden Power, Confusion, Mirror Shot, Metal Sound, Psybeam, Captivate, Flail, Attract, Psychic, Iron Head, Bug Buzz

Burmy
(Female Form)

Wormadam
(Trash Cloak)

TYPE: BUG

With the spikes on its tail, Wurmple strips away tree bark to get at the delicious sap underneath. The spikes also come in handy when fending off an attacker.

How to Say It: WERM-pull
Imperial Height: 1'00''
Imperial Weight: 7.9 lbs.
Metric Height: 0.3 m
Metric Weight: 3.6 kg

Possible Moves: Tackle, String Shot, Poison Sting, Bug Bite

WURMPLE
Worm Pokémon

Silcoon → **Beautifly**

Wurmple

Cascoon → **Dustox**

483

WYNAUT
Bright Pokémon

REGIONS:
Hoenn
Kalos
(Coastal)

TYPE: PSYCHIC

If a Wynaut is smacking its tail against the ground, that means it's angry, regardless of the big smile on its face.

How to Say It: WHY-not
Imperial Height: 2'00''
Imperial Weight: 30.9 lbs.
Metric Height: 0.6 m
Metric Weight: 14.0 kg

Possible Moves: Splash, Charm, Encore, Counter, Mirror Coat, Safeguard, Destiny Bond

Wynaut ⇨ Wobbuffet

XATU
Mystic Pokémon

REGIONS:
Alola
Johto

TYPE: PSYCHIC-FLYING

Apparently, Xatu can see into the future, but it lacks the power—or maybe just the will—to change anything. Some speculate that this is why it doesn't move much.

How to Say It: ZAH-too
Imperial Height: 4'11''
Imperial Weight: 33.1 lbs.
Metric Height: 1.5 m
Metric Weight: 15.0 kg

Possible Moves: Peck, Leer, Night Shade, Teleport, Lucky Chant, Miracle Eye, Me First, Confuse Ray, Tailwind, Wish, Psycho Shift, Future Sight, Stored Power, Ominous Wind, Power Swap, Guard Swap, Psychic, Air Slash

Natu ⇨ Xatu

XERNEAS
Life Pokémon

LEGENDARY POKÉMON

TYPE: FAIRY

Xerneas's horns shine in all the colors of the rainbow. It is said that this Legendary Pokémon can share the gift of endless life.

How to Say It: ZURR-nee-us
Imperial Height: 9'10''
Imperial Weight: 474.0 lbs.
Metric Height: 3.0 m
Metric Weight: 215.0 kg

Possible Moves: Heal Pulse, Aromatherapy, Ingrain, Take Down, Light Screen, Aurora Beam, Gravity, Geomancy, Moonblast, Megahorn, Night Slash, Horn Leech, Psych Up, Misty Terrain, Nature Power, Close Combat, Giga Impact, Outrage

Does not evolve

XURKITREE
Glowing Pokémon

REGION: Alola

ULTRA BEAST

TYPE: ELECTRIC

Xurkitree, one of the mysterious Ultra Beasts, invaded an electric plant after it emerged from the Ultra Wormhole. Some suspect it absorbs electricity into its body to power the serious shocks it gives off.

How to Say It: ZURK-ih-tree
Imperial Height: 12'06''
Imperial Weight: 220.5 lbs.
Metric Height: 3.8 m
Metric Weight: 100.0 kg

Possible Moves:
Tail Glow, Spark, Charge, Wrap, Thunder Shock, Thunder Wave, Shock Wave, Ingrain, Thunder Punch, Eerie Impulse, Signal Beam, Thunderbolt, Hypnosis, Discharge, Electric Terrain, Power Whip, Ion Deluge, Zap Cannon

Does not evolve

TYPE: GHOST

The mask that Yamask carries is said to represent its face from a former life. Sometimes, remembering that former life makes it very sad.

How to Say It: YAH-mask
Imperial Height: 1'08''
Imperial Weight: 3.3 lbs.
Metric Height: 0.5 m
Metric Weight: 1.5 kg

Possible Moves: Astonish, Protect, Disable, Haze, Night Shade, Hex, Will-O-Wisp, Ominous Wind, Curse, Power Split, Guard Split, Shadow Ball, Grudge, Mean Look, Destiny Bond

Yamask   Cofagrigus

REGION:
Unova

YAMASK
Spirit Pokémon

TYPE: BUG-FLYING

With its compound eyes, Yanma can see in every direction without moving its head. It can make quick stops and turns during flight.

How to Say It: YAN-ma
Imperial Height: 3'11''
Imperial Weight: 83.8 lbs.
Metric Height: 1.2 m
Metric Weight: 38.0 kg

Possible Moves: Tackle, Foresight, Quick Attack, Double Team, Sonic Boom, Detect, Supersonic, Uproar, Pursuit, Ancient Power, Hypnosis, Wing Attack, Screech, U-turn, Air Slash, Bug Buzz

REGIONS:
Johto
Kalos
(Coastal)

YANMA
Clear Wing Pokémon

Yanma   Yanmega

YANMEGA

Ogre Darner Pokémon

REGIONS:
Kalos
(Coastal)
Sinnoh

TYPE: BUG-FLYING

With four wings on its back and two more on its tail to keep it balanced, Yanmega is capable of extremely high-speed flight. It can carry a full-grown person through the air.

How to Say It: yan-MEG-ah
Imperial Height: 6'03''
Imperial Weight: 113.5 lbs.
Metric Height: 1.9 m
Metric Weight: 51.5 kg

Possible Moves: Bug Buzz, Air Slash, Night Slash, Bug Bite, Tackle, Foresight, Quick Attack, Double Team, Sonic Boom, Detect, Supersonic, Uproar, Pursuit, Ancient Power, Feint, Slash, Screech, U-turn

Yanma ⇨ Yanmega

YUNGOOS

Loitering Pokémon

REGION:
Alola

TYPE: NORMAL

Yungoos is always on the move during the day, looking for food—and it's not too picky about what it bites with its sharp teeth. When night comes, it immediately falls asleep no matter where it happens to be.

How to Say It: YUNG-goose
Imperial Height: 1'04''
Imperial Weight: 13.2 lbs.
Metric Height: 0.4 m
Metric Weight: 6.0 kg

Possible Moves: Tackle, Leer, Pursuit, Sand Attack, Odor Sleuth, Bide, Bite, Mud-Slap, Super Fang, Take Down, Scary Face, Crunch, Hyper Fang, Yawn, Thrash, Rest

Yungoos ⇨ Gumshoos

YVELTAL
Destruction Pokémon

LEGENDARY POKÉMON

TYPE: DARK-FLYING

When Yveltal spreads its dark wings, its feathers give off a red glow. It is said that this Legendary Pokémon can absorb the life energy of others.

How to Say It: ee-VELL-tall   **Metric Height:** 5.8 m
Imperial Height: 19'00''   **Metric Weight:** 203.0 kg
Imperial Weight: 447.5 lbs.

Possible Moves: Hurricane, Razor Wind, Taunt, Roost, Double Team, Air Slash, Snarl, Oblivion Wing, Disable, Dark Pulse, Foul Play, Phantom Force, Psychic, Dragon Rush, Focus Blast, Sucker Punch, Hyper Beam, Sky Attack

Does not evolve

ZANGOOSE
Cat Ferret Pokémon

TYPE: NORMAL

Zangoose slashes at opponents with its sharp claws extended. These Pokémon constantly feud with Seviper.

How to Say It: ZANG-goose
Imperial Height: 4'03''
Imperial Weight: 88.8 lbs.
Metric Height: 1.3 m
Metric Weight: 40.3 kg

Possible Moves: Scratch, Leer, Quick Attack, Fury Cutter, Pursuit, Slash, Embargo, Crush Claw, Revenge, False Swipe, Detect, X-Scissor, Taunt, Swords Dance, Close Combat, Hone Claws

Does not evolve

ZAPDOS
Electric Pokémon

LEGENDARY POKÉMON

TYPE: ELECTRIC-FLYING

When Zapdos is hit by a bolt of lightning, its power increases. This Legendary Pokémon can bend electricity to its will.

How to Say It: ZAP-dose
Imperial Height: 5'03''
Imperial Weight: 116.0 lbs.
Metric Height: 1.6 m
Metric Weight: 52.6 kg

Possible Moves: Roost, Zap Cannon, Drill Peck, Peck, Thunder Shock, Thunder Wave, Detect, Pluck, Ancient Power, Charge, Agility, Discharge, Rain Dance, Light Screen, Thunder, Magnetic Flux

Does not evolve

ZEBSTRIKA
Thunderbolt Pokémon

TYPE: ELECTRIC

A herd of Zebstrika running at top speed gives off a noise like thunder. If they get angry, their manes shoot off lightning.

How to Say It: zehb-STRY-kuh
Imperial Height: 5'03''
Imperial Weight: 175.3 lbs.
Metric Height: 1.6 m
Metric Weight: 79.5 kg

Possible Moves: Quick Attack, Tail Whip, Charge, Thunder Wave, Shock Wave, Flame Charge, Pursuit, Spark, Stomp, Discharge, Agility, Wild Charge, Thrash, Ion Deluge

Blitzle ⇨ Zebstrika

ZEKROM
Deep Black Pokémon

REGION: Unova

LEGENDARY POKÉMON

TYPE: DRAGON-ELECTRIC

Legends say Zekrom helps those who pursue their ideals. It surrounds itself with thunderclouds to travel unseen, and its tail can generate electricity.

How to Say It: ZECK-rahm
Imperial Height: 9'06''
Imperial Weight: 760.6 lbs.
Metric Height: 2.9 m
Metric Weight: 345.0 kg

Possible Moves: Thunder Fang, Dragon Rage, Imprison, Ancient Power, Thunderbolt, Dragon Breath, Slash, Zen Headbutt, Fusion Bolt, Dragon Claw, Noble Roar, Crunch, Thunder, Outrage, Hyper Voice, Bolt Strike

Overdrive Form

Does not evolve

TYPE: NORMAL

Zigzagoon's curiosity drives it to wander constantly and restlessly. It rubs the sturdy bristles on its back against trees to mark its territory.

REGIONS:
Hoenn
Kalos
(Central)

ZIGZAGOON
Tiny Raccoon Pokémon

How to Say It: ZIG-zag-GOON
Imperial Height: 1'04''
Imperial Weight: 38.6 lbs.
Metric Height: 0.4 m
Metric Weight: 17.5 kg

Possible Moves: Growl, Tackle, Tail Whip, Headbutt, Baby-Doll Eyes, Sand Attack, Odor Sleuth, Mud Sport, Pin Missile, Covet, Bestow, Flail, Rest, Belly Drum, Fling, Take Down

Zigzagoon ➡ **Linoone**

REGIONS:
Alola
Kalos
(Mountain)
Unova

ZOROARK
Illusion Fox Pokémon

TYPE: DARK

Unwary explorers who come close to Zoroark's den might find themselves wandering the forest aimlessly, distracted and led astray by the illusions this Pokémon spins to protect its lair. It can show these illusions to hundreds of people at once.

How to Say It: ZORE-oh-ark
Imperial Height: 5'03''
Imperial Weight: 178.8 lbs.
Metric Height: 1.6 m
Metric Weight: 81.1 kg

Possible Moves: Night Daze, Imprison, U-turn, Scratch, Leer, Pursuit, Hone Claws, Fury Swipes, Feint Attack, Scary Face, Taunt, Foul Play, Night Slash, Torment, Agility, Embargo, Punishment, Nasty Plot

Zorua ➡ **Zoroark**

ZORUA

Tricky Fox Pokémon

REGIONS:
Alola
Kalos
(Mountain)
Unova

TYPE: DARK

When Zorua is among strangers, it tends to stay camouflaged behind a shield of illusion. It can make itself look like other Pokémon, or even like people—though it can't speak, so it appears as a silent child.

How to Say It: ZORE-oo-ah
Imperial Height: 2'04''
Imperial Weight: 27.6 lbs.
Metric Height: 0.7 m
Metric Weight: 12.5 kg

Possible Moves: Scratch, Leer, Pursuit, Fake Tears, Fury Swipes, Feint Attack, Scary Face, Taunt, Foul Play, Torment, Agility, Embargo, Punishment, Nasty Plot, Imprison, Night Daze

Zorua ➡ Zoroark

ZUBAT

Bat Pokémon

REGIONS:
Alola
Kalos
(Central)
Kanto

TYPE: POISON-FLYING

Being in the sun isn't healthy for Zubat, so it spends the day sleeping in caves. Since it doesn't have eyes, it uses ultrasonic waves to detect its surroundings.

How to Say It: ZOO-bat
Imperial Height: 2'07''
Imperial Weight: 16.5 lbs.
Metric Height: 0.8 m
Metric Weight: 7.5 kg

Possible Moves: Absorb, Supersonic, Astonish, Bite, Wing Attack, Confuse Ray, Air Cutter, Swift, Poison Fang, Mean Look, Leech Life, Haze, Venoshock, Air Slash, Quick Guard

Zubat ➡ Golbat ➡ Crobat